THE HISTORY OF THE VICTORIA CROSS

The History of the Victoria Cross

BY

PHILIP A. WILKINS

BEING AN ACCOUNT OF THE 520 ACTS OF BRAVERY
FOR WHICH THE DECORATION HAS BEEN
AWARDED, AND PORTRAITS OF
392 RECIPIENTS

The Naval & Military Press Ltd

Published by
The Naval & Military Press Ltd
Unit 10, Ridgewood Industrial Park,
Uckfield, East Sussex,
TN22 5QE England
Tel: +44 (0) 1825 749494
Fax: +44 (0) 1825 765701
www.naval-military-press.com
www.military-genealogy.com

© The Naval & Military Press Ltd 2007

The Naval & Military Press ...

...offer specialist books for the serious student of conflict. The range of titles stocked covers the whole spectrum of military history with titles on uniforms, battles, official histories, specialist works containing Medal Rolls and Casualties Lists, and numismatic titles for medal collectors and researchers.

The innovative approach they have to military bookselling and their commitment to publishing have made them Britain's leading independent military bookseller.

In reprinting in facsimile from the original, any imperfections are inevitably reproduced and the quality may fall short of modern type and cartographic standards.

TO THE MEMORY OF

ENGLAND'S BRAVE SONS

WHO HAVE GIVEN THEIR LIVES

IN THE

MAKING AND UPHOLDING

OF THE

BRITISH EMPIRE

Preface

IN compiling the HISTORY OF THE VICTORIA CROSS, it has been my chief aim and care not to draw upon the imagination but to adhere strictly to the official reports given in the *London Gazette*, despatches from the various seats of war, and to information received from officers and men from all parts of the world.

I am anxious to acknowledge my gratitude to the relatives of many recipients of the Decoration who have long passed away, from whom I have received very great kindness and assistance and by whom I have been put into possession of private papers bearing on the actions for which the Decoration was awarded.

I am greatly indebted to Mr. T. E. Toomey, author of *Heroes of the Victoria Cross*, a little book written some years ago, but now out of print. Mr. Toomey not only assisted me in the compilation of details, but placed his work, as well as his great knowledge of the subject, at my disposal, and a great deal of use has been made of it by me in this volume.

The copyright of the above-mentioned work was held by Messrs. Newnes, Ltd., and these gentlemen most generously gave me full permission to make any use I pleased of it.

I must also acknowledge the great assistance I have received from Messrs. Elliott & Fry, Messrs. Maull & Fox, and other photographers, who took the greatest trouble to trace the negatives of so many portraits in this work, many of which were taken by them very many years ago.

Owing to the fact that some of those whose acts are herein described are serving abroad, I have been debarred from obtaining as much personal detail as I had wished. It is, however, my intention to continue this work, and I shall be grateful to any who will put me in possession of photographs or details omitted in the present issue, or who will draw my attention to errors which, I fear, in such a work as this, may possibly have occurred, so that, in later editions, any shortcomings may be rectified.

PHILIP A. WILKINS

14, WILTON PLACE,
       London, 1904.

The Victoria Cross

THE Decoration of the Victoria Cross was instituted in 1856 and the award made retrospective to the commencement of the Crimean War. In shape it takes the form of a Maltese Cross, measures $1\frac{2}{5}$ inch square, weighs about 434 grains,[1] and is of bronze, being cast from cannon taken by our army at Sebastopol. It is attached by a " V " to a bar, upon which is a sprig of laurel. On the obverse the Royal Crown surmounted by a lion occupies the centre, with a scroll underneath bearing the words " For Valour." The reverse is quite plain, with an indented circle in the centre, in which the date or dates of the act of bravery are engraved. At the back of the bar is the name of the recipient, and the whole is suspended by a Riband, blue for the Navy, red for the Army. The Warrant authorizes a Bar to be attached to the Riband for any further act of conspicuous bravery on the part of the owner of the Cross, but no such bar has ever yet been issued, although statements to the contrary have frequently been made.

[1] The weight varies slightly.

Wars, Campaigns, etc., in which the Victoria Cross has been gained

	Date.	No. of Crosses Awarded.
Crimea	1854–55	111
Persia	1856–57	3
Indian Mutiny (including Okamundel and Kattywar, October 1859, see General Goodfellow, V.C.)	1857–59	182
New Zealand	1860–61; 1863–66	15
China (including Taiping Rebellion, 1861–62)	1860–62	8
Umbeyla (N.W. India)	1863	2
Japan	1864	3
Bhootan (N.E. India)	1864–65	2
Canada [1]	1866	1
Africa—West (River Gambia)	1866	1
Little Andaman Island	1867	5
Abyssinia	1867–68	2
Looshai (N.E. India)	1871–72	1
Ashantee	1873–74	4
Perak	1875–76	1
Quetta (Beloochistan) [2]	1877	1
Kaffir	1877–78	1
Afghanistan	1878–80	16
Zululand	1879	23
Basutoland	1879 and 1881	6
Naga Hills (India)	1879–80	1
Boer Revolt	1880–81	6
Egypt	1882	3
Soudan (Red Sea Littoral)	1884	4
Nile Expedition	1884–85	1
Burma	1889	2
Manipur Rising (N.E. India) [3]	1891	1

[1] See Private O'Hea.   [2] See Major A. Scott.   [3] See Major C. J. W. Grant.

Wars, Campaigns, etc.

	Date.	No. of Crosses Awarded.
Hunza-Nagar (N.W. of India)	1891	3
Africa—West (River Gambia)	1892	1
Burma	1893	1
Chitral (Fort)	1895	1
Matabeleland	1896	3
Punjab Frontier	1897–98	11
Khartoum Expedition (Omdurman)	1898	4
Khartoum Expedition (Gedarif Kassala)	1898	1
Crete—Candia [1]	1898	1
Boer War	1899–1902	78
Ashantee	1900	2
China	1900	2
Somaliland	1902–03	5
Nigeria	1903	1
		520

[1] See Surgeon Maillard

List of Illustrations

	PAGE
ABLETT, *Private* Alfred	51
ADAMS, *The Reverend* James Williams	226
ADAMS, *Lieut.-Colonel* Robert Bellew, C.B.	294
ADDISON, *Private* Henry	182
AIKMAN, *Lieut.-Colonel* Frederick Robertson	154
AITKEN, *Colonel* Robert Hope Moncrieff	73
ALBRECHT, *Trooper* H.	324
ALLEN, *Sergeant-Instructor* William	247
ANDERSON, *Corporal* Charles	179
ANSON, *Captain* The Honble. Augustus Henry Archibald	120
ARTHUR, *Gunner* Thomas	38
ASHFORD, *Private* Thomas	232
ATKINSON, *Sergeant* Alfred	325
AYLMER, *Colonel* Fenton John	280
BABTIE, *Lieut.-Colonel* William, C.M.G.	314
BAKER, *Lieutenant* Charles George	178
BANKES, *Cornet* William George Hawtrey	161
BARRY, *Private* J.	352
BAXTER, *Trooper* Frank William	289
BEES, *Private* W.	360
BEET, *Sergeant* Harry Churchill	335
BELL, *Private* David	208
BELL, *Major-General* Edward, W. D.	7
BELL, *Lieutenant* F. W.	355
BELL, *Colonel* Mark Sever, C.B.	214
BERESFORD, *Colonel* Lord William Leslie de la Poer, K.C.I.E.	256
BERGIN, *Private* James	210
BERRYMAN, *Major* John	12
BISDEE, *Private* J. H.	345
BLAIR, *Lieut.-General* James, C.B.	98
BOGLE, *Major* Andrew Cathcart	87
BOISRAGON, *Major* Guy Hudleston	282
BOOTH, *Colour-Sergeant* Anthony	251
BOULGER, *Hon. Lieut.-Colonel* Abraham	84
BOURCHIER, *Colonel* Claude Thomas	27

List of Illustrations

	PAGE
BOYES, *Midshipman* Duncan Gordon	201
BRADSHAW, *Private* Joseph	33
BRENNAN, *Bombardier* Joseph	165
BROMHEAD, *Major* Gonville S.	245
BROWN, *Lieut.-Colonel* Edward Douglas (Brown-Synge-Hutchinson)	346
BROWN, *Lieutenant* Francis David Millett	138
BROWN, *Trooper* Peter	258
BROWNE, *Brigadier-General* Edward Stevenson, C.B.	255
BROWNE, *Colonel* Henry George	100
BROWNE, *General* Sir Samuel James, G.C.B., K.C.S.I.	175
BUCKLEY, *Captain* Cecil William, R.N.	36
BULLER, *General* The Right Hon. Redvers Henry, G.C.B., G.C.M.G, P.C.	253
BURGOYNE, *Captain* Hugh Talbot, R.N.	36
BURSLEM, *Captain* Nathaniel	195
BUTLER, *Colonel* Thomas Adair	155
BYRNE, *Private* Thomas	300
BYTHESEA, *Admiral* John, C.B., C.I.E.	2
CADELL, *Colonel* Thomas	69
CAFE, *Lieut.-General* William Martin	167
CAMBRIDGE, *Sergeant* Daniel	52
CAMERON, *Colonel* Aylmer Spicer, C.B.	162
CARLIN, *Private* Patrick	167
CHAMPION, *Sergeant-Major* James	172
CHANNER, *Major-General* George Nicholas, C.B.	216
CHAPLIN, *Colonel* John Worthy	196
CHARD, *Colonel* John Rouse Merriott	244
CHASE, *Lieut.-Colonel* William St. Lucien, C.B.	232
CLEMENTS, *Corporal* J. J.	328
CLIFFORD, *Major-General* The Hon. Sir Henry Hugh, K.C.M.G.	19
CLOGSTOUN, *Captain* Herbert Mackworth	183
COBBE, *Captain* Alexander Stanhope, D.S.O.	371
COCHRANE, *Colonel* Hugh Stewart	163
COCKBURN, *Major* Hampden Zane Churchill	348
COGHILL, *Lieutenant* Neville Josiah Aylmer	234
COGHLAN, *Sergeant-Major* Cornelius	67
COLLIS, *Gunner* James	231
COLVIN, *Brevet-Major* James Morris Colquhoun	296
COMMERELL, *Admiral of the Fleet* Sir John Edmund, G.C.B.	59
CONGREVE, *Lieut.-Colonel* Walter Norris, M.V.O.	311
CONOLLY, *Lieut.-Colonel* John Augustus	16
COOK, *Captain* John	219
COOPER, *Boatswain* Henry	37
CORBETT, *Private* Frederick	270

List of Illustrations

	PAGE
COSTELLO, *Captain* Edmond William	293
COULSON, *Lieutenant and Adjutant* Gustavus Hamilton Blenkinsopp, D.S.O.	356
CRANDON, *Private* H. G.	358
CREAGH, *Major-General* Sir O'Moore, K.C.B.	223
CREAN, *Surgeon-Captain* Thomas Joseph	362
CROWE, *Lieut.-Colonel* Joseph P. H.	99
CUNINGHAME, *Colonel* Sir William James Montgomery	28
CURTIS, *Corporal* A. E.	326
CURTIS, *Boatswain's-Mate* Henry	41
DALTON, *Acting-Assistant of Transport* James Langley	246
DANAHER, *Private* John	266
DAUNT, *Lieut.-Colonel* John Charles Campbell	122
DAVIS, *Major-General* Gronow	53
DAVIS, *Private* James	168
DAY, *Captain* George Fiott, C.B.	58
DIAMOND, *Sergeant* Bernard	121
DICK-CUNYNGHAM, *Lieut.-Colonel* William Henry	227
DICKSON, *General* Sir Collingwood, G.C.B.	8
DIVANE, *Private* John	101
DIXON, *Major-General* Matthew Charles	32
DOOGAN, *Private* John	268
DOUGLAS, *Brigade-Surgeon* Cpambell Millis	207
DOUGLAS, *Captain* Henry Edward Manning, D.S.O.	309
DOWELL, *Lieut.-Colonel* George Dare	48
DOWN, *Ensign* John Thornton	187
DOXAT, *Lieutenant* Alexis C.	347
DUNDAS, *Captain* James	202
DUNN, *Lieut.-Colonel* Alexander Robert	12
EDWARDS, *Private* Thomas	273
EDWARDS, *Major* William Mordaunt Marsh	270
ELPHINSTONE, *Major-General* Sir Howard Craufurd, K.C.B.	41
ELTON, *Lieut.-Colonel* Frederick Cockayne	50
ENGLEHEART, *Sergeant* H.	329
ENGLISH, *Lieutenant* W. J.	357
ESMONDE, *Lieut.-Colonel* Thomas	42
EVANS, *Private* Samuel	31
FARMER, *Sergeant* Donald	351
FARMER, *Corporal* Joseph John	268
FARQUHARSON, *Lieutenant* Francis Edward Henry	157
FINCASTLE, *Captain* Alexander Edward Murray (Viscount)	294
FINDLATER, *Piper* G.	297

List of Illustrations

	PAGE
FIRTH, *Sergeant* W.	327
FITZPATRICK, *Private* Francis	261
FLAWN, *Private* Thomas	262
FLINN, *Drummer* Thomas	149
FOSBERRY, *Lieut.-Colonel* George Vincent	198
FOWLER, *Sergeant* Edmund	252
FRASER, *Lieut.-General* Sir Charles Craufurd, K.C.B.	181
GARDINER, *Colour-Sergeant* George	30
GARDNER, *Quartermaster-Sergeant* William	170
GIFFORD, *Major* Edric Frederick (Baron)	212
GLASOCK, *Driver* H. H.	333
GOAT, *Corporal* William	155
GOODFELLOW, *General* Charles Augustus	184
GOODLAKE, *Lieut.-General* Gerald Littlehales	14
GORDON, *Captain* William Eagleson	339
GORDON, *Lance-Corporal* William James	284
GOUGH, *General* Sir Charles John Stanley G.C.B	99
GOUGH, *General* Sir Hugh Henry, G.C.B.	134
GOUGH, *Major* John Edmond	372
GRADY, *Sergeant* Thomas	9
GRAHAM, *Lieut.-General* Sir Gerald, G.C.B., G.C.M.G.	43
GRANT, *Major* Charles James William	278
GRANT, *Private* P. (93rd Regiment)	139
GREEN, *Colour-Sergeant* Patrick	101
GUISE, *Lieut.-General* John Christopher, C.B.	139
GUY, *Lieutenant* Basil John Douglas	369
HACKETT, *Lieut.-Colonel* Thomas Bernard	145
HALE, *Surgeon-Major* Thomas Egerton, M.D.	54
HALL, *Able-Seaman* William	141
HALLIDAY, *Brevet-Major* Lewis Stratford Tollemache	368
HAMILTON, *Major-General* Thomas de Courcy	35
HAMILTON, *Lieutenant* Walter Richard Pollock	222
HAMMOND, *Colonel* Sir Arthur George, K.C.B., D.S.O	229
HAMPTON, *Sergeant-Instructor* Harry	343
HANCOCK, *Private* Thomas	70
HARDHAM, *Lieutenant* W. J.	352
HARDING, *Gunner* Israel	269
HARRINGTON, *Lieutenant* Hastings Edward	136
HART, *Major-General* Sir Reginald Clare, K.C.B.	220
HARTLEY, *Colonel* Edmund Baron, C.M.G.	261
HAVELOCK-ALLAN, *Lieut.-General* Sir Henry Marshman, Bart., K.C.B.	85
HAWTHORNE, *Bugler* Robert	104

List of Illustrations

	PAGE
HEAPHY, *Major* Charles	189
HEATHCOTE, *Lieutenant* Alfred Spencer	106
HEATON, *Sergeant* William	344
HENDERSON, *Trooper* Herbert Stephen	288
HENEAGE, *Major* Clement Walker	173
HENRY, *Captain* Andrew	20
HEWETT, *Vice-Admiral* Sir William Nathan Wrighte, K.C.B., K.C.S.I.	17
HILL-WALKER, *Major* Alan Richard	267
HILLS-JOHNES, *Lieut.-General* Sir James, G.C.B.	78
HINCKLEY, *Able-Seaman* George	197
HITCH, *Private* Frederick	248
HOLLAND, *Sergeant* E.	350
HOLLOWELL, *Private* James	117
HOME, *Surgeon-General* Sir Anthony Dickson, K.C.B.	118
HOME, *Lieutenant* Duncan Charles	103
HOOK, *Private* Henry	248
HOPE, *Lieut.-Colonel* William	43
HORE-RUTHVEN, *Lieutenant* Honble. Alexander Gore Arkwright	302
HOUSE, *Private* William	341
HUGHES, *Private* Matthew	38
HUMPSTON, *Private* Robert	34
IND, *Shoeing-Smith* Alfred Ernest	363
INKSON, *Captain* Edgar Thomas	326
INNES, *Lieut.-General* John James McLeod	153
IRWIN, *Private* C.	142
JARRETT, *Colonel* Hanson Chambers Taylor	180
JEE, *Surgeon-General* Joseph, C.B.	113
JENNINGS, *Rough-Rider* Edward	137
JEROME, *Major-General* Henry Edward	164
JOHNSTONE, *Captain* R.	307
JONES, *Lieut.-Colonel* Alfred Stowell	68
JONES, *Captain* Henry Mitchell	39
JONES *Lieutenant* Robert James Thomas Digby	318
JONES, *Private* Robert	249
JONES, *Private* William	249
KAVANAGH, Thomas Henry, Esq.	128
Ditto in his disguise worn when he penetrated the Sepoy lines	388
KEATINGE, *General* Richard Harte, C.S.I.	160
KELLAWAY, *Boatswain* Joseph	57
KELLS, *Lance-Corporal* Robert	122
KENNA, *Major* Paul Aloysius	299

List of Illustrations

	PAGE
KENNEDY, *Private* Charles Thomas	350
KERR, *Lieutenant* William Alexander	83
KIRBY, *Sergeant-Major* Frank Howard	336
KNIGHT, *Corporal* H. J.	343
KNOX, *Major* John Simpson	5
LANE, *Private* Thomas	196
LAWRENCE, *Sergeant* T.	342
LAWSON, *Private* E.	298
LEACH, *Major-General* Edward Pemberton, C.V.O., C.B.	221
LEET, *Major-General* William Knox, C.B.	255
LEITCH, *Colour-Sergeant* Peter	44
LEITH, *Major* James	163
LENDRIM, *Quartermaster-Sergeant* William James	29
LENNOX, *Lieut.-General* Sir Wilbraham Oates, K.C.B.	28
LENON, *Major* Edmund Henry	195
LE QUESNE, *Surgeon-Major* Ferdinand Simeon	277
LLOYD, *Surgeon-Lieut.-Colonel* Owen Edward Pennefather	285
LOYD-LINDSAY, *Lieut.-Colonel* R. J. (Lord Wantage)	4
LODGE, *Bombardier* Isaac	332
LUCAS, *Admiral* Charles Davis, R.N.	1
LUCAS, *Sergeant-Major* John (40th Regt.)	185
LYSONS, *Lieut-Colonel* Henry	252
LYSTER, *Lieut.-General* Harry Hammon, C.B.	171
McBEAN, *Major-General* William	157
McCREA, *Surgeon* John Frederick	262
McDERMOND, *Private* John	21
McDONALD, *Captain* Henry	33
McDONELL, William Fraser, Esq.	88
McGAW, *Sergeant* Samuel	214
McGOVERN, *Sergeant* John	71
McHALE, *Private* Patrick	123
MACINTYRE, *Major-General* Donald	211
MACKAY, *Lieutenant* John Frederick	336
McKECHNIE, *Sergeant* James	5
MACKENZIE, *Captain* John	365
MACLEAN, *Lieutenant* Hector Lachlan Stewart	295
McMASTER, *Assistant-Surgeon* Valentine Munbee	114
McNEILL, *Major-General* Sir John Carstairs, K.C.B., K.C.M.G., G.C.V.O.	189
MACPHERSON, *Major-General* Sir Herbert Taylor, K.C.B.	114
McPHERSON, *Colour-Sergeant* Stewart	119
McWHEENEY, *Sergeant* William	10
MAGNER, *Drummer* Michael	210

List of Illustrations

	PAGE
MAILLARD, *Surgeon* William Job, M.D.	303
MALCOLMSON, *Captain* John Grant	62
MALONE, *Riding-Master* Joseph	13
MANGLES, Ross Lowis, Esq.	96
MANLEY, *Surgeon-General* William George Nicholas, C.B.	190
MANSEL-JONES, *Captain* Conwyn	328
MARLING, *Lieut.-Colonel* Percival Scrope, C.B.	274
MARSHALL, *Major* William Thomas	273
MARTINEAU, *Sergeant* Horace Robert	316
MARTIN-LEAKE, *Surgeon-Captain* A.	364
MASTERSON, *Brevet-Major* James Edward Ignatius	322
MAUDE, *Colonel* Francis Cornwallis, C.B.	112
MAUDE, *General* Sir Frederick Francis, G.C.B.	55
MAXWELL, *Brevet-Major* Francis Aylmer, D.S.O.	334
MAYGAR, *Lieutenant* Leslie Cecil	361
MAYO, *Midshipman* Arthur	147
MEIKLEJOHN, *Captain* Matthew Fontaine Maury	305
MELLISS, *Captain* Charles John	366
MILBANKE, *Captain* Sir John Peniston, Bart.	318
MELVILL, *Lieutenant and Adjutant* Teignmouth	233
MILLAR, *Private* Duncan	183
MILLER, *Hon.-Major* James	128
MITCHELL, *Captain of the Fore-top* Samuel	191
MONAGHAN, *Trumpeter* Thomas	179
MONGER, *Private* George	146
MONTMORENCY, Honble. Raymond Harvey Lodge Joseph de	300
MOORE, *Major-General* Arthur Thomas, C.B.	62
MOORE, *Colonel* Hans Garrett, C.B.	218
MORLEY, *Private* Samuel	169
MOUAT, *Surgeon-General* Sir James, K.C.B.	11
MOYNIHAN, *Ensign* Andrew	55
MULLANE, *Sergeant-Major* Patrick	230
MULLINS, *Major* C. H., C.M.G.	307
MUNRO, *Colour-Sergeant* James	143
MURPHY, *Private* Thomas	209
MURRAY, *Lance-Corporal* James (94th Regt.)	265
MURRAY, *Sergeant* John (68th Regt.)	192
NAPIER, *Sergeant* William	166
NASH, *Corporal* W.	159
NESBITT, *Captain* Randolph Cosby	291
NICKERSON, *Captain* William Henry Snyder	334
NORMAN, *Private* William	29
NORWOOD, *Lieutenant* John	308

List of Illustrations

	PAGE
NURSE, *Sergeant* George Edward	315
O'CONNOR, *Major-General* Luke	6
OLPHERTS, *General* Sir William, G.C.B.	115
OSBORNE, *Private* James	266
OWENS, *Corporal* James	18
OXENHAM, *Corporal* William	72
PALMER, *Captain* Anthony	22
PARKER, *Sergeant* C.	332
PATON, *Sergeant* John	143
PEARSON, *Private* John	174
PENNELL, *Captain* Henry Singleton	297
PEEL, *Captain* Sir William, K.C.B.	9
PERCY, *Colonel* Lord	23
PHIPPS-HORNBY, *Lieut.-Colonel* Edmund John	330
PICKARD, *Colonel* Arthur Frederick, C.B.	188
PITCHER, *Lieutenant* Henry William	199
PRENDERGAST, *General* Sir Henry North Dalrymple, G.C.B.	146
PRETTYJOHN, *Colour-Sergeant* John	23
PRICE-DAVIES, *Captain* Llewellyn Alberic Emilius	359
PRIDE, *Captain of the After-Guard* Thomas, R.N.	200
PROBYN, *General* Sir Dighton Macnaghten, G.C.V.O., K.C.B., K.C.S.I.	127
RABY, *Rear-Admiral* Henry James, C.B.	45
RAMSDEN, *Trooper* H. E.	317
RAVENHILL, *Private* George	315
READE, *Surgeon-General* Herbert Taylor	108
REED, *Captain* Hamilton Lyster	312
RENNIE, *Lieut.-Colonel* William	111
RENNY, *Major-General* George Alexander	109
REYNOLDS, *Surgeon-Lieut.-Colonel* James Henry	246
RICHARDSON, *Sergeant* Arthur Herbert Lindsey	338
RICHARDSON, *Private* George (34th Regt.)	184
RICKARD, *Chief Officer of Coast Guard* William	60
RIDGEWAY, *Colonel* Richard Kirby	264
ROBARTS, *Chief Gunner* John	37
ROBERTS, Honble. F. H. S.	313
ROBERTS, *Field-Marshal*, Earl of Kandahar, Pretoria, and Waterford, K.G., K.P., G.C.B., G.C.S.I., etc., etc.	150
ROBERTSON, *Hon.-Lieutenant* William	306
ROBINSON, *Seaman* Edward	160
RODDY, *Colonel* Patrick	177
ROGERS, *Major-General* Robert Montressor, C.B.	194

List of Illustrations

	PAGE
Ross, *Sergeant* John	50
Rowlands, *General* Sir Hugh, K.C.B.	24
Rushe, *Troop-Sergeant-Major* David	162
Russell, *Lieut.-Colonel* Sir Charles, Bart.	25
Salkeld, *Lieutenant* Philip	104
Salmon, *Admiral of the Fleet* Sir Nowell, G.C.B.	140
Sartorius, *Major-General* Euston Henry, C.B.	225
Sartorius, *Major-General* Reginald William, C.M.G.	213
Schofield, *Major* Harry Norton	313
Scott, *Private* Robert	323
Scott, *Lieut.-Colonel* Robert George	260
Seeley, *Seaman* William	200
Sellar, *Sergeant* George	228
Shaul, *Band-Sergeant* John David Francis	310
Shaw, *Major-General* Hugh, C.B.	192
Sheppard, *Boatswain* John	49
Simpson, *Quartermaster* John	168
Sims, *Sergeant* John J.	46
Sinnott, *Corporal* John	126
Sleavon, *Corporal* Michael	166
Smith, *Lieutenant* Clement Leslie	374
Smith, *Lieut.-Colonel* Frederick Augustus	191
Smith, *Corporal* James	296
Smith, *Major* John Manners, C.I.E.	283
Smyth, *Major* Nevill Maskelyne	301
Stagpoole, *Drummer* Dudley	187
Stanlack, *Private* William	18
Strong, *Private* George	52
Sullivan, *Boatswain's Mate* John	31
Sutton, *Bugler* William	102
Sylvester, *Surgeon* William Henry Thomas, M.D.	56
Teesdale, *Major-General* Sir Christopher Charles, K.C.M.G.	59
Temple, *Brigade-Surgeon* William	188
Thackeray, *Colonel* Sir Edward Talbot, K.C.B.	110
Thompson, *Lance-Corporal* Alexander (42nd Regt.)	169
Thompson, *Private* James (60th Regt.)	83
Tombs, *Major-General* Sir Henry, K.C.B.	79
Towse, *Captain* Ernest Beachcroft Beckwith	309
Travers, *Colonel* James	76
Trevor, *Major-General* William Spottiswoode	203
Traynor, *Sergeant* William Bernard	353
Trewavas, *Seaman* Joseph	47

List of Illustrations

	PAGE
TURNER, *Lieut.-Colonel* Richard Ernest William, D.S.O.	349
TYTLER, *Colonel* John Adam, C.B.	153
VICKERY, *Corporal* S.	298
VOUSDEN, *Major-General* William John, C.B.	230
WADESON, *Colonel* Richard	86
WALKER, *General* Sir Mark, K.C.B.	26
WALLER, *Lieutenant* William Francis Frederick	175
WANTAGE, *See* Loyd-Lindsay	4
WARD, *Private* Charles	337
WARD, *Private* Henry	116
WASSALL, *Private* Samuel	236
WATSON, *General* Sir John, G.C.B.	135
WATSON, *Captain* Thomas Colclough	295
WHITCHURCH, *Surgeon-Major* Harry Frederick	286
WHITE, *Field-Marshal* Sir George Stewart, G.C.V.O., G.C.I.E., G.C.B., G.C.S.I.	224
WILKINSON, *Bombardier* Thomas	40
WILLIAMS, *Private* John	250
WILMOT, *Colonel* Sir Henry, K.C.B.	158
WILSON, *Admiral* Sir Arthur Knyvet, K.C.B., K.C.V.O.	272
WOOD, *Field-Marshal* Sir Henry Evelyn, G.C.B., G.C.M.G.	180
WOODEN, *Quartermaster* Charles	14
WRIGHT, *Captain* Wallace Duffield	379
YOUNG, *Sergeant-Major* Alexander	358
YOUNG, *Commander* Thomas James, R.N.	141
YOUNGER, *Captain* David Reginald	340

"IL CAMPO ET LO EXERCITO DE' CAVALIERI DI DIO"

HERE, limned in lightning on the scroll of fame,
    The record of earth's bravest ye may read—
    Men to whose making fell such fiery seed,
Changed was their heart of flesh to heart of flame.
Whether of kings or cotter-folk they came,
    These all, though scions of that immortal breed
    That knows no country, doer alike and deed,
Exalt their nation, and adorn her name.

Nor lack there, by diviner frenzy driven,
    Who, fate once foiled, athwart the hail-swept sod
    Thirsty to save, the battle-ways re-trod
Triumphant. Lo! to whom such grace is given,
These, yet on earth, be paladins of heaven—
    The camp and army of the Knights of God.

JAMES RHOADES.

THE CRIMEAN WAR
1854—1855

CHARLES DAVIS LUCAS
(MATE, NOW REAR-ADMIRAL, RETIRED)

H.M.S. "HECLA," ROYAL NAVY

Photo by FRADELLE & YOUNG.

THE first act of conspicuous bravery for which the Victoria Cross was awarded was performed by Mr. Lucas, then Mate on board H.M.S. *Hecla*. During the Baltic Sea operations, while our fleet was bombarding the fortress of Bomarsund on June 21, 1854, a live shell was thrown by the enemy on to the deck. Without a moment's hesitation Mr. Lucas coolly picked it up and threw it overboard. He was immediately promoted Lieutenant, and later was awarded the Silver Medal of the Royal Humane Society.

Born in 1834, Admiral Lucas is the son of Mr. D. Lucas, of Druminargole. He served throughout the War in Burmah, taking part in the capture of Rangoon, Dalla, Pegu and Prome.

History of the Victoria Cross

JOHN BYTHESEA

(LIEUTENANT, NOW REAR-ADMIRAL, C.B., C.I.E.)

Photo by MAULL & FOX, *London.*

DURING the operations in the Baltic Sea information was obtained that despatches were about to be landed on the island of Wardo and forwarded to Bomarsund. Bythesea and Stoker Johnstone (V.C.) landed and hid themselves for three days and nights, August 9–12, 1854, when they successfully intercepted the mail, taking its guard prisoner. Although offered and advised to take more men to accompany him in his daring enterprise, Lieut. Bythesea determined to go alone with Johnstone, a larger party being more likely to attract attention and lead to failure. All arrangements being made the two were landed in a remote bay whence they made their way to a farm, Johnstone entering into conversation with the farmer, being able to speak Swedish. Owing to the Russians having "commandeered" all his horses for war purposes, thereby preventing him from gathering his crops, the farmer was only too willing to serve the Englishmen and offered them hospitality. Little by little they gleaned scraps of information, and when Bythesea referred to the mails, asking if they were valuable, their host replied that in all probability they were of considerable consequence to the Russians, seeing that they had repaired nine miles of road to enable them to be conveyed along it. Shortly after this, the enemy becoming suspicious, a close search was made of all the neighbourhood, the farmhouse itself being subjected to a very close scrutiny, but, disguised as natives, Bythesea and Johnstone excited no suspicion. On one or two occasions, when Russians were about, they got into a small boat and anchored about half a mile off the coast, cautiously returning after dusk. On the morning of August 12 the farmer informed his guests that the mail had arrived and would be sent to the fort that night, adding that great caution must be exercised as it was known to the Russians that someone from our fleet had landed. As soon as night fell, the two embarked in a small boat, changing into a larger and more serviceable one which they found on the way, and by midnight had arrived at the position they had chosen. Landing very quietly at a point near the road, they went towards it, and had hardly taken up their respective positions when the men with the mails were upon them, Bythesea being concealed so close to the road that one of them almost touched him. Johnstone, who was a few yards away in the direction in which they were making, jumped out into the road, putting his pistol to the head of the foremost man, Bythesea doing the same to one of the others. Taken so completely by surprise and imagining that the attacking party was much larger, they offered no resistance, and were promptly disarmed and bundled into the boat within a minute. The oars were given them and they were ordered to row, Bythesea steering, Johnstone sitting in the bows, both with their pistols ready. Telling the men that the first who stopped rowing would be shot, in a short time they reached their ship, handing the prisoners over to the guard and sending the valuable despatches to Sir Charles Napier and afterwards to General D'Hilliers, who wrote a very flattering letter to Bythesea's Commander, later on writing to Bythesea himself in acknowledgment of his and Johnstone's brave and invaluable action.

Rear-Admiral John Bythesea, V.C., C.B., C.I.E., son of the Rev. G. Bythesea, Freshford, Somerset, was born on June 15, 1827. Educated at Grosvenor College, Bath. Entered the Navy, 1841; Lieutenant, 1849; Commander, 1856; Captain, 1861; attained present rank, 1877. Commanded the *Locust* during Baltic operations, 1855, and the *Cruiser* in China 1858–60, during the war in that country. Was on the Royal Commission on Defence of Canada in 1862. Naval *Attaché* at Washington, 1865–7. Commanded the *Phœbe* under Admiral Hornby in 1870, and from 1874 to 1880 was Consulting Naval Officer to the Indian Government.

WILLIAM JOHNSTONE

(STOKER, ROYAL NAVY)

ASSOCIATED with Commander (now Admiral) John Bythesea, V.C., in an act of great enterprise and daring in August, 1854, on the island of Wardo in the Baltic. (See account of Bythesea.)

History of the Victoria Cross

ROBERT JAMES LINDSAY

(BREVET-MAJOR, AFTERWARDS LIEUT.-COLONEL ROBERT JAMES LOYD-LINDSAY;
THE RIGHT HONBLE. LORD WANTAGE, K.C.B.)

1ST BATT. SCOTS FUSILIER GUARDS

Photo by HEATH, *Piccadilly.*

ON September 20, 1854, at the battle of the Alma, the formation of the line of the regiment became broken. Captain Lindsay stood by the Colours, and, by his brave conduct and splendid example, helped greatly to restore confidence and order.

On November 5, 1854, at the battle of Inkerman, at a critical moment he charged and drove back with a few men a party of Russians, one of whom he ran through the body with his sword.

Lord Wantage (1st Baron, 1885, U.K.) K.C.B., V.C., son of the late General James Lindsay, of Balcarres, was born in 1832. Commander of the Legion of Honour, Commander of the Medjidie. Equerry to H.M. the King when Prince of Wales—1858–9; extra Equerry from 1874; Lieut.-Colonel H.A.C. 1866–81; Lieut.-Colonel Commandant 1st. Vol. Batt. Berkshire Regiment from 1860; Colonel commanding the Home Counties Infantry Volunteer Brigade from 1888. Conservative M.P. for Berkshire, 1865–85; Financial Secretary to the War Office, 1877–80; Lord Lieutenant of Berks from 1886.

His Lordship died at Lockinge House, Wantage, on June 10, 1901.

The Crimean War

JOHN SIMPSON KNOX

(SERGEANT, AFTERWARDS MAJOR)

1ST BATT. SCOTS (FUSILIER) GUARDS AND RIFLE BRIGADE

SERGEANT KNOX was one of the cool heads at Alma, September 20, 1854, when the "line formation" of his battalion was disordered, and to remedy this no one was more energetic than this young sergeant. When an officer in the Rifle Brigade, at the attack on the Redan, June 18, 1855, he volunteered for the ladder party, behaving admirably, and remaining with his men till twice severely wounded, losing his left arm, but, happily, he was not compelled to quit the profession. He rose to the rank of Captain in his new regiment, but retired many years ago, with Field-Officer's rank.

Major Knox died at Cheltenham, aged 78.

JAMES McKECHNIE

(SERGEANT)

SCOTS (FUSILIER) GUARDS

SERGEANT McKECHNIE was one of those who, at a critical moment at the battle of Alma, September 20, 1854, behaved admirably when the shot and shell from the batteries just in front of his battalion threw it into momentary disorder. He held up his rifle and dashed for the Colours, beside which stood, tall and erect, Captain R. J. Lindsay (afterwards Lord Wantage, V.C.). McKechnie called out, as if advancing in line on parade, "By the centre, Scots, by the centre; look to the Colours, and march by them."

History of the Victoria Cross

WILLIAM REYNOLDS
(PRIVATE)
SCOTS (FUSILIER) GUARDS

DECORATED for his gallant behaviour on September 20, 1854, at the battle of Alma, Crimea, when, the formation of the line being thrown into disorder, Reynolds rallied the men round the Colours.

LUKE O'CONNOR
(COLOUR-SERGEANT, NOW MAJOR-GENERAL, RETIRED)
23RD. THE ROYAL WELSH FUSILIERS

Photo by MAULL & FOX.

COLOUR-SERGEANT O'CONNOR is a remarkable instance of a man rising from the ranks to one of the highest positions in the army by sheer merit and bravery. On September 20, 1854, at the battle of Alma, he snatched the fallen Colours from the hands of Lieut. Anstruther, whose blood dyed them as he fell. Although severely wounded himself, being shot in the breast, he persisted in carrying the Queen's Colour throughout the day. On September 8 following, he behaved with marked gallantry at the Redan, wheie he was shot through both thighs.

General O'Connor was born on February 21, 1831. After serving through the Crimean War, he fought in the Indian Mutiny, 1857-8, and the Ashantee Expedition, 1873. He retired from the service in 1887.

The Crimean War

EDWARD W. D. BELL

(CAPTAIN, AFTERWARDS MAJOR-GENERAL, C.B.)

23RD THE ROYAL WELSH FUSILIERS

KNIGHT OF THE LEGION OF HONOUR

CAPTAIN BELL won the Victoria Cross on the heights of Alma on September 20, 1854. Though more than decimated, the gallant Welsh charged up the hill in face of the Russian batteries and dense columns of infantry. The enemy was speedily in retreat. Captain Bell, seeing the enemy's gunners in front of him preparing to ride off with one of their guns, which was actually limbered up, rushed forward, seized the leading horse, and, single-handed, captured the fieldpiece.

All his senior officers being killed or wounded, he found himself in command of the Regiment, which he successfully brought out of action.

The gun was afterwards placed at Woolwich, the horses serving for some time in what was known as the "Black Battery."

Major-General Bell became Lieutenant in April, 1842; Captain in December, 1848; Brevet-Major, 1854; Lieut.-Colonel in January, 1858, Colonel in August, 1862; and Major-General on March 6, 1868. Was appointed to the command of the Belfast District, February 28, 1875.

JOHN PARK

(SERGEANT)

77TH REGIMENT

AWARDED the Victoria Cross for many acts of bravery and devotion in the Crimean War. He was noticed for his conduct at the battles of Alma and Inkerman; highly distinguished himself on April 19, 1855, at the taking of the Russian rifle pits, earning special praise from Colonel Egerton at the time; was severely wounded, and remarked for his determined resolution at the two attacks on the Redan.

History of the Victoria Cross

COLLINGWOOD DICKSON

(BREVET LIEUT.-COLONEL, NOW GENERAL, G.C.B.)

ROYAL ARTILLERY

Photo by BASSANO *London.*

DURING the first bombardment of Sebastopol on October 17, 1854, Sir Collingwood Dickson, seeing that his men were running short of ammunition, went repeatedly with great courage under a hurricane of shot and shell, and carried barrels of powder to them from the magazine. In addition to this he stood for hours exposed to all the dangers around him, directing the unloading and storing of ammunition. This was the first Cross awarded for the *siege* of Sebastopol.

General Sir Collingwood Dickson, son of the late Major-General Sir A. Dickson, G.C.B., was born on November 20, 1817. Educated at R.M.A., Woolwich. Entered R.A., 1835, and was promoted Captain, 1846; Brevet Lieut.-Colonel, 1854; Colonel, June, 1855; General, October, 1877; Inspector-General of Artillery, 1870–75; Colonel Commandant R.A., 1875. Retired in 1885.

WILLIAM PEEL

(CAPTAIN, AFTERWARDS K.C.B.)

ROYAL NAVY

CAPTAIN PEEL was awarded the Victoria Cross for three specific acts of bravery. On October 18, 1854, at the greatest possible risk, he picked up a live shell (the fuse of which was still burning) from several powder-cases outside the Magazine, and threw it over the parapet. The shell burst as it left his hands, but his brave and prompt action saved the Magazine and the lives of all near him.

The Crimean War

At Inkerman, at the Sandbag Battery, the Grenadiers were hard pressed while defending the Colours. This officer was conspicuous for his assistance on this occasion, and specially noticed by H.R.H. the Duke of Cambridge, the Lieut.-General commanding the Division.

At the Redan, on June 18, 1855, he volunteered for the ladder party, carrying the first one himself, till he was struck down.

He took part in the Relief of Lucknow in November, 1857, and at the siege and capture in March, 1858, dying of smallpox at Cawnpore, on his way to Calcutta, on April 27, 1858.

Third son of the Right Hon. Sir Robert Peel, Bart., the distinguished Statesman, Sir William was born on November 2, 1824, and passed away, as above stated, in his thirty-third year.

THOMAS GRADY

(PRIVATE, AFTERWARDS SERGEANT)

4TH KING'S (ROYAL LANCASTER) REGIMENT

THIS brave Irishman, on October 18, 1854, volunteered to repair the embrasures of the battery on the Left Attack, assisted by another whose name has not been handed down. This act was accomplished successfully in clear daylight, under a heavy fire from a whole line of batteries. Again, on November 22, during the repulse of an attack on the most advanced trenches, although severely wounded he refused to quit his post among his comrades, but kept encouraging them to "hold on," and was the means of saving the position and preventing the guns from being spiked.

Sergeant Grady died some years ago in Victoria, New South Wales.

History of the Victoria Cross

WILLIAM McWHEENEY

(SERGEANT)

44TH (ESSEX) REGIMENT

DECORATED for his conduct on October 20, 1854, when he saved the life of Private John Keane who had been dangerously wounded when the Sharpshooters were forced to retreat from the "Quarries." He took Keane on his back and carried him for a long distance under heavy rifle-fire until he could place him in safety. On December 5, 1854, Corporal Courtney, a Sharpshooter, was severely wounded in the head. McWheeney went out into the open and, under a terrific storm of lead, brought him some distance back. He then, with his bayonet, dug up the ground to form a slight cover for him, as they were by no means out of range and the fire was still very severe, and remained with him until darkness had set in, when he was able to retire with him into safety. On June 18, 1855, he volunteered for the advance-guard of General Eyre's Brigade in the Cemetery. The *Gazette* states that he was "always vigilant and active," and that he was "never absent from duty during the war."

JOHN GRIEVE

(SERGEANT-MAJOR)

2ND DRAGOONS

AT Balaklava, October 25, 1854, in the Heavy Cavalry charge, one of Grieve's officers being surrounded by Russian horsemen, he rode to his rescue, cut off the head of one of them, disabled two others, and put them to flight, thereby saving the life of his officer.

The Crimean War

HENRY RAMAGE

(PRIVATE, AFTERWARDS SERGEANT)

2ND DRAGOONS

At the battle of Balaklava, Private McPherson, of the 2nd Dragoons, was severely wounded and surrounded by seven Russians. Private Ramage rode to his help, cut his way through the enemy and saved his comrade's life. On the same day, when the Heavy Brigade was covering the retreat of the Light Cavalry, Private Gardiner's leg was shattered by a round-shot, and he lay on the ground exposed to a very heavy cross-fire. Ramage dashed to his rescue and carried him to the rear, the place where he had fallen being almost immediately covered by Russian Cavalry. He also, when the Heavy Brigade was rallying and the enemy retiring, dismounted and brought in a prisoner from the Russian ranks.

Ramage died at Newbridge, Ireland, not long after receiving his decoration, which was sold in London on June 16, 1903, for £61.

JAMES MOUAT

(SURGEON, AFTERWARDS SURGEON-GENERAL, K.C.B.)

6TH (THE INNISKILLING) DRAGOONS

Photo by ELLIOTT & FRY.

After the retreat of the Light Cavalry at the battle of Balaklava, on October 26, 1854, Lieut.-Colonel Morris, C.B., 17th Lancers, was dangerously wounded and lying in a very exposed place. Surgeon Mouat went to his assistance and, in full view of the enemy, under a most severe fire, dressed his injuries, and by stopping a serious haemorrhage was able to save his life.

Surgeon-General Sir James Mouat, son of the late J. Mouat, M.D., was born in 1815, and died in London on January 4, 1899. Educated at University College and Hospital, London; in 1837 admitted a Member of the Royal College of Surgeons, being elected to the Fellowship in 1852. Entered the Army in 1838, serving, during the

History of the Victoria Cross

Crimean War, at Balaklava, Inkerman, and Tchernaya. Afterwards was principal Medical Officer in New Zealand, 1863-5, receiving the thanks of that Government for his special and valuable services during the war. Appointed Honorary Surgeon to Queen Victoria, 1888, and created a Military K.C.B. in 1894. Knight of the Legion of Honour.

JOHN BERRYMAN
(TROOP-SERGEANT-MAJOR, AFTERWARDS MAJOR)
17TH (THE DUKE OF CAMBRIDGE'S OWN) LANCERS

Photo by BALL, *Regent Street.*

SERGEANT-MAJOR BERRYMAN was one of the many heroes who fought right through the Crimean War. He was "mentioned" for Alma, Balaklava, Inkerman, and MacKenzie's Farm, and at the last place captured three Russian soldiers close up to their own guns. At Balaklava his horse was shot under him in the charge, yet he remained with a wounded and dying officer (Captain Webb), whom he carried out of immediate range of the cannon. For his bravery at Inkerman, on February 24, 1857, he was specially mentioned in the *London Gazette*. Born on July 28, 1825, he died on June 27, 1896.

ALEXANDER ROBERT DUNN
(LIEUTENANT, AFTERWARDS LIEUT.-COLONEL)
11TH HUSSARS

ON October 25, 1854, during the charge of the Light Cavalry at Balaklava, Lieutenant Dunn saved the life of Private Bentley by riding at, and cutting down, some Russians who were attacking him from the rear. Later on he saw Private Levett hard pressed by a Russian Hussar, and rode to his assistance, cutting down his assailant.

In 1858 Lieut.-Colonel Dunn raised and commanded the 100th Royal Canadian Regiment, now 1st Batt. Leinster. He served

The Crimean War

in the Abyssinian War of 1868 as Lieut.-Colonel of the 33rd Regiment, and lost his life during one of the hard fought actions of that year.

JOHN FARRELL
(QUARTERMASTER-SERGEANT)

17TH LANCERS

ON October 25, 1854, after the charge at the battle of Balaklava, when Farrell's horse was shot under him, Captain Webb was severely wounded. Farrell and Berryman (V.C.) carried the officer as far as the pain of his wounds would allow, and, when a stretcher was obtained, he assisted Berryman and a Private of the 13th Dragoons (Malone, V.C.) to carry him from the field. Farrell died at Secunderabad, India, on August 4, 1865.

Photo by COE, *Norwich.*

JOSEPH MALONE
(SERGEANT, AFTERWARDS RIDING MASTER)

13TH HUSSARS

ON October 25, 1854, while returning on foot from the charge at Balaklava, in which his horse had been shot, Malone stayed, under a severe fire, to take charge of Captain Webb, 17th Lancers (who had been mortally wounded), until others arrived to assist in removing him. (See Farrell and Berryman.)

SAMUEL PARKES
(PRIVATE)

4TH (LIGHT) DRAGOONS

DURING the charge of the Light Cavalry at Balaklava, October 25, 1854, Parkes' horse had been shot and he was dismounted, while that of Trumpet-Major Crawford had also fallen and its rider had lost his sword. Parkes dashed up to him, placed himself between him and two Cossacks and drove them off. When attempting to follow the retreat of the Light Cavalry, six Russians attacked them, but he kept them at bay, retiring slowly, until, after defending his friend for some time, his sword was shattered by a shot.

History of the Victoria Cross

CHARLES WOODEN

(SERGEANT-MAJOR, AFTERWARDS QUARTER-MASTER 104TH BENGAL FUSILIERS)

17TH LANCERS

ON October 26, 1854, after the battle of Balaklava, Sergeant-Major Wooden went (with Dr. Mouat, V.C.) to the assistance of Lieut.-Colonel Morris, C.B., and rescued him when lying exposed to a very heavy fire, thereby saving his life.

Photo by MAULL & FOX.

GERALD LITTLEHALES GOODLAKE

(CAPTAIN, AFTERWARDS LIEUT.-GENERAL)

1ST BATT. COLDSTREAM GUARDS

KNIGHT OF THE LEGION OF HONOUR

ON the occasion of "the powerful sortie" made chiefly against the Second Division on October 26, 1854, Major Goodlake was in command of the Sharpshooters of his battalion in the "Windmill Ravine," well in advance of the picket-house erected there. This he held against a large force, his men placing *hors-de-combat* no fewer than thirty-eight of the enemy and taking three prisoners. The Major during this combat was the only officer present, and most of his men were very young soldiers, the successors of their more matured comrades who fell at Alma and during the siege. In November following, in the same place, when commanding almost the same men, he surprised a picket, capturing their rifles and knapsacks.

The Crimean War

The following extract from Kinglake's *Crimea* gives an illustration of the invaluable work done by Captain Goodlake and his Sharpshooters during the war—

MAJOR GOODLAKE, V.C.
From Kinglake's "Crimea"

To assure himself against any ambush, Captain Goodlake (taking with him Sergeant Ashton) had gone up to examine the caves, leaving the rest of his sixty men halted across the bed of the chasm and partly, too, on each bank. Whilst thus left for a moment without their commander, Goodlake's men were suddenly confronted by the sight of the Russian Column thronging up round the corner below. The hostile force seemed like a mob, numbering about six or eight hundred men, and was pressing forward along the bed of the ravine and also along each of its banks. Goodlake's people retreated firing.

Goodlake himself, with Sergeant Ashton at his side, was still by the caves. Hemmed in by assailants and debarred by the craggy and difficult ground from any possibility of effectual retreat, he thought that he and the sergeant must needs submit to be made prisoners. Sergeant Ashton, however, suggested that if the captain and he were made prisoners they would be assuredly put to death, in vengeance for one of their recent exploits (referring to the fact that this little force under Goodlake had lately attacked a Russian picket, taking an officer and some of the men prisoners), and all notion of surrender being thereupon discarded, the alternative of course was resistance. The Russians, whilst closing in upon their two adversaries, fired at them numbers of shots, which all, however, proved harmless. On the other hand Goodlake and the sergeant fired, each of them once, into the nearest clump of Russians, and then with the butt-ends of their rifles, knocked away the foremost of their assailants, and ran down to the foot of the bank. There, however, they were in the midst of a mob of Russians advancing up the ravine. To their great surprise, no one seized them; and it was evident that, owing to the grey cloaks and plain caps they both wore, the enemy was mistaking them for his own fellow-countrymen. Shielded by this illusion, and favoured, too, by the ruggedness of the ground and obstructive thickets of brushwood, which enabled them to be constantly changing their neighbours without exciting attention, they moved on unmolested in the midst of their foes; and, though strange, it is not the less true, that this singular march was continued along a distance of more than half a mile. At length, with its two interlopers, the Russian throng came to a halt, and not without a reason, for it was confronted by the sixty men of the Guards, who, after the lengthened retreat they had made when their Chief was cut off from them, were now plainly making a stand and had posted themselves some thirty yards off, behind a little trench, which there seamed the bed of the gorge. Goodlake, with his trusty sergeant, soon crossed the intervening space which divided the Russians from the English and found himself once more amongst his own people.

Lieut.-General Goodlake, son of T. Goodlake, Esq., of Wadley, Berks, was born on May 14, 1832. Entered the Royal Welsh Fusiliers, 1848, exchanging into the Coldstream Guards in 1850; became Major in the Army, June 6, 1856; A.D.C. to Queen Victoria, 1869; Major-General to the Land Forces, 1879; Lieut.-General, 1881; and died in 1890.

JOHN AUGUSTUS CONOLLY

(LIEUTENANT, AFTERWARDS LIEUT.-COLONEL)

49TH (THE PRINCESS CHARLOTTE OF WALES') REGIMENT

(ROYAL BERKSHIRE)

Photo by MAULL & FOX.

ON the attack by the Russians outside Sebastopol during the "great sortie," on October 26, 1854 (the day after Balaklava), Lieutenant Conolly was in command of his company on outlying picket. The Russians hurled themselves on the Second Division. They were met, in the first instance, by the 49th, resolutely led by Conolly in frequent short, sharp charges, he himself engaging several of them in hand-to-hand fight, one after another, till at length, from loss of blood, he fell insensible, and had to be borne off the field. His gallant behaviour, no less than that of his men, elicited a General Order, in which all were deservedly praised. Soon afterwards he was promoted Captain into the Coldstream Guards as part reward for his bravery and devotion.

Died at the Curragh of Kildare, Ireland, in 1888.

The Crimean War

WILLIAM NATHAN WRIGHTE HEWETT
(LIEUTENANT, AFTERWARDS VICE-ADMIRAL, K.C.B., K.C.S.I.)

NAVAL BRIGADE

KNIGHT OF THE LEGION OF HONOUR

Photo by FLEMING, *Southsea.*

AT the great sortie from Sebastopol, on October 26, 1854, Lieutenant William Hewett was in charge of a battery. The Russians were swarming towards his post when the word was passed—by whom it was never ascertained—"Spike the guns and retire." Hewett replied that "such an order did not come from Captain Lushington, and he would not do it till it did." He then pulled down the parapet, and, assisted by a few soldiers, swung the gun round towards the advancing thousands, into which he poured so steady a fire that the advance was checked, and the battery saved. For his pluck at Inkerman on November 5, he was specially "named" in despatches.

Sir William Hewett died at Portsmouth on May 13, 1888, aged 54.

Son of William Hewett, Esq., he was born at Brighton in 1834. Entered the Royal Navy at the age of thirteen; became Captain in 1862; Rear-Admiral, 1878. Served in China and in Burmah; also in Ashantee, including the capture of Coomassie (K.C.B.); Egypt, 1882; and the Eastern Soudan, 1884.

History of the Victoria Cross

JAMES OWENS
(CORPORAL)
49TH REGIMENT

DECORATED for his bravery on October 30, 1854, in personal encounter with the Russians and for nobly assisting Major Conolly of the Coldstream Guards. He died on August 30, 1901, and his Victoria Cross was sold in London on October 15, 1902.

WILLIAM STANLACK
(PRIVATE)
1ST BATT. COLDSTREAM GUARDS

DECORATED for his courage in volunteering, when engaged as a Sharpshooter in October, 1854, to crawl up to within six yards of a Russian sentry, in order to enable his officer (Major Goodlake, V.C.) to effect a surprise. The danger he ran was fully explained to Private Stanlack, but it did not deter him from undertaking the perilous adventure.

THOMAS BEACH
(PRIVATE)
55TH REGIMENT

ON November 5, 1854, at the battle of Inkerman, Lieut.-Colonel Carpenter of the 41st Regiment was lying wounded and several of the enemy were robbing him. Beach was on picket at the time. Seeing what the Russians were about, he attacked and killed two of them, protecting the officer from further molestation until the arrival of some men of the 41st Regiment.

JOHN BYRNE
(PRIVATE)

68TH REGIMENT

AT the battle of Inkerman, November 5, 1854, the 68th were ordered to retire, but Byrne returned towards the enemy and brought back a wounded soldier who would otherwise have fallen into their hands. On May 11, following, he engaged in a hand-to-hand fight with a Russian on the parapet of the work he was defending. He killed his opponent and took away his arms.

HENRY HUGH CLIFFORD
(LIEUTENANT, AFTERWARDS MAJOR-GENERAL, K.C.M.G.)

RIFLE BRIGADE

Photo by FRADELLE & YOUNG.

ON November 5, 1854, at the battle of Inkerman, Lieutenant Clifford was conspicuous by his bravery in leading a charge against the Russian lines. He cut off the head of one man and the arm of another, and by his determined assault, and the splendid following of his men, drove the Russians back. During the contest he saved the life of a soldier who had been wounded.

Son of the 7th Lord Clifford of Chudleigh, he was born in Shropshire, on September 12, 1828, and died at Ugbrooke Park, Chudleigh, in Devonshire, on April 12, 1883.

EDWARD ST. JOHN DANIEL
(MIDSHIPMAN)

ROYAL NAVY

RECOMMENDED by Sir Stephen Lushington for conspicuous bravery on November 5, 1854, when a call for volunteers was made to bring up powder from a wagon which had been left in a most exposed position owing to the horses being all killed. Captain Peel (V.C.), who was in command of the battery at the time, specially reported the bravery of this young naval officer. He also accompanied Captain Peel as A.D.C. at the battle of Inkerman, and, at the attack on the Redan on June 18, 1855, when his officer was wounded, displayed the greatest devotion to him, placing a *tourniquet* on his arm under a terrific fire.

Daniel left the Navy in 1861, and his Bronze Cross found its way into the United Service Institute, Whitehall, where it now remains.

JAMES H. GORMAN

(SEAMAN)

Royal Navy

Sir S. Lushington, in a letter of June 7, 1856, mentions Gorman, Reeves and Scholefield, three seamen, for their bravery on November 5, 1854. At the battle of Inkerman the Right Lancaster Battery was attacked, and these men were the survivors of five who mounted a *banquette* and, making use of the rifles of disabled soldiers, loaded for them by their friends below, kept up a sharp fire under a hail of lead from the Russians.

Gorman died on December 27, 1889.

ANDREW HENRY

(SERGEANT-MAJOR, AFTERWARDS CAPTAIN, LAND TRANSPORT CORPS)

Royal Artillery

At the battle of Inkerman on November 5, 1854, Sergeant-Major Henry displayed great bravery in defending the guns of his battery against overwhelming numbers of the enemy, during which he was terribly wounded. His undaunted courage is thus referred to in Kinglake's *Crimea*—

"When the foremost of the enemy's troops had so closely surrounded Henry's gun as to be already but a few paces off, they charged in with loud shouts, undertaking to bayonet the gunners; but by Henry himself, and one at least of his people, they were encountered with desperate valour. Henry called upon the men to defend the gun. He and a valiant gunner named James Taylor drew their swords and stood firm. The throng of the Russians

The Crimean War

came closing in, very many of them for some reason bareheaded, and numbers of them, in the words of a victim, 'howling like mad dogs.' Henry with his left hand wrested a bayonet from one of the Russians and found means to throw the man down, fighting hard all the time with his sword arm against some of his other assailants. Soon both Henry and Taylor were closed in upon from all sides and bayoneted again and again, Taylor then receiving his death-wounds. Henry received in his chest the up-thrust of a bayonet, delivered with such power as to lift him almost from the ground, and at the same time he was stabbed in the back and stabbed in the arms. Then, from loss of blood, he became unconscious, but the raging soldiery, inflamed by religion, did not cease from stabbing his heretic body. He received twelve wounds, yet survived."

Andrew Henry "rose from the ranks" to Lieutenant in the Artillery, May 15, 1855, becoming Captain six months later. Possessed four clasps for the Crimea in addition to the Sultan's medal.

JOHN McDERMOND
(PRIVATE)

47TH REGIMENT

AT Inkerman, November 5, 1854, this soldier saved the life of Colonel Hely, who was lying wounded and surrounded by a number of Russians. McDermond rushed to his rescue and killed the soldier who had disabled him. (See also Rowlands, V.C.)

AMBROSE MADDEN
(SERGEANT-MAJOR)

41ST REGIMENT

DURING the battle of Inkerman, Madden led a party of his battalion and captured a Russian officer and fourteen soldiers, three of whom he personally accounted for.

History of the Victoria Cross

FREDERICK MILLER

(MAJOR, AFTERWARDS LIEUT.-COLONEL)

ROYAL ARTILLERY

KNIGHT OF THE LEGION OF HONOUR

AT Inkerman, November 5, 1854, the Russians had surrounded a battery, driving part of one of our Infantry Regiments through it. Major Miller, however, afterwards personally attacked three Russians, and led his men in charging the occupants of the battery, successfully preventing them from doing any damage to the guns.

Entered the Royal Artillery in December, 1848, and became Captain in April, 1855.

ANTHONY PALMER

(PRIVATE, AFTERWARDS CAPTAIN 3RD ESSEX R.V.)

3RD BATTALION GRENADIER GUARDS

DECORATED for his bravery at Inkerman on November 5, 1854, when he followed Sir Charles Russell, V.C., into the Sandbag Battery. Was also present when the charge was made in defence of the Colours. It is stated that Private Palmer saved the life of Sir Charles Russell by killing the Russian who was about to bayonet him.

His Victoria Cross is now in the United Service Institute, London.

The Crimean War

THE HONOURABLE HENRY HUGH MANVERS PERCY
(COLONEL, AFTERWARDS LORD PERCY)
GRENADIER GUARDS

On November 5, 1854, at the battle of Inkerman, Colonel Percy charged alone far ahead of his men into the Sandbag Battery, which was at the time strongly held by the enemy, who kept up a heavy fire of musketry. On the same day he found himself, with many soldiers of various regiments who had charged too far, almost surrounded by the Russians.

Without ammunition and exposed to severe fire from the enemy, their position was most precarious, but Colonel Percy, by his knowledge of the ground and skilful leading, brought the men to where fresh ammunition could be obtained, and they were able to continue the fight.

H.R.H. the Duke of Cambridge signified his approbation of his gallant conduct on the spot.

JOHN PRETTYJOHN
(CORPORAL, AFTERWARDS COLOUR-SERGEANT)
ROYAL MARINE LIGHT INFANTRY

At the battle of Inkerman, Corporal Prettyjohn greatly distinguished himself by his cool courage, in going on ahead of the men and opening fire upon the enemy, killing four of them and so checking their advance.

He died on January 20, 1887.

Photo by HAWKE, *Plymouth.*

History of the Victoria Cross

THOMAS REEVES

(SEAMAN)

ROYAL NAVY

ASSOCIATED on November 5, 1854, at Inkerman, in a heroic act described in the record of Gorman (V.C.).

HUGH ROWLANDS

(BREVET MAJOR, NOW GENERAL, K.C.B., C.B.)

41ST REGIMENT

Photo by ELLIOTT & FRY.

DECORATED for gallant conduct on November 5, 1854, in saving the life of Colonel Hely of the 47th Regiment, who was wounded and surrounded by Russian soldiers. (See MacDermond, V.C.) Also at Inkerman, at the commencement of the great battle, his bravery was most conspicuous. By his exertions and courageous leading, the advanced picket held the ground they had occupied, against the attack of the enemy.

Born in 1829, Sir Hugh Rowlands entered the army in 1849. For his services in the Crimean War, besides the decoration of the Victoria Cross, he received his Brevet-Majority, 5th Class Medjidie, and Turkish Medal, and was created Knight of the Legion of Honour. Served in the Kaffir and Zulu Wars, 1877-9, being mentioned in despatches; from 1884-9 was in command of a 1st class district in India, and from 1893-6 commanded the Scottish District.

The Crimean War

Photo by LAMBERT, WESTON & SON, *Folkestone.*

SIR CHARLES RUSSELL, BART.
(BREVET-MAJOR, AFTERWARDS LIEUT.-COLONEL)
GRENADIER GUARDS

ON November 5, 1854, at the battle of Inkerman, Sir Charles Russell offered to dislodge a party of Russians from the Sandbag Battery if any one would follow him. His call was quickly answered, Sergeant Norman, V.C., Privates Anthony Palmer, V.C., and Bailey being the first. Bailey was killed, but under the courageous leadership of Sir Charles Russell the attack proved a complete success, the enemy being driven from their position.

MARK SCHOLEFIELD
(SEAMAN)
ROYAL NAVY

AT the battle of Inkerman, November 5, 1854, Scholefield was associated with Gorman (V.C.) and Reeves (V.C.) in a heroic act described in the record of Gorman.

MARK WALKER
(LIEUTENANT AND ADJUTANT, AFTERWARDS GENERAL, K.C.B.)
30TH (CAMBRIDGESHIRE) REGIMENT

LIEUTENANT WALKER was awarded the Victoria Cross for a particularly courageous action at the battle of Inkerman on November 5, 1854. When the alarm was given by the pickets, the 30th Regiment advanced in two battalions, the right under Colonel Mauleverer, the left under Colonel Petullo. Lieutenant Walker was with the former battalion, which moved towards a low wall and lay down. Suddenly from out the thick fog, which had been hanging over the ground since daylight, two heavy columns of Russian Infantry appeared close upon them, and the 30th were ordered to open fire. In those days it was the custom to pile arms at night before the men's tents, and the stoppers of the rifles had been lost, causing the arms to become wet and useless. With the Russians coming closer and closer, the position became

History of the Victoria Cross

Photo by LAMBERT, WESTON & SON, *Folkestone.*

most critical, and under such disadvantages, there was a possibility of the men becoming nervous and out-of-hand. It was at this moment that Lieutenant Walker grasped the situation. He sprang up on the low wall, and calling on his men to follow him with the bayonet, led them straight at the Russian ranks. The suddenness of the appearance and attack of our men, and the fact that they could not see how small our party really was, caused a panic among the enemy, who, in spite of the exhortations of their officers, turned and bolted, followed some distance by the intrepid little party. The success of this affair was almost entirely due to the cool and courageous conduct of Lieutenant Walker, who, by his splendid example under sudden adverse circumstances, gave encouragement to his men, and turned what might have proved a serious reverse into a brilliant episode of the battle. Soon afterwards, Lieutenant Walker volunteered and led a party which destroyed a Russian rifle pit, and for his conduct on this occasion was promoted into the Buffs.

General Sir Mark Walker, son of Captain Alexander Walker, of Gore Port, county Westmeath, a distinguished Peninsular officer, was born on November 24, 1827. Educated at Portarlington, he entered the army in 1846 and served as Adjutant of the 30th Regiment all through the Crimean War. At the battle of Alma his horse was shot under him and he was wounded. While serving in the trenches he was again wounded, this time so seriously as to necessitate amputation of the right arm. Frequently mentioned in despatches. Served through the China War of 1860 as Brigade Major. Commanded a Brigade at Kamptu, 1875–9; at Aldershot, 1883–4; and Gibraltar, 1884–8. Colonel of the Sherwood Foresters from 1900. He died at Arlington Rectory, Barnstaple, on July 18, 1902, and is buried at Folkestone, where he had lived for many years.

The Crimean War

GEORGE WALTERS
(SERGEANT)
49TH REGIMENT

ON November 5, 1854, at the battle of Inkerman, Brigadier-General Adams, C.B., was surrounded by Russians and in a perilous position. Walters went to the officer's rescue and saved his life by bayonetting one of his assailants.

F. WHEATLEY
(PRIVATE)
1ST BATT. RIFLE BRIGADE

ON November 10, 1854, before Sebastopol, this soldier performed the plucky act of throwing over the parapet a live shell which had fallen into the trenches.

CLAUDE THOMAS BOURCHIER

Photo by MAULL & FOX.

(LIEUTENANT, AFTERWARDS COLONEL)
1ST BATT. (THE PRINCE CONSORT'S OWN) RIFLE BRIGADE
KNIGHT OF THE LEGION OF HONOUR

LIEUTENANT BOURCHIER was among those who captured and held the Russian rifle pits on November 20, 1854.

These places were appropriately called by the besiegers "ovens," or "wasps' nests," and from them Russian riflemen killed many of our men every night. To put an end to this, Major Bourchier determined that they should be captured and destroyed. In doing this he so highly distinguished himself that his name and his acts of bravery were promulgated in French General Orders. On the fall of Lieutenant Tryon he succeeded to the command of the two hundred men of his regiment engaged in effecting this important capture.

History of the Victoria Cross

WILLIAM JAMES MONTGOMERY CUNINGHAME

(CAPTAIN, AFTERWARDS COLONEL SIR WILLIAM, BART.)

1ST BATT. (PRINCE CONSORT'S OWN) RIFLE BRIGADE

On November 20, 1854, during the capture of the Russian rifle pits, Captain Cuninghame displayed great bravery. The fight was a most severe one, and his conduct was particularly distinguished. The affair attracted the attention of the French General, who recorded it in General Orders. Sir William Cuninghame, Bart., born in 1834, was present at the actions of Alma, Balaklava, Inkerman and Sebastopol.

Photo by MAULL & FOX.

WILBRAHAM OATES LENNOX

(LIEUTENANT, AFTERWARDS LIEUT.-GENERAL, K.C.B.)

ROYAL ENGINEERS

Photo by ELLIOTT & FRY.

On November 20, 1854, during the siege of Sebastopol, it became necessary to establish a lodgment in some dangerous rifle pits, overhanging the Woronzoff Road. Lieutenant Lennox was conspicuous, among many others, by his "cool and gallant conduct" in repelling the numerous and persistent assaults of the enemy. This brilliant operation drew forth the compliment of a special order from Maréchal Canrobert, of the French Army, at whose request the Rifle Brigade was selected to make the capture.

Sir Wilbraham Lennox, son of the late Colonel Lord J. G. Lennox, was born in 1830, and served through the Indian Mutiny; with the German Army in the

The Crimean War

Franco-Prussian War, 1870; and with the Turkish Army during the Russo-Turkish War, 1877. Brigadier-General in Egypt, 1884–7; and in command of the Forces at Ceylon, 1887–8; Director-General of Military Education, 1893–4.

WILLIAM NORMAN

(PRIVATE)

7TH ROYAL FUSILIERS (CITY OF LONDON REGIMENT)

Photo by TAYLOR *Manchester*

ON the night of December 19, 1854, when placed on single sentry duty a considerable distance in advance of the others in the White Horse Ravine (a task requiring much courage and vigilance, as the enemy's picket was only 300 yards distant), three Russians crept up under cover of brushwood to reconnoitre our position. Without any noise, lest he should give the alarm, Private Norman went stealthily towards them, and, single-handed, captured two of them

WILLIAM JAMES LENDRIM

(CORPORAL, AFTERWARDS QUARTERMASTER-SERGEANT)

ROYAL ENGINEERS

Photo by PHILLIPS, *Farnborough Road.*

THE Victoria Cross was awarded to this non-commissioned officer for intrepid conduct on April 11, 1855, before Sebastopol, in getting on to a parapet under a hail of lead and extinguishing a fire which had broken out among the sandbags.

He was particularly prominent in setting a fine example of courage to a party of one hundred and fifty French Chasseurs, whom he was superintending, on February 14, 1855, during the building of No. 9 Battery, Left Attack, and replacing all the capsized gabions under heavy fire. (Awarded French War Medal.) On April 20 he was one of the four volunteers to destroy the farthest Russian rifle pit.

He died in October, 1892, at Camberley, where he had long held the post of Quartermaster-Sergeant to the Staff College.

GEORGE GARDINER
(COLOUR-SERGEANT)
57TH WEST MIDDLESEX (DUKE OF CAMBRIDGE'S OWN) REGIMENT

Photo by AYTON, Edinburgh.

On March 22, 1855, Sergeant Gardiner was orderly-sergeant to the field officers on trench duty. The Russian attack was sudden, and there was a momentary retirement out of the trenches. Gardiner hastened to the threatened point, rallied the men, led them against the enemy and regained the position at the point of the bayonet. On June 18, his courage and devotion to duty was marvellous. He remained in front of the enemy, encouraging others to do the same, taking shelter in the holes made by the exploded shells, and making a parapet of the dead bodies of his comrades! From this gruesome entrenchment they kept up a steady fire until their ammunition was exhausted.

This was done, according to the official account, under a fire by which nearly half the officers and one-third of the rank and file of the party of the Regiment were placed *hors-de-combat*.

ALEXANDER WRIGHT
(PRIVATE)
77TH REGIMENT

Decorated for special bravery during the whole Crimean War. Greatly distinguished himself on the night of March 22, 1855, in repelling a *sortie*, and at the taking of the rifle pits on the night of April 19, 1855, being specially noticed on that occasion for the fine example he gave the men while holding the position under a terrible fire. Displayed great bravery also on August 30, 1855, when he was wounded.

The Crimean War

WILLIAM COFFEY
(PRIVATE)

34TH REGIMENT

DECORATED for his bravery on March 29, 1855, when he threw a lighted shell, which had fallen into the trench, over the parapet.

JOHN SULLIVAN
(BOATSWAIN'S MATE)

ROYAL NAVY

KNIGHT OF THE LEGION OF HONOUR

SIR S. LUSHINGTON recommended Sullivan for the Victoria Cross for an act of great bravery on April 10, 1855. A concealed Russian Battery was doing great execution on one of our advanced works, and, in order to enable our No. 5 Battery to open fire on it, Sullivan deliberately placed a flag on a mound in a most exposed position under a terrific fire. Commander Kennedy reported that Sullivan's gallantry was always conspicuous.

Photo by YERBURY, *Edinburgh.*

SAMUEL EVANS
(PRIVATE)

19TH (1ST YORKSHIRE) (ALEXANDRA, PRINCESS OF WALES' OWN) REGIMENT

SAMUEL EVANS volunteered, on April 13, 1855, to enter an embrasure in order to repair the damage done by a concentrated fire on one of our batteries before Sebastopol. Our gunners were nearly all killed, and while others were being brought up to take their place, Evans and Callaghan entered the battery, and, leaping into the embrasure under a heavy fire, undauntedly persevered until the breach was mended. Callaghan fell during the war. Evans was one of the sixty-two who received the Cross

History of the Victoria Cross

from Her Majesty the Queen on June 26, 1857. Originally a 26th Cameronian, which he joined in 1839, serving with it in China in 1842, gaining his first Medal, followed by the Crimean with three clasps, the French and Turkish. He died at Edinburgh in his eightieth year in October, 1901.

MATTHEW CHARLES DIXON
(CAPTAIN, NOW MAJOR-GENERAL, RETIRED)

ROYAL ARTILLERY

KNIGHT OF THE LEGION OF HONOUR

Photo by ELLIOTT & FRY, *London.*

COLONEL DIXON was in command of a battery before Sebastopol, on April 17, 1855. On the afternoon of that date, during a terrible cannonade, a shell from the enemy blew up his magazines, destroyed the parapet, killed and wounded ten men, dismounted or otherwise disabled five guns, and covered a sixth with earth. One solitary gun remained. With this he encouraged and helped his few remaining men to open fire on the enemy, keeping it in action, working as a gunner himself, until the sun went down, and being all the time (some seven hours) exposed to the concentrated fire of the enemy's line of batteries.

Major-General Dixon, son of General Matthew Dixon, R.E., was born at Avranches in Brittany in 1821. Educated R.M.A., Woolwich. Joined the R.A. on March 19, 1839; became Captain, 1848; Major, 1855; Colonel, 1860; and Major-General, 1869.

The Crimean War

HENRY McDONALD
(COLOUR-SERGEANT, AFTERWARDS CAPTAIN)
ROYAL ENGINEERS

DECORATED for conspicuous bravery on April 19, 1855, when engaged in effecting a lodgment in the enemy's rifle pits, in front of the Left Advance of the Right Attack on Sebastopol. Later on in the day, the Engineer officers being wounded and the command devolving on him, he persisted in a most determined manner in carrying on the Sap, in spite of the repeated attacks of the enemy.

He died in Glasgow, on February 15, 1893, aged 70.

JOSEPH BRADSHAW
(PRIVATE)
2ND BATT. RIFLE BRIGADE (THE PRINCE CONSORT'S OWN)

AMONG some almost impregnable rocks overhanging the Woronzoff Road the Russians had constructed rifle pits, and from these a harassing fire was kept up day and night upon our men. As this was becoming unbearable and greatly interfered with some works we were engaged upon, Bradshaw, on April 22, 1855 (accompanied by Robert Humpston, V.C.), attacked and captured one of the pits in broad daylight, holding it until support arrived, when the rest of these "wasp's nests"—as they were called—were destroyed.

For his gallant exploit he received a gratuity of £5 and was promoted on the spot.

Photo by LAMBERT, WESTON & SON, *Folkestone.*

History of the Victoria Cross

ROBERT HUMPSTON
(PRIVATE)
2ND BATT. RIFLE BRIGADE

Photo by PRICE, *Derby.*

A NEW battery was being erected by our men on the extreme right front of the 2nd Parallel Left Attack and every night the work was greatly impeded by the fire from some Russians in a rifle pit, situated among the rocks overhanging the Woronzoff Road, between the 3rd Parallel Right Attack and "the Quarries." On April 22, 1855, in broad daylight Robert Humpston and Joseph Bradshaw (V.C.) stormed and took it, and on further support being obtained, they eventually destroyed it. Both men received a gratuity of £5 and were promoted, in addition to being awarded the Victoria Cross.

R. McGREGOR
(PRIVATE)
2ND BATT. RIFLE BRIGADE

DECORATED for his conspicuous bravery when employed as a Sharpshooter in July, 1855. Two Russians occupying a rifle pit were most annoying by their continuous fire, and McGregor crossed the open space under a hail of bullets, took shelter under a rock and dislodged them, occupying the position himself.

The Crimean War

THOMAS DE COURCY HAMILTON

(CAPTAIN, AFTERWARDS MAJOR-GENERAL) 68TH DURHAM LIGHT INFANTRY

KNIGHT OF THE LEGION OF HONOUR

Photo by WHITE, *Cheltenham.*

On the night of May 11, 1855, a most determined sortie was made by the Russians from Sebastopol, but Captain Hamilton led a few men from a battery of which he held possession and boldly charged the enemy. His gallantry and daring conduct on this occasion was most conspicuous, and by his courageous initiative the works were saved from falling into the enemy's hands.

Major-General Hamilton, son of the late James John Hamilton, Esq., of Ballymacoll, Co. Meath, was born at Stranraer, Wigtonshire, July 20, 1825. Educated privately. Joined the 90th Light Infantry, 1842, serving through the Kaffir War of 1846. Present with the 68th Light Infantry at Alma, Balaklava, Inkerman and the siege and fall of Sebastopol, obtaining medal and four clasps and the Turkish medal. Retired 1874.

CECIL WILLIAM BUCKLEY

(LIEUTENANT, AFTERWARDS CAPTAIN) ROYAL NAVY

KNIGHT OF THE LEGION OF HONOUR

On May 29, 1855, while serving as Junior Lieutenant of the *Miranda*, Captain Buckley, accompanied by Lieutenant Burgoyne (V.C.) and Gunner John Robarts (V.C.), landed and set fire to immense quantities of stores belonging to the Russians at Genitchi, in the Sea of Azoff. Captain Lysons, in his despatch, remarked that these stores were in a particularly favourable position for supplying the Russian Army, and that their destruction was of the utmost importance. This act was carried out in the presence of a

History of the Victoria Cross

Photo by MAULL & FOX.

very large force of the enemy and at imminent risk.

On June 3, following, Captain Buckley, this time in company with Henry Cooper (V.C.), boatswain, performed a similar act of bravery at Taganrog, the dangers of this second desperate undertaking being equally as great as the first.

His name appears *first* in the *Gazette* as being awarded the Victoria Cross, although the *earliest* act for which the decoration has been gained was performed by Mr. Lucas. The institution of the Victoria Cross was made retrospective to the commencement of the Crimean War.

Captain Buckley died at Funchal, Madeira, on December 7, 1872.

HUGH TALBOT BURGOYNE

(LIEUTENANT, AFTERWARDS CAPTAIN)

ROYAL NAVY

HUGH TALBOT BURGOYNE was Senior Lieutenant of the *Swallow*, in the Sea of Azoff, in May, 1855, and on the 29th of that month, with Lieutenant C. W. Buckley (V.C.) and Mr. J. Robarts (V.C.), gunner, landed at Genitchi and destroyed, in spite of an overwhelming force, vast quantities of Government stores and forage for use of the Russian Army in the Crimea. At Taganrog, on June 3, he performed a similar act of daring, in face of a still stronger force.

Captain Burgoyne, fifteen years afterwards, when in command of H.M.S. *Captain*, went down with that vessel off Cape Finisterre during the night of September 6, 1870. Of the officers and crew, 490 men, only eighteen were saved. The names of the men drowned are to be found recorded on a brass tablet in St. Paul's Cathedral.

Photo by MAULL & FOX.

The Crimean War

JOHN ROBARTS
(CHIEF GUNNER) ROYAL NAVY
KNIGHT OF THE
LEGION OF HONOUR

Mr. J. Robarts, on May 29 and June 3, 1855, was one of the few who landed from the boats of the *Miranda* to destroy stores, forage and ammunition at Genitchi and Taganrog. (See Lieutenant Buckley, V.C., and Lieutenant Burgoyne, V.C.)

Mr. Robarts died October 17, 1888.

HENRY COOPER
(BOATSWAIN) ROYAL NAVY
KNIGHT OF THE LEGION OF
HONOUR

Henry Cooper accompanied his commander, Lieutenant Buckley, R.N., in his gallant and desperate exploit at Taganrog, on the night of June 3, 1855, when he landed in the face of a great force of Russians and fired the stores. (See account of Lieutenant Buckley.)

Cooper survived his chief by twenty-one years, having died at Tor Point, Devon, on July 15, 1893.

GEORGE SYMONS
(LIEUTENANT, 5TH BATT. MILITARY TRAIN)
(LATE SERGEANT ROYAL ARTILLERY)

Decorated for the heroic act on June 6, 1855, of unmasking the embrasures of a five-gun battery. The Russians commenced a terrific fire on his opening the

History of the Victoria Cross

first embrasure, and increased its ferocity in proportion as each additional one was opened. He performed the uncovering of the last one by boldly mounting the parapet and throwing down the sandbags, but was badly wounded by a shell which burst while he was performing his task. The Cross awarded him for this brave act has found its way to the United Service Institute, London.

MATTHEW HUGHES
(PRIVATE)
7TH REGIMENT

THE gallant conduct of Hughes was specially noticed by Colonel Campbell, 90th Light Infantry, on June 7, 1855, at the storming of "the Quarries." He twice went for ammunition across the open ground, also going to the front and bringing in Private John Hampton, who was lying wounded. On June 18, 1855, he volunteered to bring in Lieutenant Hobson of his regiment, who had been shot, and in performing this humane act was himself severely wounded.

THOMAS ARTHUR
(GUNNER AND DRIVER)
ROYAL ARTILLERY

ON June 7, 1855, when in charge of the Magazine in one of the batteries, Arthur carried, of his own accord, barrels of powder and ammunition for the 7th Fusiliers several times across the open. On June 18, 1855, he volunteered for and formed one of the party who spiked the guns at the assault on the Redan. Arthur fought in the China War of 1860 and died at Savernake in March, 1902, his Cross being sold in London on July 17 of that year for £47.

The Crimean War

HENRY MITCHELL JONES

(CAPTAIN)

7TH THE ROYAL FUSILIERS (CITY OF LONDON REGIMENT)

ON June 7, 1855, during the attack on the "Quarries" before Sebastopol, Captain Jones behaved with great coolness and daring in the face of overwhelming numbers. Repeatedly he led the men around him to repel the continual assaults of the enemy during the night. Although suffering from severe wounds received earlier in the day, in order to encourage his men he remained unflinchingly all night long at his dangerous post, until after daylight next morning.

Retiring in 1857, Captain Jones has occupied diplomatic positions in Tabreez, Christiania, Philippopolis, Bangkok, Lima, and Quito.

JOHN LYONS

(PRIVATE)

19TH REGIMENT

DECORATED for bravely taking up, on June 10, 1855, a live shell which had fallen among the guard in the trenches and throwing it over the parapet.

History of the Victoria Cross

THOMAS WILKINSON

(BOMBARDIER) ROYAL MARINE ARTILLERY

KNIGHT OF THE LEGION

OF HONOUR

THOMAS WILKINSON was specially recommended for his brave conduct on June 5, 1855. He was in the advanced batteries, and when the breast-work was much injured by the Russian Artillery, most courageously repaired it under a very galling fire.

He died at York on September 22, 1887.

JOSEPH PROSSER

(PRIVATE)

2ND BATT. 1ST REGIMENT

DECORATED for two acts of bravery. On June 16, 1855, when on duty before Sebastopol, he pursued and caught, under two heavy cross-fires, a soldier deserting to the enemy. On August 11, 1855, when in the most advanced trench before Sebastopol, he left it and went to the assistance of a soldier of the 95th Regiment who had fallen badly wounded, and succeeded in carrying him into safety, all the time under a heavy fire.

JOHN ALEXANDER

(PRIVATE)

90TH REGIMENT

ON June 18, 1855, after the attack on the Redan, Alexander went out of the trenches and brought in several wounded under a heavy fire.

He also, on September 6, 1855, went out and assisted to bring in Captain Buckley, of the Scots Fusilier Guards, who was lying dangerously wounded in an exposed position. He never lived to receive the Cross he so nobly earned, as he was killed in India on September 24, 1857, during the Mutiny.

The Crimean War

HENRY CURTIS
(BOATSWAIN'S MATE)
ROYAL NAVY

THE act of bravery and of humanity which gained for this " blue-jacket " the Victoria Cross, on June 18, 1855, is given in the *Record* of Admiral Henry Raby, V.C. On that day, with J. Taylor, V.C., he assisted in rescuing a young soldier of the 57th in front of the Redan. The three sallied out of the shelter of the trench and brought in the wounded man, who had been shot through both legs.

The distance they had to travel forward and back was about a hundred yards each way.

Curtis died at Buckland, Portsmouth, on November 23, 1896.

HOWARD CRAUFURD ELPHINSTONE
(LIEUTENANT, AFTERWARDS MAJOR-GENERAL, K.C.B.) ROYAL ENGINEERS
KNIGHT OF THE LEGION OF HONOUR

DURING the night of June 18, 1855, after an unsuccessful attack on the Redan, this brave officer collected together a party of volunteers of all corps and proceeded to bring back from under the enemy's guns on the ramparts the scaling-ladders left behind during the assault, thereby saving them from falling into the hands of the Russians. No sooner had he finished his task than he again set forth, leading the same gallant men, to search for the wounded who were lying close up to the Redan,

Photo by MAULL & FOX, *London.*

and whose cries for water could be heard in the distance from time to time. In this he was most successful, carrying in no less than twenty men himself. It is sad to relate that Sir Howard Elphinstone was, on March 8, 1890, washed overboard and drowned when on a voyage to Madeira on R.M.S. *Tongariro*.

Son of Captain Alexander Elphinstone, R.N., he was born at Riga, Northern Russia, on December 12, 1829. Educated abroad and at Woolwich, passing into the Royal Engineers in December, 1847; became Captain, 1856; Colonel, 1864; Major-General, 1887; A.D.C. to H.M. Queen Victoria, 1877–87. Commanded the Devonport district from 1889 until his death.

THOMAS ESMONDE

(CAPTAIN, AFTERWARDS LIEUT.-COLONEL)

18TH (THE ROYAL IRISH) REGIMENT

On June 18, 1855, during the attack on the Redan, Captain Esmonde several times displayed great gallantry in rescuing the wounded, all the time under a very heavy fire from the enemy.

On June 20, while in command of a covering-party, a fireball fell close to them, and, knowing that a heavy fire would greet any one exposing himself, he called to his men to stand aside and take shelter, and dashing out commenced to extinguish it. As he had anticipated, a terrific hail of shot and shell was directed upon him, but in spite of all he succeeded in his courageous act and escaped unscathed.

GERALD GRAHAM

(LIEUTENANT, AFTERWARDS LIEUT.-GENERAL, G.C.B., G.C.M.G.)

ROYAL ENGINEERS

KNIGHT OF THE LEGION OF HONOUR

Sir Gerald's first recorded conspicuous act of bravery happened on June 18, 1855. The Redan—in compliment to our brave allies, and in order to obliterate the memories of another June 18, just forty years before—was

The Crimean War

Photo by ELLIOTT & FRY.

to be attacked, with what result is well known. Lieutenant Graham — he was then only twenty-four — led a ladder-party right up to the cannon's mouth. Our columns were repulsed, and obliged to retire, and it was then that Lieutenant Graham sallied forth, and with great dash rescued from death and misery many wounded officers and men. Sir Gerald Graham's later campaigns have been those of China, 1860; (Medjidie) Egypt, 1882; Eastern Soudan, 1884 (El-Teb and Tamaai); and Suakin, 1885. Retired, 1890.

Son of R. H. Graham, M.D., of Eden Brows, in Cumberland, he was born on June 27, 1831, and died in his seventy-ninth year at Bideford, Devon, on December 17, 1899.

WILLIAM HOPE

(LIEUTENANT) 7TH. THE ROYAL FUSILIERS (CITY OF LONDON REGIMENT)

LATER LIEUT.-COL. CITY OF LONDON A.V.

Photo by HAWKE, Plymouth.

ON June 18, 1855, our troops were forced to retire after the attack on the Redan. Lieutenant Hope, being informed by Sergeant-Major William Bacon that an officer, Lieutenant Hobson, had been severely wounded and was lying outside the trenches, started off to search for him, and found him in the old agricultural ditch running towards the left flank of the Redan. He then went for assistance, and four men returned with him, but he saw the officer could not be removed without a stretcher, so went back across the open ground to Egerton's Pit. Having been able to secure what he needed, he again faced the rain of bullets, carrying the stretcher, and was finally able to convey Lieutenant Hobson to shelter. During the entire accomplishment of his humane action, the fire from the Russian batteries was heavy and continuous.

Colonel Hope, born April 12, 1834, is the son of the late Rt. Hon. John Hope. Educated at Hatfield and Trinity Hall, Cambridge. Besides the heroic act related above he is stated to have saved the lives of thousands of men on November 15, 1855, by his personal exertions and heroic bravery in extinguishing the fire in the roof of a magazine containing 160 tons of powder. He is the inventor of the Shrapnel Shell for rifled guns and many other improvements in war material.

PETER LEITCH

(COLOUR SERGEANT)

ROYAL ENGINEERS

ON June 18, 1855, during the assault on the Redan, Leitch behaved with great bravery. On approaching it with the leading ladders, he fearlessly tore down the gabions from the parapet, filled them with earth and placed them to form a *caponnière* across the ditch. In 1854, at Bomarsund, he had been noticed for his conspicuous gallantry, and was awarded the Legion of Honour.

JOHN PERIE

(SAPPER)

ROYAL ENGINEERS

DECORATED for bravery in leading the sailors with the ladders at the storming of the Redan on June 18, 1855, the *Gazette* stating that his services on that occasion were " invaluable." He afterwards rescued a soldier who had been shot and was lying in the open, although having himself been wounded by a bullet in the side just previously.

The Crimean War

HENRY JAMES RABY

(COMMANDER, NOW REAR-ADMIRAL, C.B.)

ROYAL NAVY

Photo by RUSSELL, *Southsea.*

THE Victoria Cross was deservedly awarded to this distinguished officer for his humane and brave conduct on June 18, 1855, after the attack on the Redan. A young soldier of the 57th Regiment was lying shot through the legs and exposed to the fire of the Russian batteries. On being informed of this, Commander Raby (with John Taylor and Henry Curtis, seamen) crossed over the open ground, about one hundred yards, and under a terrific fire carried the wounded man to shelter. They had the assistance of Lieutenant Edward Hughes D'Aeth, of H.M.S. *Sidon*, but this officer never reaped the reward he undoubtedly merited, as he died of cholera on August 7 following, Taylor, although awarded the V.C., never lived to wear it, for the reason stated in the record under his name, and Curtis died in 1896, so Commander Raby is the only living representative of the heroic act described.

Rear-Admiral Raby, son of Mr. Arthur Turnour Raby, of Llanelly, Carmarthen, was born September 26, 1827. After being educated at Sherborne School, he entered the Navy in 1842 as 1st Class Volunteer H.M.S. *Monarch*. Served for eleven months with the Naval Brigade in the Crimea, being promoted Commander for his services. In command H.M.S. *Medusa* and *Alecto*, West Coast of Africa and during the attack and destruction of Porto Novo; promoted to Captain for meritorious services in those parts, where he was engaged in combating the slave trade, in the suppression of which his name has been prominently associated. Served in command of H.M.S. *Adventure* in China, 1868–71, retiring 1877, since when he has devoted his time to charitable objects connected with the men of that branch of the Service of which he has been so distinguished a member.

History of the Victoria Cross

JOHN J. SIMS

(PRIVATE, AFTERWARDS SERGEANT)

34TH REGIMENT

DECORATED for his bravery on June 18, 1855, when, after the regiment had retired from the attack on the Redan, he went out into the open ground, under heavy fire, and brought in several wounded who had fallen outside the trenches.

PHILIP SMITH

(CORPORAL, AFTERWARDS LANCE-SERGEANT)

17TH REGIMENT

DECORATED for his bravery in continually going out under heavy fire, after the column had retired from the assault on the Great Redan, and bringing in wounded soldiers.

JOHN TAYLOR

(CAPTAIN OF THE FORECASTLE)

ROYAL NAVY

ON June 18, 1855, after the great attack on the Redan, a young soldier of the 57th Regiment had been shot through the legs and was lying in a terribly exposed position calling out for help. On their attention being called to the danger he was in, Commander Raby (V.C.), John Taylor, and Henry Curtis (V.C.) climbed over the breastwork of the advanced sap, crossed the one hundred yards of open ground, under terrific fire, and brought him into shelter. Taylor was justly awarded the Victoria Cross, but he never lived to wear the well-earned decoration, for he died on February 24, 1857, the very day on which his name appeared in the *Gazette*.

The Crimean War

CHARLES McCORRIE
(PRIVATE)
57TH REGIMENT

DECORATED for bravery on June 23, 1855, when he threw a live shell, which had fallen into the trenches, over the parapet.

JOSEPH TREWAVAS
(SEAMAN) ROYAL NAVY
KNIGHT OF THE LEGION OF HONOUR

Photo by PRESTON, *Penzance.*

ON July 3, 1855, in the Straits of Genitchi, the shore being completely lined with the enemy's troops and the adjacent houses filled with riflemen, Seaman Trewavas (one of the crew of H.M.S. *Beagle*) went forward under a heavy fire from only eighty yards distance and with great heroism cut the hawsers of the floating bridge. He was hit in the body at the moment of success, but the desired effect was accomplished and a means of conveying stores to the enemy completely destroyed. Lieut. Hewett, then only twenty-one (afterwards Admiral, V.C.), had given orders that the pontoon must be destroyed at all costs. The first attempt was at night, but was unsuccessful. On the return of the party to the ship, Hewett swore it should be done, if not by night, then by day. Under cover of a little paddle steamer with one gun, Trewavas started again in a four-oared boat. The "paddle steamer" fired one round and then the gun collapsed, remaining useless for the rest of the time. Rowing up to the "Pontoon," Trewavas leapt on to it and cut the hawsers, the Russians then realising what the little party of British sailors were doing, upon which they opened a terrific fire on them. "By coolness and pulling for dear life," says Mr. Trewavas, "and by the Russians' shocking aim we got back to the ship, the boat completely riddled and up to the thwarts in water."

Born December 14, 1835, Joseph Trewavas joined the Navy, H.M.S.

Agamemnon, in 1853. Was at the bombardment of Sebastopol, October 17, 1854, landing on the 23rd with the Naval Brigade. Took part, from 1855, in all operations in the Sea of Azoff and was paid off May 22, 1857. Has been awarded the medal for conspicuous gallantry. Was decorated with French Legion of Honour after Crimean War. Has now for many years followed the calling of a fisherman at Penzance, and at present, in spite of the wounds received from the Russians, is hale and hearty, but advance in years prevents him going to sea as often as before.

GEORGE DARE DOWELL
(LIEUTENANT, NOW LIEUT.-COLONEL)
ROYAL MARINE ARTILLERY

AN explosion took place on a rocket-boat belonging to the *Arrogant* at the naval attack on the forts near Viborg on July 13, 1855. Lieutenant Dowell was at the time on board the *Ruby*. Springing into one of her boats, with three volunteers, he pulled to the assistance of the damaged boat's crew, the Russians directing a heavy fire of grape and musketry upon them. In spite of this, Lieutenant Dowell rescued three men and took them on to the *Ruby*, and, pulling back to the cutter, kept her afloat until she could be towed into safety.

Lieutenant Dowell was born on February 15, 1831, at Chichester, and joined the Royal Marine Artillery on July 25, 1848; was promoted First Lieutenant, October 6, 1851; Captain, September 22, 1859; Brevet-Major, September 17, 1861; Brevet-Lieut.-Colonel, April 23, 1872. Took part in the action with the Russian batteries at Hangorhead, May 22, 1854. During the Baltic Expedition, 1855, was present at the actions of June 18, 23, and 30, on which latter date thirty vessels were destroyed; at Lovisa, July 5, when the Government houses were burnt; and at the shelling of a Cossack encampment and destruction of their barracks on July 10 and 12 respectively.

The Crimean War

GEORGE INGOUEVILLE
(CAPTAIN OF THE MAST)
ROYAL NAVY

ON July 13, 1855, the boats of H.M.S. *Arrogant* were engaged with the enemy's gunboats and batteries off Viborg when the second cutter, being disabled by the blowing up of her magazine, commenced to drift under a battery. Despite a wound in the arm, and the terrific fire the boat was under, Ingoueville, without waiting for orders, leapt overboard, caught the cutter's painter, and saved her. He died on January 13, 1869.

JOHN SHEPPARD
(BOATSWAIN),
ROYAL NAVY

KNIGHT OF THE LEGION OF HONOUR

Photo by WALKER, *Hull.*

ON July 15, 1855, while serving as Boatswain on the *St. Jean d'Acre*, Mr. Sheppard went in a punt with an exploding apparatus into the harbour of Sebastopol in order to try and blow up a Russian line-of-battle ship. This service, described by Lord Lyons as "a bold one and gallantly executed," was twice attempted. On the first occasion he contrived to slip past the Russian steamboats at the entrance to Careening Bay, but was prevented from going further by a long string of boats which were carrying troops from the south to the north side of Sebastopol.

The second attempt was made on the following day, from the side of Careening Bay, occupied by the French.

He died on December 17, 1884.

History of the Victoria Cross

JOHN ROSS
(CORPORAL, AFTERWARDS SERGEANT)
ROYAL ENGINEERS

On July 21, 1855, Corporal Ross displayed great bravery in connecting the 4th Parallel Right Attack with an old Russian rifle pit in front.

On August 23, when in charge of the advance from the 5th Parallel Right Attack on the Redan, he placed and filled twenty-five gabions under a most severe fire from the Russians.

On the night of September 8 he crept alone right up to the Redan and found the enemy had evacuated it, upon which he reported to his officer and our troops took possession of it.

FREDERICK COCKAYNE ELTON
(CAPTAIN, AFTERWARDS LIEUT.-COLONEL)
55TH (WESTMORELAND), 2ND BATT.
THE BORDER REGIMENT

On August 4, 1855, Major Elton was with a working-party in the trenches, close up to the "Quarries." The fire directed at them was terrible, making the work extremely dangerous, but taking a pick and shovel he boldly went into the open and began to work, stimulating by his fine example the men under his command.

Son of the Rev. W. Tierney Elton, he became Ensign on January 19, 1849; Captain, November, 1854; Brevet-Major, 1855; followed by promotion to Brevet-Lieut.-Colonel, and Lieut.-Colonel commanding the 21st Royal Scots in 1866.

Photo by KENT *Eastbourne.*

The Crimean War

JOHN COLEMAN
(SERGEANT)
97TH REGIMENT

ON August 30, 1855, the enemy made an attack on a new sap, driving the working party in. Coleman remained in the open, fully exposed to the enemy's rifle fire, until all around him had been either killed or wounded, finally carrying one of his officers, who had been injured, to the rear.

ALFRED ABLETT
(PRIVATE)
2ND BATT. GRENADIER GUARDS

ON September 2, 1855, a shell from the Russian batteries fell among a number of cases containing powder and ammunition. Ablett instantly seized it and flung it over the trench, whereupon it exploded. By his quick and courageous action, he saved the lives of all around him. Besides the Victoria Cross he was awarded the medal for Distinguished Conduct in the Field. He afterwards held the appointment of Inspector of Police, Millwall Docks, London, and died in February, 1897. His Victoria Cross was sold in London on March 20, 1903, for £62.

JAMES CRAIG
(ENSIGN AND ADJUTANT)
3RD BATT. MILITARY TRAIN
FORMERLY SERGEANT, SCOTS FUSILIER GUARDS

ON the night of September 6, 1855, when in the right advanced sap, in front of the Redan, Craig volunteered and collected other volunteers to go out under a heavy fire of grape and small arms to look for Captain Buckley, Scots Fusilier Guards, supposed at the time to be only wounded. With the assistance of a drummer, he brought in the body of that officer—whom he found dead—and while occupied in this action was himself badly wounded.

Photo by CLARKE, Tetbury.

GEORGE STRONG
(PRIVATE)

1ST BATT. COLDSTREAM GUARDS

WHEN on duty in the trenches, in September, 1855, Private Strong picked up, and threw aside, a live shell which had fallen among the men.

DANIEL CAMBRIDGE
(SERGEANT)

ROYAL ARTILLERY

AT the assault on the Redan, September 8, 1855, Cambridge volunteered for the spiking-party, and though severely wounded continued in the dangerous task. Later in the day he went out in front of the advanced trench and brought in a wounded man under very heavy fire, during which service he was himself badly injured for the second time.

The Crimean War

JOHN CONNORS
(PRIVATE)
3RD REGIMENT

ON September 8, 1855, during the assault on the Redan, Connors displayed great courage in personal conflict with the Russians. He also rescued an officer of the 30th Regiment who was surrounded by the enemy, one of whom he shot, and bayonetted another, and inside the Redan was noticed in personal combat for some time with the enemy. Selected by his comrades to receive the French War Medal.

GRONOW DAVIS
(CAPTAIN, AFTERWARDS MAJOR-GENERAL)
ROYAL ARTILLERY

Photo by LEWIS, *Clifton.*

ON September 8, 1855, at the attack on the Redan, Captain Davis was in command of the spiking-party, carrying out his dangerous duty with conspicuous coolness and bravery. Shortly afterwards he saw that Lieutenant Sanders, 30th Regiment, was lying wounded, his leg being broken. Without hesitation he sprang over the parapet, twice crossing the open space swept by a murderous fire, and, procuring help, at length succeeded in carrying him to shelter. After this brave and humane action, he returned to the Redan and removed several injured and dying men to places of comparative safety.

Captain Davis, son of Dr. Davis, at one time house-physician at St. Peter's Hospital, was born at Bristol, May 16, 1828. Educated by Mr. Exley, of Cotham, and at Bishop's College (a school which preceded Clifton College), he passed direct into the Royal Academy, Woolwich, joining the Royal Artillery, June, 1847; became Lieutenant 1848; Captain, 1855; Major, 1857; Lieut.-Colonel, 1868; Colonel, 1876; Major-General, 1881. Served through the Crimean War from July 6, 1855, including the siege and fall of Sebastopol and battle of Tchernaya, obtaining medal and clasp, 5th class Medjidie, Turkish Medal, and Brevet of Major. For five years was Inspector of the Auxiliary Forces of the Western District, and represented the Council of the Primrose League for many years at Clifton, where he died on October 18, 1891.

THOMAS EGERTON HALE, M.D.

(ASSISTANT SURGEON, NOW SURGEON-MAJOR, RETIRED)

7TH THE ROYAL FUSILIERS (CITY OF LONDON REGIMENT)

Photo by ELLIOTT & FRY, *London.*

ON September 8, 1855, Captain H. M. Jones (V.C.), 7th Regiment, had been severely wounded, and the men in the immediate vicinity had all retired excepting Surgeon Hale and Lieutenant W. Hope (V.C.). Hale, however, remained with the wounded officer and afterwards was conspicuous for his attempts to rally the men, assisted also by Lieutenant Hope. On the same day when the soldiers had retreated into the trenches, Surgeon Hale carried several wounded men from the open to the shelter of a sap, being under a very heavy fire during the entire time. He was nobly assisted in his humane action by Sergeant Charles Fisher of the same regiment.

Born in 1832, Surgeon-Major Hale is the son of Mr. George P. Hale of Faddiley, near Nantwich. He entered the army in 1854, and after the Crimean War served through the Indian Mutiny, 1857–9.

CHARLES HENRY LUMLEY

(BREVET-MAJOR)

97TH REGIMENT

ON September 8, 1855, at the assault on the Redan, Major Lumley greatly distinguished himself, being one of the first to gain the inside of the work. He at once attacked three Russian gunners who were reloading a field-piece, shot two of them with his revolver, and was himself stunned by a large stone, but recovering quickly he drew his sword and cheered on his men, and while doing so was hit by a bullet in the mouth and most severely wounded.

The Crimean War

FREDERICK FRANCIS MAUDE

(MAJOR, AFTERWARDS GENERAL, G.C.B.)

3RD BUFFS (EAST KENT REGIMENT)

KNIGHT OF THE LEGION OF HONOUR

Photo by BASSANO, *London.*

DECORATED for conspicuous and most devoted bravery, during the final attack on the Redan, on September 8, 1855.

When in command of the covering-party of the 2nd division, Major Maude, with only nine or ten of his men, all the rest having fallen and he himself being severely wounded, dashed for a traverse, which he held, and only retired when all hope of support was at an end.

Frederick Francis Maude, born December 20, 1821, died at Torquay on June 20, 1897; was the son of the Rev. Honourable J. C. Maude. In 1861 was A.A.G. at Gibraltar; commanded a division in India, 1875-80, and the 2nd of the Khyber Force during the Afghan War, 1878-9. Retired 1885.

ANDREW MOYNIHAN

(SERGEANT 90TH REGIMENT, AFTERWARDS ENSIGN 8TH REGIMENT)

AT the attack on the Redan, September 8, 1855, Moynihan, then a sergeant in the 90th Light Infantry, displayed great bravery. He himself attacked five Russians and killed every one. Afterwards under a heavy fire he rescued a wounded officer who had fallen near the Redan.

He died at Malta in 1866.

History of the Victoria Cross

ROBERT SHIELDS

(CORPORAL)

23RD REGIMENT

ON September 8, 1855, after the attack on the Redan, Shields volunteered to go out to the front from the 5th Parallel, to bring in Lieutenant Dyneley, who had fallen wounded — mortally as it afterwards proved. (See also Sylvester.)

Photo by DANIELS, *Tachorcok Street.*

WILLIAM HENRY THOMAS SYLVESTER

(ASSISTANT SURGEON, NOW M.D., L.R.C.S.EDIN., L.S.A., RETIRED),

23RD REGIMENT

KNIGHT OF THE LEGION OF HONOUR

ON September 8, 1855, under a terrific fire, Surgeon Sylvester went out near the Redan, to where Lieutenant Dyneley was lying mortally wounded, and attended to him in that exposed and dangerous position. He was also specially mentioned in General Sir James Simpson's despatch of September 18, 1855, for going to the front and attending to many wounded under very severe fire.

He served in the Indian Mutiny and took part in the Relief of Lucknow, 1857-8.

The Crimean War

JOSEPH KELLAWAY
(BOATSWAIN)
ROYAL NAVY
KNIGHT OF THE LEGION OF HONOUR

Photo by SANDS, *Old Brompton.*

IN September, 1855, in the sea of Azoff, near Mariopol, a small party from H.M.S. *Wrangler* landed in the middle of the night to destroy some boats, fishing stations, and haystacks, on the opposite side of a lake. The Russians were on the alert, and rushed upon them from their ambush, endeavouring to cut off their retreat. One of our men fell into the enemy's hands, and the others had made good their escape, when one of them (Mr. Odevaine) accidentally fell.

Kellaway, thinking he was wounded, at once returned to his rescue, and while lifting him, both were surrounded by the enemy. In spite of a gallant but hopeless resistance, they were captured.

Commander Burgoyne, V.C., stated that he was himself an observer of the zeal, gallantry, and self-devotion displayed by Kellaway on this occasion.

Mr. Kellaway died at Chatham on October 10, 1880.

GEORGE FIOTT DAY
(CAPTAIN, AFTERWARDS C.B.,)
ROYAL NAVY
KNIGHT OF THE LEGION OF HONOUR

DURING the Crimean War, in the sea of Azoff, Captain Day conceived the idea of landing at night, getting within the Russian lines at Genitchi and finding out the practicability of cutting out the enemy's gunboats lying within the Straits, close to the town. Setting off quite alone, he landed and crossed four or five miles of swamps, often waist deep, penetrating eventually to within 200 yards of the enemy's vessels. From the absolute stillness on board the boats he came to the conclusion that they were not strongly manned, and that therefore an expedition for the purpose of cutting them out was feasible.

History of the Victoria Cross

Photo by CHAFFIN, *Taunton.*

Retracing his steps, after seven hours' hard work, he reached his ship. Next day, however, from unusual signs of activity in the enemy's direction, it seemed that his surmises were incorrect, so he returned once more to again watch their movements.

Passing through the same dangerous swamps, he reached his former place of observation and found, to his great disappointment, that the boats were all manned and ready for action, so he turned back, wandering through the swamps again for nine hours, and the idea had to be abandoned. The plucky nature of this act is the more apparent when it is mentioned that, while making a similar *reconnaissance* previously, Captain l'Allemand, of the French steamer *Monette*, had lost his life. The decorations worn by Captain Day in the portrait above are :—St. Jean d'Acre—Syria, 1840 ; China, 1841 ; Burmah, 1852 ; South Africa, 1853 ; Baltic, 1854 ; Crimean and Turkish, 1855 ; Victoria Cross ; Legion of Honour ; Order of the Bath (C.B.), and Medjidie. Promoted Commander, 1855 ; Captain, 1861 ; he died at Weston-super-Mare, December 18, 1876.

CHRISTOPHER CHARLES TEESDALE

(LIEUTENANT, AFTERWARDS MAJOR-GENERAL, K.C.M.G.)

ROYAL ARTILLERY

KNIGHT OF THE LEGION OF HONOUR

ON September 29, 1855, when acting as A.D.C. to Sir William Fenwick Williams, Bart., K.C.B., at Kars, Lieutenant Teesdale volunteered to take command of the force placed to defend the most advanced part of the works —the key of the position—against the attack of the Russian army.

The enemy had forced their way into the redoubt, whereupon he flung himself into their midst, and so encouraged the garrison by his splendid example, that, after a hard struggle, the Russians were driven out and the position saved from capture. During the crisis of the action, when the fury of the Russian fire was such that the Turkish artillerymen were driven from the guns, he rallied them, and, by his gallant conduct and leading, induced them to return to their post. He led the final charge which completed the victory for the day, and afterwards, at a terrible risk to himself, flung him-

The Crimean War

Photo by BASSANO, London.

self among several infuriated Turkish soldiers and prevented them from killing wounded Russians lying outside the works. This marvellous act of humanity and courage was witnessed, and gratefully acknowledged, by the Russian Commander, General Mouravieff.

Son of Lieut.-General H. G. Teesdale, he was born on June 1, 1883, entered the Royal Artillery 1851, and served as A.D.C. to Sir Fenwick Williams, at Kars and Erzeroun, in 1854. Was also Colonel in the Turkish army and received the second class Medjidie. Had been, since 1890, Master of the Ceremonies to the Queen. He entered the army in 1851, becoming Captain, 1858; Brevet-Major, 1858; Major, 1862; Lieut.-Colonel, 1868; Colonel, 1877; and attained the rank of Major-General on April 22, 1887. He died at Bognor, on November 1, 1893.

JOHN EDMUND COMMERELL
(COMMANDER, AFTERWARDS ADMIRAL OF THE FLEET, G.C.B.)
ROYAL NAVY
KNIGHT OF THE LEGION OF HONOUR

ON the night of October 11, 1855, Commander Commerell, accompanied by Quartermaster William Rickard and Seaman George Milestone, landed and destroyed 400 tons of corn and forage belonging to the Russians. He was at the time Commander of the *Weser*, in the sea of Azoff. The three men, waiting until darkness could cover their movements, rowed ashore and hauled their small boat across the Spit of Arabat, then traversed the Sivash to the Crimean shore of the Putrid Sea. In order to reach the magazine of corn, which lay distant about

Photo by ELLIOTT & FRY, London.

History of the Victoria Cross

two and a half miles, they had to ford the Kara-su and Salghir Rivers, and, creeping to the stacks, they contrived to ignite them. The flames from the burning forage roused the Cossacks, of whom there was a guard of thirty in the vicinity, and these pursued the three intrepid sailors to the shore. However, in spite of the heavy rifle-fire directed at them, they managed to escape and rejoin their ship.

Admiral Sir Edmund Commerell, son of the late J. W. Commerell, of Horsham, was born January 13, 1829, and died at Rutland Gate, Hyde Park, on May 21, 1901.

He served in South America, 1846, the Baltic in 1854, and after the Crimean War, in China, 1859-60, and Ashanti, 1873, in which campaign he was dangerously wounded. A.D.C. to the Queen, 1872-6; Naval Lord of the Admiralty; Commander-in-Chief on American and West Indian station, 1882; Portsmouth, 1888; Admiral of the Fleet, 1892; M.P. for Southampton, 1885-8.

WILLIAM RICKARD

(QUARTERMASTER, ROYAL NAVY, NOW CHIEF OFFICER OF COAST GUARD, KNIGHT OF THE LEGION OF HONOUR)

Photo by HUGHES & MULLINS, *Ryde.*

ON October 11, 1855, Quartermaster Rickard accompanied Lieutenant Commerell, V.C., commander of the *Weser*, to the Crimean shore of the Sivash, and his gallant conduct on that occasion was brought to the notice of the authorities by his officer, in the following despatch—

"I must bring to your notice the excellent conduct of the small party who accompanied me, more especially that of William Rickard, Quartermaster, who, though much fatigued himself, remained to assist the other seaman (George Milestone), who from exhaustion had fallen in the mud and was unable to extricate himself, notwithstanding the enemy were keeping up a heavy fire on us at the distance of thirty or forty yards as we crossed the mud."

THE PERSIAN WAR

1856—1857

JOHN AUGUSTUS WOOD

(CAPTAIN, AFTERWARDS COLONEL)

20TH BOMBAY NATIVE INFANTRY

AT Bushire, Persia, on December 9, 1856, Captain Wood led the Grenadier company which formed the head of the assaulting column. He sprang on the parapet of the fort, being the first to reach it, and was instantly attacked by a number of the enemy. They fired a volley when only a yard distant from him, and, although hit by seven bullets, he flung himself upon the enemy, killed their leader with his sword, and with his own company, who were following close behind him, routed the enemy, and took their position. His decision, energy, and determined valour, undoubtedly (to use the words of the *Gazette*) contributed in a high degree to the success of the attack. His wounds compelled him to leave the force for a time, but, with the pluck and spirit of a good soldier, he rejoined his regiment, and returned to his duty at Bushire before the wounds were properly healed.

Captain Wood joined the Army in 1839 and saw service in the Afghan War of 1842.

ARTHUR THOMAS MOORE

(LIEUTENANT AND ADJUTANT, NOW MAJOR-GENERAL, C.B.)

3RD BOMBAY LIGHT CAVALRY

ON February 8, 1857, at the battle of Khoosh-ab, Persia, Lieutenant Moore charged an infantry square at the head of his regiment, jumping his horse over the bayonets of the enemy, a feat perhaps never accomplished

History of the Victoria Cross

Photo by ELLIOTT & FRY.

before. His charger fell dead, pinning him to the ground. Extricating himself with great difficulty, he attempted to cut his way through the press, but, his sword being broken by the fall, he could barely defend himself and would certainly have been killed but for the prompt assistance of Lieutenant Malcolmson, whose record will be found below.

General Moore was born on September 20, 1830, entered the Army in 1850, serving in the Persian War, 1857, and the Indian Mutiny, 1857, being mentioned in despatches in the latter campaign. Was afterwards through the operations in Central India under Sir Hugh Rose.

JOHN GRANT MALCOLMSON

(LIEUTENANT, AFTERWARDS CAPTAIN)

3RD BOMBAY LIGHT CAVALRY

Photo by ELLIOTT & FRY.

AT the battle of Khoosh-ab, on February 8, 1857, Lieutenant Malcolmson, seeing that Lieutenant and Adjutant Moore, V.C. (to whose heroic act we have referred above) was surrounded by a crowd of the enemy and practically unarmed, his sword being broken, cut his way through the mass of fighting Persians, and, giving his stirrup to his brother officer, succeeded in conveying him to a place of safety. But for his gallant conduct, Lieutenant Moore must have been killed. The *Gazette* states that the thoughtfulness for others, cool determination, devoted courage and ready activity shown in a moment of extreme danger by Lieutenant Malcolmson, appear to have been most admirable, rendering him worthy of the highest honour.

The Persian War

Captain Malcolmson, M.V.O., son of the late James Malcolmson, of Muchrach, Inverness-shire, was born in 1835. Present at the capture of Reshire and surrender of Bushire in the Persian War; through the Indian Mutiny, 1857, and took part in the Central India operations, from the siege of Ratghur to the fall of Calpee. Was, from 1870, one of Her Majesty Queen Victoria's Gentlemen-at-Arms. He died on August 14, 1902.

THE INDIAN MUTINY
1857—1859
(including Okamundel and Kattywar—October, 1859)

GEORGE FORREST [1]
(LIEUTENANT)

WILLIAM RAYNOR
(LIEUTENANT)

JOHN BUCKLEY
(CONDUCTOR)

BENGAL ORDNANCE

THE troublous times of the Indian Mutiny brought to light many examples of bravery, devotion and self-sacrifice, but it was left to a little band of nine resolute men to perform the act which, of all the heroic ones of those days, will be the last to be obliterated by the hand of time. On May 11, 1857, the great Delhi Magazine, full of enormous stores of warlike material, was in charge of Lieutenant George Willoughby, Bengal Artillery, and with him were Lieutenants Forrest and Raynor, and six European soldiers. In the early hours of that day Willoughby was in the magazine when Forrest arrived with the Magistrate, Sir Theophilus Metcalfe, and informed him that the mutineers had crossed the river and entered the palace gates. Knowing well the value of the magazine to the enemy should they contrive to storm and take it, and how much to our cause could he but hold it, Willoughby resolved to defend it to the last, always with the hope that our troops at Meerut would soon arrive to his relief. There were many natives on the establishment of the magazine, but

[1] The author much regrets that no portrait of Lieutenant Forrest is procurable. There once was a miniature of him, which, unfortunately, was destroyed at Delhi in 1857.

The Indian Mutiny

the officer saw they were not to be trusted, and he formed the heroic resolution with his eight British comrades to defend the magazine as long as possible against the enormous odds and then at last, when overpowered, to blow the building into the air with all its inflammable contents and themselves to die at their posts.

The gates were closed and barricaded, and guns were brought out, loaded with grape shot and placed so as to command the entrances. Should the enemy force their way in through these channels, their ranks would be torn to pieces by the point blank fire of the six pounders, and then if the little band should be overpowered, at a signal—preconcerted by Willoughby—the entire place was to be blown up and any within its walls would perish. To this end a train of powder was laid from the outside to the magazine, Scully, with heroic resolution, undertaking the firing of the train, this duty making death a certainty for him should the signal be given.

Shortly afterwards a summons was brought from the King of Delhi, ordering the surrender of the magazine. Contemptuous silence was the only reply given, upon which the enemy, bringing ladders, commenced to scale the walls, the natives in the establishment promptly joining their friends the attackers. Thus the resolute nine, left alone, faced Death with fearless hearts, and soon the guns sent volleys of grape into the midst of the storming parties. Gun after gun fired its rounds, served coolly and steadily, the heroic gunners under a hail of bullets from those of the enemy who had now scaled the walls. After a while the supply of ammunition brought up from the magazine began to give out, and it was impossible for more to be fetched, no one being able to leave the guns for that purpose. Two of the gallant nine were wounded and the rebels were forcing their way in now on every side, so, true to his intention, and to his country's cause, Willoughby raised his hat—the signal arranged—John Scully applied the port-fire to the train and with an appalling explosion, the magazine was blown into the air, more than one thousand mutineers being killed. Of the nine heroic men, only four escaped; Willoughby and Forrest joined a party of Europeans at the Main Guard in Delhi, so blackened as to be almost unrecognizable; the former being shortly afterwards killed in an encounter with the mutineers. Raynor and Buckley, taking different directions, eventually reached Meerut in safety. The splendour of this achievement, the nobility of heart of those who deliberately offered their lives in the furtherance of their country's cause, makes the Victoria Cross almost an insufficient reward. But, added to that decoration, and to perpetuate the memory of the heroic lives given for such a cause, a memorial tablet was placed over the gate of the old magazine with the following inscription—

History of the Victoria Cross

ON MAY 11, 1857,
NINE RESOLUTE ENGLISHMEN,
LT. GEO. DOBREE WILLOUGHBY, BENGAL ARTILLERY,
IN COMMAND,
LIEUTENANT WILLIAM RAYNOR, LIEUTENANT GEO. FORREST,
CONDUCTOR G. WILLIAM SHAW, CONDUCTOR JOHN BUCKLEY,
CONDUCTOR JOHN SCULLY, SUB-CONDUCTOR WILLIAM CROW,
SERGEANT BRYAN EDWARDS, SERGEANT PETER STEWART

Defended the magazine of Delhi for more than four hours against large numbers of the rebels and mutineers, until, the walls being scaled, and all hope of succour gone, these brave men fired the magazine. Five of the gallant band perished in the explosion, which at the same time destroyed many of the enemy.

This Tablet,
marking the former entrance gate to the magazine, is placed here by the Government of India.

PETER GILL

(SERGEANT-MAJOR)

LOODIANA REGIMENT

ON June 4, 1857, Sergeant-Major Peter Gill was at Benares, and the mutineers were firing the bungalows and killing the European inhabitants round that station. In company with Sergeant-Major Rosamond (V.C.) he made his way to the residence of Captain Brown and his family, who were in great peril and cut off from their friends, and by his noble exertions succeeded in bringing them all safely within the lines. He also saved the life of a sergeant of the 25th Bengal Native Infantry, who, having been bayonetted, was about to receive the *coup de grace*, when Gill hewed off the head of his assailant. On the same evening, with only a sergeant's sword, he faced a guard of twenty-seven mutineers, and twice saved the life of Major Barrett, 27th Regiment, when that officer was attacked and in great danger of being overpowered.

JOHN KIRK

(PRIVATE)

10TH REGIMENT

ON June, 4, 1857, this soldier was associated with Sergeants-Major Rosamond (V.C.) and Gill (V.C.). When, on the outbreak at Benares the mutineers fired the bungalows and massacred so many Europeans, he and his comrades were able to rescue Captain Brown and his family, bringing them into the lines in safety. His Victoria Cross is in the United Service Institute, London.

The Indian Mutiny

M. ROSAMOND
(SERGEANT-MAJOR)
37TH BENGAL NATIVE INFANTRY

ON June 4, 1857, at Benares, Rosamond volunteered with Lieut.-Colonel Spottiswoode, his commanding officer, to set fire to the Sepoy lines so as to drive out the enemy. He also accompanied Sergeant-Major Gill (V.C.) and Private Kirk (V.C.) when they rescued Captain Brown and his family from their bungalow which the Sepoys had set on fire. His conduct was specially noted as "meritorious" and he was promoted. His Cross was sold in London on November 25, 1903, for £54.

CORNELIUS COGHLAN
(COLOUR-SERGEANT, AFTERWARDS SERGEANT-MAJOR)
75TH (STIRLINGSHIRE) REGIMENT (NOW 1ST BATT. THE GORDON HIGHLANDERS)

DURING the siege of Delhi, Sergeant Coghlan became conspicuous by his numerous acts of bravery. On June 8, 1857, at Budle-Ke-Serai, under a heavy fire, he entered a building held by the rebels in great force, and rescued from it Private Corbett, of his regiment, who was severely wounded. On July 18, 1857, he cheered and encouraged a party which showed signs of hesitation in charging into a lane, which was filled with armed mutineers, not one of whom escaped. He then returned to procure dhoolies for the wounded, being the whole time exposed to a heavy cross fire. In this he also succeeded, receiving on the spot public praise from his officers for his chivalrous conduct.

He was, until a few years ago, Sergeant-Major of a Militia Battalion in Co. Mayo, Ireland.

History of the Victoria Cross

ALFRED STOWELL JONES

(LIEUTENANT, NOW LIEUT.-COLONEL)

9TH (QUEEN'S ROYAL) LANCERS

Photo by MAULL & FOX.

On June 8, 1857, at Budle-Ke-Serai, Delhi, the squadron commanded by Lieutenant Jones charged the rebels and, although they offered a stout resistance, rode straight through them, killing the drivers, and capturing one of their guns. With the assistance of Colonel Yule, he turned it upon a village, strongly held by the mutineers, and drove them out. Sir Hope Grant stated in his despatch that nothing could have been better done or more gallantly executed. At Agra, on October 10 following, Lieutenant Jones received no fewer than twenty-two wounds, part of his head being cut away, and one eye destroyed, in spite of which he recovered.

Born at Liverpool, January 24, 1832, Lieut.-Colonel Jones is the son of the late Archdeacon Jones. Educated at Liverpool College and Staff College, Sandhurst, he entered the 9th Lancers in 1852. Throughout the siege of Delhi served as D.A.Q.M G. to the cavalry, being three times mentioned in despatches, and promoted Captain and Brevet-Major.

Graduated at the Staff College, 1861, served on the Staff at the Cape, 1861–7, retiring 1872.

H. HARTIGAN

(SERGEANT)

9TH LANCERS

At the battle of Budle-Ke-Serai, near Delhi, on June 8, 1857, Hartigan performed an act of special daring and devotion. During a particularly severe charge, Sergeant Helstone was wounded and fell from his horse, being quickly surrounded by the fanatical enemy. At the risk of his own life Hartigan cut his way through the press and carried his wounded comrade to the rear.

On October 10, following, at Agra, under circumstances of great bravery,

The Indian Mutiny

he saved the life of Sergeant Crews, who was attacked by four rebels (who had crept into the camp), and though quite unarmed, Hartigan dashed for the nearest, wrenched a tulwar from his hand, hitting him a blow in the mouth with his fist, then turned and attacked the other three, one of whom he killed, and wounded the two remaining. He was, however, by that time so terribly wounded himself, that he was unable to continue the combat, and was obliged to retire on assistance arriving.

THOMAS CADELL
(LIEUTENANT, NOW COLONEL, I.S.C.)
2ND BENGAL FUSILIERS (LATE 104TH FOOT) THE ROYAL MUNSTER FUSILIERS

Photo by ELLIOTT & FRY.

THE flag staff on the historic "Ridge" at Delhi was often a point of attack by the enemy when they attempted a sortie, as well as by their friends outside, in their many efforts to raise the siege. On June 12, 1857, a vigorous attack was made, and the pickets of the 75th and of the Bengal European Fusiliers were forced to retire before overwhelming numbers. Lieutenant Cadell, seeing a bugler fall severely wounded, went to his assistance and, carrying him from among the enemy under a heavy fire, saved him from certain death. Again, on the same evening, when his regiment was ordered to retire on Metcalfe's house, learning that a wounded man of the 75th was left behind, he immediately went back towards the advancing mutineers, taking with him three men, and brought him in. This act of devotion he and his men accomplished under a terrible fire of cannon and musketry.

Colonel Cadell, V.C., son of the late H. F. Cadell, of Cockenzie, Haddingtonshire, and a younger brother of the late General Sir Robert Cadell, K.C.B., was born on September 5, 1835. Educated at Edinburgh Academy; Grange, Sunderland; and abroad. Has held various political appointments in India. From 1879 to 1892 was Governor of the Andaman and Nicobar Islands.

History of the Victoria Cross

THOMAS HANCOCK
(PRIVATE)
9TH LANCERS

This gallant soldier was specially mentioned by Sir Hope Grant, in command of the Field Force, for his courageous conduct on June 19, 1857. When that brave leader's horse was shot under him at Delhi, Hancock remained by him and, giving him his own mount, enabled him to be taken out of the hot corner the cavalry were in at the time. With him was Private Purcell (V.C.) and a Sowar, Roopur Khan. The former was awarded the chief of decorations, but the Sowar's name unfortunately does not figure in the list of recipients.

JOHN PURCELL
(PRIVATE)
9TH LANCERS

At Delhi, June 19, 1857, Purcell, with another brave lancer, Thomas Hancock (V.C.) and Sowar Roopur Khan, saved the life of Sir Hope Grant, by staying with him, offering him one of their horses, and getting him out of the *mêlée* when surrounded by rebel cavalry. Purcell's horse was killed in the contest.

SAMUEL TURNER
(PRIVATE)
1ST BATT. 60TH RIFLES

On June 19, 1857, when before Delhi, Lieutenant Humphreys, of the Indian Service, was mortally wounded, and had he been allowed to remain where he fell, he would have been mutilated beyond recognition, a fate unfortunately too often met by many another soldier during that terrible time. Turner carried him to the rear on his shoulders under a brisk fire from the enemy posted around, and, at one time, even at close quarters. During his humane act he was severely wounded by a sabre cut.

The Indian Mutiny

STEPHEN GARVIN
(COLOUR-SERGEANT)

1ST BATT. 60TH RIFLES

BESIDES being brought into prominent notice for his gallant conduct during the entire operations before Delhi, Garvin was specially noticed for his bravery on June 23, 1857, when he led a little party of men under a terrific fire to assault the "Sammy House," a well-defended post which gave particular trouble to our advancing troops. After a sharp contest this hostile post was captured, chiefly by his noble example and daring conduct.

JOHN McGOVERN
(PRIVATE, AFTERWARDS SERGEANT)

1ST BENGAL FUSILIERS (NOW ROYAL MUNSTER FUSILIERS, 101ST)

DECORATED for his great gallantry during the siege of Delhi, and for saving the life of a wounded comrade on June 23, 1857, by carrying him into camp under a very heavy fire from the enemy's battery.

WILLIAM GEORGE CUBITT
(LIEUTENANT, AFTERWARDS COLONEL, D.S.O.)

13TH BENGAL NATIVE INFANTRY

WHEN the Lucknow Residency was on the point of being invested, Sir Henry Lawrence sent a force to meet and fight the advancing rebels at Chinhut on June 30, 1857. The result was a dismal failure, and the beaten troops returned to the Residency with a loss they could ill spare. At this battle Lieutenant Cubitt was prominently noticed, and, when the retreat to Lucknow began, he saved the lives of three men at imminent risk when the surging mass of fanatics had penetrated among our own disorganized soldiery.

Born on October 19, 1835, son of Major W. Cubitt, of the Bengal Army, he was educated privately and entered the Regiment of Native Infantry in 1853. His first active service was during the Santhal campaign, after which he served through the Mutiny, taking part in the defence of the Residency, the Duffla Expedition of 1875, Afghan War, 1880, the Akha Expedition of 1883, and the Burmah War of 1886, for which latter campaign he was awarded the D.S.O. He died at Camberley on January 25, 1903, and was buried at Frimley, Surrey.

WILLIAM OXENHAM

(CORPORAL)

32ND REGIMENT

On June 30, 1857, on the same date as the disastrous battle of, and retreat from, Chinhut, Mr. Capper, an Indian Civil Service official, was buried beneath the ruins of a verandah which had fallen. Corporal Oxenham, in spite of a tremendous fire from the enemy directed upon him for ten minutes, contrived to extricate Mr. Capper from his perilous position, and by his noble exertions saved his life.

ROBERT HOPE MONCRIEFF AITKEN

(LIEUTENANT, AFTERWARDS COLONEL)

13TH BENGAL NATIVE INFANTRY

"For various acts of gallantry performed during the defence of the Residency of Lucknow from June 30 to November 22, 1857."

So states the *London Gazette* in its matter of fact record.

Although only a few of the gallant acts of bravery and devotion to his country and to his comrades are stated here, those who served under or with Colonel Aitken have in remembrance the invaluable services rendered by him throughout the now historic defence.

Twice he sallied out to bring in cattle as food for the beleaguered garrison. On another occasion, the enemy having set fire to the Bhoosa Stock in the garden, which threatened to spread and ignite the powder magazine, Aitken dashed out, cut down all the tents which might have communicated the flames to the powder, and saved the garrison from fearful danger. Whilst thus occupied he was under a terrific fire from the enemy's loop-holes and house-tops.

The Indian Mutiny

On August 20 the mutineers set fire to the Baillie Guard Gate, by placing inflammable material against it. Aitken was the first to dash out, partially open the gate, and remove the combustibles. On September 25, by a plucky sortie, he, with his native soldiers, attacked and seized two guns to prevent their being turned against General Havelock's column, which was advancing to their rescue.

On the 26th he led a small party of his regiment to the assault of a barricaded gateway of the Furreed Buksh Palace. By throwing himself against the gate he was able to prevent it being closed, thus giving time for his men to run to his help and force the door. The capture of this position was entirely due to his splendid bravery.

On the 29th, during a sortie of the garrison, he volunteered to capture a gun which harassed our troops by its continuous fire upon them. With four of his men he worked his way through the lanes and houses, shot at the whole time by the enemy from the surrounding houses, and succeeded in reaching the gun. Here he and his little party held their ground until reinforced, when the gun was upset from its carriage and taken back by them to the Residency.

(Lieutenant Digby-Jones, a relative of Colonel Aitken, greatly distinguished himself during the Boer War of 1899–1902, the *Gazette* stating that the V.C. would have been awarded to him had he survived, for his heroism at the great attack on the British at Ladysmith, January 6, 1900. See account.)

Colonel Aitken became Ensign in 1847; Lieutenant in 1853; Captain on February 18, 1861; Brevet-Major, February 19, 1861; Major, September, 1867; Lieut.-Colonel, August 1, 1869. He was the son of Mr. J. Aitken, of Cupar, Fife, N.B., and was born on April 14, 1828. He went to India in 1847 and served with the Honourable Company's 13th Regiment of Bengal Native Infantry in the Punjab campaign, 1848–9. Present at the action of Ramnugger, at the passage of the Chenab, Battle of Goojerat, and with the column which, under Major-General Sir Walter Gilbert, pursued the Sikh and Afghan Army. Medal and clasp. Served with the 13th Regiment Bengal Native Infantry in the Santhal Rebellion of 1855. Present in some skirmishes with the Santhals, and, assisted by Lieutenant Loughnan, 13th N.I., personally took prisoner Koulea, a Santhal chief, for whose capture a reward of Rs. 5,000 was offered (reward not paid to captors on the ground that soldiers were not entitled to it). Served with the 13th N.I. throughout the Indian Mutiny in 1857–8.

Engaged, 1st. In action against the mutineers in Lucknow Cantonments on May 30 and 31, 1857.

2nd. In battle of Chinhut on June 30, 1857.

3rd. Commanded, throughout the Defence of Lucknow, the whole of the Hindostanee Sepoys of the 13th Bengal N.I., who remained faithful; and, with them alone, held the Baillie Guard Post stated by Sir John Inglis to be " perhaps the most important position in the whole of the Defences."

4th. Commanded in two sorties and was present in two others.

5th. Commanded the remains of the 13th N.I. (both Hindostanees and Sikhs) in the movement of retreat from the Residency on the night of November 22, under General Sir Colin Campbell, G.C.B., Commander-in-Chief.

Present (as Paymaster of the Army under General Sir Colin Campbell) in the fighting against the Gwalior contingent in Cawnpore, from November 29 to December 5, 1857, and at the defeat of the rebels on December 6 in the Battle of Cawnpore. Raised the Cawnpore Levy and commanded it in Futtehpore district in support of the troops engaged under Sir Colin Campbell (Commander-in-Chief) in the Baiswarah Campaign (Oudh), 1858. Was mentioned ten times in the despatches connected with the defence of Lucknow and received the thanks of His Excellency the Governor-General in Council for having " commanded an important position in the Defence with signal courage and success." The following are two extracts from the Lucknow siege despatches of Brigadier-General Inglis, commanding the garrison, which bear directly on the services of Lieut.-Colonel Aitken in the command of the 13th N.I., and of the Baillie Guard Post—

First Extract from Despatches:

" Lieutenant Aitken, with the whole of the 13th N.I., which remained to us, with the exception of the Sikhs, commanded the Baillie Guard, perhaps the most important position in the whole of the defences."

Second Extract from Despatches:

" With respect to the native troops, I am of opinion that their loyalty has never been surpassed. They were indifferently fed and worse housed. They were exposed, especially the 13th Regiment, under the gallant Lieutenant Aitken, to a most galling fire of round shot and musketry, which materially

The Indian Mutiny

decreased their numbers. They were so near the enemy that conversation could be carried on between them, and every effort, persuasion, promise, and threat was alternately resorted to in vain, to seduce them from their allegiance to the handful of Europeans who, in all probability, would have been sacrificed by their desertion."

The following is a copy of the address which General Sir Hugh Rose, G.C.B., Commander-in-Chief in India, was pleased to make in conferring the decoration of the Victoria Cross on Lieut.-Colonel (then Major) Aitken:—

"The army knows, and history will tell, the stand which the garrison of the Residency made for all the rights which loyal soldiers and good men hold most dear.

"History will tell how, with entrenchments hastily and rudely constructed, commanded from above and mined from below, a few English, badly off for artillery and supplies, and exposed to the worst of India's seasons, repulsed for five months the incessant attacks of a rebel army which, protected by a treacherous city, besieged and hemmed them in on every side.

"You, Major Aitken, were conspicuous amongst those who at Lucknow upheld the cause of their country, of humanity, and of civilization.

"Not satisfied with a resistance within the Residency, which never yielded an inch, you acted on the offensive and carried the war into the enemy's camp. Assisted by only a few faithful Sepoys of the 13th Native Infantry, who, with pleasure I say it, were as resolute and devoted as British soldiers, you captured on two different occasions enemy's guns, and on two others fortified houses.

"Of all his duties, there is not one which a commander values more than giving a good soldier his meed.

"You may then judge, sir, with what pleasure I give you the recompense conferred on you by our most Illustrious Sovereign for your brilliant services; and you may judge how that pleasure is enhanced by presenting you the Victoria Cross in the midst of those scenes to which you and your gallant companions-in-arms have imparted a celebrity which can never pass away."

In April, 1871, was recommended for the Companionship of the Bath by His Excellency Lord Napier, G.C.B., Commander-in-Chief of the Indian Army, and His Excellency the Earl of Mayo, G.C.B., Governor-General of India.

Colonel Aitken died in September, 1887.

History of the Victoria Cross

JAMES TRAVERS
(COLONEL)
(LATE) 2ND BENGAL NATIVE INFANTRY

Photo by FRADELLE & YOUNG.

ON July 1, 1857, Holkar's mutinous troops made a sudden attack upon Indore. Colonel Travers, with only five men, charged straight for the guns, drove the mutineers from their battery, and by his sudden attack gave time to the Bhopal artillery to man their guns. Many European fugitives were also, by the diversion caused by his gallant attack, enabled to escape from their pursuers, and these lives may be considered as owed to that officer's brave initiative. His horse was shot in three places, and his clothing riddled with bullets.

Colonel Travers, son of Major-General Sir Robert Travers, was born on October 6, 1820. Educated at Addiscombe. Served in Afghanistan, 1840-42, at the operations at Zamindawar, capture of Ghuzni, action of Mydan. Served in Bhopal, and at Kullea Karee, 1846. In 1856 served against the rebel Sunker Sing, receiving the thanks of the Agent to the Governor-General of Central India for his services.

WILLIAM DOWLING
(PRIVATE)
32ND REGIMENT

THIS soldier on three occasions, July 4 and 9, and September 27, 1857, went out to spike the Sepoy guns. On all occasions he came under a very heavy fire, and was successful on the first and third attempts. His second was, however, unsuccessful owing to the spike being too small to be serviceable.

WILLIAM CONNOLLY
(GUNNER)
BENGAL HORSE ARTILLERY

THERE have been many acts of heroism recorded in this volume, but few which can surpass the devotion to duty and strength of will exhibited by this gunner.

The Indian Mutiny

At Jhelum, on July 7, 1857, Connolly's troop became engaged with the enemy at short range. A "sponge man" of one of the guns having been wounded, Connolly took his place, and before he had served many minutes received a bullet through the left thigh, which laid him alongside the gun. The "retire" was then sounded, but he was helped on to his horse in the gun-team and rode to the next position taken up, refusing to leave his post though the nature of his wound was pointed out to him. From the fresh position he manfully sponged out his gun, firing round after round, until a bullet again struck him, this time in the hip, from which he fell to the ground, remaining partly unconscious, the pain being very severe and blood flowing freely from his injured limb. On Lieutenant Cookes ordering his removal, Connolly exclaimed, " No, sir, I'll not go there while I can work here," and staggering to his feet he resumed his duties at the gun. Later in the day, when the battery were pounding at a village wall, a hail of bullets raining on the devoted crew, Connolly still was serving his gun with a courage which excited the admiration of all present, and he called for more ammunition and cheered his men to continue in their heroic task, till he was again struck, the bullet tearing through the muscles of his right leg. Even then he did not relinquish his post, but served his gun until it had been fired six times more, when from loss of blood, agony from his wounds and exhaustion of body, he fell into the arms of his officer and was carried unconscious from the fight.

SAMUEL HILL LAWRENCE

(LIEUTENANT)

32ND REGIMENT

This officer was awarded the Victoria Cross for conspicuous bravery during two sorties on different occasions, July 7 and September 26, 1857.

Major Wilson, D.A.A.G., of the Lucknow garrison, reports, on the first occasion, to the effect that he himself was an eye-witness of the personal gallantry of Lieutenant Lawrence, who was the first to mount the ladder and enter the window of a house to discover whether or not a mine was being laid from it, during which act he had his pistol knocked from his hand by one of the enemy.

On the second occasion, with only two of his men, he charged well in advance of his party and recaptured a 9-pounder gun.

History of the Victoria Cross

JAMES HILLS

(LIEUTENANT, NOW LIEUT.-GENERAL SIR JAMES-HILLS JOHNES, G.C.B.)

ROYAL (BENGAL) ARTILLERY

Photo by ELLIOTT & FRY, *London.*

THIS distinguished officer was the second gazetted for the protracted and trying siege of Delhi, which was invested shortly after the outbreak at Meerut on May 10, and only captured, on September 20, after seven days of hard fighting, day and night.

On July 9, 1857, Lieutenant Hills was placed in command of two guns of his battery in a specially selected and dangerous position to be ready at a moment's notice to move to any given point in case of a sortie by the garrison, or to repel outside attack, or an attempt to raise the siege.

Here this young officer, then hardly twenty-four, was attacked, frequently, by cavalry at close quarters, on each occasion defending the post most gallantly, being aided by his commanding officer, Major—late Major-General—Sir Henry Tombs, V.C., K.C.B.

The following is *his own* account of another incident on the same day, when his life was heroically saved by the late Sir Henry Tombs, for which the latter was awarded the Victoria Cross. The *official* despatch of Lieutenant Colonel Mackenzie to Brigadier Wilson reporting the bravery of Lieutenant Hills and Major Tombs is given in the record of the latter officer (*page* 80).

"I thought that by charging them I might make a commotion, and give the gun time to load, so in I went at the front rank, cut down the first fellow, slashed the next across the face as hard as I could, when two Sowars charged me. Both their horses crashed into mine at the same moment, and, of course, both horse and myself were sent flying. We went down at such a pace that I escaped the cuts made at me, one of them giving my jacket an awful slice just below the left arm; it only, however, cut the jacket. Well, I lay quite snug until all had passed over me, and then got up and looked about for my sword. I found it full ten yards off. I had hardly got hold of it when three fellows returned, two on horseback. The first I wounded, and dropped him from

The Indian Mutiny

his horse. The second charged me with a lance. I put it aside and caught him an awful gash on the head and face. I thought I had killed him. Apparently he must have clung to his horse, for he disappeared. The wounded man then came up, but got his skull split. Then came on the third man—a young, active fellow. I found myself getting very weak from want of breath, the fall from my horse having pumped me considerably; and my cloak, somehow or other, had got tightly fixed round my throat, and was actually choking me. I went, however, at the fellow, and cut him on the shoulder, but some cloth on it apparently turned the blow. He managed to seize the hilt of my sword, and twisted it out of my hand, and then we had a hand-to-hand fight, I punching his head with my fists, and he trying to cut me, but I was too close to him. Somehow or other I fell, and then was the time, fortunately for me, that Tombs came up and shot the fellow. I was so choked by my cloak that move I could not until I got it loosened. By the bye, I forgot to say that I fired at this chap twice, but the pistol snapped, and I was so enraged I drove it at the fellow's head, missing him, however."

Lieut.-General Sir James Hills-Johnes, son of the late James Hills, of Neechindipore, Bengal, was born on August 20, 1833. After the Indian Mutiny he served in Abyssinia, 1868, and the Looshai Expedition, 1871; in 1880 was Military Governor of Cabul; commanded the 3rd Division Field Force in Northern Afghanistan, 1879-1880; took part, during Afghan War, in actions of Kurrum Valley, Charasiab, Padkoa Valley, and received thanks of Houses of Parliament for his services. Retired 1888.

HENRY TOMBS, C.B.

(LIEUT.-COLONEL, AFTERWARDS MAJOR-GENERAL, K.C.B.)

Bengal Artillery

Lieut.-Colonel Mackenzie, in command of the Bengal Horse Artillery, mentioned this officer for his noble conduct before Delhi on July 9, 1857, when he twice saved his subaltern's life, and on both occasions killed his assailants. The official account of his bravery, as reported by Lieut.-Colonel Mackenzie, is given below, and Lieutenant Hills' own version of the incident is set out in the record of that officer.

History of the Victoria Cross

Despatch No. 40, Lieut.-Colonel M. Mackenzie, commanding 1st Brigade Horse Artillery, to Brigadier A. Wilson, Commandant of Artillery.

"CAMP NEAR DELHI,
"*July* 10, 1857.

"SIR,—

"It is with great pleasure I submit, for the information of the Brigadier-Commandant, the following account of the very gallant conduct of Second-Lieut. James Hills, of the 2nd Troop, 1st Brigade Horse Artillery, and the noble behaviour of his commanding officer, Major H. Tombs, in twice coming to his subaltern's rescue and on each occasion killing his man.

"Yesterday, the 9th inst., Second-Lieut. J. Hills was on picket-duty, with two guns, at the mound to the right of the camp. About eleven o'clock a.m. there was a rumour that the enemy's cavalry were coming down on this post. Lieut. Hills proceeded to take up the position assigned in case of alarm, but before he reached the spot he saw the enemy close upon his guns, before he had time to form up. To enable him to do this, Lieut. Hills boldly charged, single-handed, the head of the enemy's column, cut down the first man, struck the second and was then ridden down, horse and all. On getting up and searching for his sword, three more men came at him (two mounted). The first man he wounded with his pistol, he caught the lance of the second with his left hand, and wounded him with his sword. The first man then came on again and was cut down; the third man (on foot) then came up and wrenched the sword from the hand of Lieut. Hills (who fell in the struggle), and the enemy was about to cut him down when Major Tombs (who had gone up to visit his two guns) saw what was going on, rushed in and shot the man and saved Lieut. Hills. By this time the enemy's cavalry had passed by, and Major Tombs and Lieut. Hills went to look after the wounded men, when Lieut. Hills observed one of the enemy passing with his (Lieut. Hills') pistol. They walked towards him. The man began flourishing his sword and dancing about. He first cut at Lieut. Hills, who parried the blow, and he then turned on Major Tombs, who received the blow in the same manner. His second attack on Lieut. Hills was, I regret to say, more successful, as he was cut down with a bad sword-cut on the head, and would have been no doubt killed had not Major Tombs rushed in and put his sword through the man. I feel convinced that such gallant conduct on the part of these two officers has only to be brought properly forward to meet with an appropriate reward. Major Tombs was saved from a severe sword cut on the head by the wadded head-dress he wore.

"(Signed) M. MACKENZIE,
"Lieut.-Colonel."

The Indian Mutiny

The following two references to Major-General Henry Tombs, V.C., are made by Earl Roberts in his book, *Forty-one Years in India*—

I

"Henry Tombs, of the Bengal Horse Artillery, an unusually handsome man and a thorough soldier. His gallantry in the attack on the Idgah[1] and wherever he had been engaged was the general talk of the camp. I had always heard of Tombs as one of the best officers in the regiment, and it was with feelings of respectful admiration that I made his acquaintance a few days later. As a cool, bold leader of men, Tombs was unsurpassed; no fire, however hot, and no crisis, however unexpected, could take him by surprise; he grasped the situation in a moment and issued his orders without hesitation, inspiring all ranks with confidence in his power and capacity. He was somewhat of a martinet, and was more feared than liked by his men until they realized what a grand leader he was, when they gave him their entire confidence and were ready to follow him anywhere and everywhere."

II

"On the 17th (September, 1857) we were attacked from almost every direction—a manœuvre intended to prevent our observing a battery which was being constructed close to an Idgah situated on a hill to our right, from which to enfilade our position on the Ridge. As it was very important to prevent the completion of this battery, Barnard ordered it to be attacked by two small columns, one commanded by Tombs, of the Bengal Horse Artillery, the other by Reid. Tombs, with 400 of the 60th Rifles and 1st Bengal Fusiliers, thirty of the Guides Cavalry, twenty Sappers and Miners and his own troop of Horse Artillery, moved towards the enemy's left. . . . Tombs drove the rebels through a succession of gardens, till they reached the Idgah, where they made an obstinate but unavailing resistance. The gates of the mosque were blown open and thirty-nine of its defenders were killed. Tombs himself was slightly wounded and had two horses killed, making five which had been shot under this gallant soldier since the commencement of the campaign."

Born on November 10, 1825, son of Major-General Tombs, Bengal Cavalry. Educated at Addiscombe. Served in Gwalior Campaign at battle of

[1] A Mahomedan place of worship and sacrifice.

History of the Victoria Cross

Punniar, 1843 ; Sutley Campaign, 1845–6, as A.D.C. to Sir Harry Smith; present at actions of Moodkee and Ferozeshah, Budiwal and Aliwal ; Punjab Campaign, 1848–9, as D.A.Q.M.G. of Artillery, and present at actions of Ramnuggur, Chillianwallah and Goojerat. In the Mutiny was present at the siege of Delhi, battle of Nujjufghur, siege and capture of Lucknow, Allygunge, Bareilly, and Rohilcund Campaign, receiving C.B., V.C., and brevets of Lieut.-Colonel and Colonel. In every action he was mentioned in despatches in eulogistic terms, and was referred to by Lord Panmure in the House of Lords. Was in 1851 in command of the force at the capture of Dewangiri, when the Victoria Cross was so nobly won by Trevor and Dundas. On receipt of the news of his death, Lord Napier of Magdala, then Commander-in-Chief, issued the following G.O. : " The army of India will share with the Right Honourable the Commander-in-Chief the deep regret with which he has received the intelligence of the death in England of Major-General Sir Henry Tombs, K.C.B., V.C., of the Royal (late Bengal) Artillery. The career of this distinguished officer is identified with the history of this country for the last thirty years. The decorations which he bore on his breast for Gwalior, the Sutley Campaign, the Campaign of the Punjab, the siege of Delhi and capture of Lucknow, and for the recapture of Dewangiri, in Bhootan, under his independent command, bore testimony to the conspicuous part he took in nearly all the more important military events that have taken place during that period. Appointed to the command of a division in 1871, Sir Henry Tombs displayed all those attributes of a general of which his early career had given promise, and fully justified his selection for the high trust which had been confided to him. Firm in the maintenance of discipline, courteous in his demeanour, strict and impartial in the exercise of his command, he acquired in a remarkable degree the respect, confidence and affection of all with whom he was associated. His premature death, which Lord Napier of Magdala so greatly deplores, has deprived the Government and country of an accomplished and devoted servant, the Commander-in-Chief of a valued friend and trusted lieutenant and the Army of a gallant comrade and one of its most brilliant ornaments."

The Indian Mutiny

Photo by NICHOLLS, *Lichfield.*

JAMES THOMPSON
(PRIVATE)
60TH REGIMENT

ON July 9, 1857, at Delhi, this soldier saved the life of his captain (Wilmot) when surrounded by a party of Ghazees who had dashed upon him from a Serai. Before any assistance had arrived, Thompson killed two of the enemy. During the siege of Delhi, where he was wounded, his conduct was most conspicuous and he was elected for the award of the Victoria Cross under Rule 13 of the Warrant.

WILLIAM ALEXANDER KERR
(LIEUTENANT)
24TH BOMBAY NATIVE INFANTRY

Photo by BROUGHTON, *Lowestoft.*

THE 27th Bombay N.I. mutinied in July, 1857, and a large body of them made for the stronghold of Kolapore, midway between Belgaum and Satara. They were quickly followed up for eighty miles by Lieutenant Kerr, then Adjutant of the Southern Mahratta Horse. On reaching the mutineers' place of defence, he, on the 9th, with a few of his men, made a dash at the gate and broke it down. All within it were either killed, wounded or captured, a result due to his heroic dash and bravery. The mutiny was thus practically at one stroke stamped out on the Malabar coast. Had there been more men of such calibre at some of the military stations in India at that time, the Mutiny would probably have been checked at its outbreak and might never have assumed such awful proportions in so short a time.

History of the Victoria Cross

ABRAHAM BOULGER

(LANCE-CORPORAL, AFTERWARDS HON. LIEUT.-COLONEL)

84TH (THE YORK AND LANCASTER) REGIMENT

Photo by CHANCELLOR, *Dublin.*

FROM the date of the departure of Havelock's force from Allahabad for the relief of Lucknow early in July, 1857, until its entry on September 25, Abraham Boulger was practically engaged daily with the enemy, either in pitched battle with his regiment or as a scout and skirmisher. Twelve severe actions were fought, and in all of these he took part. In Lucknow he helped to storm a bridge and was the first man to dash into a masked battery.

His rank in 1857 and that which he lately held is a sufficient indication of his meritorious services. After serving for many years as Sergeant-Major he became Quartermaster in 1872, and after taking part in the storming of Tel-el-Kebir, retired as Lieut.-Colonel in November, 1887. Died in Ireland, his native country, in January, 1900.

P. MYLOTT

(PRIVATE)

84TH REGIMENT

ELECTED by his fellow soldiers in the regiment under Rule 13 of the V.C. Warrant for conspicuous bravery at every engagement in which he was present, from July 12, 1857, to the Relief of the Lucknow Garrison. On one occasion he specially distinguished himself by rushing across a road, under a terrific fire, to seize an enclosure on the opposite side.

The Indian Mutiny

HENRY MARSHMAN HAVELOCK

(LIEUTENANT, AFTERWARDS LIEUT.-GENERAL SIR H. M. HAVELOCK-ALLAN, BART., K.C.B.)

10TH REGIMENT

Photo by BASSANO, *London.*

On July 16, 1857, when Lieutenant Havelock was Aide-de-camp to his father, the renowned Sir Henry Havelock, the 64th Regiment had come under terrible artillery fire from the mutineers when advancing on Cawnpore, and, seeing a 24-pounder being brought up in action against us, the general gave the order to rise and advance. With the greatest coolness young Havelock rode at a foot-pace ahead of the regiment, opposite the muzzle of the gun, which commenced firing, and, cheering on the men, he dashed forward and carried the battery.

At Lucknow—at the Char Bagh Bridge—he again led a charge with conspicuous bravery, routing and inflicting heavy loss on the enemy.

Lieut.-General Sir Henry Havelock-Allan, son of Major-General Sir Henry Havelock, K.C.B., was born at Chinsurah, Bengal, August 6, 1830. Served in Persian Expedition, 1857, as A.Q.M.G., and was A.A.G. to his father during the march to the Relief (or Reinforcement) of Lucknow, and on September 21, 1857, he was credited with having twice saved the life of General Outram. He met his death on December 30, 1897, during the campaign in the North West Frontier of India, under Sir William Lockhart. When with an escort riding from Lala Cheena down the Khyber Pass from Lundi Kotal, and almost on British ground, Sir Henry, thinking all danger passed, galloped far ahead of his party. As he did not return, a search was organized, and he was eventually found quite dead, having been shot by some Afridi sharpshooter from a long distance.

History of the Victoria Cross

Photo by MAULL & FOX.

RICHARD WADESON

(LIEUTENANT, AFTERWARDS COLONEL)

75TH REGIMENT (1ST GORDON HIGHLANDERS)

ON July 18, 1857, during the action in the Subjee Munjee at Delhi, Lieutenant Wadeson saved the life of Private Michael Farrell by killing a Sowar who had attacked him when wounded and lying on the ground.

On the same day, Private John Barry, who had fallen, severely injured, owed his life to Lieutenant Wadeson, who came up and cut down a cavalry Sowar who was attacking him. After service in the Army as a non-commissioned officer, the late Colonel Wadeson rose to command the regiment. He died while Lieut.-Governor of Chelsea Hospital a few years ago.

GEORGE LAMBERT

(SERGEANT-MAJOR)

84TH REGIMENT

MENTIONED by Sir Henry Havelock for distinguished bravery at Oonao, July 29; Bithoor, August 16; and Lucknow, September 25, 1857.

The Indian Mutiny

ANDREW CATHCART BOGLE

(LIEUTENANT, AFTERWARDS MAJOR)

78TH ROSS-SHIRE BUFFS—2ND SEAFORTH HIGHLANDERS

Photo by WINDOW & GROVE, *London.*

UNDER Havelock, on July 29, 1857, the gates of Oonao were blown in by the 78th. Bogle, then a lieutenant (fresh from recent victories in Persia), got together a few men and stormed a contested passage, opening a way for the force to advance.

He and his handful of men, exposed to a most harassing fire, attacked a loopholed house strongly held by Sepoys. This they succeeded in capturing, clearing it of the enemy. During the attack he was terribly wounded. After twenty-five years' retirement, Major Bogle died in December, 1890.

He entered the 78th Highlanders as Ensign on December 28, 1849, and took part in the Persian War, 1856; was promoted Captain in the 10th Foot on August 31, 1858.

DENIS DEMPSEY

(PRIVATE)

1ST BATT. 10TH REGIMENT

DURING the disastrous retreat from Arrah in July, 1857, when Mr. Mangles and Mr. McDonell both won the Victoria Cross by acts of heroic devotion, Dempsey was one of the retreating party, and helped to carry Ensign Erskine of his regiment from the pursuing Sepoys. On August 12, 1857, he was the first man to enter the village of Jugdispore under a terrific fire, and further, on March 14, 1858, he carried a bag of powder through a burning village in order to mine a passage in rear of the enemy's position. As the sparks from the burning houses were falling in showers around him, and the path he took was open and exposed to a terrific fire from the enemy, who were behind loopholed walls, his brave act appears all the finer.

Dempsey died in Canada, January 10, 1886.

History of the Victoria Cross

WILLIAM FRASER McDONELL, ESQ.
Bengal Civil Service

Photo by Jacolette, *Queen's Gate.*

Mr. McDonell was Magistrate at Sarun, India, and gained his Victoria Cross in the Mutiny on the same date as Mr. Mangles, another Civil Service official. It was during the retreat of the relief force of Arrah that our little party had to contend against fearful odds and terrible hardship. In those times of peril soldiers and civilians alike lent their aid to suppress the revolt, and thus it is that brave deeds in action are recorded of those whose vocation in life was never intended to be combatant. Ever in the van, ever in any engagement where danger was greatest, Mr. McDonell handled his rifle with unerring aim, and did terrible execution among the Sepoys. He was standing by Dunbar when that brave leader fell, being splashed with his chief's blood. Though himself wounded, he still fought on, and reached the boats, when it was found that the mutineers had taken away the oars, and tied the rudders, rendering this way of escape for the moment impossible.

The following is the official account of Mr. McDonell's act as given by Captain J. W. Medhurst, 60th Rifles, previously of the 10th Foot—

"On the ill-fated expedition retiring from Arrah on the morning of July 30, 1857, and on arriving at the village and stream of Bherara, as is well known, the men, exhausted and dispirited, broke and made for the only six large country boats moored close to the right bank. After assisting some wounded men into the furthest boat, and being myself pulled in, I saw that Mr. McDonell, who was

The Indian Mutiny

one of our number, was exerting himself with a sergeant to move the boat into the stream. It being discovered that the boat was bound to the bank, one or two men jumped out and loosened the rope, and the boat moved. Assisted by the less-exhausted of my party, I was keeping up a fire of Enfields on the enemy, whose musketry was very galling. Whilst so employed, I heard Mr. McDonell call out for a knife to cut away some rope which bound the rudder to the right, causing the lumbering boat to veer round into the right shore again, and for a time causing it to stick fast. On looking round I saw him seated on the stern extremity of the boat in full view of the enemy and quite exposed to their fire. He cut away the mentioned rope, and guiding the rudder himself, a fortunate breeze carried our boat across the stream, grounding at about ten yards from the left bank, whereby all those who were alive were enabled to jump out and reach the steamer in safety. The number of men thus saved was about thirty-five; and during the passage across three men were shot dead; one was mortally, and two or three slightly, wounded. I may safely assert that it was owing to Mr. McDonell's presence of mind, and at his personal risk, that our boat got across on that day.

The following is an account of the affair written by Mr. McDonell and published in the *Times* of 1857—

"THE DISASTER AT ARRAH.

"*To the Editor of* THE TIMES.

"SIR,—The columns of *The Times* have ever been ready to do justice to the gallantry and heroism which have been displayed by all classes during recent events in India, but in a letter signed 'Indophilus,' which appeared in *The Times* on the 24th of October, censure is implied on some who rather merit praise. In alluding to the abandonment of Chuprah and other stations by the civil authorities, in consequence of orders from Mr. Tayler, Commissioner at Patna, 'Indophilus' says—

"'Chuprah was abandoned with somewhat more reason, because it was threatened by a strong party of Holmes' Irregular Horse. Still, the flight was unnecessarily hastened, and had the Commissioner's orders not given an excuse to the timid, it is probable the station would not have been abandoned.'

"The recent mail has brought the enclosed letter from Mr. William McDonell, Magistrate of Chuprah, and, as it contains the most graphic account I have seen of the disastrous expedition for the relief of Arrah and of the vacillation and mismanagement at Dinapore, which mainly caused the disaster, I think you may deem portions of the letter as deserving a place in your columns. As one nearly connected with ... Mr. McDonell, I can assure you that implicit confidence may be placed in the accuracy of every statement made by him; and I am sure that those who read this letter will feel that he is not justly liable to the imputation of having deserted his post of duty in the hour of danger.

"I have the honour to remain,

"Your obedient servant,

"H. H. LINDSAY.

"WEST DEAN-HOUSE,
   "CHICHESTER.
      "*Nov.* 3, 1857."

"CHUPRAH,
   "*September* 3.

"On the evening of the 25th of July, or rather in the middle of the night, a note came from Dinapore, saying that the troops were very shaky, but that Her Majesty's 10th and the guns were ready for them. Next morning we got an official despatch from the Brigade Office, telling us that all three native corps had gone off in a westerly direction (this was at 11 a.m.), and that the 10th were after them. About half an hour afterwards we got a note from Daunt at Peiprah, an indigo factory about fifty miles north of Chuprah, that the 12th Irregular Cavalry had, on the 23rd, mutinied, murdered all their officers and their wives, and had then set off towards Sewan. He said he wrote on the chance of our not having heard it, though it had occurred three days before. On hearing this we held a Cabinet Council, and determined that Chuprah was no longer safe. So Martin, Richardson and his wife set off at once; the doctor and his wife followed soon afterwards; and about 2 o'clock I was thinking of following them when I remembered that all my prisoners, owing to cholera having broken out in the gaol, were in the opium go-down. Now, as they could easily escape from there, I went and saw them all into the gaol. By this time everybody knew that the officials had bolted, and people seemed so alarmed that I determined on staying on a little longer. About 6 p.m. I got a note from Mr. Garston, asking if I was in the station, as he heard I was alone. He was returning from the district. I said I was, but I advised him to bolt; but, instead of that, he very pluckily came in and stayed with me. We rode round the town, to show the people we had not bolted, and then came home, and went to bed without undressing; and we had our horses, saddled, standing all night at the door. About 12 o'clock that night I got a pencil note, not signed, but written, I saw, by Lynch, saying he had escaped from Sewan with his life, and that the

The Indian Mutiny

cavalry were there. Early in the morning I got a second note, saying that the troopers had come down the Chuprah road searching for Lynch, and McDonell, the Deputy Opium Agent. About 10 a.m. I heard that the Dinapore mutineers had reached Arrah, and while in *cutcherry*, about 3 o'clock, a man on a pony came galloping in, saying that the cavalry were within ten miles of Chuprah. I finished the case I was about, and I fear rather hastily, and then wrote home, and Garston and I agreed it was time to bolt, so we made a start for it, going through the town, and to the police station, and also to the missionaries to tell them we were going, and advising them to do the same. We rode down to Doreegunge, about eight miles, and saw the smoke of a steamer in the distance, so we waited until she came near. We found Martin and Richardson and the doctor on board, with a party of the 5th Fusiliers and some thirteen Sikhs. On hearing that the cavalry were on their way here, and that the rebels were at Arrah, all agreed it would be folly to go back with only thirteen Sikhs, so we got a party of the 5th Fusiliers to go with us, and we started off in boats for Chuprah, which we reached at 11 p.m. We went to the collector's, and all assisted in packing treasure, and we started back for the steamer with some 90,000 rupees. If they had left me fifty men I would have stopped at Chuprah, but not with only thirteen Sikhs. As the men could not be spared, back we went, and on the way we heard that the Arrah people, consisting of my friend Wake,[1] Officiating Magistrate; Littledale, the Judge; Coombes, the Collector; Boyle, Railway Engineer, and some six or seven others, were besieged in a small bungalow by the three Dinapore corps. On reaching Dinapore I found that 200 men of the 37th Queen's and fifty Sikhs had been sent to relieve Arrah, but unfortunately the steamer grounded, through treachery, I believe, on the part of the pilot. There the steamer lay quite close to Dinapore, and the authorities doing nothing. I went to the General and urged upon him that unless relieved soon the garrison must all be murdered, and that if he would send another detachment in boats I could show them another way to Arrah where the steamer was sure not to stick, and that I knew the road from the Ghât to Arrah. He said if I would really go with them he would send some of the 10th. Just then another steamer came in; it was agreed that all the passengers were to be landed and put into the church, and that 500 of the 10th were to start at 3 next morning. While making arrangements I got a note from Tayler, the Commissioner, saying he had heard I had volunteered to show the way, but that he could not spare me; so I at once got into a native cart at 10 at night, and drove to Patna, which I reached about half-past eleven p.m. I saw Tayler, and begged him

---

[1] The late Herwald Crawfurd Wake, C.B., son of Sir Charles Wake, Bart. His brave conduct during the Defence of Arrah was particularly noticed. (P.A.W.)

History of the Victoria Cross

to let me go, as, humanly speaking, it was the only way of saving the little garrison. At last he said that if the General really laid any stress on my going he would not object. He ordered his carriage, and I drove down with him and young Mangles,[1] to Dinapore. It was then nearly 2 o'clock. We woke up the General, and he told Tayler that it was very important that I should go, as I knew the road and he would trust to me. By this time it was the hour fixed to start. We drove down to the steamer, and to my disgust found all the passengers still on board. There was great delay and squabbling, and at 5 a.m. the General said, ' Oh, if there is not room in the steamer, never mind ; the flat takes only 150 men.' So all the others went back. This caused endless confusion. Colonel Fenwick would not go with only 150 of his men ; he ordered Captain Dunbar to take the command. At last we got off and came up to the other steamer, got her flat containing 200 of the 37th, and fifty Sikhs, steamed on, and landed at Berara Ghât about 2 p.m. Of the disasters that befell us on that occasion you must have seen a long account, but I will give a brief sketch. About two miles from the Ghât there is a river, after crossing which you get on the public road to Arrah from Chuprah, a distance of about twelve miles. As I was not sure I should find boats, as we were in an enemy's country, I offered to go on with a small party of Sikhs, and secure the boats while the Europeans had their dinner on the bank. So off Ingelby of the 7th Native Infantry, who volunteered, and commanded the Sikhs, Garston, and myself, with twenty men, went to the riverside. On reaching the river's bank we found all the boats drawn up on the other side, and about 200 men assembled. They had four or five of those long native guns stuck on three sticks, and began blazing at us, whereupon two of our party said they would return for aid. We told them particularly not to disturb the Europeans, but to ask for the rest of the Sikhs, fifty being sufficient to dislodge the enemy. We immediately set to work and blazed across the river, and soon set all the fellows running. Two Sikhs then swam across, and got a small boat, in which Ingelby, Garston, and myself, with ten Sikhs, crossed. We were hardly across, when, to our disgust, we saw all the Europeans coming up at double quick, these fools having reported that we were surrounded ; so the 10th came away without getting their dinners, or even a drop of grog, and had brought nothing with them. We all crossed, and by the time we were in marching order it was 4 o'clock. Ingelby, Garston, myself, and twenty Sikhs formed the Vanguard ; then came 150 of the 10th ; then fifty Sikhs ; and lastly, 200 of the 37th Queen's. We marched four miles all right, when we saw some ten or twelve horsemen in front. However, they galloped off before any damage could be done to them. The

[1] Ross Lowis Mangles, V.C.

The Indian Mutiny

men got very footsore, and we halted at the Kaimnugger Bridge, about three miles from Arrah, at 10 p.m., and here we ought to have remained for the night, but, after stopping about half an hour, on we marched. I fancy poor Dunbar thought it useless halting, considering his men had nothing with them, and that it would be better to push on. What possessed us, I know not; up to this time we had made the Sikhs throw out skirmishers, but now we marched in a body—Ingelby and Dunbar, who was talking to me, with about twenty Sikhs, some 200 yards in advance of the main body. After marching to within half a mile of Arrah, we arrived at a thick tope of trees, and the moonlight hardly showed through; in fact the moon was setting. Well, we had got nearly through, when, like a flash of lightning, all along our left side came one blaze of musketry, and then another, and a third volley. By the light the firing made we could see we were surrounded. We got behind the trees and tried to return the fire; Dunbar, myself, three of the 10th, and two Sikhs got together and blazed away. Foolishly I had given my powder-flask and bullets, etc., to a native to carry; of course he disappeared, and after firing off two barrels I was powerless; not for long, however, for the next minute we got a volley into us. I fancy our firing showed where we were. Poor Dunbar fell against me mortally wounded; I was covered with his blood. A ball hit me in the thigh, cutting it slightly only; at the same time two of the 10th and one Sikh also fell. I immediately picked up an Enfield rifle belonging to the 10th man, and his cartridge box, and began blazing away. I then shouted out that Dunbar was killed; that the first officer in command had best give orders. This brought another volley on us, and another man dropped. We then tried to join the main body, and ran from tree to tree; the Europeans, seeing us coming, all Sikhs, nearly, thought we were the enemy, and fired into us, killing several; in fact, I fear as many of our men were killed by their own comrades as by the enemy. In the night it was difficult to tell friend from foe; and after having to dodge round a tree, you in the dark could hardly tell where your friends were, and where your foes. At last most of us got together and beat a retreat towards a tank, near which was a high bank; we got to the other side of this bank and lay there all night, the enemy firing into us every five minutes, and foolishly our men would return the shot. It was bad policy; it showed where we were, and we could not afford to throw away a single shot. Young Anderson, a very nice young fellow, of the 22nd Native Infantry, a volunteer, was standing up behind the hedge; he was shot through the head, and jumped up like a buck—of course killed on the spot. About daylight we counted our forces, and found that we were about 350 strong, 100 missing; afterwards about fifty of these joined us, being concealed in a village close by; the rest were killed. We could see the enemy and tried to make out their number ; there were the three Dinapore regiments drawn up in order, with bugles sounding the advance. About 2,000 men, with long matchlocks, belonging to and headed by Baboo Koor Sing, and more than 1,000 of the disbanded Sepoys who had managed to join him, and a large rabble armed with swords, spears, etc., not formidable in themselves, but who made themselves useful, killing all the wounded, beating them like dogs. We tried to make the men charge, but they were tired, wet, and a great number wounded. My leg, from lying on the damp ground and from the bleeding, was so stiff I could hardly walk ; however, I soon warmed up. Unfortunately, the doctor was one of the first wounded, and, though he did his best, poor fellow, he could not bind up the wounds properly. There were no dhoolies, so that the wounded had to march with the rest. Then commenced our retreat. They completely surrounded us, and fired into us all the way back—twelve miles ; men dropping every minute, and some, badly wounded, were, I fear, left behind and killed by the enemy. By the time we reached the boats 100 must have been killed, and then commenced the massacre. The boats, which we expected to have been taken away, were all there, so with a cheer we all rushed to them, when, to our dismay, we found they had fastened them securely to the shore, and had dragged them up out of the water and had placed about 300 yards off a small cannon, with which they blazed into us. (I forgot to say that all the way they pitched into us with four small cannon.) The men, to escape the shot, got into the boats, and, of course, as long as they were in them, it was impossible to push the boats off. So a number of men stripped themselves, throwing away their rifles and everything, and some of them managed to reach the other side. The wounded men, of course, could not swim, and some of us knew we could never reach the shore, so out we jumped, and managed to get two of the boats off ; well, then we were at the mercy of the wind and stream, for not an oar had they left us. The wind was favourable, and we started off splendidly, when, lo and behold, we gradually turned towards the shore, and then I saw they had tied our rudder, so as to bring us in again. I told the men to cut it, but no one moved, and so I got a knife and climbed up to the rudder. It was one of those country boats, covered in except just at the stern. The moment they saw what I was at they blazed at me, but God in His mercy preserved me. Two bullets went through my hat, but I was not touched. The rope was cut, and we were saved ; but about half way across we struck on a sandbank, and then the bullets poured in so fast that nearly every one jumped overboard. One young officer jumped over as he was, with his sword on, and down he went ; another, Ingelby, was shot in the head, and either drowned or killed. I threw my pistol overboard ; my coat I had thrown away early in the morning, as, being a coloured one, it made

The Indian Mutiny

me conspicuous among the soldiers, who were all in white. How I swam on shore I know not, as it is not an accomplishment I am a ' dab ' at. When once on shore we were pretty safe, and 250 out of 450 reached the steamer alive. Since then nearly 100 more, from wounds, exposure, etc., have died, making a loss of 300 out of 450—the worst that has befallen us yet; nearly every one was wounded. Of the eight volunteers who went with the troops six were killed, two wounded, poor Garston badly, shot right through the body from hip to hip, myself slightly in two places, the thigh and on the shin, the latter cutting my trousers in two places, cutting two holes in a Wellington boot, and luckily only cutting a flesh wound. The eighth volunteer, young Mangles, John Lowis's brother-in-law, was knocked on the head and stunned for some ten minutes. He had a great lump on his head, but the bullet did no more damage; it must have just glanced off. This account, I fear, is rather egotistical, but it is too late to alter it. I have since then been on another expedition in charge of 150 Sikhs, this second time as commander. We had not much fighting, but burnt several villages, more especially the village of Behara, where we were so awfully punished. It is just post time, so I must stop. Chuprah is, I trust, now pretty safe. Our only fear is from Lucknow; the bordering districts of Goruckpore and Azimghur have been deserted. The latter, however, is by this time occupied by 3,000 Nepaulese troops, but in Goruckpore there is no one. A Lucknow man, named Mohamed Hassen, has made himself Chuck-ledar or Negrim to the King of Oude, and issues orders. He has some 8,000 men with him, but mostly rabble. One English regiment, or half a regiment, and two guns, would drive him out, whereas now we have to watch him. In another month the Mutiny will be nearly over, I think. Lots of work left in punishing these brutes, but there will not be any fresh outbreaks. I trust Lucknow may weather the storm, but it is a near business. They have been entreated to hold out to extremities, and not to make terms. General Outram will relieve them if he can."

William Fraser McDonell passed into the Bengal Civil Service from Haileybury in 1850, and was Assistant-Magistrate and Collector at Sarun until 1857. After the Mutiny he acted as Settlement-Officer in Shahabad till 1860, when he spent three years on furlough. From 1863 to 1870 he was Judge at Nuddea and from 1874 to 1886 Judge of the High Court of Judicature at Calcutta, when he retired from the Service. He died at Cheltenham on July 31, 1894.

History of the Victoria Cross

ROSS LOWIS MANGLES

(ASSISTANT-MAGISTRATE AT PATNA)

BENGAL CIVIL SERVICE

Photo by KIRK, *Freshwater.*

MR. MANGLES volunteered and served with the little force sent to the relief[1] of the garrison at Arrah, where fifteen Europeans and fifty of Rattray's Sikhs were holding out against 4,000 mutineers. They fell into an ambush on the night of July 29, 1857, and lost 300 of the 450 men. A retreat was made next morning under a blazing Indian sun, and a terrible fire from the Sepoys. At the first attack Mr. Mangles was wounded, but, regardless of that, he assisted the surgeon in his care of the injured, fetching water, when able, in order to alleviate their sufferings.

"In the flower of his youth, a man of fine presence, with a long stride and a firm hand on his two-barrel, our men looked to him, as to one who, though without official command, had natural right to be obeyed."[2] He was a magnificent shot, and kept a hot fire from his post upon the enemy, a little knot of men he kept together, handing him loaded muskets.[3] During the retreat a soldier of the 37th had been shot and, as he lay on the ground, implored Mangles not to leave him, well knowing that Death, not in too fast or painless a manner, would be his on the arrival of the mutineers.

Under a hail of lead, Mangles turned to the man, bound up his wounds, and, though no food had passed his lips for twenty-four hours, and no sleep had he had for forty-eight, yet he lifted him upon his back and marched away with him. The man he carried was as big as himself, the ground over which he marched was swampy, rough and dangerous; yet for six long miles did he tramp, only putting down his heavy burden to stand over him while firing at the harassing enemy to keep them in check and enable him to accomplish his act of mercy and of love. At last he reached the river, into which he plunged, holding up his comrade until he could get him into a boat, when, under medical care, his life was eventually saved. His name was Richard Taylor, and this story of as fine an act of English heroism as has ever been recorded, was only brought to light by the surgeon to whom the man recorded his marvellous deliverance. It was this act which was instrumental in bringing about the alteration of the

---

[1] A detailed account of the disaster to the Relief Force is given in the Record of Mr. McDonell, V.C.

[2] Kaye's *Sepoy War.*   [3] Trevelyan.

The Indian Mutiny

V.C. Warrant, as, up to that time, none but military or naval men were eligible for the decoration. Not until more than a year had passed was the incident just recorded brought to the knowledge of Lord Canning by Sir James Outram, who, on hearing of it, had decided to recommend Mr. Mangles for the V.C. Meanwhile, another splendid act had been done by another civilian in Oude, but the decision of the authorities was, in spite of it, against the alteration of the Warrant. The Governor-General thereupon, on receipt of Outram's letter, wrote to the Home Government, forwarding it for their information and emphatically endorsing its contents, remarking that " the modesty which has allowed the event to remain unknown to those in authority until after the lapse of a twelvemonth, is not the least remarkable feature in the story.[1] " Afterwards the Warrant was altered in favour of " Soldier-Civilians," and no one will regret the withdrawal of so invidious a distinction.

Ross Lowis Mangles, born at Calcutta, April 14, 1833, is the son of R. D. Mangles, member of the Bengal Civil Service, and, after his retirement, M.P. for Guildford and a Director of the Old East India Company. Educated at Bath Grammar School and Haileybury College, entering Bengal Civil Service 1853. In 1857 was Assistant-Magistrate at Patna, accompanying the 45th (Rattray's) Sikhs in quelling a disturbance in Patna City, subsequently joining the Arrah Relief Force as described. Immediately after the retreat the Sepoys were driven out of Arrah and Behar by Sir Vincent Eyre. He was then appointed Magistrate in the Chunparun District, North Behar, being engaged there in procuring supplies and carriage for the Ghoorkas under Jung Behadur, who had marched down from Nepal to our assistance. Early in 1858 held the station of Jewan in the Chuprah district until the Sepoys under Koer Singh returned to Behar, upon which, having only a guard of a few native police, armed with swords, he escaped from one end of the station as the rebels entered at the other, and, after a ride of forty miles, reached Chuprah in safety. Held subsequently the appointments of Commissioner of Revenue and Circuit in several districts in Bengal; Judicial Commissioner of Mysore and Coorg in Madras; Secretary to the Government of Bengal and Member of the Board of Revenue, Lower Provinces. Gazetted to his nobly earned Victoria Cross July 8, 1859, which he received from the hands of Queen Victoria at Windsor Castle, on January 4, 1860.

[1] Kaye.

History of the Victoria Cross

JAMES BLAIR

(CAPTAIN, NOW LIEUT.-GENERAL, C.B.)

2ND BOMBAY LIGHT CAVALRY

Photo by ELLIOTT & FRY.

During the night of August 12, 1857, at Neemuch, Captain Blair volunteered to capture seven or eight mutineers who had shut themselves up in a house near at hand. He burst open the door, and rushed upon them, when, to avoid him, they fled by way of the roof. In the struggle he was badly wounded, but in spite of this he pursued them, being, however, unable to overtake them owing to the darkness of the night.

At Jeerum, on October 23, 1857, he was literally surrounded by a party of rebels. In an encounter with one of them, on whose head he broke his sword, he received a terrible cut on the arm. Fighting his way through them he rejoined his men, where he at once, wounded as he was, placed himself at the head of the troop and with no other weapon than the hilt of his broken sword, pursued the enemy for miles, completely routing them.

General Blair was born on January 27, 1828. Entered the Army in 1844; became Captain, 1857; Colonel, 1873; and attained his present rank in 1894.

The Indian Mutiny

JOSEPH P. H. CROWE
(LIEUTENANT, AFTERWARDS LIEUT.-COLONEL 10TH FOOT)

78TH THE ROSS-SHIRE BUFFS (2ND SEAFORTH HIGHLANDERS)

THE 78th were hotly engaged at Busherut Gunge on August 12, 1857. Here a redoubt was strongly held by the enemy from which they were firing heavily on our men. Preparations were made to carry the place by storm, there being no guns at hand, darkness setting in, and men falling fast. While marksmen played on the place to keep down the fire, the gallant Highlanders dashed forward, each man trying to be "first in." The race was won by Lieutenant Crowe, who outstripped all the others and, being followed by his men, in a few minutes the place was captured and the enemy scattered.

Colonel Crowe, after being some years in command of a battalion of the Lincoln Regiment, died in February, 1876.

CHARLES JOHN STANLEY GOUGH
(MAJOR, NOW GENERAL, G.C.B.)

5TH BENGAL EUROPEAN CAVALRY

SIR CHARLES GOUGH, one of two brothers who have been awarded the Victoria Cross, was decorated for bravery on four different occasions.

On August 15, 1857, he saved the life of his brother, Sir Hugh Gough (V.C.), killing two of his assailants. On August 18, 1857, he led a troop of the Guide Cavalry in a charge against the enemy, cutting down and killing two Sowars.

On January 27, 1858, at Shumsabad, he attacked the leader of the enemy's cavalry,

Photo by FRADELLE & YOUNG.

and ran him through with his sword, which, however, was carried out of his hand in the *mêlée*. He then defended himself with his revolver and shot two of the enemy.

On February 23, 1858, at Meangunge, seeing Brevet-Major O. H. St. George Anson in great danger, he dashed to his assistance, killed his opponent, and immediately afterwards cut down another of the enemy in a similarly gallant manner.

Born in 1832, Sir Charles Gough entered the Bengal Cavalry in 1848. Served in the Punjab Campaign, 1848–9; throughout the Mutiny, 1857–8; the Bhootan War, 1864–5; and both Afghan Wars, 1878–9 and 1879–80. In 1881 was Commandant of the Hyderabad Contingent, and from 1886–90 commanded a division of the Bengal Army.

His son, Major J. E. Gough, was awarded the Victoria Cross for bravery in Somaliland, on April 22, 1903. Thus three members of one family hold the decoration.

HENRY GEORGE BROWNE

(CAPTAIN, NOW COLONEL, RETIRED)

32ND THE DUKE OF CORNWALL'S LIGHT INFANTRY

Photo by FRADELLE & YOUNG.

DECORATED for his bravery on August 21, 1857, during the siege of Lucknow in leading a sortie to spike two heavy guns which were causing great havoc to our defences.

He was the first to enter the battery which was protected by high pallisades, the embrasures being closed with sliding shutters, which he most courageously removed, and attacked the gunners. About one hundred of the enemy were killed, and the two guns were spiked.

Colonel Browne, son of Mr. Arthur Browne, Newtown, Roscommon, was born in Ireland in 1830. Educated at Trinity College, Dublin. Gazetted to 32nd Light Infantry in 1855. Mentioned repeatedly in despatches during the Mutiny, apart from the act described above, and promoted to a company for his meritorious services.

The Indian Mutiny

JOHN DIVANE
(PRIVATE)
1ST BATT. 60TH RIFLES

ELECTED by the privates of his regiment under Rule 13 of the Warrant, for his distinguished conduct at Delhi, September 10, 1857, when he headed a charge made by the Beloochee and Sikh troops upon the enemy's trenches. Followed closely by the native troops, he jumped from our trenches and, making straight for the enemy's breast-works, was shot down when within a few yards of the goal.

PATRICK GREEN
(PRIVATE, AFTERWARDS COLOUR-SERGEANT)
75TH REGIMENT

ON September 11, 1857, Patrick Green performed an act of daring for which he was, in the name of the Queen, awarded the decoration almost on the spot by the Commander-in-Chief in India, an occurrence most rare and only found in one other instance, viz., that of Patrick Carlin. The General Order, being almost unique, is copied verbatim—

" Headquarters, Allahabad, July 28, 1858. The Commander-in-Chief in

History of the Victoria Cross

India is pleased to approve that the under-mentioned soldier be presented, in the name of Her Most Gracious Majesty, with a medal of the Victoria Cross for valour and daring in the field, viz.—

"Private Patrick Green,
"Her Majesty's 75th Foot,

for having on September 11, 1857, when the picquet at the Koodsia Bagh at Delhi was hotly pressed by a large body of the enemy, successfully rescued a comrade who had fallen wounded as a skirmisher.

"(Signed) C. Campbell, General,
"Commander-in-Chief, East Indies."

WILLIAM SUTTON

(BUGLER)

1st Batt. 60th Rifles

Elected by the privates of his regiment under Rule 13 of the Warrant, for his brave conduct at Delhi, September 13, 1857, the day before the great assault, when he volunteered to make a reconnaissance to ascertain the state of the breach. Throughout the operations of the siege his behaviour was most noticeable, especially on August 2, when, seeing a bugler of the enemy during the attack about to sound an order, he rushed forward and killed him before he could carry out his purpose.

The Indian Mutiny

DUNCAN CHARLES HOME
(LIEUTENANT)
BENGAL ENGINEERS

PHILIP SALKELD
(LIEUTENANT)
BENGAL ENGINEERS

JOHN SMITH
(SERGEANT)
BENGAL SAPPERS AND MINERS

ROBERT HAWTHORNE
(BUGLER)
52ND REGIMENT

DUNCAN CHARLES HOME.

No more magnificent example of heroism has ever been added to the glorious deeds of British soldiers than that of the four men Home, Salkeld, Smith and Hawthorne, who, on September 14, 1857, blew up the Cashmere Gate at Delhi, prior to the great assault on that city in the Indian Mutiny. The account written by Sergeant John Smith gives so vivid a description of the heroic actions of all concerned that it has been set out here almost word for word as given in Kaye's *Sepoy War*. Lieutenant Salkeld, as will be seen, never survived his wounds to receive the Victoria Cross, and Lieutenant Home only escaped the frightful perils of the 14th September to die on October 1 following, from the effects of the premature explosion of a mine after the capture of the fort of Malagurh. All having been prepared, the slow-match was lighted, but as no explosion followed in the ordinary time, Lieutenant Home went forward to re-light the match, which he supposed had gone out. At that instant the explosion occurred. His death was extraordinarily similar

History of the Victoria Cross

to that of Lieutenant Dundas, V.C., reference to whom will be found in this volume.

Sergeant John Smith's account—

"The party for blowing in the gate, the 60th Rifles leading, went off at a double from the Ludlow Castle, until they arrived at the cross-road leading to the Customs, and the men, when they opened out right and left, the Sappers going to the gate led by Lieutenant Home and one bugler (Hawthorne), Lieutenant Salkeld, with the party carrying the powder a few paces behind, the three European non-commissioned officers, and nine natives with twelve bags of twenty-five pounds each. My duty was to bring up the rear, and see

PHILIP SALKELD.  ROBERT HAWTHORNE.

From a Photo of the Monument in Delhi.

that none of them remained behind. Lieutenant Salkeld had passed through the temporary Burn Gate with Sergeants Carmichael and Burgess, but four of the natives had stopped behind the above gate and refused to go on. I had put down my bag and taken my gun, and threatened to shoot them, when Lieutenant Salkeld came running back and said, 'Why the —— don't you come on?' I told him there were four men behind the gate, and that I was going to shoot them. He said, 'Shoot them, d——n their eyes, shoot them!' I said, 'You hear the orders, and I will shoot you,' raising the gun slowly to 'present' to give fair time, when two men went on. Lieutenant Salkeld said, 'Do not shoot; with your own bag it will be enough.' I went on, and only Lieutenant Salkeld and Sergeant Burgess were there; Lieutenant Home and

The Indian Mutiny

the bugler had jumped into the ditch, and Sergeant Carmichael was killed as he went up with his powder on his shoulder, evidently having been shot from the wicket while crossing the broken part of the bridge along one of the beams. I placed my bag, and then at great risk reached Carmichael's bag from in front of the wicket, placed it, arranged the fusee for the explosion, and reported all ready to Lieutenant Salkeld, who held the slow match (*not a port-fire*, as I have seen stated). In stooping down to light the quick match, he put out his foot, and was shot through the thigh from the wicket, and in falling had the presence of mind to hold out the slow match, and told me to fire the charge. Burgess was next him and took it. I told him to fire the charge and keep cool. He turned round and said, 'It won't go off, sir ; it has gone out, sir' (not knowing that one officer had fallen into the ditch). I gave him a box of lucifers, and, as he took them, he let them fall into my hand, he being shot through the body from the wicket also, and fell over after Lieutenant Salkeld. I was then left alone, and keeping close to the charge, seeing from where the others where shot, I struck a light, when the port-fire in the fuse went off in my face, the light not having gone out as we thought. I took up my gun and jumped into the ditch, but before I had reached the ground the charge went off, and filled the ditch with smoke, so that I saw no one. I turned while in the act of jumping so that my back would come to the wall to save me from falling. I stuck close to the wall, and by that I escaped being smashed to pieces, only getting a severe bruise on the leg, the leather helmet saving my head.

"I put my hands along the wall and touched some one, and asked who it was. 'Lieutenant Home,' was the answer. I said, 'Has God spared you? are you hurt?' He said 'No,' and asked the same from me. As soon as the dust cleared a little we saw Lieutenant Salkeld and Burgess covered with dust; their lying in the middle of the ditch had saved them from being smashed to pieces and covered by the *débris* from the top of the wall, the shock only toppling the stones over, which fell between where we stood and where they lay. I went to Lieutenant Salkeld and called the bugler to help me to remove him under the bridge as the fire had covered upon us, and Lieutenant Salkeld's arms were broken. Lieutenant Home came to assist, but I begged him to keep out of the fire and that (*sic*) we would do all that could be done. Lieutenant Salkeld would not let us remove him, so I put a bag of powder under his head for a pillow, and with the bugler's puggery bound up his arms and thigh, and I left the bugler to look to him and went to Burgess, took off his sword, which I put on, and done (*sic*) what I could for him. I got some brandy from Lieutenant Home and gave to both, also to a Havildar (Pelluck Singh), who had his thigh shot through, and was under the bridge by a ladder that had been put into the ditch by mistake by the Rifles. Lieutenant Home got out of the ditch, leaving me in charge of the wounded, and went to the front after the Rifles had gone in, and the 52nd followed them.

* * * * *

"I then went to the rear for three stretchers and brought them, one of which was taken from me for an officer of the Rifles. I had to draw my sword and threaten to run any one through who took the other two. I put them into the ditch, and with the bugler's assistance got Lieutenant Salkeld into one and sent him with him, charging him strictly not to leave him until he had placed him in the hands of a surgeon, and with the assistance of a Naick who had come to the Havildar, got Burgess into one and sent the Naick with him, I being scarcely able to walk, and in a few minutes he returned to say he was dead, and asked for further orders. I told him to take him to the hospital.' After assisting to clear away the gate and make the roadway again, I went on to the front to see what was going on."

ALFRED SPENCER HEATHCOTE

(LIEUTENANT)

60TH RIFLES

LIEUTENANT ALFRED SPENCER HEATHCOTE was elected by the officers of his regiment under Rule 13 of the Victoria Cross Warrant, for his daring conduct during the siege of Delhi from June to September, 1857, during which he was wounded. He volunteered for services of extreme danger, especially during the terrible six days of the assault by our troops, when such severe fighting took place in the streets of the city.

He was born in London, March 29, 1832.

The Indian Mutiny

J. McGUIRE

(SERGEANT)

1st EUROPEAN BENGAL FUSILIERS

On September 14, 1857, during the great assault on Delhi, the brigade had reached the Cabul Gate and the 1st Fusiliers and the 75th Regiment with many Sikhs were awaiting orders, while ammunition was being served out for the various regiments. From some unaccountable cause, five boxes of ammunition caught fire, three of which exploded, and the two remaining were fully alight when Sergeant McGuire and Drummer M. Ryan (V.C.) dashed for them, and one after the other flung them over the parapet into the water. At the explosion of the first three, soldiers and natives in the vicinity rushed about, not knowing where it had taken place, and they were running towards the burning mass to certain destruction. These two soldiers, in risking their lives and by their brave conduct, saved those of all around them.

M. RYAN

(DRUMMER)

1st EUROPEAN BENGAL FUSILIERS

This soldier was associated with John McGuire (V.C.) on September 14, 1857, when he threw the boxes of ammunition which had caught fire into the water, thereby saving the lives of many men. Further details of this noble act are given in the record of McGuire.

EVERARD ALOYSIUS LISLE PHILLIPPS

(ENSIGN)

11TH REGIMENT BENGAL NATIVE INFANTRY

For the many gallant acts performed by him during the siege of Delhi, it was intended to recommend this young officer for the Victoria Cross, but during the street fighting in the city on September 18, 1857, he met his death. He was specially noticed for his bravery in capturing, with only a small handful of men, the Water Bastion of Delhi.

History of the Victoria Cross

HERBERT TAYLOR READE

(SURGEON, AFTERWARDS SURGEON-GENERAL)

61ST (SOUTH) GLOUCESTER REGIMENT

ON September 14, 1857, during the siege of Delhi, while Surgeon Reade was attending to the wounded at the end of one of the streets in the city, the rebels established themselves in the houses overlooking him and commenced firing from the roofs.

Seeing the precarious position of affairs, he drew his sword and, calling upon the few available soldiers near at hand to follow, succeeded under a heavy fire in dislodging the enemy from their position. His brave little party consisted of only ten men, of whom two were killed and six wounded during the encounter.

On September 16, at the assault of Delhi, he was one of the first up at the breach in the magazine, and on this occasion, with a sergeant of the 61st Regiment, spiked the enemy's guns.

Surgeon-General Reade, son of the late Colonel G. H. Reade, Canadian Militia, was born in 1828. Principal Medical Officer, Southern District, 1886, retiring in 1887. Died at Bath, in June, 1897, aged 68.

ROBERT HAYDON SHEBBEARE

(BREVET-CAPTAIN)

60TH BENGAL NATIVE INFANTRY

ON September 14, 1857, at the assault on Delhi, Captain (then Lieutenant) Shebbeare, at the head of the Guides, twice charged a loopholed serai to enable the breach to be attained, but, owing to the terrible fire, he was unable to accomplish his task, one third of his European soldiers having fallen. For this reason he was prevented from reorganizing his men for another attempt, but he conducted the rearguard of the retreat most successfully across the canal. His immunity from death is noted as miraculous, although he received one bullet through the cheek and a very severe scalp wound along the back of the head. This gallant officer was killed in the China War of 1860.

The Indian Mutiny

HENRY SMITH
(LANCE-CORPORAL)
52ND REGIMENT

MENTIONED in General Order of Major-General Sir Archdale Wilson, K.C.B., for his gallantry on September 14, 1857, when, through a murderous fire of grape, he carried a wounded comrade from the Chandin Chouk.

Henry Smith died some years ago, and his Victoria Cross was sold in July, 1896, for £70.

GEORGE WALLER
(COLOUR-SERGEANT)
1ST BATT. 60TH RIFLES

ELECTED by the non-commissioned officers of his regiment under Rule 13 of the Warrant, for conspicuous gallantry before Delhi, when he charged and captured the enemy's guns near the Cabul Gate, on September 14, 1857; and again, four days later, when the Sepoys made a most determined attack on a gun near the Chandin Chouk, his conduct was particularly noticeable.

GEORGE ALEXANDER RENNY
(CAPTAIN, AFTERWARDS MAJOR-GENERAL)
ROYAL (BENGAL) HORSE ARTILLERY

Photo by HAWKINS, *Brighton.*

ON September 16, 1857, after our capture of the Delhi magazine, a very determined attack was made upon the post by the enemy, and was kept up with great violence for a considerable time. Under cover of a heavy cross-fire from the high houses on the right flank of the magazine, from Selinghur and the palace, the enemy advanced to the high wall and endeavoured to fire the thatched roof. In this they partially succeeded, but it was extinguished by a soldier of the Belooch Battalion. On repeating the attempt, which was more successful, Captain Renny, with the greatest courage, mounted to the top of the wall of the magazine and flung several shells with lighted fuses into the midst of the enemy, which had a most beneficial effect, as the attack almost at once became less severe at that point, and shortly afterwards entirely ceased.

General Renny, born in 1827, was educated at Addiscombe, obtaining his commission in June, 1844. Served through Sutlej Campaign, present at battle of Sobraon.

He died at Bath on January 5, 1887.

EDWARD TALBOT THACKERAY
(LIEUTENANT, NOW COLONEL, K.C.B.)
ROYAL (BENGAL) ENGINEERS

Photo by ELLIOTT & FRY, *London.*

On September 16, 1857, fire broke out in a shed in the Delhi magazine in which large quantities of ammunition were lying about. Lieutenant Thackeray, although under a very heavy fire from the Sepoys, and notwithstanding that the flames were all round the combustible stores, most daringly rushed in, and, by his exertions, contrived to extinguish them.

Colonel Sir Edward Thackeray, son of the Rev. Francis Thackeray, first cousin of Thackeray the novelist, was born on October 19, 1836, educated at Marlborough and Addiscombe, and entered the R.E. in 1854. Served in Afghan War, 1879. Promoted Captain, 1865; Major, 1872; Lieut.-Colonel, 1880; Colonel, 1884; and retired in 1888. Was from 1880 Commandant of the Bengal Sappers and Miners.

PATRICK MAHONEY
(SERGEANT)
1ST MADRAS FUSILIERS

On September 21, 1857, at Mungulwar, the 1st Regiment of Native Infantry had mutinied, and Mahoney, when doing duty with the volunteer cavalry, was most prominent in capturing the regimental colour of the mutineers.

The Indian Mutiny

WILLIAM RENNIE

(LIEUTENANT AND ADJUTANT, AFTERWARDS LIEUT.-COLONEL)

90TH PERTHSHIRE VOLUNTEER LIGHT INFANTRY (2ND THE SCOTTISH RIFLES).

On September 21, 1857, during the advance on Lucknow by the force under Outram and Havelock, Lieutenant Rennie, under a heavy musketry fire, charged upon the Sepoy guns far in advance of the skirmishers of his regiment, and prevented the piece being carried off. Upon the arrival of support it was captured and used by us.

On September 25 he again dashed ahead of his men, when advancing upon a battery which was firing grape, and forced the enemy to abandon the guns.

Colonel Rennie, when a young officer of the 73rd (Perthshire)—now 2nd Black Watch—served at the blockade of Monte Video, 1846, and, during the four following years, in the war against the Kaffirs, received special promotion for his distinguished service.

He died at Elgin, in August, 1896, aged 75.

ROBERT GRANT

(SERGEANT)

1ST BATT. 5TH REGIMENT

On September 24, 1857, some of the stiffest fighting of the Indian Mutiny took place at the Alumbagh, and during the action Private Deveney was terribly wounded, his leg being shot away.

Grant proceeded under a terrific fire to his friend's assistance, carried him out of range and, with the help of the late Lieutenant Brown and some soldiers, contrived to bring him safely into camp. This gallant soldier's name was originally gazetted on June 19, 1860, as "Ewart," but corrected in the issue of October 12, following.

History of the Victoria Cross

FRANCIS CORNWALLIS MAUDE

(CAPTAIN, AFTERWARDS COLONEL, C.B.)

ROYAL ARTILLERY

Photo by ELLIOTT & FRY, *London.*

CAPTAIN FRANCIS CORNWALLIS MAUDE was in command of a battery in the force led by Outram and Havelock to the relief of the Lucknow Residency. His fearless behaviour under a most terrific fire of cannon and musketry was most noticeable on every occasion during that trying time, and his name was constantly mentioned in despatches.

He was entrusted with the terrible duty of blowing the mutineers from the guns, when that drastic and frightful punishment was meted out to the murderers of our helpless women and children. Sir James Outram, in his report, referring to the splendid conduct of Captain Maude during the relief says, "This attack appeared to him to indicate no reckless or foolhardy daring, but the calm heroism of a true soldier, who fully appreciates the difficulties and dangers of the task he has undertaken, and that, but for Captain Maude's nerve and coolness on this trying occasion, the army could not have advanced."

Born in October, 1828, Colonel Maude was the son of Captain the Honourable Francis Maude, R.N. After retiring from the service, was Consul-General at Warsaw from 1876 to 1886. He died at Windsor Castle, of which he was a Military Knight, on October 19, 1900.

JOEL HOLMES

(PRIVATE)

84TH REGIMENT

IN the record of Captain F. C. Maude, V.C., mention was made of the terrific fire through which that gallant officer's gunners had to force their way and work the guns, and when those in charge had been shot down, volunteers had to be requisitioned to carry on the work. One of these was Joel Holmes, whose conduct through the terrible ordeal was specially noticed in Major General Havelock's Field Force Orders of October 17, 1857.

The Indian Mutiny

JOSEPH JEE

(SURGEON, AFTERWARDS INSPECTOR-GENERAL, C.B.)

78TH REGIMENT (ROSS-SHIRE BUFFS; 2ND SEAFORTH HIGHLANDERS)

Photo by NUMA BLANC, *Cannes.*

ON September 25, 1857, when Havelock's relieving column was forcing its way into Lucknow, Surgeon Jee displayed the greatest courage and devotion to the wounded who had fallen during the charge of the 78th Highlanders at the Char Bagh Bridge. He succeeded in getting them to some cots and by this means, as well as on the backs of his men, he was able to have them conveyed in the direction of the Residency until the dhoolie-bearers who had fled were collected and persuaded to carry out their duties. Later in the day, while still occupied in directing the conveyance of the wounded, he and his party were besieged in the Mote-Mehal by an overwhelming number of the enemy. Here he remained during the whole night and following morning, exposing himself freely to the hail of bullets while proceeding to tend the wounded who had fallen while serving a 24-pounder gun, in a most open position, and, by his endeavours and intrepid conduct, was enabled to get many of them safely into the Residency by way of the river bank through a heavy cross-fire of ordnance, although he had been repeatedly warned not to attempt the perilous task.

Surgeon-General Jee was the son of Christopher Preston Jee, of Atherstone, Warwickshire, and joined the 1st Dragoons as Assistant-Surgeon in 1842, becoming Surgeon, 1854. Served through Persian War, 1857–8, including battle of Koosh-ab and bombardment of Mohammera; Indian Mutiny under Havelock in first relief of Lucknow Residency, and its subsequent defence, also taking part in the operations in Rohilkund, 1858, and capture of Bareilly. After many years of retirement died at Queeniborough Hall, Leicestershire, March 17, 1899.

History of the Victoria Cross

VALENTINE MUNBEE McMASTER

(ASSISTANT-SURGEON)

78TH REGIMENT (THE ROSS-SHIRE BUFFS; 2ND SEAFORTH HIGHLANDERS)

ON September 25, 1857, during the relief of Lucknow by Havelock and Outram, Surgeon McMaster behaved with conspicuous bravery and humanity, all night long exposing himself to the heavy fire of the enemy while bringing in, and attending to, the many wounded.

HERBERT TAYLOR MACPHERSON

(LIEUTENANT, AFTERWARDS MAJOR-GENERAL, K.C.B.)

78TH REGIMENT

ON September 25, 1857, Lieutenant Macpherson was with the force under Outram and Havelock, and, during the heavy fighting at Lucknow between the outskirts of the city and the Residency, to whose relief they were forcing their way, he led his men to the attack and capture of two brass 9-pounder guns, setting them an example of heroic gallantry.

He died in Burma in 1886.

Major-General Sir H. T. Macpherson entered the Army on February 28, 1845; became Captain October 6, 1857; Brevet-Major, February, 1865; Brevet-Lieut.-Colonel, 1867; Colonel, 1871; and attained the rank he held at his death on July 1, 1882. He served in Persia in 1857, as

Photo by FRADELLE & YOUNG.

The Indian Mutiny

Adjutant of the 78th, and in every engagement leading to the relief of the Residency, and was at the final capture of Lucknow.

WILLIAM OLPHERTS
(CAPTAIN, AFTERWARDS GENERAL, G.C.B.)
BENGAL ARTILLERY

Photo by ELLIOTT & FRY.

ALTHOUGH the conduct of Captain Olpherts was brought to notice continually during the severe fighting which took place during the march to Lucknow under Outram and Havelock, he was specially prominent on September 25, 1857, when the force penetrated into the city itself. He charged on horseback with the 90th Regiment, led by Colonel Campbell, and, in the face of a heavy fire of grape-shot, captured two Sepoy guns, after which he again braved the storm of lead to bring up horses and limbers to carry off the captured ordnance.

The heroic manner in which Olpherts served the guns of his battery during Havelock's advance to the Residency has been mentioned too often in chronicles of the Mutiny to allow it to be related here, but the characteristic sobriquet of " Hell Fire Olpherts " which he earned in the Army tells sufficiently its own story.

Sir William, son of Wm. Olpherts, of Dartrey, Co. Armagh, was born on March 8, 1822, and educated at Gracehill and Dungannon Schools, and Addiscombe Military College. Entered Bengal Artillery, June 11, 1839; became Captain, 1853; Brevet-Major and Lieut.-Colonel, 1858; Colonel, 1872; and General, March 31, 1883. Served through Gwalior and Sinde campaigns under Sir Hugh (Lord) Gough and Sir C. Napier respectively; and in the Peshawar Valley under Sir Colin Campbell, 1852. On outbreak of Russian War was employed on special service with Sir Fenwick Williams at Kars and Erzeroun in Armenia.

In 1859 accompanied the expedition against the Wazarees as volunteer under Sir N. Chamberlain. On his return in 1868 was presented with a sword of honour by the County and City of Armagh. He died at Norwood on April

History of the Victoria Cross

30, 1902, his body being escorted to the cemetery by a detachment of the Royal Horse Artillery. During the service the rain poured in such torrents and with such ferocity that, as a writer expressed it afterwards, " it seemed as if the very elements were rehearsing the battle scenes of the life that had ceased."

HENRY WARD

(PRIVATE)

78TH REGIMENT (ROSS-SHIRE BUFFS; 2ND SEAFORTH HIGHLANDERS)

ON the night of September 25, 1857, during the advance of Outram's relieving force into Lucknow, Captain Havelock (afterwards Lieut.-General Sir H. M. Havelock-Allan, V.C.) was severely wounded. He was placed in a dhoolie and Private Ward remained by him all through the night, guarding it. The next morning Private Thomas Pilkington was wounded and took refuge in the same dhoolie. Ward escorted both men through a terrific fire of ordnance and musketry, keeping the bearers to their work by his exertions, bravery, and splendid example, finally succeeding in having both safely conveyed to the Baillie Guard.

WILLIAM BRADSHAW

(ASSISTANT SURGEON)

90TH REGIMENT

WHEN, on September 26, 1857, the Lucknow Residency was reinforced (although not relieved) by Sir Henry Havelock, his troops forced their way into the beleaguered garrison's entrenchments, and many wounded had to be left behind in the city streets. Sir Anthony Home, V.C., whose heroic conduct gained him the Victoria Cross, was accompanied by Surgeon Bradshaw, and that gallant member of the medical profession was conspicuous for his devotion in the removal of the wounded. In spite of the swarms of Sepoys around them keeping up a heavy fire, the dhoolie-bearers were prevailed on by this man to rally and return to their duties, and when his party of about twenty bearers became separated from the rest of our troops, his exertions and splendid example enabled

The Indian Mutiny

the wounded under his care to be successfully brought into the Residency by way of the river bank.

THOMAS DUFFY

(PRIVATE)

1ST MADRAS FUSILIERS

SPECIALLY mentioned by Sir James Outram for his cool intrepidity and daring conduct, whereby a 24-pounder gun was prevented from being captured by the Sepoys, on September 26, 1857, at Lucknow.

Thomas Duffy died some years ago, and his Victoria Cross was sold in London on October 28, 1902, for £53.

JAMES HOLLOWELL

(PRIVATE)

78TH REGIMENT (THE ROSS-SHIRE BUFFS; 2ND SEAFORTH HIGHLANDERS)

ON September 26, 1857, nine men were shut in and besieged in a house in Lucknow by the Sepoys during the advance of Outram and Havelock to the relief of the Residency. James Hollowell, one of the party, displayed conspicuous courage, exposing himself most bravely, and by his fine example prevailed on the men with him to keep up a splendid defence, in the face of terrible odds and fearful circumstances. The Sepoys set fire to the house, and crept near enough to shoot through four of the windows, but the little defending party held out until ultimately rescued. (See McManus and Ryan.)

ANTHONY DICKSON HOME

(SURGEON, NOW SURGEON-GENERAL, K.C.B.)

90TH PERTHSHIRE VOLUNTEER LIGHT INFANTRY (2ND SCOTTISH RIFLES)

SIR ANTHONY HOME was, when Havelock entered Lucknow on September 26, 1857, in charge of the wounded in rear of the column. The small escort left with him had been nearly all wounded, and the whole became separated

History of the Victoria Cross

Photo by ELLIOT & FRY.

from the main body. The few remaining men were forced to enter a house, which they defended till it was set on fire, upon which they took shelter in a shed which they held for twenty-two hours, till at length only six men and Dr. Home were able to fire. The four officers with him being all wounded, the command devolved on him. By his energy and example he stimulated all to action, and through him the defence was successful and the wounded eventually saved.

Three of the wounded officers died soon afterwards, owing to the hardships they had undergone.

Sir Anthony Dickson Home, V.C., K.C.B. (1874), was born in 1823. Entered the Army Medical Department in 1848. Served in the Crimean War; the Indian Mutiny; the China War of 1860; New Zealand Campaign, 1863-5, and the Ashantee War of 1873; in the latter war he served as Principal Medical Officer, and held the same position in Cyprus during 1878-9, and to the forces in India from 1881 to 1885. Was promoted to Surgeon-General in 1880, retiring in 1886.

PETER McMANUS

(PRIVATE)

5TH REGIMENT

ON September 26, 1857, McManus was one of the band of men whose bravery is described in the record of James Hollowell, V.C. He remained outside the house in which the party were shut up, and from behind a pillar kept up a most telling fire on the Sepoys, thereby preventing their making a rush on the building. With Private John Ryan, V.C., he rushed into the street under a terrific fire and carried in Captain Arnold, 1st Madras Fusiliers, who received another wound while being taken into the house. After serving through the Mutiny this gallant soldier died of smallpox at Allahabad, in 1859.

The Indian Mutiny

STEWART McPHERSON
(COLOUR-SERGEANT)

78TH REGIMENT (THE ROSS-SHIRE BUFFS; 2ND SEAFORTH HIGHLANDERS)

ON September 26, 1857, at the relief of the Lucknow Residency, one of our men was lying badly wounded, in a most exposed situation, under a very heavy fire. McPherson rushed out and, with great coolness, under a storm of bullets, lifted him up and carried him into safety.

He was also distinguished on many other occasions by his daring, and gallantry in action.

JOHN RYAN
(PRIVATE)

1ST MADRAS FUSILIERS

ON September 26, 1857, John Ryan was associated with Surgeon Home and Privates Hollowell and McManus in their heroic stand at a small house in which they were defending the wounded under their care. Ryan was particularly conspicuous for his daring rescue of many wounded from the dhoolies into which the mutineers were firing and some of which they set on fire. Many lives were owed that day to his bravery.

J. THOMAS
(BOMBARDIER)

4TH COMPANY 1ST BATT. BENGAL ARTILLERY

ON September 27, 1857, the party to which Thomas belonged was returning from a sortie and one of his comrades fell severely wounded. He took the injured man on his back and carried him a long distance, under a very heavy fire and in circumstances of considerable difficulty, to prevent him from falling into the hands of the Sepoys, who would otherwise have despatched him by their own slow methods of torture.

THE HONBLE. AUGUSTUS HENRY ARCHIBALD ANSON
(CAPTAIN)
84TH REGIMENT

On September 28, 1857, at Boolundshuhur, the conduct of this officer was especially distinguished. The 9th Light Dragoons had charged through the town, and, on reaching the serai, commenced to reform their ranks. To prevent them making their way out, the enemy blocked the entrance by drawing their carts across the gateway, on seeing which Captain Anson dashed out and, with a lance, knocked the drivers over. Suffering at the time from a severely wounded hand, he was unable to control his horse, which carried him into the middle of the enemy's ranks, and although fired at by them with a volley, a bullet passing through his coat, he contrived to make his way out without further mishap. On November 16 following, at the assault of the Secundrabagh, he was one of the foremost of the storming party, being slightly wounded and having his horse shot under him. Major-General Sir Hope Grant referred to him in his despatch of August 12, 1858, saying, "He has shown the greatest gallantry on every occasion and has slain many enemies in fight."

ROBERT BLAIR
(LIEUTENANT)
2ND DRAGOON GUARDS

Major-General Sir James Hope Grant, K.C.B., brought this officer's gallant conduct forward in his despatch of January 10, 1858.

He states that at Boolundshuhur, on September 28, 1857, Lieutenant Blair was ordered to take a sergeant and twelve men to bring in a deserted

The Indian Mutiny

ammunition wagon. On his nearing the wagon, about sixty of the enemy's horsemen, who had been unobserved up to that time, swooped down upon them, but Lieutenant Blair, taking no thought of the heavy odds he had to face, led his little party against the oncoming troop and fought his way through them, killing four of them with his own hand. Not one of his men was killed, and all were by his skilful leadership safely brought back to camp, although he himself was most severely wounded by a native officer, whom he had run through with his sword. The native turned and slashed at Lieutenant Blair, the blow nearly severing the joint of his shoulder. (See Private Donohoe, V.C.)

BERNARD DIAMOND
(SERGEANT)
BENGAL HORSE ARTILLERY

Photo by PRICE, *New Zealand.*

THE gallantry of this soldier was mentioned by Major Turner, Bengal Horse Artillery, in his despatch of October 2, 1857. At Boolundshuhur, on September 28, 1857, he was conspicuous for his determined bravery in working a gun in company with Richard Fitzgerald (V.C.) after every other man had been either killed or wounded who belonged to it. By the devoted conduct of these two men the road was completely cleared of the enemy.

P. DONOHOE
(PRIVATE)
9TH LANCERS

ON September 28, 1857, at Boolundshuhur, during the charge in which Lieutenant Robert Blair (V.C.) so gallantly distinguished himself, Donohoe was greatly instrumental in assisting his officer in returning to camp after going to his support when so terribly wounded.

RICHARD FITZGERALD
(GUNNER)
BENGAL HORSE ARTILLERY

ASSOCIATED with Sergeant Diamond (V.C.), in an act of determined bravery at Boolundshuhur, September 28, 1857, as recorded in the sketch of that soldier.

History of the Victoria Cross

Photo by BALL, Regent Street.

ROBERT KELLS
(LANCE-CORPORAL)

9TH LANCERS

ON September 28, 1857, at Boolundshuhur, Captain Drysdale's horse was shot, and he was thrown heavily, breaking his collar-bone. Kells, dashing to his rescue, kept the enemy at bay until help arrived, and was the means of saving him from certain death. The portrait of this gallant lancer shows him in the uniform of the Yeomen of the Guard, in which corps he is still serving. In July 1901 was presented with the Royal Victorian Medal by H.M. The King.

J. R. ROBERTS
(PRIVATE)

9TH LANCERS

DECORATED for conspicuous gallantry and devotion at Boolundshuhur, September 28, 1857, when, under a most galling fire, he brought a wounded comrade through the streets, being himself badly injured during his humane act.

Photo by Cox, Clifton.

JOHN CHARLES CAMPBELL DAUNT
(LIEUTENANT, AFTERWARDS LIEUT.-COLONEL)

11TH (LATE 70TH) BENGAL NATIVE INFANTRY

DECORATED for conspicuous courage at Chota Behar, on October 2, 1857, when in action against the mutineers of the Ramgurh Battalion. One-third of the detachment had been mown down by grape-shot from two guns, when Daunt, in company with Dennis Dynon (V.C.), charged at the gunners, shot them down and captured both pieces.

The Indian Mutiny

Lieutenant Daunt was also specially mentioned for his gallantry on November 2, 1857, when he pursued the mutineers of the 32nd Bengal Native Infantry. Driving them across a plain into a thick cultivation, he, with a small party of Rattray's Sikhs, followed and attacked them, being himself dangerously wounded in the struggle. The mutineers greatly outnumbered Daunt's little force, and the ultimate preservation of any of the Sikhs was due to his courageous conduct and skilful leading.

DENIS DYNON
(SERGEANT)
53RD REGIMENT

ASSOCIATED with Lieutenant J. C. C. Daunt, V.C., in heroically dashing at and capturing two guns from the mutineers of the Ramgurh Battalion on October 2, 1857, at Chota Behar.

PATRICK McHALE
(PRIVATE)
1ST BATT. 5TH REGIMENT

DECORATED for conspicuous bravery at Lucknow, October 2, 1857, when, at the capture of the guns of the Cawnpore Battery, he was the first man to arrive. On December 22 following he was again the first in another battery which was assaulted, and its guns, which had poured grape into our advancing columns, captured. The *Gazette* stated that "upon every occasion of attack McHale had been the first to meet the enemy, amongst whom he caused such consternation by his terrific onslaught that little work was left to his comrades coming up behind. His habitual coolness, daring and sustained bravery in action, has rendered his name a household word for gallantry among his comrades."

The following account of McHale's career, copied from the *Regimental Records*, was given to the author some years ago—

History of the Victoria Cross

"No. 2626, 'Pat' McHale, as he was generally called, enlisted for the 5th Fusiliers on December 18, 1847. He was then twenty-one years old, and joined the depôt at Parkhurst Barracks, Isle of Wight.

"Having passed his recruit's drill he embarked for foreign service on board the *Lady Edmondsbury*, and sailed from Cowes on the following 8th of May for the Island of Mauritius. At this time McHale was a most powerful man, standing about six feet two inches, and with square shoulders and chest in proportion; he was what we call a 'fine soldier.' His complexion was fair, hair sandy, and his face much freckled. Pat was no scholar; he could neither read nor write.

* * * * *

"Landing at the Mauritius on August 19, 1848, Pat served nine years in that beautiful island, doing his duty as a good and steady soldier.

"Arriving with the headquarter of the regiment in India in 1857, he proceeded with his company towards the North-Western Provinces and was at the relief of Arrah and the operations in the Jugdeespore district.

"On September 3, Pat with his detachment rejoined the headquarter at Allahabad and marched with it on the 5th towards Cawnpore. Proceeding with Havelock's column for the relief of Lucknow Residency, he was present at the Battle of Mungulwar, the capture of the Alumbagh, and the first relief of Lucknow on September 25. In these actions Pat was always to the front, and, without fear for himself, performed valorous deeds with his bayonet, when the Sepoys would allow him to get near enough.

"We have now arrived at the period when the regiment was besieged for nearly two months in the Lucknow Residency. McHale shared cheerfully the hardships and privations of that time and took part in the various sallies made for the purpose of capturing guns from the enemy and clearing the surrounding houses and other obstacles too closely situated, which gave shelter to the mutineers. On October 2, at the capture of the 'Cawnpore Battery,' he was the first man to leap into the embrasure, and some of the Sepoy gunners were bayonetted by him.

"On being relieved by Sir Colin Campbell in November the regiment was encamped at the Alumbagh, and was attached to the 1st Brigade of Sir James Outram's force. There McHale found plenty of hard picquet duties, besides being almost constantly harassed by attacks of the enemy, but it was not until December 22 that an opportunity occurred for the display of his undaunted courage.

"Sir James Outram, through the medium of his spies, had heard that the mutineers were about to attack him in great force. In order to defeat this purpose he, in the dead of the night, left his camp standing, and with the greater

The Indian Mutiny

part of his force proceeded to surprise the enemy, who was bivouacked some two or three miles off in a village. Marching slowly in dead silence, and with unmeasured and broken tread, the force reached a mosque, where a halt was made. At break of day Outram in a loud voice ordered the 'advance'; the enemy's vedettes fired their carbines and bolted. Colonel Guy (5th Fusiliers) ordered the 'double,' and, as the regiment cleared the street and issued into open space, it formed line. While this movement was being completed a gun belonging to the Sepoys situated in a *tope*, about 100 yards in front, was firing grape into it, and independent firing commenced as the companies formed up. No sooner was the regiment in line than the colonel gave the command to 'charge,' and away it went with a cheer at a steady double. Here the first gun was captured on that day by Captain Bigge (now Major-General Bigge, retired). The enemy had bolted, leaving one gun behind them. The regiment then pursued the enemy. Our men advanced so rapidly that they drove everything before them, and the Sepoys did not do anything but run away. The enemy, however, opened fire upon them with their artillery from the village of Guilee, where their main body was stationed. Our skirmishers quickly pushed the rebels through the village. They had just loaded a gun which they had discharged at us, but they fled without stopping to fire it, for they could not force on the bullocks quickly enough to get away. The gallant McHale, one of the finest and bravest of our men (where many were fine and themselves brave), was down upon them, followed by others who were not so quick as he. With a stroke from the butt of his rifle he turned the bullocks round, then set the gun and fired into the rebels the charge they had loaded it with.

"For this act, together with his bravery at the 'Cawnpore Battery,' he was unanimously elected by his comrades as one of the candidates for the V.C. The number of these decorations to be given to the regiment was limited to three, but there were others that deserved the distinction; the three fortunate recipients were elected by their comrades.

"McHale was at the final capture of Lucknow and also in the Campaign in Oude in 1858-9. During all this time he was never absent from his duty for a single day, and it is almost wonderful to relate that he escaped without a single scratch.

"Returning to England in 1861, he served with the regiment until it embarked for India in 1866, when he was sent with the rest of the old soldiers to Shorncliffe to form the regimental depôt.

"In addition to having the Victoria Cross he was in possession of the Indian Mutiny medal with clasps for the '*Defence of Lucknow*,' and '*Lucknow*,' the good conduct medal and the regimental medal of merit. He died at Shorncliffe on October 26, 1866, and a stone erected by his comrades marks the spot where rests the remains of as good and plucky a soldier as ever served in the ranks of the Fighting Fifth."

JOHN SINNOTT

(LANCE-CORPORAL, AFTERWARDS CORPORAL)

84TH (YORK AND LANCASTER) REGIMENT

Photo by MAULL & FOX.

ON October 6, 1857, at Lucknow, Lieutenant Gibaut went several times, carrying water, to extinguish a fire which had occurred in a breastwork, and he was accompanied by Lance-Corporal John Sinnott on almost every occasion. At last Lieutenant Gibaut fell mortally wounded, upon which Sinnott, together with Sergeants Glinn and Mullins, and Private Mullins, went out, and carried him into shelter under a heavy fire. He was twice wounded during the performance of this act, and was elected by his fellow-soldiers to receive the Victoria Cross under Rule 13 of the Warrant.

He died at Livingstone Road, Clapham, on July 20, 1896, aged 63.

DIGHTON MACNAGHTEN PROBYN

(CAPTAIN, NOW GENERAL, G.C.V.O., K.C.B., K.C.S.I., P.C.)

2ND PUNJAUB CAVALRY

GENERAL SIR HOPE GRANT, K.C.B., in his despatch dated January 10, 1858, says of Captain Probyn : " Has been distinguished for gallantry and daring throughout the campaign."

During the charge of his squadron upon the rebel infantry at the Battle of Agra he became separated from his men and surrounded by five or six Sepoys, who attacked him, but he defended himself from the many cuts made at him, and by the time his men had joined him had killed two of his assailants.

At another time, in fighting with a Sepoy, his horse was wounded, and he

The Indian Mutiny

Photo by STEREOSCOPIC CO., *London.*

received a severe cut on the wrist from the bayonet, but after a desperate encounter he cut him down. Later on in the same day he singled out a standard-bearer, and, in face of a number of the enemy, killed him and captured the colours.

These are only a few of the many gallant deeds recorded of this brave officer.

General Probyn, born January 21, 1833, son of the late Captain G. Probyn, entered the Army in 1849. His active services include, apart from the Mutiny, the fighting on the Trans-Indian Frontier, 1852-7; China, 1860, and Umbeyla Campaign, 1863.

Has been Comptroller of the Royal Household, Keeper of the Privy Purse, Member of the Council of the Duchy of Cornwall, and also of Lancaster. Equerry at present to H.M. the King. He became Captain in 1857; Major, 1858; Lieut.-Colonel, 1861; Colonel, 1866; Major-General, 1870; Lieut.-General, 1877; and attained his present rank in 1888. Was at Delhi during the siege, and fought at the actions of Boolundshuhur, Allyghur and Agra, being four times mentioned in despatches; also at the battle of Kanouje, and the relief of Lucknow under Sir Colin Campbell. Received the thanks of the Governor-General (Lord Canning), and was twice mentioned in despatches. Fought at the battles of Cawnpore and Kalle Nuddee, and the storming of Lucknow in March, 1858.

J. FREEMAN

(PRIVATE)

9TH LANCERS

AT Agra, on October 10, 1857, Lieutenant Jones had been shot and severely wounded. Freeman, dashing to his officer's assistance, killed the leader of the enemy's cavalry and kept at bay the Sepoys surrounding him. His Cross is in the United Service Institute, London.

History of the Victoria Cross

JAMES MILLER
(CONDUCTOR, AFTERWARDS HON. MAJOR)
ORDNANCE DEPARTMENT, BENGAL

ON October 28, 1857, Miller was employed with heavy howitzers and ordnance stores, and attached to a detachment under the command of Colonel Cotton, C.B. The rebels had taken up their position in the serai at Futtehpore Sekra, near Agra, and, in the attack upon them, Lieutenant Glubb, of the late 38th Bengal Native Infantry, was severely wounded. Miller went to his assistance, and, at great personal risk, carried him out of action. He was himself subsequently wounded and sent to Agra.

THOMAS HENRY KAVANAGH
ASSISTANT-COMMISSIONER IN OUDE

ALTHOUGH the garrison of the Residency of Lucknow was reached on September 26, 1857, after hard fighting by the force under Outram and Havelock, it was not actually *relieved* until Sir Colin Campbell's force succeeded in fighting its way through the strongly held positions of the enemy a few weeks later. Outram and Havelock, owing to their loss in killed and wounded, were only able to form a *reinforcement* of the beleaguered garrison, being too weak to bring away the many wounded and the women and children. When Sir Colin Campbell's force was approaching the city Mr. Kavanagh determined to attempt to pass through the Sepoy lines, and reach him, in order to place at his disposal his own intimate knowledge of the city and the enemy's position. Mr. Kavanagh's own account of his adventures on

The Indian Mutiny

the night of November 9[1] gives an idea of the terrible perils he had to face, but does not make sufficiently clear the invaluable service to his country which resulted from his superhumanly heroic action. Oude was annexed in 1856, and by 1857 there were no plans of Lucknow to show Sir Colin Campbell the intricacies of the streets. Outram and his gallant men had had to force their way through miles of narrow lanes to reach the Residency, and as every yard of the way was fiercely contested great loss of life resulted before the object was attained. Mr. Kavanagh was not only able to bring Outram's plans for concerted action between the Residency and the relieving force, but, by his own intimate knowledge of the city, was able to guide the columns by a different route from that originally intended [2] and, avoiding the city streets, reached the Residency by way of the Dilkoosha Park. By this means much fighting in the well-defended narrow lanes was avoided, and therefore the relief was attained with the loss of many less lives. The indomitable courage of Mr. Kavanagh places his name among the most worthy recipients of the decoration, and there can be none who remember the terrible times of the Indian Mutiny but will be glad that the Victoria Cross Warrant was altered to enable the list to include the name of " Lucknow Kavanagh," the second of three " civilians " who have been similarly rewarded.

Thomas Henry Kavanagh was born at Mullingar, Co. Westmeath, in 1820, and went to India in 1839. He was a Member of the Punjab Commission and went to Lucknow with Sir James Lawrence. He retired in 1875 as First Grade Deputy Commissioner, and died at Gibraltar, at the house of his friend, Lord Napier of Magdala, on November 11, 1882. The Victoria Cross was given to him at Windsor by Queen Victoria on January 4, 1860, and in 1897 it was presented to a Museum in Lucknow by his son, Mr. Hope Kavanagh, District Superintendent of Police at Saharunpore.

Mr. Kavanagh's own account of his exploit is given below, and his portrait in the disguise he wore on the eventful night is given in Appendix III.

Mr. Thomas Henry Kavanagh's Narrative of his Escape from the British Entrenchments at Lucknow to the Camp of Sir Colin Campbell, near Bunnee, for the Purpose of Acting as his Guide in his Advance for the Relief of the Besieged Garrison.

While passing through the entrenchments of Lucknow about 10 o'clock a.m. on the 9th instant, I learnt that a spy had come in from Cawnpore, and that he was going back in the night as far as Alum Bagh with despatches to His

---

[1] The *Gazette* states the 8th (P. A. W.).

[2] It was originally intended to follow the same route taken by Outram (P. A. W.).

History of the Victoria Cross

Excellency Sir Colin Campbell, the Commander-in-Chief, who—it is said—was approaching Lucknow with five or six thousand men.

I sought out the spy, whose name was Kunoujee Lall, and who was a *nazir* in the Court of the Deputy Commissioner of Durriabad before the outbreak in Oudh. He had taken letters from the entrenchments before; but I had never seen him till now. I found him intelligent, and imparted to him my desire to venture in disguise to Alum Bagh in his company. He hesitated a great deal at acting as my guide, but made no attempt to exaggerate the danger of the road. He merely urged that there was more chance of detection by our going together, and proposed that we should take different roads, and meet outside of the city; to which I objected. I left him to transact some business, my mind dwelling all the time on the means of accomplishing my object.

I had some days previously witnessed the preparation of plans which were being made by direction of Sir James Outram to assist the Commander-in-Chief in his march into Lucknow for the relief of the besieged, and it then occurred to me that some one with the requisite local knowledge ought to attempt to reach His Excellency's camp beyond or at the Alum Bagh. The news of Sir Colin Campbell's advance revived the idea, and I made up my mind to go myself.

At 2 o'clock, after finishing the business I was engaged upon, I mentioned to Colonel R. Napier, Chief of Sir James Outram's Staff, that I was willing to proceed through the enemy to Alum Bagh, if the General thought my doing so would be of service to the Commander-in-Chief. He was surprised at the offer, and seemed to regard the enterprise as fraught with too much danger to be assented to; but did me the favour of communicating the offer to Sir James Outram, because he considered that my zeal deserved to be brought to his notice.

Sir James did not encourage me to undertake the journey, declaring that he thought it so dangerous that he would not himself have asked any officer to attempt it. I, however, spoke so confidently of success, and treated the danger so lightly, that he at last yielded, and did me the honour of adding that if I succeeded in reaching the Commander-in-Chief my knowledge would be of great help to him.

I secretly arranged for a disguise so that my departure might not be known to my wife, as she was not well enough to bear the prospect of an eternal separation. When I left home about seven o'clock in the evening, she thought I was gone on duty for the night to the mines; for I was working as an Assistant Field Engineer, by order of Sir James Outram.

By 7¼ o'clock my disguise was completed and when I entered the room

The Indian Mutiny

of Colonel Napier no one in it recognized me. I was dressed as a *bud mash*, or as an irregular soldier of the city, with sword and shield, native-made shoes, tight trousers, a yellow silk *koortah* (coat) over a tight-fitting white muslin shirt, a yellow-coloured chintz sheet thrown round my shoulders, a cream-coloured turban, and a white waist-band or *kummerbund*. My face, down to the shoulders, and my hands to the wrists, were coloured with lamp-black, the cork used being dipped in oil, to cause the colour to adhere a little; I could get nothing better. I had little confidence in the disguise of my features, and I trusted more to the darkness of the night; but Sir James Outram and his Staff seemed satisfied, and after being provided with a small double-barrelled pistol and a pair of broad *pyjamahs* (trousers) over the tight drawers, I proceeded with Kunoujee Lall to the right bank of the River Goompty, running north of our entrenchments, accompanied by Captain Harding of the Irregular Cavalry.

Here we undressed, and quietly forded the river, which was only about four and a half feet deep, and about a hundred yards wide at this point. My courage failed me while in the water, and if my guide had been within reach I should, perhaps, have pulled him back and abandoned the enterprise. But he waded quickly through the stream, and, reaching the opposite bank, went crouching up a ditch for three hundred yards to a grove of low trees on the edge of a pond, where we stopped to dress. While we were here a man came down to the pond to wash, and went away again without observing us.

My confidence now returned to me, and with my *tulwar* (sword) resting on my shoulder, we advanced into the huts in front, where I accosted a matchlockman, who answered to my remark (that the night was cold): "It is very cold; in fact it is a cold night." I passed him, adding that it would be colder by-and-bye.

After going six or seven hundred yards further, we reached the iron bridge over the Goompty, where we were stopped and called over by a native officer who was in an upper-storied house, and seemed to be in command of a cavalry picquet, whose horses were near the place—saddled. My guide advanced to the light, and I stayed a little back in the shade. After being told that we had come from Mundeon (our old cantonment, and then in possession of the enemy) and that we were going into the city to our homes, he let us proceed. We continued on along the left bank of the river to the stone bridge, which is about eight or nine hundred yards from the iron bridge; passing unnoticed through a number of Sepoys and matchlockmen, some of whom were escorting persons of rank in *palankeens* (litters) preceded by torches.

Recrossing the Goompty by the stone bridge, we went by a sentry unobserved, who was closely questioning a dirtily dressed native, and into the *Chouk*, or principal street of the city of Lucknow, which was not illuminated so much as it used to be previous to the siege; nor was it so crowded. I jostled against several armed men in the street without being spoken to; and only met one guard of seven Sepoys, who were amusing themselves with some women of pleasure.

When issuing from the city into the country, we were challenged by a *chokeydar* or watchman, who, without stopping us, merely asked who we were. The part of the city traversed by me that night seemed to have been deserted by at least a third of its inhabitants.

I was in great spirits when we reached the green fields, into which I had not been for five months. Everything around me smelt sweet, and a carrot I took from the roadside was the most delicious I had ever tasted. I gave vent to my feelings in a conversation with Kunoujee Lall, who joined me in my admiration of the province of Oudh, and lamented that it was now in the hands of wretches whose misgovernment and rapacity was ruining it. A further walk of a few miles was accomplished in high spirits. But there was trouble before us. We had taken the wrong road, and were now quite out of our way—in the Dilkoosha Park, which was occupied by the enemy. I went within twenty yards of two guns, to see what strength they were, and returned to the guide, who was in great alarm and begged I would not distrust him because of the mistake, as it was caused by his anxiety to take me away from the picquet of the enemy. I bade him not to be frightened of me, for I was not annoyed, as such accidents were not unfrequent, even when there was no danger to be avoided. It was now about midnight. We endeavoured to persuade a cultivator who was watching his crop to show us the way for a short distance, but he urged old age and lameness; and another, whom I peremptorily told to come with us, ran off screaming, and alarmed the whole village. We walked quickly away into the canal running under the Char Bagh, in which I fell several times, owing to my shoes being wet and slippery and my feet sore. The shoes were hard and tight, and had rubbed the skin off my toes, and cut the flesh above the heels.

In two hours more we were again in the right direction, two women in a village we passed having kindly helped us to find it. About 1 o'clock we reached an advanced picquet of Sepoys, who told us the way, after asking where we had come from, and whither we were going. I thought it safest to go up to the picquet than to try and pass them unobserved. Kunoujee Lall now begged I would not press him to take me into Alum Bagh, as he did not know the way in, and the enemy were strongly posted around the place. I was tired, and in pain from the shoes, and would therefore have preferred going into Alum Bagh,

The Indian Mutiny

but as the guide feared attempting it, I desired him to go on to the camp of the Commander-in-Chief, which he said was near Bunnee (a village eighteen miles from Lucknow) upon the Cawnpore road. The moon had risen by this time, and we could see well ahead.

By 3 o'clock we arrived at a grove of mango trees, situated on a plain, in which a man was singing at the top of his voice; I thought he was a villager, but he got alarmed on hearing us approach, and astonished us too by calling out a guard of twenty-five Sepoys, all of whom asked questions. Kunoujee Lall here lost heart for the first time, and threw away the letter entrusted to him for Sir Colin Campbell; I kept mine safe in my turban. We satisfied the guard that we were poor men travelling to Umroula, a village two miles this side of the Commander-in-Chief's camp, to inform a friend of the death of his brother by a shot from the British entrenchment at Lucknow, and they told us the road. They appeared to be greatly relieved on discovering that it was not their terrible foe who was only a few miles in advance of them. We went in the direction indicated by them, and after walking for half-an-hour we got into a *jheel* or swamp, which are numerous and large in Oudh. We had to wade through it for two hours, up to our waists in water, and through weeds; for before we found out that we were in a *jheel* we had gone too far to recede. I was nearly exhausted on getting out of the water, having made great exertions to force our way through the weeds, and to prevent the colour being washed off my face—it was nearly gone from my hands.

I now rested for fifteen minutes, despite the remonstrances of the guide, and went forward, passing between two picquets of the enemy, who had no sentries thrown out. It was near 4 o'clock in the morning when I stopped at the corner of a *tope*, or grove of trees, to sleep for an hour, which Kunoujee Lall entreated I would not do; but I thought he over-rated the danger, and, lying down, I told him to see if there was any one in the grove who would tell him where we then were.

He had not gone far when I heard the English challenge, "Who goes there?" with a native accent: we had reached a British cavalry outpost! My eyes filled with joyful tears; I shook the Sikh officer in charge of the picquet by the hand; the old soldier was as pleased as myself when he heard from whence I had come, and he was good enough to send two of his men to conduct me to the camp of the advance guard.

An officer of H.M.'s 9th Lancers, who was visiting his picquets, met me on the way, and took me to his tent, where I got dry stockings and trousers, and —what I much needed—a glass of brandy, a liquor I had not tasted for nearly two months.

History of the Victoria Cross

I thanked God for having safely conducted me through this dangerous enterprise; and Kunoujee Lall for the courage and intelligence with which he had conducted himself during this trying night. When we were questioned he let me speak as little as possible; he always had a ready answer, and I feel that I am indebted to him in a great measure more than to myself for my escape. It would give me great satisfaction to hear that he had been suitably rewarded.

In undertaking this enterprise, I was actuated by a sense of duty, believing that I could be of use to His Excellency the Commander-in-Chief when approaching for the relief of the besieged garrison, which had heroically resisted the attack of thirty times its own number for nearly five months within a weak and irregular entrenchment; and secondly, because I was anxious to perform some service which would ensure to me the honour of wearing our Most Gracious Majesty's Cross.

My reception by Sir Colin Campbell and his Staff was cordial and kind to the utmost degree, and if I never have more than the remembrance of their condescension and of the heartfelt congratulations of Sir James Outram and of all officers of his garrison on my safe return to them, I should not repine; though—to be sure—having the Victoria Cross would make me a prouder and happier man.

(Signed) HENRY KAVANAGH.

ALUM BAGH, *November* 24, 1857.

[TRUE COPY.—HOPE KAVANAGH, Dist. Supt. of Police, United Provinces and Oudh, 25/1/'04.]

Photo by ELLIOTT & FRY.

HUGH HENRY GOUGH

(LIEUTENANT, NOW GENERAL, G.C.B.)

1ST EUROPEAN LIGHT CAVALRY

WHEN in command of a party of Hodson's Horse on November 12, 1857, Lieutenant Gough displayed great bravery near the Alumbagh by charging across a swamp and attacking the defenders of two guns. Though the enemy were in greatly superior numbers he succeeded in capturing the two cannon, his turban being cut through by sword cuts while in combat with three Sepoys. On February 25, 1858, near Jellalabad, he set a very fine

The Indian Mutiny

example to his men when ordered to charge the enemy's guns. By his courageous leading they were taken, and during the attack he was engaged in several single combats until disabled by a bullet wound in the leg when in the act of charging two Sepoys with fixed bayonets. On that day two horses were killed under him, and he received a bullet through his helmet and one through his scabbard.

Son of Mr. George Gough, of Rathronan House, Clonmel, Ireland, Sir Hugh was born on November 14, 1833. Educated privately, he entered the Bengal Army in 1853. Has served through the Abyssinian War and Afghan War, having been often wounded and frequently mentioned in despatches. He is a brother of Sir Charles Gough, V.C., and uncle of Major J. E. Gough, V.C., who was decorated for bravery in Somaliland on April 22, 1903.

JOHN WATSON

(LIEUTENANT, NOW GENERAL, G.C.B.)

1ST PUNJAB CAVALRY

On November 14, 1857, Lieutenant Watson, with his own squadron, came across a body of the enemy's cavalry. The Ressaldar in command rode out at once to the front, and was singled out by him. As they approached one another the rebel fired at him at only a yard's distance, but without effect. (The bullet, it is believed, had previously fallen out. In those days the pistols were muzzle loaders.) A hand to hand struggle took place, and the Ressaldar, run through the body by Lieutenant Watson, was dismounted, but, nothing daunted, drew his tulwar, and, with the help of his men, returned to the attack. Our cavalry just then coming up, the enemy were routed, losing a number killed. Lieutenant Watson had received a blow on the head from a tulwar, another on the left arm, severing the chain gauntlet-glove, another on the right arm, dividing the sleeve of his jacket, and a blow on the leg, which lamed him for some days. He also received a bullet through his coat.

Sir John Watson was born in 1829, entering the Bombay Army 1848.

History of the Victoria Cross

Served in the Punjab, 1848-9; Bozdar, 1857; through the Mutiny as above; and the Afghan War, 1879-80. From 1881 to 1888 was Governor General's Agent at Baroda.

HASTINGS EDWARD HARRINGTON
(LIEUTENANT)
BENGAL ARTILLERY

For his conspicuous bravery at the relief of Lucknow from November 14 to 22, 1857, this officer was elected to receive the Victoria Cross under Rule 13 of the Warrant.

The late Colonel F. C. Maude, V.C., in his *Memoirs of the Mutiny*, gives the following details of the career of Hastings Harrington, V.C., as an illustration of the temper of the times (1857) —

He (Harrington) was at Oxford pursuing his studies. The Crimean War came. Studies seemed derogatory at such a crisis, and he volunteered for service; but the authorities would only allow him to go out in the transport. He went out and worked hard at Kertch and other places, coming home through Hungary, and landed at Dover with sixpence in his pocket. Bought rolls, drank water, slept under a haystack, and reached at last the old parsonage where he had been born. Then he returned to Oxford, and took a "second," which, considering all interruptions, was very fair. But the charms of adventure had been tasted, and the quiet academical career seemed impossible. He must go somewhere. "To India," said O'Shaughnessy, "in my telegraph service, the finest service in the world." (This expression was, in a measure, hyperbolical.) So in the telegraph he came, arriving at Agra in the cold weather, and, taking his sword off the roof of the dâk carriage, exclaimed, "My old Crimean sword—I shall not want *that* again." However, the summer found him in the Volunteer Cavalry—only too glad to have it still in his possession.

He died at Agra on July 20, 1861.

The Indian Mutiny

EDWARD JENNINGS
(ROUGH RIDER)
ROYAL (BENGAL) ARTILLERY

EDWARD JENNINGS was one of those engaged at the second relief of Lucknow, under Sir Colin Campbell, in November, 1857. During the struggle, day and night, from the capture of the Secundra Bagh on the 16th until the actual accomplishment of the heroic enterprise on the 22nd, Jennings' bravery in working the guns was noticed by all, and especially by the Commander-in-Chief himself, who, although wounded, had scarcely quitted the saddle the whole time. With him are associated Lieutenant H. E. Harrington, Gunners J. Park, T. Laughnan, and H. McInnes, all of whom, under Clause 13 of the Royal Warrant, were elected by their comrades, and in due course (Christmas Eve, 1858) were gazetted. Jennings survived his comrades by many years, working to the last as a corporation street labourer at Shields, and died a few years ago, aged 74.

T. LAUGHNAN
(GUNNER)
BENGAL ARTILLERY

ELECTED under Rule 13 of the Victoria Cross Warrant, for conspicuous bravery during the relief of Lucknow from November 14 to 22, 1857.

H. McINNES
(GUNNER)
BENGAL ARTILLERY

ELECTED under Rule 13 of the Victoria Cross Warrant, for conspicuous bravery during the relief of Lucknow from November 14 to 22, 1857.

History of the Victoria Cross

J. PARK
(GUNNER)

BENGAL ARTILLERY

ELECTED under Rule 13 of the Victoria Cross Warrant, for his conspicuous bravery during the relief of Lucknow from November 14 to 22, 1857.

Photo by MUDFORD, Tiverton.

FRANCIS DAVID MILLETT BROWN
(LIEUTENANT)

1ST EUROPEAN BENGAL FUSILIERS

AT Narnoul on November 16, 1857, this officer rushed to the assistance of a wounded soldier of his regiment and, although the enemy's cavalry were within fifty yards of him at the time, he carried him away to safety.

J. DUNLEY
(LANCE-CORPORAL)

93RD REGIMENT

AT the attack on the Secundra Bagh at Lucknow, November 16, 1857, Dunley was the first surviving man of his regiment who entered the trench. He was particularly noticeable in his conduct, gallantly supporting Captain Burroughs against heavy odds. Elected by the private soldiers of the 93rd Regiment under Rule 13 of the Warrant.

ALFRED KIRKE FFRENCH
(LIEUTENANT)

53RD REGIMENT

THE conduct of this officer was highly praised by the whole of the Grenadier company which he was commanding at the taking of the Secundra Bagh,

The Indian Mutiny

Lucknow, November 16, 1857, and he was elected to receive the Victoria Cross under Rule 13 of the Warrant. He was one of the first to enter the building

P. GRANT
(PRIVATE)
93RD REGIMENT

ELECTED under Rule 13 of the Victoria Cross Warrant, for his bravery at the storming of the Secundra Bagh, Lucknow, November 16, 1857. Lieut.-Colonel Ewart had most gallantly captured a colour from the mutineers, and, while striving to get it away through the masses of Sepoys, was furiously attacked by them. Grant kept close to his colonel, and defended him, and having seized one of the enemy's swords, killed five of them himself. The colour was eventually safely carried out.

JOHN CHRISTOPHER GUISE
(MAJOR, AFTERWARDS LIEUT.-GENERAL, C.B.)
90TH (PERTHSHIRE VOLUNTEERS L.I.) THE SCOTTISH RIFLES

MAJOR GUISE was awarded the Cross for conspicuous gallantry in action at Lucknow, on November 16 and 17, 1857. The act or acts of gallantry being of a general character, no details as to the specific instances are given in the official documents, beyond that he was chosen by the officers of the regiment as being the most worthy and distinguished among them all, some thirty-five or forty in number, including the present Field-Marshal Viscount Wolseley, then a young captain with the 90th.

General Guise died on February 5, 1895 (on the same day as Major-General Montresor Rogers, V.C., who had served with him before Sebastopol). He was the son of General Sir J. Guise, Bart., G.C.B., and was born on July 27, 1826. Ensign, June, 1845, and forty-five years afterwards became Colonel of the Leicestershire Regiment.

Photo by FRADELLE & YOUNG.

History of the Victoria Cross

NOWELL SALMON

(LIEUTENANT, NOW ADMIRAL OF THE FLEET, G.C.B.)

ROYAL NAVY

Photo by STEREOSCOPIC Co., *London.*

ON November 16, 1857, at the attack on the Shah Nujjiff at Lucknow, a very severe fire was poured upon the Naval Brigade by the rebels, who were posted behind the gateway. As no sufficiently effective reply could be given from the front, Captain Peel, V.C., called for volunteers to climb a tree overlooking the gate, and fire at the enemy. Lieutenant Salmon promptly answered, and, in company with Boatswain Harrison (V.C.), shot so well from the advantageous position that the enemy's defence was considerably weakened, and shortly afterwards the place was captured.

Admiral Salmon, son of the Rev. H. Salmon, Rector of Swarraton, Hants, was born on February 20, 1835. Educated at Marlborough. Served in the Baltic operations, 1854, and the Mutiny as stated above. Was A.D.C. to the Queen, 1875-9; Commander-in-Chief on the Cape and West African Station, 1881-5; held the same position in China, 1888-90; and at Portsmouth, 1894.

JOHN HARRISON

(BOATSWAIN'S MATE)

ROYAL NAVY

WHEN Sir Colin Campbell reached the city of Lucknow at the end of his famous march to the relief of the beleaguered Residency, the Shah Nujjiff was one of the most stubbornly defended posts held by the mutineers on November 16, 1857. A very heavy fire was poured upon us from a gate at the angle of the defences, and Captain Peel, V.C., called for volunteers to climb a large tree overlooking the inner fortifications and fire upon the enemy. Harrison and Lieutenant Nowell Salmon (V.C.) (now Admiral, G.C.B.) performed this dangerous service, and worked great havoc on those inside.

Harrison died on December 25, 1865.

The Indian Mutiny

THOMAS JAMES YOUNG
(LIEUTENANT, AFTERWARDS COMMANDER)
ROYAL NAVY

LIEUTENANT YOUNG was recommended for the Victoria Cross by Captain Peel, V.C., for his conspicuous courage while serving the naval guns at the attack on the Shah Nujjiff, at Lucknow, on November 16, 1857.

He died at Caen, France, on March 20, 1869.

WILLIAM HALL
(ABLE SEAMAN)
NAVAL BRIGADE, ROYAL NAVY

DURING Sir Colin Campbell's advance to the final relief of the Lucknow Residency on November 16, 1857, William Hall, "Captain of the Foretop" of H.M.S. *Shannon*, was with the guns of Peel's Naval Brigade, and was conspicuous for his fearless bravery at the attack on the Shah Nujjiff, one of the stoutest defences of the mutineers around Lucknow. Hall is one of the three men of colour who have been awarded the Victoria Cross. The other two are Samuel Hodge and W. J. Gordon.

S. HILL
(SERGEANT)
90TH REGIMENT

ON November 16 and 17, 1857, Hill's bravery was most conspicuous. At the storming of the Secundra Bagh he saved the life of Captain Irby, by warding off a blow, aimed at his head with a tulwar, by a Sepoy. He also went out under a heavy fire to the assistance of two wounded men. Throughout the entire operations for the relief of Lucknow this man's conduct was very noticeable, and he was elected under Rule 13 of the Victoria Cross Warrant.

C. IRWIN
(PRIVATE)

53RD REGIMENT

ELECTED by the private soldiers of his regiment for his conspicuous bravery at the taking of the Secundra Bagh, Lucknow, November 16, 1857, when, although severely wounded in the shoulder, he was one of the first of his regiment to enter the place under a terrific fire.

J. KENNY
(PRIVATE)

53RD REGIMENT

ELECTED by the private soldiers of his regiment for his gallant conduct and fearless bravery at the assault on the Secundra Bagh, Lucknow, on November 16, 1857, when, in spite of a most heavy cross-fire, he volunteered to bring up fresh ammunition to his company.

D. MACKAY
(PRIVATE)

93RD REGIMENT

AT the capture of the Secundra Bagh at Lucknow, November 16, 1857, Mackay displayed the greatest gallantry in capturing one of the standards of the enemy, after a most obstinate resistance on their part. Afterwards, at the capture of that strong defence, the Shah Nujjiff, he was severely wounded. His comrades elected him to receive the decoration of the Victoria Cross under Rule 13 of the Warrant.

The Indian Mutiny

JAMES MUNRO

(COLOUR-SERGEANT)

93RD REGIMENT (ARGYLL AND SUTHERLAND HIGHLANDERS)

DECORATED for his devoted gallantry on November 16, 1857, at the attack on the Secundra Bagh, Lucknow, during Sir Colin Campbell's advance to the relief of the Residency. Captain Walsh had fallen severely wounded and was in imminent danger of being killed by the Sepoys, when Munro rushed to his assistance, carried him to a place of safety, and saved his life. He himself was shortly afterwards brought in dangerously wounded.

His Victoria Cross is in the United Service Institute, in London.

JOHN PATON

(SERGEANT)

93RD REGIMENT (ARGYLL AND SUTHERLAND HIGHLANDERS)

At the Shah Nujjiff, November 16, 1857, Peel's naval guns had been firing point blank at the walls, endeavouring to force a breach for the eager Highlanders to rush in, but the strength of the masonry was such that it seemed a hopeless task. An attempt was about to be made to carry the place by assault, when Sergeant Paton hurried up with the report that he had found an opening. On his own initiative, and quite alone, he had crept round the stronghold to, if possible, discover a means of entry, and found that the shots from our heavy guns had at the commencement gone over the front and made a breach in the rear defences, through which he guided his regi-

Photo by CHARLEMONT, *Sydney.*

ment. The enemy were taken in rear, and a general stampede took place, leaving the Shah Nujjiff in our hands. Born on December 23, 1883, at Stirling, Paton enlisted in the 42nd Highlanders on March 20, 1848, but volunteered into the 93rd at the outbreak of the Crimean War. After the Mutiny, he left the Army in 1861, went to Sydney, joined the Prison Service, and eventually became Governor of Goulburn Gaol, retiring in 1896. See appendix 7.

J. SMITH
(PRIVATE)
1st Madras Fusiliers

This gallant soldier was elected to receive the Victoria Cross under Rule 13 of the Warrant by the soldiers of the detachment of his regiment. His bravery was most marked at the storming of the Secundra Bagh, November 16, 1857. When the gateway on the north side had been burst open, he was one of the first to enter, being instantly surrounded by a mass of the enemy, from whom he received a sword cut on the head, a bayonet wound in the left side, and a blow from the butt-end of a musket on the right shoulder. In spite of all those wounds he gallantly held out and for the rest of the day continued fighting most splendidly.

WILLIAM GEORGE DRUMMOND STEWART
(CAPTAIN, AFTERWARDS MAJOR SIR W. G. D. STEWART, BART.)
93rd Regiment

On November 16, 1857, this officer led a brilliant charge upon two of the enemy's guns which were brought to bear upon our troops, and inflicting severe damage. By the capture of these cannon the position of the mess-house was secured. Under Rule 13 of the Warrant this officer was decorated with the Victoria Cross.

P. GRAHAM
(PRIVATE)
90th Regiment

Elected by his comrades of the regiment under Rule 13 of the Warrant, for his conspicuous bravery at Lucknow, November 17, 1857, when he carried a wounded soldier under heavy fire to a place of safety.

The Indian Mutiny

CHARLES PYE

(SERGEANT-MAJOR, AFTERWARDS ENSIGN)

53RD REGIMENT

ELECTED by the non-commissioned officers of his regiment for steadiness and fearless conduct on every occasion when his regiment was in action, and particularly on November 17, 1857, at Lucknow, when he carried up ammunition to the mess-house under terrific fire.

THOMAS BERNARD HACKETT

(LIEUTENANT, AFTERWARDS LIEUT.-COLONEL)

23RD REGIMENT

AT the Secundra Bagh, Lucknow, on November 18, 1857, a young corporal of the 23rd was dangerously wounded, and lay in an exposed position under fire of the enemy. Lieutenant Hackett and George Monger (V.C.), seeing his danger, rushed out and, placing him between them, brought him under cover, and, promptly procuring medical aid, his life was saved. On the same date Lieutenant Hackett displayed conspicuous courage in getting on to the roof of a burning bungalow, from which he tore the thatch to prevent the fire spreading. While doing this he became the target for hundreds of Sepoys in the houses close by, who poured on him an incessant fire. It is sad to relate that he eventually met his death by the explosion of his own gun some years ago in Ireland.

History of the Victoria Cross

GEORGE MONGER

(PRIVATE)

23RD REGIMENT

AT the Secundra Bagh, Lucknow, on November 18, 1857, Monger displayed great bravery in accompanying Lieutenant Hackett (V.C.) to assist in carrying in a corporal of his regiment who, being wounded, was lying in a most exposed position.

HENRY NORTH DALRYMPLE PRENDERGAST

(LIEUTENANT, NOW GENERAL, G.C.B.)

ROYAL (MADRAS) ENGINEERS

ON November 21, 1857, at Mundisore, Lieutenant G. Dew, of the 14th Hussars, was in imminent danger of being shot by a Velaitee, who covered him from the rear with his musket. Lieutenant Prendergast rushed at him and cut him down, but not before being wounded himself by the discharge of the piece. His gallant action saved the life of Lieutenant Dew, but he was almost cut down in his turn, had not Major Orr killed the rebel. He also distinguished himself at the actions of Ratgurh and Betwa, being severely wounded.

Major-General Sir Hugh Rose, in forwarding his recommendation of this officer, states—

Photo by ELLIOTT & FRY.

The Indian Mutiny

" Lieutenant Prendergast was specially mentioned by Brigadier Stuart for the gallant act at Mundisore when he was severely wounded; secondly, he was specially mentioned by me when acting as my A.D.C. in the action before besieging Ratgurh on the Beena River for gallant conduct. His horse was killed on that occasion. Thirdly, at the action of the 'Betwa,' he again voluntarily acted as my A.D.C. and distinguished himself by his bravery in the charge which I made with Captain Need's troop, against the left of the Peishwa's army under Tantia Topee. He was severely wounded on that occasion."

Son of Thomas Prendergast, Madras Civil Service, Sir Henry Prendergast was born in India, October 15, 1834. Educated at Cheam School, Brighton College and Addiscombe, he entered the Army in 1854, serving in the Persian War, 1856–7; with the Malwa Field Force, 1857, and the Central India Field Force, 1858, in the two latter services being severely wounded and mentioned in despatches; through the Abyssinian War, 1868, and the Indian Expedition to the Mediterranean, 1878; Upper Burma, 1885–6, being thanked by Her Majesty Queen Victoria and the Government of India. Has held many distinguished positions in Travancore and Cochin, 1887; Mysore and Coorg, 1887 and 1891; Baroda, 1889; Baluchistan, 1889.

ARTHUR MAYO

(MIDSHIPMAN)

ROYAL (INDIAN) NAVY

ON November 22, 1857, the Indian Naval Brigade (abolished in 1863) was quartered at Dacca, in Bengal, and under the command of Lieutenant T. E. Lewis, R.N. The Sepoys at that station having mutinied, orders were received to disarm them, and three of their " Guards " showed no resistance. The fourth, however, drawn up on the Lall Bagh with two 6-pounder field guns, had loop-holed the hospital and their barracks, and on the Naval Brigade entering the enclosure and forming into line, the native officer gave the order to fire, which was promptly responded to by his troops. The sailors replied with a volley, and charged the barracks on the hill, breaking down the doors, their howitzers firing at the enemy's two guns, one of which commenced to blaze away at those of our men who had worked their way along the higher ground. When at the further end of the hill, the officer in command gave the order, "Take those guns," whereupon Mr. Mayo, collecting a few men, called on them to follow him, and with a cheer they rushed down the hill. The Sepoys working the gun for which Mayo's party were making, now depressed the muzzle, and when the sailors were within a few yards of it one of them was in the act of applying a port-fire, when he was fortunately shot. A second Sepoy sprang forward to finish the work, but Mr. Mayo and his men were on him, and, before he could reach the powder, was cut down, and all his rebellious crew round the gun promptly slain, the two guns being turned upon the now retreating rebels. During the charge Mr. Mayo was fully twenty yards ahead of his party. On another occasion, during an expedition into the Abor Hills, on February 27, 1859, seven well-defended stockades were taken by the Naval Brigade. One of these was across a nullah over which was a wooden bridge. The bugle from headquarters sounded "Cease firing," but arrows were raining round Mr. Mayo's party, and he asked the C.O. not to hear it, urging that the party should push on. Though warned that the bridge across the nullah was probably cut, he led his men across it, and, reaching the opposite side in safety, dashed for the stockade and got over it. The last was stubbornly defended by natives with arrows, spears and stones, and during the attack upon it he was struck in the hand by a poisoned arrow. Stopping to suck the wound, the men thought he was badly injured, and hesitated to go on, but he dashed forward again, calling out that he was not hurt, and the place was taken. The fighting lasted for five hours, and Mr. Mayo was mentioned in despatches for his gallantry throughout the entire time.

Born in 1840, Mr. Mayo was just 17 years old when he won the Victoria Cross—one of the youngest of its recipients. He was invalided home in 1860, matriculated at Oxford in 1862, took his B.A. degree 1865, and was ordained Deacon of the Exeter Diocese in 1866. He served as Assistant-Curate at St. Peter's, Plymouth, for one year and eight months, and was received into the Catholic Church November 5, 1867, at Farm Street.

The Indian Mutiny

THOMAS FLINN
(DRUMMER)
64TH REGIMENT

AT Lucknow, on November 28, 1857, Flinn displayed the utmost bravery in charging on the enemy's guns, and, though severely wounded, he engaged in a hand-to-hand encounter with two rebel artillerymen.

FREDERICK SLEIGH ROBERTS
(LIEUTENANT, NOW FIELD-MARSHAL EARL ROBERTS OF KANDAHAR, PRETORIA AND WATERFORD, P.C., K.G., K.P., G.C.B., O.M., G.C.S.I., G.C.I.E., D.C.L., LL.D.)
COMMANDER-IN-CHIEF
BENGAL ARTILLERY

THE Victoria Cross was awarded to this officer, now the best known soldier throughout the British Empire, for two special acts of bravery and devotion during the Indian Mutiny, and for conspicuous gallantry throughout the entire operations of that troublous time. He received the decoration from the hands of H.M. the Queen at Buckingham Palace on June 8, 1859. At Khodagunge on January 2, 1858, while following up the retreating enemy, he saw two Sepoys escaping with a standard. Riding straight for them, he overtook them as they were entering a village. Both men turned and faced him, but Roberts dashed at them, and, while wrenching the standard from the hands of one of them, whom he cut down, the other levelled his musket point-blank at him and pulled the trigger, but fortunately it missed fire, and Roberts rode off with the standard. On the same day he went to the rescue of a Sowar, who was being attacked by a rebel armed with a bayonet. Riding up to them, he engaged the Sepoy, parried a blow aimed at him, and cut his assailant a terrific blow across the face with his sword, killing him instantly.

Earl Roberts, son of General Sir Abraham Roberts, was born at Cawnpore, India, on September 30, 1832. Educated at Eton, Sandhurst and Addiscombe,

History of the Victoria Cross

Photo by ELLIOTT & FRY.

he obtained his 2nd Lieutenancy in the Bengal Artillery in 1851, becoming 1st Lieutenant 1857; Captain, 1860; Brevet-Major, 1860; Brevet Lieut. - Colonel, 1868; Brevet-Colonel, 1875; Major-General, 1878; Lieut.-General, 1883; General, 1890; Field-Marshal, 1895. His war records number more battles than any other soldier, and his services to his country are too numerous to mention in these pages. He served through the Indian Mutiny, and took part in the siege and capture of Delhi, and the actions of Boolundshuhur, Aligarh, Agra, Kanauj, Bantharra, relief of Lucknow, Cawnpore, Khodagunge, Futtehghur, storming of Mianganj, siege of Lucknow, storming of Laloo; capture of Umbeyla; destruction of Malka. Served in Abyssinian Expedition, 1867–8; Lushai Expedition, 1871–2; capture of Kholel villages and attack on Murtland Range. In command of the Kuram Valley Field Force, at capture of Peiwar Kotal; attack in Sapari Pass; occupation of Khost, and reconnaissance up Kuram River. Commander Kabul Field Force at battle of Charasiah, capture of Kabul, and operations near Sherpur in December, 1879. Commanded the Field Force which marched to the relief of Kandahar, and fought the battle of that name. In command of the army in Burma, 1886. In December, 1899, went out to South Africa as Commander-in-Chief; relieved Kimberley, and on the nineteenth anniversary of "Majuba" took Cronje and the Boer army in the west prisoners.

Has been twice thanked by both Houses of Parliament, August 4, 1879, and May 5, 1881, and on several occasions by the Indian Government.; D.A.Q.M.G. during Indian Mutiny; A.Q.M.G. (Bengal), 1863–8; 1st A.Q.M.G., 1869–72; D.Q.M.G., 1872–5; Q.M.G. in India, 1875–8. Commander-in-Chief, Madras, 1881–5; India, 1885–93; of the Forces in Ireland, 1895. Up to the year 1879 had been twenty-three times mentioned in despatches, and possesses the following medals: Indian Mutiny clasps for Delhi, Relief of Lucknow, Siege of Luck-

The Indian Mutiny

now. Indian Frontier medal with clasps for Umbeyla, Lushai and Burma; Abyssinia; Afghan War, with clasps for Peiwar Kotal, Charasia, Kabul, and Kandahar; Kabul-Kandahar bronze star; Queen's South African with six clasps. Received the following honorary degrees: D.C.L., Oxford, 1881; LL.D., Dublin, 1880; LL.D., Cambridge, 1893; LL.D., Edinburgh, 1893. Has received the freedom of the following cities: London, Edinburgh, Glasgow, Bristol, Newcastle-on-Tyne, Dundee, Waterford, Cardiff, Chesterfield, Inverness, Wick and Dunbar.

Lieutenant Hon. F. H. S. Roberts, son of the Commander-in-Chief, was recommended for, and would have received, the Victoria Cross for his heroic attempts to save the guns at Colenso in 1899 had he survived the wounds received on that occasion.

Earl Roberts retired in February, 1904, and the following appeared in the *Times* of February 19—

"The following Special Army Order, expressing the King's thanks to Lord Roberts on his retirement, was issued last night by the Army Council, and as it is the first Army Order published under the new organization, is reproduced by us in the exact form in which it was issued—

"ARMY ORDER.

"Special

"WAR OFFICE,
"*February* 18, 1904.

"The following is promulgated to the Army by direction of the Army Council—

"RETIREMENT OF FIELD-MARSHAL EARL ROBERTS, K.G., V.C.

"His Majesty the King has been graciously pleased to direct the issue of the following Order to the Army—

"BUCKINGHAM PALACE,
"*February* 18, 1904.

"I desire on behalf of My Army to express My deep regret at taking leave of Field-Marshal Earl Roberts, K.G., V.C., who retires from active employment

History of the Victoria Cross

on relinquishing the high office of Commander-in-Chief, which will not again be filled.

"For over fifty years, the Field-Marshal has served Queen Victoria, My beloved and lamented Mother, and Myself, in India, in Africa, and at Home with the highest distinction. During that long period he has performed every duty entrusted to him with unswerving zeal and unfailing success.

"I am unable to part with My Commander-in-Chief, without returning publicly to him My thanks, and those of My Army which he has commanded, for the invaluable services he has rendered to My Empire, and I ask all ranks of My Army to profit by the example of his illustrious career, and of his single-minded devotion to his Sovereign and to his country.

"EDWARD R. et I.

"By order of the Army Council,
"E. W. D. WARD."

BERNARD MCQUIRT

(PRIVATE)

95TH REGIMENT

DECORATED for great gallantry at the capture of Rowa, an entrenched town, on January 6, 1858. He engaged in a hand-to-hand fight with three men, killing one, and wounding two others. He received five severe sabre-cuts, and a bullet-wound during this action.

D. SPENCE

(TROOP SERGEANT-MAJOR)

9TH LANCERS

DECORATED for conspicuous bravery at Shumsabad, on January 17, 1858, when he rescued Private Kidd from the centre of a band of rebels. Kidd's horse had fallen and he was badly wounded, and to reach him Spence had to cut his way through several of the enemy.

The Indian Mutiny

JOHN ADAM TYTLER
(LIEUTENANT, AFTERWARDS COLONEL, C.B.)
66TH (GHOORKA) BENGAL NATIVE INFANTRY

DECORATED for his conspicuous courage on February 10, 1858, on the occasion of the action at Choorpoorah. The attacking parties were approaching the enemy's position under a heavy fire of round-shot, grape and musketry, when Lieutenant Tytler dashed, ahead of his men, straight for the guns and engaged the rebels in a hand-to-hand fight until support came up.

He was shot through the left arm, received a spear-wound in the chest, and a bullet through the right sleeve of his coat.

Colonel Tytler became Ensign in the East India Company's service on Dec. 10, 1844; Captain, April, 1859; Major, 1864; and Colonel, 1870. Served against the tribesmen round Peshawur, 1851–3. In 1863 commanded a Ghoorka battalion in the Black Mountain Expedition.

JOHN JAMES McLEOD INNES
(LIEUTENANT, NOW LIEUT.-GENERAL, RETIRED)
ROYAL (BENGAL) ENGINEERS

Photo by ELLIOTT & FRY.

SULTANPORE was held in force by the rebels, and was attacked on February 23, 1858. A line of skirmishers covered the advance. In the far distance the guns of the enemy could be seen. They were being closely pressed by our skirmishers, and, abandoning a gun, they were retiring, only to take up a fresh position. Here they had loaded a heavy piece, the fire from which would have ploughed through the column, had not Lieutenant Innes dashed ahead alone and shot the gunner before he could fire, remaining, undaunted, the mark for hundreds of matchlock and riflemen sheltered in huts close by, and beating back the gunners until aid reached him. By his courageous act the guns were captured, the rebels routed, and many lives were saved.

FREDERICK ROBERTSON AIKMAN
(LIEUTENANT, AFTERWARDS LIEUT.-COLONEL)
4TH BENGAL NATIVE INFANTRY

Photo by ELLIOTT & FRY.

AT daybreak on March 1, 1858, near Lucknow, Lieutenant Aikman obtained information that 500 rebel cavalry, 200 horse and two guns under Moosahib Ali Chuckbdar, were three miles off the high road. With only 100 of his men he attacked them without hesitation, utterly routed them, killed 100 of them, captured the guns, and drove the survivors into and over the river Goomtee. This splendid feat was accomplished under the great disadvantage of broken ground, and under the heavy flanking fire of an adjacent fort. During the encounter Lieutenant Aikman received a severe sabre-cut across the face.

Colonel Aikman was Commandant for many years of the Royal East Middlesex Militia, and had been a member of the Honourable Corps of Gentlemen-at-Arms from May 13, 1865. On October 6, 1888, he dropped dead while attending a ball in Scotland.

The Indian Mutiny

WILLIAM GOAT
(CORPORAL)
9TH (QUEEN'S ROYAL) LANCERS

THIS brave young soldier took part in the siege and capture of Lucknow in 1858. On March 6, while in action with the enemy's cavalry, he coolly dismounted, took up Major Smyth, 2nd Dragoon Guards, who was thought to be only severely wounded, and attempted to remove him off the field. This, at first, he was unable to accomplish, being surrounded by the enemy's horse. Nothing daunted, he made a second attempt, this time under a heavy fire, and, succeeding in his endeavours—in defiance of the rabble around him—removed the officer's body out of reach of those waiting to mutilate it.

William Goat's Cross with Mutiny medal was sold in London, in May, 1902, for £85.

THOMAS ADAIR BUTLER
(LIEUTENANT, AFTERWARDS COLONEL)
1ST BENGAL FUSILIERS (LATE 101ST)

ON March 9, 1858, during the capture of Lucknow, the heavy guns were being placed in position when Major Lothair Nicholson, Outram's Commanding Engineer, thought that he saw the enemy's first line being abandoned, but could not be quite sure. It was most necessary to ascertain for certain whether this was the case, as the infantry of Hope's brigade, which had attacked and driven the rebels out of the Martinière, could be seen preparing to assault the works at the other side of the river. Lieutenant Butler volunteered to swim across the Goomtee river,

History of the Victoria Cross

and, if he found the enemy had retired, communicate the fact to Hope's men.[1]

This feat was successfully accomplished by the brave young officer, who, swimming across, mounted a parapet, and, until the completion of his dangerous task, was exposed to a heavy fire from the enemy's guns.

Fitchett relates [2] an extraordinary incident which happened to Lieutenant Butler at the storming of Delhi on September 14, 1857, at the Burn Bastion. While some of our men were fighting up a narrow lane where the fire of the enemy, concentrated on so narrow a space, was perfectly murderous, we were compelled to retire for awhile, but some refused to do so and actually reached the screen through which the Sepoys were firing their guns. One of these was Lieutenant Butler, of the 1st Bengal Fusiliers. As he came at the run through the white smoke he struck the screen heavily with his body; at that moment two Sepoys on the inner side thrust through the screen with their bayonets. The shining deadly points of steel passed on either side of Butler's body and he was pinned between them as between the prongs of a fork! Butler, twisting his head, saw through a loophole the faces of the two Sepoys, who held the bayonets and who were still vehemently pushing, under the belief that they held their enemy impaled. With his revolver he coolly shot them both, and then fell back, pelted with bullets, but somehow unhurt, to his comrades who were re-forming for a second charge at the head of the lane.

Colonel Thomas Adair Butler, born in 1836, was the son of the Rev. Stephen Butler. Educated privately, joining the Army in 1854. Served through the Great Mutiny from June 10, 1857; in all the engagements under the walls of Delhi; galloper to Brigadier-General Nicholson at the action of Nujjufguhr and took part in the storming of the Mogul capital, being wounded in that action; took part in the actions of Gungeree, Puttialee, and Mynpoorie, and was present at the storming of Lucknow, where he gained the Victoria Cross as described; served in the North-West Frontier Campaign, 1863; present at the attack on the Crag Picket, Conical Hill and Umbeyla. He died at Lyndale, Camberley, in November, 1901.

[1] Earl Roberts' *Forty-one Years in India*.
[2] *Tale of the Great Mutiny*.

The Indian Mutiny

FRANCIS EDWARD HENRY FARQUHARSON

(LIEUTENANT)

42ND REGIMENT

DECORATED for conspicuous bravery before Lucknow, on March 9, 1858, when he led a party of men and stormed a bastion, mounting two guns, which he succeeded in spiking. By his gallant action the advanced position taken and held by our men during the night was made secure from the fire of artillery.

Lieutenant Farquharson was severely wounded on the following day while holding an advanced position.

WILLIAM McBEAN

(LIEUTENANT AND ADJUTANT, AFTERWARDS MAJOR-GENERAL)

93RD (ARGYLL AND SUTHERLAND) HIGHLANDERS

DECORATED for his extraordinary bravery on March 11, 1858, when, quite alone, he attacked and killed eleven of the enemy in the main breach of the Begum Bagh, Lucknow.

Forbes-Mitchell, in his *Reminiscences of the Great Mutiny*, relates how Lieutenant McBean, with Sergeant Hutchinson and Drummer Ross, a boy of about twelve years of age, climbed to the top of the dome of the Shah Nujjiff by means of a rude rope-ladder which was fixed on it. This was during the relief of Lucknow by Sir Colin Campbell's force, and the reason for this daring adventure (for the enemy on the Badshahibagh saw them and turned their guns on them) was in order to signal to the garrison of the Residency to let them know the position of the relieving force.

Photo by MAULL & FOX, *London.*

History of the Victoria Cross

Describing the assault on the Begum's Kothee, the same author relates the act for which William McBean was awarded the Victoria Cross. After the assault the men were broken up into small parties in a series of separate fights all over the different detached buildings of the palace. "Willie" McBean, as he was known to the officers, but "Paddy" McBean to the men, encountered a *havildar*, a *naik*, and nine Sepoys at one gate, and killed the whole eleven one after the other. The havildar was the last; and, by the time he got out through the narrow gate, several men came to the assistance of McBean, but he called to them not to interfere, and the havildar and he went at it with their swords. At length McBean made a feint cut, but instead gave the point, and put his sword through the chest of his opponent.

McBean was an Inverness-shire ploughman before he enlisted, and rose from the ranks to command the regiment and died a major-general. It is said of him that when he first joined the regiment he walked with a rolling gait and the drill-corporal was rather abusive with him when learning his drill. At last he became so offensive that another recruit proposed to McBean, who was a very powerful man, that they should call the corporal behind the canteen in the barrack yard and give him a good thrashing, to which proposal McBean replied: "Toots, toots, man, that would never do. I am going to command this regiment before I leave it and it would be an ill beginning to be brought before the colonel for thrashing the drill-corporal." McBean kept to his purpose and *did* live to command the regiment, going through every rank from private to major-general.

HENRY WILMOT

(CAPTAIN, AFTERWARDS COLONEL, K.C.B.)

2ND BATT. RIFLE BRIGADE

Photo by ELLIOTT & FRY.

ON March 11, 1858, Captain Wilmot, when his company was engaged with a large force of the enemy near the Iron Bridge, Lucknow, found himself with only four men at the end of a street, and a very large body of the enemy opposed to him. One of the men fell, shot through both legs. Corporal Nash and Private D. Hawkes (although the latter was wounded) took him up and carried him away a very long distance, under a severe fire from the enemy, while Captain Wilmot covered their retreat, using the men's rifles in turn.

The Indian Mutiny

Sir Henry Wilmot, born February 3, 1831, was the son of the late Sir Henry Sacheverel Wilmot. Educated at Rugby, he joined the 43rd Light Infantry in 1849. In 1851, on obtaining his company, he was transferred to the Rifle Brigade, the 2nd Battalion of which he joined in the Crimean War, January, 1856. In July, 1857, he sailed for India, and after the siege of Lucknow, where he so greatly distinguished himself, he served on the staff of Sir Hope Grant as Deputy-Judge-Advocate-General in Oude. In 1860, as Judge-Advocate-General of the expeditionary force, he took part in the campaign in China, which terminated his active services.

He died at his residence, Chaltenden, on April 7, 1901.

DAVID HAWKES
(PRIVATE)
2ND BATT. RIFLE BRIGADE

ASSOCIATED with the late Sir H. Wilmot (V.C.), in a very brave act at the Iron Bridge, Lucknow, on March 11, 1858. (See account of Wilmot.)

Hawkes died in 1859, shortly after being gazetted.

Photo by BURNHAM, *Brixton.*

W. NASH
(CORPORAL)
2ND BATT. RIFLE BRIGADE

ASSOCIATED with Sir Henry Wilmot (V.C.), in a most courageous and humane action near the Iron Bridge at Lucknow, March 11, 1858. (See account of that officer.)

History of the Victoria Cross

EDWARD ROBINSON
(SEAMAN)
ROYAL NAVY

ON March 13, 1858, at the siege of Lucknow, the battery served by the Naval Brigade ignited, owing to the sandbags catching fire. Edward Robinson dashed up and, under a terrific fire from the enemy, who were only fifty yards distant, succeeded in extinguishing the flames, being dangerously wounded during this heroic act.

He died at Windsor on October 2, 1896.

RICHARD HARTE KEATINGE
(MAJOR, AFTERWARDS GENERAL, C.S.I.)
ROYAL (BOMBAY) ARTILLERY

MAJOR KEATINGE rendered most efficient aid at the assault and capture of the stronghold of Chandairee on March 17, 1858. Placing himself at the head of the column, he led it through the breach, which was protected by a heavy cross-fire, and was first to enter, where he fell severely wounded. He had been, the night before, with his servant to examine a small path leading across the ditch, and his knowledge of this saved the column from dreadful loss. Having cleared the breach, he struggled up and led his men into the fort, where he was again struck down by another bullet.

The Commander-in-Chief (Sir Colin Campbell) states "that the success at Chandairee was mainly owing to this

Photo by ELLIOTT & FRY, *London.*

officer, whose gallantry, really brilliant, he considers was equalled by his ability and devotion." Major Keatinge was at the time Political Officer with a Brigade of the Central India Field Force.

The Indian Mutiny

General Keatinge, son of the late Right Honourable Richard Keatinge, was born at Dublin on June 17, 1825. After the Mutiny he served in the Sathpoora Hills in 1858 and again in 1859, and with Parke's Brigade in pursuit of Tantia Topee in 1858. Commanded Field Detachments against the Wagheers in 1865. Died at Horsham, May 25, 1904.

WILLIAM GEORGE HAWTREY BANKES
(CORNET)
7TH HUSSARS

ON March 19, 1858, near the Moosa Bagh, Lucknow, this young officer twice charged a body of infuriated fanatics who had rushed on the guns employed in shelling a small mud-fort. He received terrible wounds on that occasion, and died eighteen days later, April 6, 1858. It is stated that his conduct in the action referred to excited the admiration of all, whilst universal sympathy was extended to him for the terrible sufferings he had to undergo, borne with great fortitude by him until his death, both his arms and legs being mutilated. The Victoria Cross was provisionally conferred upon him before his death by the Commander-in-Chief in India, and a notice appeared in the *Gazette* of December 24, 1858, stating that Her Majesty Queen Victoria would have confirmed the award had he survived.

Born on September 11, 1836, William Bankes was the son of the Right Honourable George Bankes, M.P., of Kingston Lacy and Corfe Castle. Educated at Westminster School, he joined the Army in April, 1857. He served in the Indian Mutiny under Sir Colin Campbell in Oude, including the repulse of the enemy at the Alumbagh, February 25; the siege of Lucknow from March 2 to 16; and the advance on the Moosa Bagh, where he met his death.

R. NEWELL
(PRIVATE)
9TH LANCERS

DECORATED for his bravery at Lucknow on March 19, 1858, when, under a heavy fire of musketry, he went to the assistance of a comrade whose horse had fallen on bad ground, and brought him away to safety.

History of the Victoria Cross

Photo by SCOTT & SMITH, Great Marlow.

DAVID RUSHE
(TROOP SERGEANT-MAJOR)
9TH LANCERS

ON March 19, 1858, this non-commissioned officer displayed conspicuous bravery near Lucknow in having, with one other soldier, attacked eight mutineers posted in a nullah, and killed three of them.

AYLMER SPICER CAMERON
(LIEUTENANT, NOW COLONEL, C.B.)
72ND REGIMENT (1ST SEAFORTH HIGHLANDERS)

IN March, 1858, the 72nd were marching and fighting day and night in the jungle—between Neemuch and Gwalior. On the 30th an armed band, which was strongly posted in a loop-holed building in Kotah, was attacked. Lieutenant Cameron headed a small party of his regiment and stormed the place, killing, single-handed, three of the defenders. He was severely wounded, losing half of one hand by a tulwar (native sword) cut.

Colonel Cameron, born August 12, 1833, son of Lieut.-Colonel W. G. Cameron, of the Grenadier Guards, served also in the Crimean War. Was A.A.G. 1877-81; commanded the King's Own Borderers, 1881-3; Chief of Intelligence Branch, 1883-5; and from 1886 to 1888 was Commandant of the Royal Military College, Sandhurst.

Photo by BIRD, Bath.

The Indian Mutiny

HUGH STEWART COCHRANE

(LIEUTENANT AND ADJUTANT, AFTERWARDS COLONEL)

86TH ROYAL COUNTY DOWN (NOW 2ND ROYAL IRISH RIFLES)

Photo by BOURNE & SHEPHERD, *India.*

AT Jhansi on April 1, 1858, a company (No. 1) of the 86th Regiment was ordered to charge and capture a gun. Being mounted, Lieutenant Cochrane dashed forward—greatly in advance of his men—exposed to the musketry fire of the rebel infantry in rear of the battery as well as that from the gun itself. Charging headlong on the gunners, who gave way almost to a man, he kept possession of the piece till support came up, afterwards charging the enemy's rear-guard, who shot three horses from under him, his attack upon them being so close and resolute.

He became Ensign in 1849; Captain in the 7th Fusiliers in 1858; and afterwards Lieut.-Colonel in the 43rd Light Infantry, which he commanded in India from February, 1878, until his retirement.

JAMES LEITH

(LIEUTENANT, AFTERWARDS MAJOR)

14TH (THE KING'S) HUSSARS

DURING the action on April 1, 1858, the troops engaged at Betwah, under Sir Hugh Rose (afterwards Lord Strathnairn), had a powerful force to contend with. The enemy surrounded them, killing and wounding a great many. Captain Need was later on attacked by a rabble of infantry mutineers, and on the point of being bayonetted, when Lieutenant Leith, seeing his danger, charged the Sepoys single-handed, and rescued him from certain death.

History of the Victoria Cross

FREDERICK WHIRLPOOL
(PRIVATE)
3RD BOMBAY EUROPEAN REGIMENT

DECORATED for his bravery at the attack of Jhansi on April 3, 1858, when he twice most gallantly volunteered to go out and bring in the wounded under a very heavy fire from the wall of the fort. He also displayed conspicuous courage at the assault of Lohari on May 2, 1858, in rushing to the rescue of Lieutenant Doune, of his regiment. His conduct during the day, and the example he showed the men, greatly contributed to the successful issue of the battle. When Whirlpool went to the rescue of Lieutenant Doune he received seventeen desperate wounds, one of which almost severed his head from his body. In spite of this he lived for many years, and only died in New South Wales on June 24, 1899.

HENRY EDWARD JEROME
(CAPTAIN, AFTERWARDS MAJOR-GENERAL)
86TH THE ROYAL COUNTY DOWN (NOW 2ND BATT. ROYAL IRISH RIFLES)

Photo by LEWIS, *Bath.*

ON April 3, 1858, at Jhansi, Captain Henry Edward Jerome, assisted by Private James Byrne (V.C.), of his regiment, brought out of action, under a very heavy fire, Lieutenant Sewell, who had fallen severely wounded at a very exposed part of the attack. Again on May 28, at the capture of the Fort of Chandairee, at the storming of Jhansi, and in action with a powerful force, his bravery was most conspicuous. In the last action he had part of his head torn away, his recovery being considered marvellous.

Major-General Jerome afterwards served through the Hazara Campaign, retiring in 1885. He was born on February 2, 1830, and died at Bath, February 25, 1901.

The Indian Mutiny

JOSEPH BRENNAN
(BOMBARDIER)
ROYAL ARTILLERY

DECORATED for great bravery at the assault of Jhansi on April 3, 1858. He brought up two guns of the Hyderabad Contingent, manned by natives, from a position open to a heavy fire from the enemy, and directed them so well that the Sepoys were forced to abandon their battery.

JAMES BYRNE
(PRIVATE)
86TH REGIMENT

ON April 3, 1858, at the storming of the Fort of Jhansi, Byrne carried Lieutenant Sewell, who had been badly wounded, to a place of safety, being assisted by Captain (afterwards Major-General) Jerome, V.C. This act was performed under a very heavy rifle fire. His Victoria Cross was sold in London, June, 1893, for £35.

History of the Victoria Cross

MICHAEL SLEAVON
(CORPORAL)
ROYAL ENGINEERS

DECORATED for conspicuous bravery on April 3, 1858, at the attack on the Fort of Jhansi, when, in the words of the *Gazette*, he " maintained his position at the head of a Sap, and continued the work under a heavy fire with a cool and steady determination worthy of the highest praise." Sleavon died some years ago. His Victoria Cross was sold in London, on January 22, 1903, for £53.

JAMES PEARSON
(PRIVATE)
86TH REGIMENT, AFTERWARDS OF THE 56TH

ON April 3, 1858, at the storming of Jhansi this soldier bravely attacked several armed rebels, killing one and bayonetting two, being himself severely wounded in the fight. He, also, at Calpee, under a severe fire, carried into safety Private Michael Burns, who was wounded, but who unfortunately died soon afterwards.

Photo by CHEVALIER, *Sandhurst, Victoria.*

WILLIAM NAPIER
(SERGEANT)
1ST BATT. 13TH REGIMENT (THE PRINCE CONSORT'S OWN SOMERSETSHIRE LIGHT INFANTRY)

ON April 6, 1858, when on baggage-guard near Azimghur, Private Benjamin Milner was severely wounded. Sergeant Napier at the risk of his life stood by him, and, though surrounded by Sepoys, bandaged his wound and then carried him to the convoy.

William Napier enlisted on December 10, 1846, and was discharged, at his own request, on the same date, 1862.

The Indian Mutiny

PATRICK CARLIN
(PRIVATE)
13TH REGIMENT

Photo by BLAIR, Belfast.

THE only other case where a Victoria Cross was awarded to a soldier by a Commander-in-Chief almost on the spot is that of Patrick Green (V.C.), and the General Order issued in the case of Carlin is identical with that of the former. The decoration was awarded to Carlin for rescuing a wounded *naik* of the 4th Madras Rifles, on April 6, 1858.

As Carlin proceeded to carry him off on his shoulders, a mutineer fired at them, upon which he took the *naik's* sword, after placing him on the ground, attacked and killed his assailant, and succeeded in conveying the wounded man to safety.

WILLIAM MARTIN CAFE
(CAPTAIN, NOW LIEUT.-GENERAL)
56TH BENGAL NATIVE INFANTRY

AT the fort of Ruhya on April 15, 1858, Lieutenant Willoughby, of the 14th Punjab Rifles, was shot down as he was capturing a position. Captain Cafe, under a heavy fire, went out and brought back his body, being assisted by four men of the 42nd—Lance-Corporal Thompson (V.C.), Private Cook (V.C.), E. Spence (V.C.), and Crowie. While doing so Spence was mortally wounded, and Captain Cafe immediately ran to his assistance, leaving the others to carry his comrade's body. Spence died of his wounds on the 17th. Crowie's name does not appear among those gazetted to the Cross, owing, most probably, to his early death.

General Cafe was born on March 23, 1826.

History of the Victoria Cross

JAMES DAVIS

(PRIVATE)

42ND REGIMENT (THE BLACK WATCH)

Photo by MASTERS, *Aldershot.*

On April 15, 1858, the Black Watch attacked the fort of Ruhya. Davis was one of the advanced party accompanying the officer of Engineers, who was reconnoitring the place in order to ascertain the position of the entrance. Here Lieutenant Bramley was shot dead. There being no dhoolies, bearers, or any mode of conveyance, Davis at once, though exposed to a heavy fire, offered to remove the body. Though close under the walls, in the heat of a midday sun, with no shelter whatever, he took up the body and carried it away for some miles through the jungle.

This brave man died in his native city, Edinburgh, in 1891. His Cross and medals, including clasps for Alma, Balaclava and Sebastopol, have passed into the hands of a private collector in London.

JOHN SIMPSON

(QUARTERMASTER-SERGEANT, AFTERWARDS QUARTERMASTER)

42ND REGIMENT (THE BLACK WATCH)

On April 15, 1858, during the attack on the Fort of Ruhya, Quartermaster-Sergeant John Simpson volunteered to go to an exposed point within forty yards of the Fort, and bring in, under a severe fire, first Lieutenant Douglas, and afterwards a private soldier, both of whom had been seriously wounded.

He died at Perth on October 20, 1883.

Photo by HENDERSON, *Perth.*

The Indian Mutiny

EDWARD SPENCE
(PRIVATE)
42ND REGIMENT (THE BLACK WATCH)

THIS soldier would have been recommended to Her Majesty for the Victoria Cross had he survived the wounds received at the attack on the Fort of Ruhya, on April 15, 1858. On that occasion he assisted Captain (afterwards General) Cafe (V.C.), in bringing in the body of Lieutenant Willoughby, and exposed himself fearlessly to a heavy fire to cover the retreat of the party bearing the body. He died two days afterwards.

Photo by BOURKE, *Perth*.

ALEXANDER THOMPSON
(LANCE-CORPORAL)
42ND REGIMENT (THE BLACK WATCH)

ON April 15, 1858, during the attack on the Fort of Ruhya, Lance-Corporal Thompson volunteered to assist Captain Cafe (V.C.) to bring in the body of Lieutenant Willoughby from the top of the *glacis*, under a most severe fire. (See Private E. Spence, V.C.)

He died some years ago at Perth.

SAMUEL MORLEY
(PRIVATE)
MILITARY TRAIN

ON April 15, 1858, on the evacuation of Azimghur by Koer Singh's army, a squadron of the military train and some Horse Artillery were sent in pursuit. On coming into action, with their rear-guard the former were ordered to charge. Lieutenant Hamilton, commanding the 3rd

History of the Victoria Cross

Cavalry, was unhorsed and at once set upon by the enemy, who commenced cutting and hacking at him on the ground. Morley, whose horse had also been shot, immediately dashed up on foot to his assistance and, in conjunction with Farrier Murphy (V.C.), cut down the Sepoys, defended him and fought hand-to-hand until assistance arrived, when they carried him into safety.

MICHAEL MURPHY
(FARRIER) PRIVATE
2ND BATT. MILITARY TRAIN

ON April 15, 1858, while pursuing the army of Koer Singh from Azimghur, Lieutenant Hamilton of the 3rd Sikh Cavalry was wounded, unhorsed and surrounded by the enemy. Murphy dashed to his assistance, cut down several of them and, although himself wounded, remained by his side till support came up.

WILLIAM GARDNER
(COLOUR-SERGEANT, AFTERWARDS QUARTERMASTER-SERGEANT)
42ND REGIMENT (THE BLACK WATCH)

THE battle of Bareilly took place on May 5, 1858, the Black Watch early in the day being hotly engaged. During the action Lieut.-Colonel Cameron, the commanding officer, was knocked off his horse and, while lying on the ground stunned, was at once set upon by three ghazees (fanatics). Colour-Sergeant Gardner rushed to his aid, and in a moment bayonetted two of them. He then attacked the third, who was, however, despatched by a man of the regiment. (Letter from Captain Macpherson to officer commanding the regiment.)

Died in November, 1897, being the last of the eight men of his regiment gazetted to the Victoria Cross during the Indian Mutiny.

The Indian Mutiny

V. BAMBRICK
(PRIVATE)
1ST BATT. 60TH REGIMENT

ON May 6, 1858, Bambrick was in a serai at Bareilly and displayed great courage when set upon by three ghazees, one of whom he cut down, being twice wounded on this occasion.

HARRY HAMMON LYSTER
(LIEUTENANT, NOW LIEUT.-GENERAL, C.B.)
72ND BENGAL NATIVE INFANTRY

Photo by ELLIOTT & FRY, *London.*

ON May 23, 1858, this officer charged singly at, and broke, a skirmishing square of the rebel army near Calpee, and killed two or three mutineers with his own hand. This gallant act was witnessed and reported upon by Major-General Sir Hugh Rose, G.C.B., and Lieut.-Colonel Gall, C.B., of the 14th Light Dragoons.

Lieut.-General Lyster, son of Mr. A. Lyster, was born on December 24, 1830. Served through the Indian Mutiny, 1857-8; Afghan Campaign, 1878-9; and during the Chartist Riots of 1847 served as a Special Constable in London.

He entered the Army in 1848; became Captain in 1861; Lieut.-Colonel, 1870; Colonel, 1877; Major-General, 1887; and attained his present rank in 1891, retiring in 1892.

SAMIE SHAW
(PRIVATE)
3RD BATT. RIFLE BRIGADE

IN a despatch, dated June 17, 1858, from Nowabgunge, Major-General Hope Grant, K.C.B., brought the conduct of this soldier to the notice of the D.A.G. of the Army, saying that he trusted his Excellency would allow him to recommend

History of the Victoria Cross

Shaw for the Victoria Cross, and would approve of his having issued a divisional order stating that he had done so. The act was as follows :—On June 13, 1858, an armed mutineer, a ghazee, was seen to enter a " tope " of trees, and some officers and men dashed after him. Shaw, armed only with a short sword, rushed in single-handed and killed him after a desperate struggle, in which he himself received a severe wound from the rebel's tulwar.

GEORGE RODGERS

(PRIVATE)

71ST REGIMENT

On June 16, 1858, at Marar, in Gwalior, Rodgers attacked seven rebels by himself, killing one of them. This exploit was stated to have been a most useful one, as the party of the enemy were well-armed, and had taken up a strong position in advance of a detachment of the 71st Regiment.

JAMES CHAMPION

(SERGEANT-MAJOR)

8TH HUSSARS

At the action and pursuit of Beejapore, in Central India, on September 5, 1858, Sergeant-Major Champion highly distinguished himself. Both his troop officers were wounded early in the day, and he himself soon afterwards was shot through the body. Left thus in command of his troop, and though badly wounded, he remained in the saddle the whole day throughout the pursuit, killing many of the enemy with his revolver. Before this, at the battle of Gwalior, on June 17, he had already greatly distinguished himself in the charge with his regiment.

The Indian Mutiny

CLEMENT WALKER-HENEAGE

(CAPTAIN, AFTERWARDS MAJOR)

8TH HUSSARS

CAPTAIN CLEMENT WALKER-HENEAGE was elected under Rule 13 of the Victoria Cross Warrant, for his bravery on June 17, 1858. A squadron of his regiment made a most gallant charge upon the enemy, who were advancing against the position held by Brigadier Smith. Under a heavy and converging fire from the fort and town, they cut through the rebel camp into two batteries, captured and brought back two of the enemy's guns.

Major Walker-Heneage, son of the late Mr. G. H. Walker-Heneage, of Compton Basset, was born in 1831. He served through the Crimean War, being present at Alma, Inkerman, Balaklava, and Tchernaya, the actions of Bulganac and McKenzie's Farm, siege and fall of Sebastopol, and the Kertch Expedition. Proceeding to India immediately afterwards, he served through the Indian Mutiny, being engaged in the suppression of the rebels in Rajputana and Central India. He was present at the capture of Kotah, re-occupation of Chundaree, battle of Kotah-Ke-Serai, capture of Gwalior and of Powree, battle of Sindwaho, action of Koorwye and Naharghur. In the action at Gwalior, where he gained the Victoria Cross, he was in command of a squadron of his regiment, and with him were associated Sergeant Joseph Ward, Farrier George Hollis, and Private John Pearson, all of whom were awarded the Decoration.

He entered the Army in August, 1851, as Cornet; became Captain in May, 1857; Brevet-Major in 1858; and Major in November, 1860. Retired in 1868.

He died at Compton Basset on December 9, 1901.

History of the Victoria Cross

GEORGE HOLLIS
(FARRIER)
8TH HUSSARS

ASSOCIATED with the late Major Clement Walker-Heneage (V.C.), in a gallant charge made on the enemy at Gwalior, June 17, 1858.

JOHN PEARSON
(PRIVATE)
8TH HUSSARS

ASSOCIATED with Major Clement Walker-Heneage (V.C.), at Gwalior, June 17, 1858.

JOSEPH WARD
(SERGEANT)
8TH HUSSARS

ASSOCIATED with Major Clement Walker-Heneage (V.C.), at Gwalior, June 17, 1858.

The Indian Mutiny

WILLIAM FRANCIS FREDERICK WALLER
(LIEUTENANT)

25TH BOMBAY LIGHT INFANTRY

DECORATED for his conspicuous daring at the capture of the Gwalior Fortress, June 20, 1858, when, in company with Lieutenant Rose, who was killed, he attacked it with only a handful of men. Climbing on the roof of a house, he shot the gunners opposing them, captured the Fort, and killed every mutineer in it. He and Lieutenant Rose were the only Europeans present. Born in 1840, he died on January 29, 1885.

SAMUEL JAMES BROWNE
(CAPTAIN, AFTERWARDS GENERAL, G.C.B., K.C.S.I.)

46TH BENGAL NATIVE INFANTRY

Photo by RUSSELL, *Baker Street, London.*

IN an engagement with the rebels, under Khan Ali Khan, at daybreak on August 31, 1858, at Seerporah, Captain Browne charged ahead with only a native orderly, at a 9-pounder gun, placed to command the approach to the enemy's well-chosen position, to prevent it being re-loaded and fired upon our men who were coming on with the bayonet. A fight between the officer and gunners ensued, in which, after cutting down several of them, he was slashed across the left knee, afterwards receiving another sword-stroke which severed the left arm at the shoulder. His chivalrous object was, however, fulfilled, the gun being captured by the infantry, and the gunners slain.

General Sir Samuel Browne, son of the late J. Browne, H.E.I.C.S., was born in India October 3, 1824. Served in

History of the Victoria Cross

Punjab campaign, 1848-9, being present at Chillianwallah and Goojerat; in operations against the Oomerzale Wuzerees, 1851-2; through the Bozdar Belooch Expedition in March, 1857; in many other tribal campaigns, including the attacks on Narinjee, in July and August, 1857; commanded the 1st Division Peshawur Field Force at the capture of Ali Musjid; the forcing of the Khyber Pass, November, 1878; and throughout the Afghan War, 1878-9, for which he received the thanks of the Government and both Houses of Parliament, and the K.C.B. For nineteen years (1850-69) was in command of the Punjab Cavalry and Corps of Guides on the Derejat and Peshawur Frontier. Inventor of the "Sam Browne" belt, known throughout the British Army.

He died at Ryde, March 14, 1901.

Not long after the death of this gallant officer, one of the makers and upholders of our Indian Empire, a tablet and monument was unveiled in St. Paul's Cathedral by one of his fellow officers—Earl Roberts of Kandahar; and four of his contemporaries, wearing the Victoria Cross, were present to do honour to his memory. No greater tribute could have been paid to the splendid soldier whose days were done, than to have a monument to his memory placed, as it was, close to the great Iron Duke of Wellington, and unveiled by the most illustrious, brave, and popular soldier of modern times. The memorial is of pure white marble, carved in low relief, with a figure of a Punjab Cavalryman holding a scroll on which are the words—

"To the Glory of God and in perpetual memory of General Sir Samuel Browne, V.C., G.C.B., K.C.S.I., a distinguished soldier of the Indian Army. This tablet is erected by friends who loved, and comrades who trusted him."

A replica of this memorial will be set up in the Cathedral of Lahore, India. Speaking on the above occasion, Earl Roberts said that there never was "a truer man, a firmer friend, a braver soldier, or one more worthy of a memorial in that venerable cathedral than Sir Samuel Browne."

The Indian Mutiny

PATRICK RODDY

(ENSIGN, AFTERWARDS COLONEL)

BENGAL ARMY

ON September 27, 1858, when the Kuppurthulla Contingent were returning from Kuthirga, a rebel, armed with a percussion-musket, knelt and levelled it at any who attempted to approach him. This did not deter Ensign Roddy, who rode boldly at him. When within six yards the rebel fired, killing the horse. While he was trying to get himself free, the rebel attempted to cut him down. However, Roddy seized and held him until able to get at his sword, when he ran him through the body.

Colonel Patrick Roddy rose from the ranks to the position he held at his death. He enlisted in the Bengal Artillery and received a commission as Ensign. During the Indian Mutiny he served under Sir James Outram at the "first" relief of Lucknow, the siege of the Bailly Guard, the defence of the Alumbagh, capture of Lucknow, and in almost every subsequent engagement until the rebels were suppressed on the Oude Frontier in 1860. He was frequently mentioned in despatches, and received the thanks of the Indian Government. His later services were in the Abyssinian War, 1873, and Afghan War, 1879.

He retired in 1887, after having been thirty-nine years in the Bengal Service, and died at Jersey on November 21, 1895.

History of the Victoria Cross

CHARLES GEORGE BAKER

(LIEUTENANT)

BENGAL POLICE BATTALION

Photo by ABDULLAH, *Constantinople.*

THE act of charging, with only sixty horsemen, and scattering a force of 1,000 infantry—fully armed and backed up by a troop of cavalry—as Lieutenant Baker did on September 27, 1858, at Suhejnee, near Peroo, may well be described, as it was by Lord Clyde, " the most gallant of any during the war." Not a shot was fired by Lieutenant Baker's Mounted Police in their charge upon the enemy, who were taken in the centre and flank by Lieutenant Broughton. A half-hearted stand was made, and a few scattered volleys fired, after which they broke and fled, pursued for miles through the jungle. The horses, however, being exhausted, many of the rebels escaped. Lieutenant Baker was for many years in command of the Egyptian Police, and held the rank of Pasha in that country.

GEORGE BELL CHICKEN

(LATE INDIAN) NAVAL BRIGADE

THIS gallant man was a volunteer with the Naval Brigade in the Mutiny, and was deservedly awarded the Victoria Cross for his bravery at Suhejnee, near Peroo, on September 27, 1858. Seeing that a number of rebels were about to rally and open fire on their scattered pursuers, he charged them by himself. Surrounded on all sides, he continued fighting desperately, and killed five rebels before being himself cut down, when he would most certainly have been killed but for the fortunate arrival of some of the Bengal Police and Sikh Cavalry, who dashed into the crowd to his rescue and routed it, killing many of the enemy.

The Indian Mutiny

Photo by WINTER, Waterford.

CHARLES ANDERSON
(PRIVATE, AFTERWARDS CORPORAL)

2ND DRAGOON GUARDS (QUEEN'S BAYS)

AT Sundeela, October 8, 1858, Private Anderson behaved with great gallantry when his party was attacked by Sepoys in the jungle, on which occasion he saved his colonel's life. Further details of his brave conduct are given in the record of Trumpeter Monaghan (V.C.). His Victoria Cross is now in the United Service Institute, London.

THOMAS MONAGHAN
(TRUMPETER)

2ND DRAGOON GUARDS (QUEEN'S BAYS)

ASSOCIATED with Corporal Charles Anderson in saving the life of Lieut.-Colonel Seymour, C.B. (in command of their regiment), on October 8, 1858. Soon after the action fought at Sundeela, in Oude, a sudden attack was made upon our men in a dense jungle of sugar-canes, from which an attempt had been made to dislodge a body of thirty or forty mutineers.

Our party was fired upon at a few yards range and then attacked by the enemy with drawn swords. Colonel Seymour shot one man, fired his pistol into the oncoming mass of Sepoys, and was then cut down by two blows from a sword.

Photo by COBB, Woolwich.

Monaghan, with Anderson, at once rushed to his help, the former shooting one of the enemy who was about to cut at him, and by the exertions of these two men, who made a terrific onslaught upon them, they were kept at bay until the colonel could rise, when every one of the enemy was killed.

Monaghan's Victoria Cross was sold in London on November 5, 1903, for £43.

History of the Victoria Cross

HANSON CHAMBERS TAYLOR JARRETT

(LIEUTENANT, AFTERWARDS COLONEL)

26TH BENGAL NATIVE INFANTRY

ON October 14, 1858, at the village of Baroun, near Lucknow, a party of Sepoys—seventy in number—had fortified themselves in a strong brick building, the only approach to which was through a very narrow street, commanded by the enemy's fire. Lieutenant Jarrett called on the men of his regiment to follow him, and four responded. With only these he made a dash for the entrance, and through a shower of bullets pushed his way up to the walls. Beating up the bayonets of the rebels with his sword, he endeavoured to force his way in, but unfortunately, his support being so feeble, he was not successful, and under a hail of lead was forced to rejoin the main body.

This brave officer died in India some years ago, whilst holding the post of Conservator of Forests.

HENRY EVELYN WOOD

(LIEUTENANT, NOW FIELD-MARSHAL, G.C.B., G.C.M.G., D.L.)

17TH LANCERS

Photo by ELLIOTT & FRY.

ON October 19, 1858, at Sindwaho, during the Indian Mutiny, Lieutenant Wood was in command of a troop of the 3rd Light Cavalry. He attacked, almost single-handed, a body of mutineers who were making a stand, and routed them completely.

A short time afterwards, near Sindhora, a Pâtel, named Chemmum Singh, had been seized by the enemy. Hearing that they intended to hang the wretched man for his loyalty to us, Lieutenant Wood took about twelve men, and started in pursuit.

The Indian Mutiny

After a ride of some miles they came upon the mutineers, about seventy in number, encamped and asleep. Taking two men, he crept up to them, fired a volley, dashed among them, and rescued the man.

General Sir Evelyn Wood, son of the Rev. Sir John Page Wood, Bart., was born at Braintree, Essex, February 9, 1838. Educated at Marlborough, he entered the Navy in 1852, and was A.D.C. to Captain Peel, V.C., in the Crimean War, when only sixteen, behaving with such gallantry that Captain Lushington recommended him for the Victoria Cross, which was, however, not awarded him. He was severely wounded at the attack on the Redan, mentioned in despatches, made Knight of the Legion of Honour, and obtained the medal and two clasps, Medjidie and Turkish medal. Invalided home, he left the Navy, and in 1855 joined the 13th Light Dragoons as Cornet, becoming later Lieutenant, and in 1857 exchanged into the 17th Lancers, serving with that fine body of men through the Indian Mutiny. He organized the native Forces in the Ashanti War, 1873; commanded a column in the Gaika War, 1878; also in the Zulu War, 1879; was in command of the Forces in Transvaal War, 1881; commanded a brigade in Egyptian War, 1882; and was head of the lines of communication in Nile Expedition, 1884; commanded the Chatham District, 1882–3; Eastern District, 1886–8; Aldershot Division, 1889–93; Q.G. to the Forces, 1893–7; A.G., 1897–1901.

CHARLES CRAUFURD FRASER

(MAJOR, AFTERWARDS LIEUT.-GENERAL, K.C.B.)

7TH (QUEEN'S OWN) HUSSARS

Photo by ELLIOTT & FRY.

SIR CHARLES FRASER (late Colonel, 8th King's Royal Irish Hussars) was awarded the Victoria Cross for an exceptionally gallant act of bravery and humanity on December 31, 1858. An officer (Captain Stisted) and some men of his regiment were drowning in the river Raptee, Oude, on the borders of Nepal, having plunged in, in pursuit of mutineers. Major Fraser, as he then was, at once jumped in to their rescue, under a terrible musketry fire from the opposite bank and succeeded in saving the officer and men, although at the time partially disabled by a wound received on June 13, at Nawabgunge, when charging with his squadron.

History of the Victoria Cross

Sir Charles Fraser, born August 31, 1829, served also in the Abyssinian War of 1868. Was A.D.C. to H.R.H. the Duke of Cambridge, 1873-7, and Inspector-General of Cavalry, 1880-4. Sat in Parliament as Conservative member for North Lambeth from 1885-92. For the act of bravery recorded above, he was also awarded the medal of the Royal Humane Society.

Sir Charles died in London on June 7, 1895, aged 66.

Photo by CLARKE, *Bury.*

HENRY ADDISON
(PRIVATE)
43RD THE MONMOUTHSHIRE LIGHT INFANTRY
(NOW 1ST OXFORD LIGHT INFANTRY)

AT Kurrereah on January 2, 1859, a political agent, Lieutenant Osborn, was attacked by a large force of mutineers, and Addison rushed to his aid. With the greatest difficulty they managed to keep the enemy at bay until support came up, and during the encounter Addison was twice terribly wounded, losing a leg.

He died at Bardwell some years ago.

WALTER COOK
(PRIVATE)
42ND REGIMENT

BRIGADIER-GENERAL WALPOLE reported that at the action at Maylah Ghaut, January 15, 1859, the conduct of Walter Cook and Duncan Millar deserved to be particularly pointed out. These two men, when their only officer was severely wounded and the colour-sergeant killed, took command and led on the men with conspicuous bravery. The fighting was most severe, and the few men of the 42nd were skirmishing so close to the enemy, who were in great numbers, that many of them were wounded by sword cuts. They displayed a courage, coolness and discipline (in the words of the report), which was the admiration of all who witnessed it. For another act of Walter Cook, see account of Captain Cafe, V.C.

The Indian Mutiny

DUNCAN MILLAR
(PRIVATE)
42ND REGIMENT

AT the action at Maylah Ghaut on January 15, 1859, Duncan Millar's conduct was so admirable that special report was made of it. A more detailed account is given in the record of Walter Cook (V.C.), and the eulogistic remarks in the *Gazette* upon that soldier apply equally to Millar.

HERBERT MACKWORTH CLOGSTOUN
(CAPTAIN)
19TH MADRAS NATIVE INFANTRY

AT Chickumbah, January 15, 1859, this officer, with only eight men of his regiment (2nd Cavalry, Hyderabad Contingent), charged the rebels and forced them back into the town, causing them to drop the loot they had secured. He was severely wounded, and lost seven out of the eight men whom he led.

He died in 1861.

History of the Victoria Cross

Photo by BRACEBRIDGE, *Ontario.*

GEORGE RICHARDSON

(PRIVATE)

34TH REGIMENT

AT Kewanie, Trans-Gogra, on April 27, 1859, Richardson showed determined bravery in closing with and securing a rebel armed with a loaded revolver, he himself being severely wounded at the time—one arm quite disabled.

CHARLES AUGUSTUS GOODFELLOW

(LIEUTENANT, NOW GENERAL)

ROYAL (BOMBAY) ENGINEERS

THIS was the last Victoria Cross granted in connexion with the Indian Mutiny, and the place of action appears to have been where the last stand was made, at Beyet, in Katty war, Western India. On October 6, 1859, Lieutenant Goodfellow highly distinguished himself, as he had already done throughout the Mutiny. A soldier of the 28th Regiment having been shot under the walls of the fort, Lieutenant Goodfellow rushed to his rescue, being exposed the whole time to heavy rifle and matchlock fire. Although he succeeded in conveying him, after great difficulty, into shelter, he discovered that, in spite of his efforts, the man was dead.

Photo by BOURNE & SHEPHERD, *India.*

THE NEW ZEALAND WAR

1860—1861 and 1863—1866

WILLIAM ODGERS
(LEADING SEAMAN, H.M.S. "NIGER")
ROYAL NAVY

DECORATED for his gallantry on March 28, 1860, at the attack on a native *pah*, at Taranaki, during the campaign against the rebels in New Zealand, when he was the first to mount the stockade; and on getting into the stronghold under a heavy fire, assisted in hauling down the enemy's colours.

He died on December 20, 1873. His Cross was sold in London on June 28, 1904 (together with his New Zealand Medal), for £110.

JOHN LUCAS
(COLOUR-SERGEANT, AFTERWARDS SERGEANT-MAJOR)
40TH (2ND SOMERSETSHIRE; NOW SOUTH LANCASHIRE) REGIMENT.

Photo by CHANCELLOR, *Dublin.*

ON March 18, 1861, Colour-Sergeant Lucas acted as sergeant of a party of the 40th Regiment, who were skirmishing close to the Huirangi Bush, in New Zealand. About 4 o'clock in the afternoon the natives suddenly opened a very heavy and well-directed fire upon them from the bush and high ground to the left, wounding simultaneously three men, two mortally. Volunteers were called for, to convey them to the rear, and a file of men came up, one of whom was immediately shot. Lieutenant Rees was wounded at the same time, and under a fierce fire from the natives, not more than thirty yards distant, Lucas ran to him and carried him to shelter, sending one of his men with him to the rear. He then took the arms of the men who had been killed or wounded, and keeping up a hot fire maintained his position until support was brought up by Lieutenants Gibson and Whelan.

Sergeant-Major Lucas died in Dublin, in 1893.

EDWARD MACKENNA

(COLOUR-SERGEANT, AFTERWARDS ENSIGN)

65TH REGIMENT

THIS non-commissioned officer greatly distinguished himself in New Zealand during the campaign against the Rebel Maories. On September 7, 1863, an action was fought near Cameron-town, and Captain Swift and Lieutenant Butler were both shot. Mackenna took command of the small force left, consisting of two sergeants, a bugler, and thirty-five men. At their head, he charged through the enemy's position, although heavily outnumbered by them, and drew off his little party, with the loss of only two men, though the country was most dangerous and rugged. Lieut.-General Cameron, C.B., in command of the forces, reported that Mackenna's coolness, intrepidity, and judgment justified the confidence placed in him by the soldiers, brought so suddenly under his command.

JOHN RYAN

(LANCE-CORPORAL)

65TH REGIMENT

AT Cameron-town, New Zealand, where an action was fought on September 7, 1863, Captain Swift was mortally wounded. Ryan, with Privates Bulford and Talbot of his regiment, removed the body of their officer from the field and remained with it all night in the bush, surrounded by the enemy. Bulford and Talbot were both awarded the Medal for Distinguished Conduct, and Ryan was awarded the Victoria Cross, but he never lived to own it long, being drowned near Tuakan while attempting to rescue a comrade.

His Victoria Cross was sold in London on April 17, 1902, for £58.

The New Zealand War

JOHN THORNTON DOWN
(ENSIGN)

57TH (WEST) MIDDLESEX REGIMENT (THE DUKE OF CAMBRIDGE'S OWN)

AT Pontoko, New Zealand, on October 2, 1863, a soldier fell wounded within fifty yards of the bush, which was swarming with natives. At their colonel's call for volunteers to bring the man into shelter, Ensign Down and Drummer Stagpoole (V.C.) promptly responded, and succeeded in carrying in the wounded man, though a heavy fire was directed upon them by the enemy.

John Thornton Down died of fever in New Zealand during the war, which lasted from 1860-6. His name (together with those of his fellow-officers in the regiment who fell during those years) is recorded in St. Paul's Cathedral on a brass tablet.

DUDLEY STAGPOOLE
(DRUMMER)

57TH (WEST) MIDDLESEX (THE DUKE OF CAMBRIDGE'S OWN)

THE brave act for which Drummer Stagpoole was awarded the Victoria Cross is described in the record of John Thornton Down (V.C.). For many years he has proudly carried his decoration while employed at the Arsenal, Woolwich. He was also decorated with the Distinguished Conduct Medal for his gallant behaviour at Kaipakopako, New Zealand, on September 25, 1863, for having, although wounded in the head, twice volunteered and brought in wounded men.

Photo by DALBY, *Woolwich.*

History of the Victoria Cross

WILLIAM TEMPLE

(ASSIST.-SURGEON, NOW BRIGADE-SURGEON, B.A., M.B., L.R.C.S.I., RETIRED)

ROYAL ARTILLERY

Photo by DEBENHAM, *Southsea.*

ASSOCIATED with Lieutenant Pickard (V.C.), in most nobly exposing his life at Rangiriri, New Zealand, on November 20, 1863, to render assistance to Captain Mercer, R.A., and others who had fallen wounded in the assault on the Maori stronghold. To reach them he was obliged to cross the entrance of the Keep, upon which the enemy were concentrating a terrific fire.

Born on November 7, 1833, son of the late William Temple, M.D., of Monaghan. Educated privately and at Trinity College, Dublin. Entered the Army 1858. Has served in the Taranaki (New Zealand) Campaign 1860–1, and in that in which he won the Victoria Cross. Was present at the actions of Teairei and Rangeawhia.

ARTHUR FREDERICK PICKARD

(LIEUTENANT, AFTERWARDS COLONEL, C.B.)

ROYAL ARTILLERY

ON November 20, 1863, during the assault at Rangiriri, New Zealand, Captain Mercer, R.A., and many other officers and men were wounded, and lying in an exposed position. Lieutenant Pickard and Surgeon Temple (V.C.), in imminent danger of their lives, crossed the entrance of the Maori Keep, a point upon which the enemy had concentrated their fire, and rendered great assistance to the injured.

Lieutenant Pickard crossed and recrossed the parapet, exposed all the while to a

Photo by MAULL & FOX.

The New Zealand War

heavy cross fire, to procure water for them, when none of the other men could be induced to perform this service, and testimony is borne to the calmness displayed by him, and also by Surgeon Temple, under the trying circumstances in which they were placed.

CHARLES HEAPHY
(MAJOR)
AUCKLAND MILITIA

DURING a skirmish on the banks of the Mangapiko River in New Zealand, on February 11, 1864, Major Heaphy went to the assistance of a soldier of the 40th Regiment who, having been shot, had fallen into a hollow where the Maories were concealed in great numbers. Immediately he became a target for a volley from the enemy at a few feet distant. His clothes were struck by five bullets, and he was shot in three places, but he nevertheless kept with the wounded man, aiding him all that day.

JOHN CARSTAIRS McNEILL
(LIEUT.-COLONEL, NOW MAJOR-GENERAL, K.C.B., K.C.M.G., G.C.V.O.)

107TH BENGAL INFANTRY (NOW THE ROYAL SUSSEX)

ON March 30, 1860, when Aide-de-Camp to Sir Duncan Cameron, Lieut.-Colonel McNeill was proceeding to Awamutu with Privates Gibson and Vosper. On their return journey, when about a mile from Ohanpu, they sighted a body of the enemy. Gibson was sent to bring infantry, the remaining two staying to watch the enemy. Suddenly a heavy fire was opened upon them from the bush, and their only chance was to ride for their lives. They had hardly gone any

Photo by ELLIOTT & FRY.

distance before Vosper's horse was shot, causing it to fall and throw him. On perceiving this, Lieut.-Colonel McNeill returned, caught the horse, which fortunately was not badly hurt, helped his man to mount, and by galloping as hard as possible, both managed to escape. Vosper states that but for his officer's help he must have been killed.

Sir John McNeill, son of Captain Alexander McNeill of Colonsay, was born March 29, 1831. Educated at St. Andrews and Addiscombe. During the Mutiny was A.D.C. to Sir E. Lugard, and in the Fenian Disturbance of 1867 in command of the Tipperary Flying Column. On the staff of Lord Wolseley during Red River Expedition, and also during Ashanti War. Served through Egyptian Campaign in 1882; commanded a brigade in 1885 in the same country, taking part in the battles of Suakin and Tofrik. Bath King at Arms. A.D.C. to His Majesty. Died at St. James' Palace on May 25, 1904.

WILLIAM GEORGE NICHOLAS MANLEY
(ASSISTANT-SURGEON, AFTERWARDS SURGEON-GENERAL, C.B.)
ROYAL ARTILLERY

Photo by ELLIOTT & FRY.

On April 29, 1864, at the attack on the Maori Pah near Tauranga, New Zealand, Surgeon Manley risked his life in a most noble manner in an endeavour to save that of Commander Hay, R.N., and others. He volunteered to accompany the storming party into the stronghold, and when (as is stated in the record of Samuel Mitchell, V.C.) the mortally wounded officer was carried away, he attended to him, and afterwards again volunteered to return to see if he could find any more requiring assistance. The natives were swarming around at the time, keeping up a heavy fire, and Surgeon Manley was one of the last to quit the place.

Surgeon-General Manley, son of the Rev. Wm. Nicholas Manley, was born in Dublin, in 1831. Served through the Crimean War, 1854-5; Afghan War, 1878-9; Egyptian War, 1882, taking part in the battle of Tel-el-Kebir (3rd Class Osmanieh), retiring 1884. During the Franco-Prussian War of 1870, accom-

The New Zealand War

panied the British Ambulance, and for his devotion to the wounded and unflinching courage on all occasions received the thanks of the Prussian General in command of the division to which he was attached. For his devoted conduct during the action at Chateauneuf and Bretoncelles, and at Orleans and Cravant, he was granted the Steel War Medal and 2nd Class of the Iron Cross. He also obtained the Bavarian Order of Merit, and possessed the R.H.S. Medal, for saving the life of a man of the R.A., who had fallen overboard in the Waitotara River, New Zealand, on July 21, 1865.

He died on November 16, 1901.

Photo by TAIT, *Hokitika.*

SAMUEL MITCHELL

(CAPTAIN OF THE FORE-TOP)

H.M.S. "HARRIER," ROYAL NAVY

COMMODORE SIR WILLIAM WISEMAN brought the name of Samuel Mitchell to special notice for his devotion and bravery on April 29, 1864. During the attack on Te Papa, Tauranga, New Zealand, he entered the *pah* with Commander Hay, and when that officer was mortally wounded, carried him out, although ordered by him to leave him and look after his own safety.

Mitchell died on March 16, 1894.

FREDERICK AUGUSTUS SMITH

(CAPTAIN, AFTERWARDS LIEUT.-COLONEL)

43RD REGIMENT

ON June 21, 1864, during the engagement at Tauranga, Captain Smith led his company in a most gallant manner at the attack on the Maori position. Although wounded before he reached their rifle-pits, he jumped down into the midst of them and commenced a hand-to-hand encounter, greatly encouraging his men, and setting them a fine example.

He died on July 22, 1887.

History of the Victoria Cross

JOHN MURRAY
(SERGEANT)

68TH REGIMENT (DURHAM LIGHT INFANTRY)

ON June 21, 1864, at the storming of the Maori position, at Tauranga, New Zealand, Sergeant John Murray behaved in a most brave manner. He ran up to one of the rifle-pits, containing ten men, and, absolutely by himself, killed or wounded every one of them. He then proceeded up the works, fighting in a most desperate manner, bayonetting several more.

HUGH SHAW
(CAPTAIN, NOW MAJOR-GENERAL, C.B.)

2ND BATT. 18TH (ROYAL IRISH) REGIMENT

ON January 24, 1865, at the skirmish near Nukumaru, in New Zealand, Captain Shaw had been ordered to occupy a position about half a mile from the camp, and, advancing in skirmishing order to about thirty yards from the bush, he thought it prudent to retire to a palisade about thirty yards further back, as two of his men had fallen wounded. Noticing that one of them, Peter Conolly, was too badly injured to move, he called for volunteers, and, with four privates who responded, went out to the wounded man within thirty yards of the enemy, and under a heavy fire, succeeded in conveying him to shelter.

Major-General Shaw, C.B., born on Feb-

The New Zealand War

ruary 4, 1839, is son of Mr. James Shaw, formerly Principal Inspector of Hospitals, Madras. Educated at Sandhurst, he became ensign in 1855 and served through the Crimean War, the Indian Mutiny, the Afghan War, 1879; and the Egyptian War, 1884. In the latter he commanded the 1st Battalion of his gallant Irish Regiment during the march for the Relief of Gordon, which, with the 2nd East Surrey, was brought from India. His command on this occasion gained the £100 prize offered by Lord Wolseley for the quickest and smartest voyage in the whale boats between Sarras and Korti (December 16, 1884, to January 24, 1885), from which point it marched on foot, through the Bayuda Desert, 175 miles, to Metemmeh in eleven days. He retired from command of his old battalion in 1887.

THE CHINA WAR

1860—1862

(including Taiping Rebellion, 1861—1862)

ROBERT MONTRESOR ROGERS
(LIEUTENANT, AFTERWARDS MAJOR-GENERAL, C.B.)
44TH (EAST) ESSEX REGIMENT

Photo by BASSANO, *London.*

DECORATED for his bravery at the assault on the North Taku Fort in China on August 21, 1860, when, in company with Lieutenant Lenon (V.C.) and Private McDougall (V.C.), he swam the ditch and entered by an embrasure. He was the first Englishman to gain a footing on the wall.

General Rogers, born September 4, 1834, entered the Army in February, 1855; took part in the siege of Sebastopol, and became Lieutenant in August, 1855; Captain in November, 1860. After a few years he exchanged into the 90th Light Infantry, becoming Major in April, 1873.

He died on February 5, 1895.

The China War

JOHN McDOUGALL
(PRIVATE)
44TH REGIMENT

GREATLY distinguished himself on August 21, 1860, at the storming of the North Taku Forts in China, by swimming across the ditch and entering the embrasure. He was the second of the first three men to gain the wall, his companions being Lieutenants Rogers and Lenon.

EDMUND HENRY LENON
(LIEUTENANT, AFTERWARDS MAJOR)
67TH (SOUTH) HAMPSHIRE REGIMENT

ON August 21, 1860, the Taku Forts were attacked and captured—about 500 of our men being killed and wounded. When the moment of assault came, Lieutenant Lenon, with some others, sprang into the ditch, which was filled with water, and swam across, entering through the embrasures. He was the third to gain a footing on the walls.

NATHANIEL BURSLEM
(LIEUTENANT, AFTERWARDS CAPTAIN)
67TH (SOUTH) HAMPSHIRE REGIMENT

ASSOCIATED on August 21, 1860, with Thomas Lane (V.C.), in a most gallant act during the storming of the North Taku Forts in China. These two men swam the ditch, and, before the entrance of the fort had been effected by any one, persevered in their endeavours to enlarge an opening in the wall, through which they eventually forced their way, both being severely wounded.

Afterwards, on obtaining his company, he exchanged into the 60th Rifles.

History of the Victoria Cross

THOMAS LANE
(PRIVATE)
67TH REGIMENT

ON August 21, 1860, at the attack on the North Taku Forts, in China, Lane and his officer, Lieutenant Nathaniel Burslem (V.C.), swam the ditch, and, persevering in their attempts to enlarge the opening in the wall of the fort, made a breach, through which they forced their way, before an entrance had been effected by any of our troops. During this courageous act they were both severely wounded. Lane died in 1887.

JOHN WORTHY CHAPLIN
(ENSIGN, 67TH REGIMENT)
AFTERWARDS COLONEL 107TH REGIMENT

ON August 21, 1860, at the storming of the North Taku Forts, in the China War, this officer behaved with distinguished gallantry. He carried the Queen's colour of the regiment, and planted it upon the breach made by the storming party, later on doing the same on the *cavalier* of the fort, he being the first man to mount it. He was severely wounded.

Colonel Chaplin, born on July 23, 1840, was educated at Harrow, and entered the Army in 1858. Served also in Afghan War, 1879-80. Attained his present rank in 1883.

Photo by BALE, *Leicester.*

The China War

ARTHUR F. FITZGIBBON
(HOSPITAL APPRENTICE)
INDIAN MEDICAL ESTABLISHMENT

DECORATED for his gallant and cool behaviour and great courage on August 21, 1860, at the storming of the North Taku Forts in China. He proceeded with part of the 67th regiment to a position within 500 yards of the fort, and from cover he went out under a heavy fire to attend to the wounds of a dhoolie-bearer. Having performed his duty to this man, he crossed another open and exposed space, still under a hail of lead, and ministered to the sufferings of others, during which humane act he was himself severely wounded.

GEORGE HINCKLEY
(ABLE SEAMAN)
H.M. SLOOP "SPHINX," ROYAL NAVY

Photo by MAULL & FOX.

AT Fung-wha, in China, on October 9, 1862, while our men were attacking the East Gate of the city, Hinckley volunteered to carry Mr. Coker, Master's Assistant of the *Sphinx*, from the place where he had fallen wounded during the advance on the Gate, to a joss-house, 150 yards distant. Under a heavy fire he successfully accomplished his humane act, and on returning went to the assistance of Mr. Bremen, an officer of Ward's force. This man had also been wounded during the advance, and, still under the same raking fire, Hinckley carried him to the joss-house, returning afterwards and taking his place in the fighting at the Gate.

Of the eight officers and men awarded the Cross during that campaign, Hinckley and Colonel Chaplin, C.B., are now the only surviving recipients.

THE UMBEYLA EXPEDITION (N.W. INDIA)
1863

GEORGE VINCENT FOSBERY
(LIEUTENANT, NOW LIEUT.-COLONEL)
(LATE) 4TH BENGAL EUROPEAN REGIMENT

Photo by MAULL & FOX.

DECORATED for his gallantry and daring conduct while a volunteer at the recapture of the "Crag Picket" during the Umbeyla Campaign. On October 30, 1863, Lieut.-Colonel Keyes, C.B., directed Lieutenant Fosbery to push up one of the two paths leading to the top of the cliff, while he himself ascended by the other. There was only room for the attackers to proceed about two abreast, and with the greatest coolness and intrepidity Lieutenant Fosbery led his party of men, being himself the first to gain the top of the crag. Afterwards, Lieut.-Colonel Keyes being wounded, Lieutenant Fosbery assembled a party of his men, pursued the routed enemy, inflicting great loss on them, and confirming the possession of the "Crag Picket."

Lieut.-Colonel Fosbery, son of the Rev. T. V. Fosbery, was born at Sturt, near Devizes. Educated at Eton, he entered the Bengal Army in 1852; became Captain, 1864; Major, 1866; and attained his present rank in 1876. Took part in every engagement of importance in the Umbeyla Expedition, and retired in 1877, since when he has devoted himself to the perfecting of machine guns, being the first to introduce them to

The Umbeyla Expedition (N.W. India)

the British Government. Invented the " Paradox Gun," and an automatic revolver. Also introduced the explosive bullet, as a means of ascertaining range for infantry and mountain-guns.

HENRY WILLIAM PITCHER

(LIEUTENANT BENGAL STAFF CORPS), ADJUTANT 4TH PUNJAB INFANTRY

Photo by MAULL & FOX.

ON October 30, 1863, Lieutenant Pitcher led a party in a most gallant manner, to recapture the " Crag Picket," after the enemy had driven in the garrison, killing sixty of them in a stubborn hand-to-hand fight. Major Keyes, in command of the 1st Punjab Infantry, relates that Lieutenant Pitcher led his party in a most cool and daring manner up to the last rock, until he was knocked down and stunned by a large stone thrown from above. The nature of the approach to the top of the " Crag " was such that only one man could advance at a time. On November 13, following, Lieutenant Pitcher led the first charge during the recapture of the same post, it having again fallen into the enemy's hands. He was, on this occasion, many yards in advance of his men, his conduct being the admiration of all present. Major Keyes stated that it was impossible to over-estimate his services, and that during the assault the lieutenant was severely wounded, and had to be carried back.

JAPAN

1864

WILLIAM SEELEY
(SEAMAN)

H.M.S. "EURYALUS," ROYAL NAVY

Photo by KIVLAN, *Leominster, Mass.*

DECORATED for his intelligence and conspicuous courage at the attack on the batteries, and defences of Simonisaki, in Japan, on September 6, 1864. This seaman went ashore first and ascertained quite alone the strength and position of the enemy, his valuable information and services being specially mentioned by Lieutenant Edwards, commanding the Third Company. Later, when our sailors charged the position, he led them with great gallantry, even though he had been previously wounded.

THOMAS PRIDE
(CAPTAIN OF THE AFTER-GUARD)

H.M.S. "EURYALUS," ROYAL NAVY

ASSOCIATED with Midshipman Boyes (V.C.), in a gallant rush made on the batteries at Simonisaki, in Japan, on September 6, 1864. Thomas Pride was the survivor of the two colour-sergeants who supported him on that occasion, and was dangerously wounded.

He died at Parkstone, Dorset, on July 16, 1893.

Photo by BISHOP, *Poole.*

Japan

DUNCAN GORDON BOYES
(MIDSHIPMAN)
H.M.S. "EURYALUS," ROYAL NAVY

ACCORDING to the testimony of Captain Alexander, C.B., Mr. Boyes displayed great courage on September 6, 1864, during the capture of the enemy's stockade at Simonisaki, in Japan. The two colour-sergeants having been wounded—one mortally—he carried the colour ahead of the storming party under a very severe fire, and was only stopped from advancing still further by order of his commanding officer. The colour was pierced six times by musket-balls.

Mr. Boyes died in 1869.

(See Thomas Pride, V.C.)

THE BHOOTAN WAR (N.E. INDIA)

1864—1865

JAMES DUNDAS
(LIEUTENANT, AFTERWARDS CAPTAIN)
ROYAL (LATE BENGAL) ENGINEERS

THIS officer was associated with Major-General Trevor (V.C.), in a particularly daring act of bravery at Dewan-Giri in Bhootan, on April 30, 1865. Further details of the heroic conduct of these officers are given in the account of Major-General Trevor.

Captain Dundas was killed on December 23, 1879, during the Afghan War, under circumstances which showed that he had lost none of that bravery which had so characterized him fourteen years previously. Several forts were being blown up by our Engineers, and at one of them Captain Dundas and Lieutenant Nugent constructed three mines. All being ready, the officers withdrew all their men to safety and lighted the three fuses, but two being defective exploded almost instantly, burying Captain Dundas and his gallant companion in the ruins of the fort.

Captain Dundas was born on September 12, 1843. He was the son of George Dundas, a Judge of the Court of Session in Scotland, was educated at Edinburgh and Addiscombe, and entered the Bengal Engineers in 1860. Colonel Vibart, in his work *Addiscombe*, relates that Captain Dundas saved the life of a native in 1878 at Simla, under particularly courageous circumstances. A house in the Bazaar having caught fire, the roof had fallen in, burying the native, who,

The Bhootan War (N.E. India)

unable to get out, was in great danger of being burnt alive. Captain Dundas attempted to save the man by himself, but failed, so calling for a volunteer to help him, the two together succeeded in accomplishing the difficult and dangerous task.

WILLIAM SPOTTISWOODE TREVOR
(MAJOR, NOW MAJOR-GENERAL, RETIRED)
ROYAL (BENGAL) ENGINEERS

ASSOCIATED with Lieutenant Dundas (V.C.), in a most gallant and courageous exploit during an attack on a blockhouse at Dewan-Giri, in Bhootan, on April 30, 1865. Major-General Tombs (V.C.), the officer in command, reported that about 200 of the enemy had barricaded themselves in a blockhouse after the rest had been attacked and driven off. Being the key to the enemy's position, and considering it most necessary to act promptly before the main body of the Bhooteas should return and rally, and as our men had been fighting for three hours in a broiling sun, Major-General Tombs gave orders to Lieutenant Dundas and Major Trevor to lead the attack. They had to climb up a wall which was fourteen feet high, and then to enter a house occupied by some 200 desperate men, head foremost through an opening not more than two feet wide, between the top of the wall and the roof of the blockhouse. Major-General Tombs states that on speaking to the Sikh soldiers around him and telling them in Hindustani to swarm up the wall, none of them responded to the call, until these two officers had shown them the way, when they followed with the greatest alacrity. How Trevor and Dundas escaped death was a marvel. Perhaps the very restricted space at the point of entrance had something to do with their success, the defenders being unable to use their swords effectively and getting jammed in their eagerness to close with them ; while the officers used their revolvers with fatal effect until they cleared the gallery and enabled the storming party to effect a lodgement. About sixty of the garrison, mostly wounded, surrendered; the rest were killed, fighting to the last. (Col. Vibart: *Addiscombe: Its Heroes and Men of Note*.)

Major-General Trevor, born in India, on October 9, 1831, was the son of Captain R. S. Trevor, who was murdered by Akbar Khan, at Cabul, in 1841, at the same time as Sir Wm. McNaghten was done to death. Educated at Addiscombe, he entered the Army in 1849. Served through the Burma Campaign, 1852–3, being severely wounded at the taking of the White House Picket Stockade at Rangoon, April 12, 1852, and for his conduct was mentioned in despatches. Present at the action at Donabew, March 19, 1853, and again wounded and mentioned for his gallant conduct. Served against the Dacca Mutineers in 1857, and through the Bhootan War of 1865, when he gained the Victoria Cross. Has been employed a great deal in the Public Works Department of India, having been Provincial Chief Engineer, Director-General of Railways, and Secretary to the Indian Government.

CANADA

1866

TIMOTHY O'HEA
(PRIVATE)
1ST BATT. RIFLE BRIGADE

As will be seen on referring to Rule 5 of the Victoria Cross Warrant, the decoration could not originally be awarded except for acts performed " in the presence of the enemy," but on August 10, 1858, a new clause was inserted in the Order [1] and under that rule Private O'Hea was awarded the decoration eight years later, being the only man who has benefited by the change. On June 9, 1866, a railway van, carrying 2,000 pounds of ammunition, caught fire at Danville Station while on the way from Quebec to Montreal, in Canada. While the guard was hesitating what to do under such terrible circumstances, O'Hea kept his nerve and, seizing the keys, opened the van doors, calling for water and a ladder. He tore the covering from the cases, discovered the source of the fire, and by his example it was suppressed, and a frightful explosion averted. Some years ago this brave man was lost in the Australian Bush, and no trace of him ever found.

[1] See V.C. Warrant in Appendix.

THE WEST AFRICAN (RIVER GAMBIA) EXPEDITION

1866

SAMUEL HODGE

(PRIVATE)

4TH WEST INDIA REGIMENT

ON June 30, 1866, at the storming of the town of Jubabecolong, in the kingdom of Barra, River Gambia, West Africa, this private soldier behaved with very great bravery. Colonel D'Arcy having called for volunteers to hew down the stockade with axes, Hodge and another soldier (afterwards killed) sprang forward and commenced the work. On our troops gaining an entrance Hodge followed his officer through the town, opening two gates from the inside, which were barricaded, and thereby allowing the supports to enter, upon which the enemy were cleared out at the point of the bayonet. As soon as the troops had issued through the West Gate of the town, the colonel, in the presence of all the men, acknowledged Hodge as the bravest soldier in the regiment.

He is one of three men of colour who have gained the Victoria Cross. The two others are William Hall, of Peel's Naval Brigade, in the Mutiny, and W. J. Gordon (West India Regiment), at Toniatabe, West Africa, 1892.

LITTLE ANDAMAN ISLAND

1867

CAMPBELL MILLIS DOUGLAS

(ASSISTANT-SURGEON, NOW BRIGADE-SURGEON, RETIRED M.D., L.R.C.P.)

2ND BATT. 24TH (2ND WARWICKSHIRE) SOUTH WALES BORDERERS

Photo by YOUNG, *Burnt Island.*

ONE of our ships, the *Assam Valley*, had put in at the island of Little Andaman, in the Bay of Bengal, and some of the crew went ashore. Apparently they must have been set upon and murdered by the natives, for none of them ever returned. To ascertain their fate, a part of the 24th Regiment was sent by steamer from Rangoon, and on some of them landing on May 7, 1867, they were attacked by the natives. Meantime a storm arose and turned the surf into a raging sea, and the soldiers on shore being in great peril, Dr. Douglas and four men most gallantly manned a gig and attempted to reach them. They very nearly succeeded in their endeavours, but, the boat beginning to fill rapidly, they were forced to retire. They then made a second attempt and were successful in reaching the shore, taking off five men. On these being placed safely on board, the doctor and his four brave men turned once more to the rescue of the rest of the soldiers, and by their strenuous efforts the entire party was eventually taken off the island. The *London Gazette* states that Dr. Douglas accomplished his trips through the surf by no ordinary exertion. He stood in the bows of the boat and worked her in an intrepid and seamanlike manner, cool to a degree. The four privates behaved in an equally cool and collected manner, rowing through the roughest surf when the slightest hesitation or want of pluck would have been attended with the gravest results. Their bravery and devotion were the means of saving seventeen men from an awful fate. The four privates with Dr. Douglas were Thomas Murphy, James Cooper, David Bell and William Griffiths, and the Victoria Cross was awarded to them all. They were the first recipients of the decoration in the "Old Green Howards," which famous Regiment has now sixteen to its credit, of which seven were gained at Rorke's Drift in the Zulu War, 1879. Fortunately it has been possible to reproduce photographs of Bell and Murphy, but those of Cooper and Griffiths, in spite of many inquiries, have not been able to be found.

Dr. Douglas retired in 1882. He is the son of Dr. G. M. Douglas, and was born in Quebec, being educated at St. John's, Canada, and Laval's University, Edinburgh. Joined the 24th Regiment in 1863; was Medical Officer in charge of Field Hospital during the 2nd Riel Expedition, 1885.

DAVID BELL

(PRIVATE)

2ND BATT. 24TH REGIMENT

WITH Dr. Douglas and three privates, Bell saved the lives of seventeen of his comrades on May 7, 1867, at Little Andaman Island, under circumstances of great bravery and pluck.

(See account of Dr. Douglas, V.C.)

JAMES COOPER

(PRIVATE)

2ND BATT. 24TH REGIMENT

WAS one of a party of five, including Dr. Douglas (V.C.), who at Little Andaman Island, May 7, 1867, rescued a party of seventeen men of the regiment from almost certain death in a most gallant manner. (See account of Dr. Douglas.)

James Cooper died about fifteen years ago, at Birmingham, and it has not been possible to find any trace of a likeness of him to reproduce.

Little Andaman Island

WILLIAM GRIFFITHS
(PRIVATE)

2ND BATT. 24TH REGIMENT

AT Little Andaman Island, Bay of Bengal, on May 7, 1867, William Griffiths, Dr. Douglas, and three privates, saved the lives of seventeen men of their regiment by an act of fearless devotion and bravery. Unfortunately no portrait of this gallant man could be found to reproduce, or details of him to be given, excepting to state that he fell on January 22, 1879, at the massacre of Isandlwana, in Zululand, where, with hundreds of his regiment, he fought to the last against fearful odds, keeping untarnished the name and fame of one of the finest regiments in the British Army. (See account of Dr. Douglas, V.C.)

Photo by FRITSCH, *Pittston, Pa.*

THOMAS MURPHY
(PRIVATE)

2ND BATT. 24TH REGIMENT

ACCOMPANIED Dr. Douglas (V.C.), when with Privates Bell, Griffiths, and Cooper (James), they rescued seventeen men of the regiment on May 7, 1867, from a most perilous position at Little Andaman Island, under circumstances of very great bravery and devotion. A detailed account is given under the heading of Dr. Douglas.

THE ABYSSINIAN WAR
1867—1868

Photo by OLDHAM, *Colchester.*

MICHAEL MAGNER
(DRUMMER)

33RD REGIMENT

ASSOCIATED with James Bergin in a most heroic and courageous action at the storming of Magdala, Abyssinia, on April 13, 1868. He and Bergin were the first two men to enter the city, after meeting with very severe difficulties.

JAMES BERGIN
(PRIVATE)

33RD (DUKE OF WELLINGTON'S) REGIMENT

AT the storming of Magdala, under Sir Robert Napier, April 13, 1868, Bergin was one of the first to force his way through the defences of the town.

Born at Killbricken, Queen's County, Ireland, June 29, 1845. Enlisted in the 10th Regiment, 1862, the following year volunteering into the 108th, with which he sailed for India in 1863. In 1867 transferred into the 33rd, with which he served through the Abyssinian War. Later served in the 78th Highlanders.

He died many years ago.

THE LOOSHAI (N.E. INDIA) EXPEDITION
1871—1872

DONALD MACINTYRE
(MAJOR, AFTERWARDS MAJOR-GENERAL)
BENGAL STAFF CORPS

Photo by BASSANO.

ON January 4, 1872, during the expedition against the Looshais, under Generals Nuttall and Bourchier, their chief stockaded village, Lalgnoora, was attacked. The assault by a small party of Goorkhas, up the steep and rugged hillside, was led by Major Macintyre. On reaching it, it was found to be on fire, but this did not deter him, and, undaunted, he sprang up the stockade, eight or nine feet high, and with his party successfully stormed the place. This was carried out under the heaviest fire delivered that day by the enemy.

Born in 1831, at Kincraig, Ross-shire; educated at Addiscombe, entering the Army in 1850. Served with the 66th Goorkhas in 1852, in the expeditions against the Peshawur Hill tribes, being present at the destruction of Pranghur and the battle at Ishkakot. Served also in 1853 against the Boree Afridi, and in 1856 in the Koorum Valley, under Sir N. Chamberlain. Also in 1864 with the Doaba Field Force. His next active service was in the Looshai Expedition, as detailed above, in which he gained the Victoria Cross, and his last was in the Afghan War of 1879.

He retired in 1880, and died April 15, 1903, at Fortrose.

THE ASHANTEE WAR

1873—1874

EDRIC FREDERICK (LORD) GIFFORD

(LIEUTENANT, NOW MAJOR, RETIRED)

24TH REGIMENT, SOUTH WALES BORDERERS

Photo by MAULL & FOX.

As a young lieutenant of the 24th (late of the 63rd), Lord Gifford proceeded to Ashantee in 1873. Soon after arrival he was placed in command of the Native Scouts. His conduct throughout the entire operations was conspicuously fine, and in all his duties he carried his life in his hands. He hung upon the rear of the enemy, dogging their movements, noting their positions, and, unattended by any other white man, captured many prisoners. His finest act was performed before the taking of Becquah, February 1, 1874, when he entered the "city," before our troops had arrived, and took note of all the enemy's positions. The information he was able to place before his Commanding Officer, Sir Garnet Wolseley, contributed most materially to the subsequently successful capture of that town.

In 1879, at the close of the Zulu War, the capture of Cetewayo was nearly brought about by Lord Gifford. Had he been a few hours sooner, the credit would have been his. He had been on the search for the Zulu King for fifteen days

The Ashantee War

and nights, and when he was finally successful in finding his whereabouts, his party of scouts was utterly worn out. For this reason he decided to wait till nightfall, before attempting the capture. Meanwhile, Major Marter, who had also been searching, heard of the king's hiding-place, marched direct to it, and brought him away captive.

Edric Frederick, Lord Gifford (3rd Baron), born July 5, 1849, was educated at Harrow. Entered Army, 1869; Lieutenant, 63rd Regiment, 1870; 24th Regiment, 1873; Captain, 57th Regiment, 1876; Brevet-Major, 1st Batt. Middlesex Regiment, 1880. Colonial Secretary for West Australia and Senior Member Legislative Council, 1880–3; Colonial Secretary of Gibraltar, 1883–8. Decorated by H.M. the late Queen at the review in Windsor Park, in April, 1874.

REGINALD WILLIAM SARTORIUS

(MAJOR, NOW MAJOR-GENERAL, C.M.G., RETIRED)

6TH BENGAL CAVALRY

DECORATED for conspicuous bravery on January 17, 1874, during the attack on Abogoo in the Ashanti War, when, under a heavy fire, he saved the life of Sergeant Major Braimah Doctor, a Houssa non-commissioned officer, who had been severely wounded.

He performed another splendid act during the war, by undertaking to ride fifty miles across the enemy's country, accompanied by twenty natives, with the object of establishing connexion between Captain Glover, who was marching through unknown country, and Sir Garnet Wolseley, whose whereabouts had to be discovered. Starting on March 9, he accomplished his mission on the 11th.

Son of the late Admiral Sir George Rose Sartorius, G.C.B. Has served in the Indian Mutiny, Bhutan War, Kossi Campaign, Volta Expedition, 1874, under Sir John Glover, and Afghan War, 1879.

History of the Victoria Cross

SAMUEL McGAW
(LANCE-SERGEANT, AFTERWARDS SERGEANT)

42ND ROYAL HIGHLANDERS (THE BLACK WATCH)

DECORATED for his bravery on January 31, 1874, at the battle of Amoaful in Ashanti, when, in spite of a very severe wound, he led his section through the heavy fighting in the bush during the whole day. This gallant Highlander, when landing in Cyprus four years later, dropped dead from sunstroke.

MARK SEVER BELL
(LIEUTENANT, NOW COLONEL, C.B., RETIRED)

ROYAL ENGINEERS

THIS officer was decorated with the Victoria Cross for his conduct at Ordahsu on February 4, 1874, which was stated—in the words of the Gazette—to be "zealous," "resolute," and "self-devoted."

Sir John McLeod, commanding the 42nd, was an eye-witness and testified to his courage and fearless bearing. He urged on and encouraged an unarmed working party of Fantee labourers—who were exposed not only to the fire of the enemy, but also to that of our own native troops in the rear—to do what no European party was ever required to do in warfare, namely,

Photo by ELLIOTT & FRY.

to work under fire in the face of the enemy, without a covering party. His splendid example very materially contributed to the success of the day.

Colonel Bell, P.S.C., C.B., son of Mr. Hutchinson Bell, Leconfield, Yorkshire, was born at Sydney, New South Wales, May 15, 1843. Educated at King's College, London. Entered R.E. 1862; Captain, 1874; Major, 1882; Brevet Lieut.-Colonel, 1884; Brevet-Colonel, 1887; Colonel on Staff and commanding R.E., Western District, 1894–8; commanded R.E. and Bengal Sappers and Miners, and Assistant Field Engineer Bhutan Campaign, 1865–6 (medal and clasp); commanded R.E., and Assistant Field Engineer, Hazara Campaign, 1868. His conduct in this latter campaign was brought to notice, and his forced march of 600 miles specially mentioned. During the Ashanti War of 1873–4 he was Adjutant R.E. Brigade, and Special Service officer, being mentioned in despatches for other acts than that for which he was awarded the Cross; Intelligence Officer during Burman Expedition, 1886–7; A.Q.M.G. for Intelligence 1880–85; D.Q.M.G. 1885–8; A.D.C. to Her late Majesty, 1887–1900; C.B., 1893. Well known as a great traveller in the East and an author of military and geographical articles. Fellow of King's College, London. McGregor Gold Medallist, U.S. Institute, India.

PERAK

1875—1876

GEORGE NICHOLAS CHANNER
(CAPTAIN, NOW MAJOR-GENERAL, C.B.)
BENGAL STAFF CORPS

Photo by WARSCHAWSKI, *St. Leonards.*

ON December 20, 1875, during the Expedition in Perak, Captain Channer performed the hazardous and courageous act of creeping alone to the rear of the enemy's stockade which we were about to attack. He got so close to it that he could hear their voices, and discovered that no watch was being kept; upon which he beckoned to his men, and the party crept quietly forward, and, under Captain Channer's lead, dashed into it, this officer shooting the first man dead with his revolver. The stockade was of a most formidable nature, and had it not been taken in the manner described, owing to the foresight and courage of Captain Channer, a great loss of life would in all probability have resulted before it could have been seized at the point of the bayonet, as guns could not have been brought to bear on it owing to its position.

Major-General Channer, born in 1843, was educated at Truro and Cheltenham. Entered the army in 1859, and served through the Umbeyla Campaign 1863; Malay Campaign, 1875; Jowaki-Afridi Expedition, 1877; Afghan War, 1879; Hazara Expedition, 1888. Has been continually mentioned in despatches, and received a good service pension in 1892.

QUETTA (BELOOCHISTAN)

1877

ANDREW SCOTT
(CAPTAIN, AFTERWARDS MAJOR)
BENGAL STAFF CORPS

ON July 26, 1877, at Quetta, in Beloochistan, Captain Scott was serving in the 4th Sikh Infantry. On the evening of that day, while on duty at the Regimental Parade Ground, this officer heard that some Pathans were attacking two Engineer Officers, Lieutenants Hewson and Kunhardt, upon which he at once rushed to their assistance. On reaching the scene he saw that Lieutenant Hewson had been cut down, and that Lieutenant Kunhardt had only Sepoy Ruchpal Singh to protect him from the fury of his assailants, before whom he was retiring hard pressed, and wounded. Captain Scott attacked the Pathans most bravely, with his own hand bayonetting two of them and closing with a third, who was killed during the struggle by a Sepoy of the regiment. By his courageous conduct the life of Lieutenant Kunhardt was saved.

Major Scott entered the Army on March 4, 1860; was promoted Lieutenant January 1, 1862; and Captain March 4, 1872.

THE KAFFIR WAR

1877--1878

HANS GARRETT MOORE
(MAJOR, AFTERWARDS COLONEL, C.B.)
88TH THE CONNAUGHT RANGERS

Photo by KNIGHT, *Aldershot.*

DURING the action near Komgha against the Gaikas on December 29, 1877, a small party of Frontier Mounted Police was forced to retire before a large body of the enemy. Private Giese was unable to mount his horse, and the enemy was rapidly approaching. Major Moore saw the terrible plight he was in, and heroically rode back to attempt to save his life. By the time he reached him he was completely surrounded by the Gaikas, but he did not desist in his attempt until the unfortunate man was killed. Before he himself could escape, he shot two of the enemy, and was severely wounded in the arm by an assagai.

Major Moore was drowned, some years after, while attempting to save life in one of the lakes in Ireland.

THE AFGHAN WAR

1878—1880

JOHN COOK
(CAPTAIN)
BENGAL STAFF CORPS

ON December 2, 1878, Captain Cook displayed signal gallantry at the attack on the Peiwar Kotal. Under a terrific fire he charged out of the entrenchments with such vigour and daring that the enemy fled before him. At that moment he caught sight of Major Galbraith, A.A.G. Kurrum Field Force, who was in great danger, being in personal conflict with an Afghan soldier. He rushed to his rescue, cut at the Douranee with his sword, which the enemy avoided, sprang at him and grasped him by the throat. The Douranee, who was a most powerful adversary, while still endeavouring to get hold of and use his rifle, seized Captain Cook's arm in his teeth, but was shortly afterwards shot through the head. Captain Cook was severely wounded in the operations around Cabul on December 12, 1879, and died on December 19. The following divisional order was published by the Lieut.-General commanding—

"It is with deep regret the Lieut.-General announces to the Cabul Field Force the death, from a wound received on December 12, of Major John Cook, V.C., 5th Goorkhas. While yet a young officer, Major Cook served at Umbeyla in 1863, where he distinguished himself, and in the Black Mountain Campaign in 1868. Joining the Kurrum Field Force on its formation, Major

History of the Victoria Cross

Cook was present at the capture of the Peiwar Kotal, his conduct on that occasion earning for him the admiration of the whole force, and the Victoria Cross. In the return in the Monghyr Pass he again brought himself prominently to notice by his cool and gallant bearing. In the capture of the heights at Sang-i-Nawishta Major Cook again distinguished himself, and in the attack on the Takht-i-Shah Peak on December 12 he ended a noble career in a manner worthy even of his great name for bravery.

"By Major Cook's death Her Majesty has lost the services of an officer who would, had he been spared, have risen to the highest honours of his profession, and Sir F. Roberts feels sure the whole Cabul Field Force will share in the pain his loss has occasioned him."

REGINALD CLARE HART

(LIEUTENANT, NOW MAJOR-GENERAL, K.C.B.)

ROYAL ENGINEERS

Photo by MAULL & FOX.

THE Lieut.-General commanding the 2nd Division Peshawur Field Force brought the name of this officer to notice for a particularly fine act of courage and humanity near Dakkah. Lieutenant Hart was on convoy duty at the time, January 31, 1879, and the force was attacked by a large body of the enemy, who poured a very heavy fire upon it from the hills. A Sowar of the 13th Bengal Lancers fell seriously wounded, 1,200 yards distant from Lieutenant Hart, who, on seeing the precarious position of the man, ran to him, drove off his assailants, and, with the assistance of some men who came up shortly afterwards, carried him under cover. During the entire time he was exposed to the rifle fire of the enemy from the banks of the river, and also from a party of them in the river bed itself. Major-General Hart has the R.H.S. medal for saving life at Boulogne on July 27, 1869, and another medal from the Mayor of that city; a Medal of Honour, first class, from the President of the French Republic; a Silver Clasp, R.H.S.,

The Afghan War

for saving the life of a gunner in the Ganges Canal, Roorkee, December 15, 1884.

Sir R. C. Hart, son of the late Lieut.-General H. G. Hart, was born at Scarif, Co. Clare, Ireland, on June 11, 1848. Educated at Marlborough Cheltenham, and R.M. Academy. Lieutenant R.E. 1869; Brevet-Colonel, 1886; Assistant Garrison Instructor, 1874-8; Garrison Instructor, 1885-8; Director of Military Education in India, 1888-96. Besides the Afghan War, has served through Egyptian War 1882, in which he was twice mentioned in despatches, receiving Brevet of Lieut.-Colonel, the medal and clasp, 4th class Osmanie and Khedive's Star; through the Tirah Campaign, 1897-8, in which he commanded the 1st Brigade, for his services in which he was mentioned in despatches, received medal and two clasps, and created K.C.B. From 1896-9 commanded the Belgaum District of Madras, and since 1899 the Quetta District of India. Now commands at Chatham.

EDWARD PEMBERTON LEACH

(CAPTAIN, NOW MAJOR-GENERAL, C.V.O., C.B.)

ROYAL ENGINEERS

THE action in which General Leach gained the Victoria Cross was fought among the hills of Afghanistan, far away in the Khyber Pass, against the Shinwarris, at Maidanah, on March 17, 1879. Captain Leach's command was covering the retirement of a survey escort bearing Lieutenant Barclay (45th Rattray's Sikhs), who was mortally wounded. The escort was sorely pressed on all sides. Leach placed himself at the head of the brave Sikhs, and dashed against overwhelming numbers of the tribesmen. In the encounter he slew three of them, himself receiving a severe wound from an Afghan knife on the left arm. But for his determination and gallantry the whole party would have been annihilated.

Major-General Leach, son of Sir George Leach, K.C.B., R.E., was born on April 2, 1847, at Londonderry. Educated at Highgate School and R.M.A. Woolwich, entering the Royal Engineers in 1866. In the

History of the Victoria Cross

Looshai Expedition, 1871, his first active service, he was mentioned in despatches and received the thanks of the Government of India. Later he served in the Afghan War from the first to the last, and, besides the Victoria Cross, was mentioned in despatches, obtaining Brevets of Major and Lieut.-Colonel. Took part in the operations at Suakin 1885 (despatches and C.B.), commanded the troops at Korosko 1885-6, and the British Brigade at Assouan in 1886-7. In command of the 9th Division 3rd Army Corps. Since 1900 has commanded the Belfast District.

WALTER RICHARD POLLOCK HAMILTON

(LIEUTENANT)

BENGAL STAFF CORPS (FORMERLY 70TH FOOT)

ON April 2, 1879, at the battle of Futtehabad, Lieutenant Hamilton's commanding officer, Major Wigram Battye, had been killed, in a charge made by the Guides Cavalry against the Afghans. Finding that he was the only officer left with the regiment, he promptly placed himself at the head of the men, led a most brilliant charge, and thoroughly routed the enemy. His bravery was most marked during this engagement. He saved the life of a Sowar, Dowlut Ram, whose horse had fallen, pinning him to the ground, and who was being attacked by three Afghans. Hamilton went to the man's rescue, cut down the three assailants, and brought him out of the *mêlée*. Although recommended for the Victoria Cross on account of this daring act, the War Office at first refused to grant it, and it was only on October 7, 1879, that tardy recognition was paid to him. He, however, never lived to know that they had recognized his conduct, for he accompanied the ill-fated mission under Cavagnari to Cabul, and fell on September 3, 1879, when the entire party was massacred in that city.

The Afghan War

O'MOORE CREAGH

(CAPTAIN, NOW MAJOR-GENERAL, K.C.B.)

BENGAL STAFF CORPS

THE decoration was won by Sir O'Moore Creagh on April 21, 1879. At the village of Kam Dakka on the Cabul River, Captain Creagh set out with two companies to attack the Mohmunds. The enemy, about 1,500 strong, advanced upon them, and the little force had to retire on a neighbouring Afghan cemetery, which was made as defensible as possible. Here his men repelled attacks with the bayonet all day up to 3 o'clock, when relief reached them. A charge by the 10th Bengal Lancers, under Captain (late Major-General) D. M. Strong, completely routed them, many being driven into the river. Sir F. Haines, then Commander-in-Chief in India, stated that had it not been for the admirable conduct displayed by Captain Creagh, the little party would probably have been cut off and destroyed.

Sir O'Moore Creagh served in China during the troubles in 1900, and for some years, during the occupation by European troops of part of that country, commanded those of England.

Son of Captain Creagh, R.N., he was born at Cahirbane, Co. Clare, Ireland. Educated privately and at R.M. College, Sandhurst. Ensign 95th, 1866; Staff Corps, 1870. Commanded the 2nd Baluchis, 1889. A.Q.M.G. Bombay Command, 1895. Political Resident at Aden, 1898–1900. Since January, 1904, has been in command of the Mhow District, India, in succession to Major-General Sir Richard Westmacott.

GEORGE STEWART WHITE

(MAJOR, NOW FIELD-MARSHAL, G.C.V.O., G.C.I.E., G.C.B., G.C.S.I.)

92ND REGIMENT

AT the battle of Charasiah, Afghanistan, on October 6, 1879, our artillery and rifle-fire failed to dislodge the enemy from a hill which, strongly fortified, it was necessary should be taken by us. It was determined to attempt the

History of the Victoria Cross

Photo by STEREOSCOPIC Co., London.

capture by assault, and Major White led his men up the precipitous rocks, climbing from ledge to ledge until they found themselves face to face with a force outnumbering them by eight to one. The Highlanders were most exhausted, but it was necessary to take immediate action, and Major White, taking a rifle, deliberately went straight at the enemy *by himself*, and shot the leader of the Afghans. His action so intimidated the rest that they fled down the hill, and the post was taken. On September 1, 1880, at the Battle of Kandahar, Major White led a charge upon the enemy with the greatest dash and gallantry. A heavy fire was being brought to bear upon his party from the Afghan rifles and two guns; but, nothing daunted, he charged the gunners and captured one of the pieces, the enemy retiring in all directions.

Born on July 6, 1835, Sir George White is the son of Mr. J. R. White, of Whitehall, Co. Antrim. Educated at Sandhurst, he entered the 27th Inniskillings in 1853, with which he served in the Indian Mutiny, 1857. Became Captain in the Gordon Highlanders in 1863; Major, 1873; and fought through the Afghan War, taking part in the Battle of Charasiah, occupation of Cabul, expedition to Maidan, Sherpur and capture of Takti Shah; accompanied Lord Roberts in the march from Cabul to Kandahar, being frequently mentioned in despatches and receiving Brevet of Lieut.-Colonel. Promoted Lieut.-Colonel, 1881, in which year he was Military Secretary to the Viceroy of India; took part in Nile Expedition, 1884; became Colonel, 1885; Lieut.-General, 1895; A.A.Q.G. in Egypt during expedition for the Khartoum Relief; in command of a brigade in Burma, 1885-6, being promoted Major-General for his distinguished services, and thanked by the Indian Government. In command of the Zhob Expedition, and of the Indian Forces, 1893-8. Q.G. to the Forces, 1898-9.

His latest services to his country have been during the Boer War, when from almost the outbreak of hostilities until the "Relief" by General Sir Redvers Buller, V.C., he commanded the garrison of Ladysmith, keeping the British flag flying against enormous odds, heavier armaments, and the privations and disease of a severe siege of 119 days (November 2, 1899–March 1, 1900).

The Afghan War

Since 1900 has been Governor of Gibraltar, and was promoted in 1903 to the rank of Field-Marshal.

EUSTON HENRY SARTORIUS
(CAPTAIN, NOW MAJOR-GENERAL, C.B.)
59TH REGIMENT

Photo by WEST, *Southsea.*

THIS gallant officer and his brother, Major-General R. W. Sartorius, are both wearers of the Victoria Cross. On October 24, 1879, Captain Sartorius behaved with conspicuous bravery during the action of Shah-jui. The Ghilzais had prepared a surprise attack on the British camp, but the information was brought to our command and the tables were turned on the enemy. Captain Sartorius led a small party of only five or six men, to a surprise attack on their stronghold at Tazi, on the top of an almost inaccessible hill. First creeping up and dashing unawares on the picket, the place was taken by assault with the loss of only one man. Captain Sartorius was himself, however, severely wounded in both hands by sword cuts.

Born at Cintra, near Lisbon, in 1844, Captain Sartorius is the son of the late Admiral of the Fleet, Sir G. R. Sartorius, G.C.B. Educated at Woolwich and R.M. College, Sandhurst, he joined the 59th Regiment in 1862, and passed Staff College. Besides being mentioned in despatches in the Afghan War, was thanked by the Indian Government for his services on the Survey, and obtained Brevet-Majority. Served in Egyptian War, 1882, D.A.A.G.; Brevet-Lieut.-Colonel, and mentioned in despatches. Military *Attaché* in Japan. For saving the lives of three girls from drowning at Broadstairs, June 29, 1869, received the Bronze Medal of the Royal Humane Society.

History of the Victoria Cross

THE REV. JAMES WILLIAMS ADAMS, B.A.
BENGAL ECCLESIASTICAL ESTABLISHMENT
Chaplain, Cabul Field Force

Photo by Elliott & Fry.

At the village of Bhagwana, on December 11, 1879, two troopers of the 9th Lancers were, during a charge, hurled with their horses into a wide and deep nullah, the enemy close upon them. The Rev. J. W. Adams rushed into the water and dragged the men one after the other from under the horses, being at the time under a heavy fire and up to his waist in water. While this took place, the Afghans were pressing on most vigorously, the leading men getting within a few yards of Mr. Adams, who having, previous to the above act, let go his horse in order to render more effectual aid to a young lancer whom he had rescued from the Afghan horsemen, was compelled to escape on foot.

Lord Roberts refers in his memoirs to this latter act of bravery and devotion performed by "The Fighting Parson," as the Rev. J. W. Adams has been often called. Seeing a wounded man of the 9th Lancers staggering towards him, he dismounted and tried to lift the man on to his own horse. Unfortunately, the mare broke loose, and was never seen again. He managed, however, to support the lancer until he was able to make him over to some of his own comrades. Referring also to the act for which the "Padre" was awarded the Cross, the same authority states that, on seeing the two lancers struggling under their horses, Adams did not hesitate an instant, but jumped into the ditch. He was an unusually powerful man, and by sheer strength dragged the lancers clear of the struggling animals. The Afghans had by this time reached Bhagwana, and were so close to the ditch that he thought Adams could not possibly escape. He called out to him to look after himself, but until he had pulled the almost exhausted lancers to the top of the slippery bank, Adams paid no heed to his own safety or the warnings of his commanding officer.

It was not only at Cabul that this Irish clergyman distinguished himself, for just a year previously, during the first days of the war in Afghanistan, when

The Afghan War

acting as " aide " to Sir Frederick (Lord) Roberts, Peiwar Kotal way, he rode forth alone, early one winter's morning, into the ravines, in search of a missing column, which he found, together with other benighted troops, led them to their position, and Peiwar Kotal was won.

He took part in that historic and splendid march under (then) Sir Frederick Roberts, from Cabul to Kandahar in August, 1880, and was present at the battle with, and defeat of, Ayub Khan on September 1. Five years later was again in the field, this time among the Paddi fields of Burma, obtaining medal and clasp. This terminated his services in the East.

In 1887 Mr. Adams became rector of Postwick, Norfolk, and of Stow Bardolf, in the same county, in 1895, finally holding the living of Ashwell, Oakham, where he died on October 20, 1903, aged 63.

WILLIAM HENRY DICK-CUNYNGHAM
(LIEUTENANT, AFTERWARDS LIEUT.-COLONEL)
2ND GORDON HIGHLANDERS

Photo by STEREOSCOPIC Co., *London.*

THIS gallant officer was decorated for conspicuous bravery at the attack on the Afghans, at the Sherpur Pass, December 13, 1879. On this occasion, owing to the terrible fire brought to bear on them, the men were forced back, and for a moment were inclined to waver. Although facing the full fire of the Afghans, Lieutenant Dick-Cunyngham sprang forward and, calling on his men to follow him (which order with renewed confidence they promptly obeyed), the attack was successfully carried out.

Born in 1851, Lieut.-Colonel Dick-Cunyngham joined the 2nd Gordon Highlanders in 1872; became Captain, 1881; Major, 1891; and Lieut.-Colonel, 1897. Serving through the Afghan War, he was engaged on transport duty in the advance to Kandahar and Khelat-i-Ghilzie under Sir Donald Stewart, and was with the Thull Chotiali Force under Major-General Biddulph, being mentioned in despatches. With Sir Frederick (now Earl) Roberts, V.C., in the Kurum Valley operations (including the action at Ali

History of the Victoria Cross

Kheyl), and in the fighting round Cabul in 1879. With the Maidan Expedition as Acting-Adjutant of a wing of the Gordon Highlanders, including the action of Charasiah. Took part in the historic march from Cabul to Kandahar, and was present at the battle of the latter place. During the entire War was frequently mentioned in despatches. In 1881 he served against the Boers as Adjutant to the Gordon Highlanders, and on the declaration of War against the same enemy in 1899, went to the front in command of the 2nd Battalion of his famous regiment, leading them into action at the battle of Elandslaagte, where he was wounded in the leg, necessitating his forced inaction during the early part of the siege of Ladysmith.

On January 6, 1900, almost the first day on which he had resumed his active duties, while the great attack on the town was in progress, he was killed by a chance shot at nearly 3,000 yards range.

Photo by KNIGHT, *Newport.*

GEORGE SELLAR

(LANCE-CORPORAL, AFTERWARDS SERGEANT)

72ND (SEAFORTH) HIGHLANDERS

ON December 14, 1879, during the attack on the Asmai Heights, round Cabul, Lance-Corporal Sellar, in a most gallant manner, led the attack and, under a very severe fire, dashed up the slope in front of his party, and engaged in a desperate hand-to-hand combat with an Afghan who sprang out to meet him. He was severely wounded.

ARTHUR GEORGE HAMMOND

(CAPTAIN, NOW COLONEL, K.C.B., D.S.O.)

BENGAL STAFF CORPS

DURING the severe fighting around Cabul in December, 1879, the troops were frequently hard pressed. The numbers to be met and defeated or kept in

The Afghan War

check were overwhelming, as the hilltops were alive with men keeping up a long-range fire. This became so harassing and annoying that it was at length resolved to storm the crags and drive them from their fastnesses once for all, and, on the 14th, vigorous action was taken, with splendid results. The position occupied by Colonel Hammond's men was such an exposed and dangerous one, that a short retirement became necessary for strategic reasons, seeing which the exultant Afghans seized this opportunity to press on. Colonel Hammond took a rifle and, hanging in rear of his men, opened so deadly a fire upon them that their advance was effectually checked. Later on, when a Sepoy fell severely wounded, he rushed to his assistance and helped to rescue him from the Afghans.

Son of Major T. G. Hammond, he was born in 1843, and educated at Sherborne and Addiscombe.

Served in the Jowaki Afridi Expedition, 1877, with the Guides under General Keyes; against the Ranizai village at Skhakat, March 14, 1878; and attack on Utman Kheyl villages, March 21. Through Hazara Expedition, 1888 (obtaining the D.S.O.), and Hazara, 1891; Izazai Expedition, 1892; Chitral Relief, 1895, receiving the thanks of the Indian Government; Tirah Campaign, 1897. In 1890 was appointed A.D.C. to the Queen, and received his Colonelcy. Has a good service pension.

WILLIAM JOHN VOUSDEN

(CAPTAIN, AFTERWARDS MAJOR-GENERAL, C.B.)

5TH PUNJAB CAVALRY

DECORATED for his exceptional gallantry on December 14, 1879, on the Koh Asmai Heights, near Cabul, when, with a small party, he charged into the centre of the line of Kohistanis, who were retreating. Although greatly outnumbered by the enemy, who repeatedly attempted to close round them, he led his men through and through their ranks, backwards and forwards, several times, afterwards sweeping off round the opposite side of the village and rejoining the rest of the troop.

History of the Victoria Cross

Photo by BASSANO, London.

Major-General Vousden, son of the late Captain Vousden, 21st R.N.B. Fusiliers, was born at Perth, Scotland, on September 20, 1845. Educated at King's School, Canterbury; R.M.C., Sandhurst. Joining the 35th Regiment in 1864, was transferred in 1867 to the 5th Punjab Cavalry, serving in the Afridi Expedition on the staff, and the two Afghan Campaigns, in which he obtained Brevet of Major. His subsequent active service was in the Miranzai Expedition, Tochi Field Force and Tirah Campaign, and the fighting on the north-west of India, 1897–8. In every one of these campaigns he was specially mentioned in despatches—during the Afghan no less than three times.

He died at Lahore, India, November 12, 1902.

PATRICK MULLANE

(SERGEANT, AFTERWARDS SERGEANT-MAJOR)

ROYAL HORSE ARTILLERY

ON July 27, 1880, after the disaster at Maiwand, our small force was retreating to Kandahar, when Driver Pickwell Istead fell badly wounded. Although the enemy were only ten or fifteen yards distant, Patrick Mullane, seeing the driver's danger, unhesitatingly ran back two yards and lifted him on to the limber of his gun, where he unfortunately died almost immediately.

Later on, he volunteered to fetch water for the wounded, going for it to a village near, where already so many of our men had been killed.

The Afghan War

JAMES COLLIS
(GUNNER)
ROYAL HORSE ARTILLERY

Photo by FARLIE, *Woolwich.*

AFTER the fearful disaster at Maiwand, on July 27, 1880, a retreat was made to Kandahar by the remnant of our force. The road became blocked by masses of fugitives, and the sufferings of the wounded were increased by terrible thirst. The conduct of James Collis was most noticeable, for, time after time, he went into the villages on the road to procure water for them, running the greatest risk in so doing, by reason of the bands of Afghans who hovered around, attacking our disorganized soldiers whenever an opportunity presented itself. His finest act took place at the bend of a road through a narrow defile. A body of Afghan cavalry bore down upon the gun-carriage he was guarding and directed a hail of bullets on the wounded, who had been placed upon the limber. In order to draw their attention from the helpless men, Collis sprang to the side of the road and returned the fire of the pursuing horsemen, making himself their target, and by his heroic act the limber was dragged round the bend of the road and the wounded saved. Later on he again distinguished himself by volunteering to carry a message from the beleaguered garrison to General Dewberry, entrenched some distance off. This he successfully accomplished though fired at by the enemy both when going and returning.

James Collis was born at Cambridge in 1860. His Cross was presented to him on Poona Racecourse by Sir Frederick (now Earl) Roberts.

WILLIAM ST. LUCIEN CHASE
(LIEUTENANT, NOW LIEUT.-COLONEL, C.B.)
BOMBAY STAFF CORPS

ON August 16, 1880, during the Afghan War, the Kandahar garrison made a sortie against the village of Deh Khoja. Private Massey, of the Royal Fusiliers, having been severely wounded, took shelter in a blockhouse, and from there Lieutenant Chase carried him for over 200 yards to a more safe position, the whole time exposed to a heavy fire from the enemy. Private

History of the Victoria Cross

Photo by BOURNE & SHEPHERD, *India*.

Ashford (V.C.) most bravely assisted him, remaining with him all the time.

Lieut.-Colonel Chase, son of the late Captain R. H. Chase, Commissary of Ordnance, was born at St. Lucia, West Indies. Joined the 15th Regiment in 1876; Indian Staff Corps, 1878; and served through the Afghan War, 1879-80, taking part in the Defence of Kandahar, the sortie above described, and the battle of Kandahar; Zhob Campaign, 1884; Chin-Lushai Expedition and advance on Fort Haka; Naga Hills Campaign and Manipur, 1893; Mohmund Expedition, 1897; Tirah Campaign, 1897-8; actions of Sampagha Pass; occupation of Maidan and Bagh Valleys, and operations in Dwatoi Defile, Rajghul Valley, and Bara Valley. Mentioned continually in despatches for his bravery and gallant services. Now in command of the 28th Bombay Pioneers.

Photo by BRIGGS, *St. John's Wood*.

THOMAS ASHFORD
(PRIVATE)
ROYAL FUSILIERS

ASSOCIATED with Lieutenant Chase (V.C.), in an act of conspicuous bravery on August 16, 1880, during the sortie from Kandahar against the village of Deh Khoja.

THE ZULU WAR

1879

TEIGNMOUTH MELVILL

(LIEUTENANT AND ADJUTANT)

24TH REGIMENT

Photo by HEATH, *Plymouth.*

ON January 22, 1879, when the camp at Isandlwana was attacked by the Zulus and nearly every man killed, Colonel Pulleine, seeing the disastrous turn that affairs were taking, called to Lieutenant and Adjutant Melvill to take the colours of the regiment and endeavour to cut his way through the enemy to save them. His heroic conduct is described more fully in the record of Lieutenant Coghill (V.C.), with whom he was associated, and with whom, on the banks of the Buffalo River, he met his death.

Teignmouth Melvill, born in London on September 8, 1842, was the son of Philip Melvill, Secretary in the Military Department to the East India Company. Educated at Harrow, Cheltenham, and Cambridge, he graduated B.A. in 1865. Entered the Army in 1865, and received his Lieutenancy December 2, 1868. Proceeded with his regiment to Malta, Gibraltar, and (in 1875) the Cape. Passed examination for Staff College and was ordered home to join that establishment when the Galeka War broke out, upon which he obtained permission to rejoin his regiment, and served through the suppression of the outbreak. At the commencement of the Zulu War he joined the Headquarters' Column, and, with his regiment, took part in the attack and capture of Sirayo's stronghold on January 13, 1879.

Her Majesty the late Queen Victoria, as a mark of her appreciation and recognition of his heroic conduct, caused his name to be placed upon the colour-pole of the 24th Regiment, together with those of Lieutenants Coghill, Chard and Bromhead. (See appendix VI.)

NEVILL JOSIAH AYLMER COGHILL
(LIEUTENANT)
24TH REGIMENT

NEVILL JOSIAH AYLMER COGHILL, eldest son of Sir John Joscelyn Coghill, Bart., J.P., of Castle Townshend, Co. Cork, Ireland, was born on January 25, 1852.

He was educated at Haileybury, and passed direct commission in 24th Regiment; became Aide-de-Camp to General Sir Arthur Cunynhame during the Galeka War, 1877, afterwards serving in a similar capacity to Sir Bartle Frere, who, at his own request, gave him six weeks' leave to join the fighting column in the Zulu War, under Lord Chelmsford.

He had been told off to act as galloper to Colonel Glyn on the unfortunate reconnaissance made from Isandlwana Camp, on January 22, 1879, but that officer, seeing he was quite lame, insisted he should remain behind and nurse his knee, injured while out foraging a few days before. He therefore remained in the camp, which, as soon as the Zulus had drawn off Lord Chelmsford and the main body of our troops, was attacked by an impi of 25,000 men, completely surrounded, and practically annihilated.

Colonel Pulleine, who was in command, seeing the desperate state of affairs, called to Lieutenant and Adjutant Melvill to take the Queen's colour of the regiment and endeavour to cut his way through the mass of Zulus, to prevent its falling into the enemy's hands. This order Lieutenant Melvill proceeded to carry out, and, with Lieutenant Coghill, spurred his horse over the rocky and dangerous ground to the Buffalo River, six miles distant. The direction chosen was the only one possible which gave any hope of success, for the road

The Zulu War

to Rorke's Drift was now seen completely blocked by dense masses of Zulus. As it was, they had to fight nearly the whole way, for the enemy, whose running powers enabled them to keep up with the horses, were assagaing from the saddle most of the fugitives who had followed these officers. In company with one mounted soldier, Melvill and Coghill reached the Buffalo and plunged in, the soldier being at once carried away by the whirling stream and drowned. Coghill reached the Natal side in safety, and, turning round, saw Melvill, whose horse had been drowned, being carried down by the rushing torrent, and that the colour he had tried so hard to save, had been wrenched from his grasp and was floating away down the river. Though unable to walk owing to his injured knee, and knowing, as he did, that any accident to his horse meant certain death to him, with safety and life at hand if he chose to take them, yet Coghill refused to consider himself, and, turning his horse's head, rode back again into the stream to Melvill's assistance. The Zulus kept up a hot fire upon both men, and shortly afterwards Coghill's horse was shot. With the greatest difficulty both managed to reach and climb the steep bank, and took shelter beneath some huge boulders. Higginson, an officer of the Natal Native Contingent, who had succeeded in escaping thus far from Isandlwana, saw them at this point and joined them, but both Melvill and Coghill persuaded him to save himself by flight, as, being unarmed, he could render no assistance and, when discovered, would only add another to the two lives whose tide was so nearly at the ebb.

Leaving them, he had gone some distance, when he heard shots fired, and, looking round, saw them both surrounded by Zulus. Of their actual end no living man has ever borne witness, but when the search party under Major Black discovered the bodies of these brave men,[1] a ring of dead Zulus around them bore silent testimony that they had sold their lives dearly and had fought it out to the last.

The Queen, whose colour these officers had died to save, was quick to recognize such heroic bravery, and sent two wreaths[1] to be placed on the arms of the cross which marks their grave by the Buffalo River, and later presented to the 24th Regiment a silver wreath to be hung on the colour pole for ever, upon which were inscribed four names:—Bromhead and Chard, of Rorke's Drift, and Melvill and Coghill, of Isandlwana.

---

[1] In Appendix No. VI will be found—

Account from Colonel Glyn of the finding of the bodies and also the recovery of the colour from the bed of the river.

Letter to the Queen from the Empress Eugenie, who placed the wreaths on their grave.

Letter to Sir J. Coghill, Bart., from General Dillon, stating the admiration of the Army for his son and Melvill's heroic bravery.

History of the Victoria Cross

SAMUEL WASSALL
(PRIVATE)
80TH REGIMENT

Photo by CHANCELLOR, *Dublin.*

WITH the exception of Lieutenants Melvill and Coghill and Private Griffiths (who was killed), this is the only man on the Victoria Cross list who was present at the terrible disaster of Isandlwana, January 22, 1879. When the camp was sacked and nearly every man massacred, there were a few fugitives who succeeded in reaching the Buffalo River, six miles away. Wassall had just commenced to ford the river when he saw one of his comrades, Private Westwood, being carried down the stream, almost certain to be drowned. Though the Zulus were close behind him, without hesitation he sprang from his horse, which he tied up *to the Zulu bank* of the river, swam out to the man's assistance and brought him back to the shore. Then, again mounting his horse, he urged the animal across the river, dragging the exhausted man by the hand, and succeeded in getting him safely to the opposite side, in spite of a brisk fire kept up on him by the enemy, who had by then arrived at the river.

THE DEFENCE OF RORKE'S DRIFT (ZULU WAR)

January 22—23, 1879

JOHN ROUSE MERRIOTT CHARD
  LIEUTENANT, ROYAL ENGINEERS

GONVILL S. BROMHEAD,
  LIEUTENANT, 2ND BATT. 24TH REGIMENT

JOHN WILLIAMS	PRIVATE	
HENRY HOOK	PRIVATE	
WILLIAM JONES	PRIVATE	2ND BATT. 24TH REGIMENT.
ROBERT JONES	PRIVATE	
WILLIAM ALLEN	CORPORAL	
FREDERICK HITCH	PRIVATE	

JAMES HENRY REYNOLDS,
  SURGEON-MAJOR, ARMY MEDICAL DEPARTMENT

JAMES LANGLEY DALTON
  ACTING ASSISTANT, COMMISSARIAT AND TRANSPORT DEPARTMENT.

F. C. SCHIESS
  CORPORAL, NATAL NATIVE CONTINGENT.

THE Zulu War of 1879 is full of individual acts of heroism and devotion, and of situations of the gravest peril; yet, from among so much that is splendid in the behaviour of our troops against the fearful odds they had to face in that fierce conflict, the famous defence of Rorke's Drift stands out as one of the finest examples of discipline and valour ever recorded to the credit of British soldiers. Coming, as it did, within a few hours of one of the most terrible disasters which has ever befallen a British force—that of the battle of Isandlwana, which was followed shortly after by the reverses sustained at Intombi and

History of the Victoria Cross

Inhlobane—the heart of the nation went out in admiration and gratitude to the little band of about a hundred men which held Rorke's Drift against 4,000 Zulus, whose natural ferocity and reckless disregard of death was rendered more dangerous by the confidence of recent victory.

On the morning of January 22, orders had come to Colonel Durnford to move up with all his command from Rorke's Drift to the camp at Isandlwana. Thus the Post was denuded of troops, a fact which is the more astonishing in view of its tactical importance as a point on the direct route from Zululand into Natal. The position was further left without any preparation for its defence, although it constituted a base for supplies, and an enormous quantity of provisions and commissariat was collected and kept there. The Post was a mission station, and consisted of two buildings standing about thirty yards apart, the walls being constructed of sun-dried clay bricks, and the roofs of thatch. The Mission House was, at the time, used as a hospital, and contained a number of wounded and convalescent soldiers. The fate of Colonel Durnford and his men at Isandlwana is well known. After the massacre and complete annihilation of the force, the Zulus advanced towards Rorke's Drift with the intention of overwhelming the small guard which occupied it, and then a successful attack upon the garrison at Helpmakaar, fourteen miles distant, would have left them free to overrun and devastate the Colony of Natal.

About 3.30 p.m. Lieutenant Chard, R.E., the officer in command of the Post, was on duty at the river superintending work on the pontoons, when he saw, in the distance, two horsemen riding hard for the Drift. On reaching the bank they shouted to be taken across. They were Lieutenant Adendorff of the Natal Native Contingent, and a trooper, and were survivors of Durnford's force. They informed him of the disaster at Isandlwana, and warned him that the enemy were advancing on Rorke's Drift. The trooper then rode on to warn the garrison at Helpmakaar, while Lieutenant Adendorff remained and subsequently assisted in the defence. Lieutenant Chard was at once preparing to return, when he received a message from Lieutenant Bromhead, who was in command of the Company of the 24th Regiment at the Post, asking him to return there immediately, which he proceeded to do after mooring the pontoons in mid stream. Lieutenant Bromhead had also received warning of their peril from Captain Gardner, 14th Hussars, with orders to defend the Post at any cost. Immediately the message was received, defences were erected, as far as was possible, in the time and with the materials at their disposal.

It was decided to form a laager, by connecting the two small buildings

The Defence of Rorke's Drift

with barricades, so that a square or oblong enclosure would be formed on two sides by the barricades, and at the ends by the walls of the two buildings, which faced each other. The barricades, to a height of four feet, were hastily constructed with bags of mealies and biscuit boxes. The buildings were loopholed, their interiors constituting, in a sense, two separate extensions of the central laager. A number of natives at the station deserted in a panic at the approach of danger, and this handicapped the construction of the defences in the loss of so much labour. Further, the garrison were thereby reduced to about eighty men, slightly reinforced by a few of the patients in the hospital who turned out to give what help they could. While the defences were hurriedly being constructed—Mr. Dalton's energies being particularly noticed by Lieutenant Chard in his report—it occurred to the officers that they would necessitate dispositions too extended for the effective handling of the small force at their command, and therefore the laager was divided into half by a transverse barricade of biscuit boxes. The foresight which resulted in the construction of this extra defence ultimately proved the salvation of the little force from certain annihilation. So swiftly did the attack follow the warning received by the garrison, that only half an hour elapsed between the appearance of the fugitive horsemen at the drift, and the actual appearance of the enemy. Consequently, the garrison had not time to complete the laager before they were compelled to defend it for their lives. About thirteen feet of the barricade connecting the two buildings remained unfinished on one side, and it was at this point that the fiercest fighting throughout the attack took place, preceding the retirement of the defenders into the completely finished half of the laager. Unfortunately for the defenders, cover for the attack, afforded by the trees of the mission orchard, ran right up to this gap in the barricade. It was about 4 p.m. when the first of the enemy came in sight. Private Hitch, of the 24th Regiment, posted as a look-out on the roof of the hospital, saw a Zulu on the crest of the hill and fired at him. This was the first shot of the action of Rorke's Drift.

The laager was situated at a short distance from a small kopje which rose above the mission buildings. On the other three sides stretched the bare undulating veldt which hid the river and was devoid of all cover beyond the hollows between rise and ridge. Near the laager, however, on the side of the kopje, a number of ovens afforded cover, while the orchard, already mentioned, also afforded advanced cover for the attack in the trees which grew right up to the gap in the barricade. No sooner had Private Hitch fired, than the Zulus emerged from the cover of the kopje. They extended swiftly and silently in the horn-shaped formation of Zulu attack, and, constantly preserving the direction of this curve, extended, under cover of the hollows of the veldt, until they completely encircled the little laager with its desperate defenders. Then, with a yell, the circle closed in a combined attack upon the laager. The enemy advanced, firing, and attempted to carry the barricade with the rush of a sudden assault. As has already been stated, the weak point in the defences was the incompleted portion of the barricade. Here the fiercest fighting took place through the desperate hours of succeeding attacks. It was a hand-to-hand conflict. The Zulus burst through the orchard trees till within a few yards of the gap, and hurled themselves repeatedly upon the men who held this point. And it was the bayonet work which held the gap.

Mr. Dalton's conduct at this point was exceptionally fine. He directed the fire of the men, and by his own unerring aim during the Zulu rush, and his courageous behaviour when they closed on the bayonet, contributed very considerably towards the repulse. The general nature of the attack, throughout, was a succession of desperate attempts to force and climb over the barricades, and the strain upon the defenders can be imagined under the stress of the circumstances in which they were placed. For twelve long hours, without cessation, this magnificent defence continued. The heroic bravery of the two young officers in command stimulated their men in the continual repulse of rush after rush of the fearless enemy. Lieutenant Chard, standing in the centre of the laager, directed men from one point to another, as he saw that any particular part of the barricade required extra assistance. Lieutenant Bromhead bayonetted Zulu after Zulu, and, throughout the action, led his men where the attack was fiercest. But a much more serious and terrible defect in the defence, due under the circumstances to, perhaps, a venial want of foresight rather than to want of time, became apparent when the attack developed. It has already been stated, that the two mission buildings constituted extensions of the laager formed in the square by barricades connecting the two. Therefore, each of these buildings was truly outside the laager altogether. Moreover the doors of the mission house—used as a hospital—were so arranged that the inmates could only gain exit in the face of the enemy's attack, when they would find themselves outside the barricades of the laager. With the exception of a tiny window in the wall opening into the laager, no communication could possibly be made between those in the hospital and their comrades. This window, moreover, could not be reached from any of the rooms, as, with one exception, there was no interior communication from one to another of the several rooms, which all opened outwards towards the enemy. Now the terrible situation of the sick and helpless men in this building

The Defence of Rorke's Drift

when the attack developed, can be fully realized. On three sides of them surged their fierce relentless enemy; yet escape from room to room was impossible, and the wall not only barred them from refuge into the laager, but shut them effectually from the succour of their comrades. Private John Williams was posted with Privates Joseph Williams and Horrigan in one of these isolated rooms, having three patients under their care. For upwards of an hour, they held the door against the Zulus, John Williams working to cut a hole in the partition to enable him to get his patients through to safety. At last the Zulus forced the door, and dragged out Joseph Williams and Horrigan, and killed them, together with one of the patients; but John Williams contrived to get the other two through the wall and joined Henry Hook, who was in a room farthest from the laager, with six wounded men under his care. These two men rescued every one of their charges by the exercise of splendid valour and devotion. The doors of the hospital were blocked up with mealie-bags, and the attack upon both doors and windows was defended by Hook and Williams, for some time, by rifle-fire through loopholes, which the former had made with a pick-axe in the wall of the building. But at last the door was carried, and the Zulus attempted to rush into the room. While Hook held the door single-handed against the enemy, Williams moved the patients out of this room into the next one nearer the laager.[1] Hook retreated last, carrying in his arms one of the patients whose leg was broken. The enemy rushed the room, and again Hook held the inner door, while Williams, with the pickaxe, attacked the partition wall of clay bricks to make an aperture large enough to enable them to continue their escape. Happily the door of this room, which opened outwards, resisted the attacks of the enemy to batter it in, so that Hook's attention was concentrated in the defence of the inner door by which they had entered. By now the roof of the building was in flames. The Zulus, tying lighted material to assagais, had flung them on to the thatch, which caught readily, and the interior soon became filled with smoke, in the choking fumes of which this desperate conflict continued. When, at last, Williams had succeeded in breaking through the wall, the party retreated into another room still nearer the laager, while Hook again retreated last with his disabled comrade in his arms, only to turn again and defend this aperture against the rush of their pursuers, while Williams once more attacked the wall leading into the last room that now divided them from refuge in the laager. The retreat into this room was successfully accomplished. They were now in the room nearest to the laager, but their only means of exit was through the small window to which reference has already been made. This window, too small to allow a man to

---

[1] This was the only room having communication with the next by a door.

pass through, much less to drag wounded men through it, had to be enlarged by Williams with the pickaxe. Hook defended the aperture till all had passed through with safety while the Zulus stabbed at him through blinding and almost suffocating smoke. When the window was enlarged, Williams lifted the patients through into the laager. Then he himself followed, pulling Hook after him, just in time to evade a final rush of the Zulus.

The fact that the enemy were now in possession of a building actually commanding the laager, would have proved a matter of extreme peril for its defenders, had not a greater part of the blazing roof fallen in with a crash upon its inmates, very shortly after its evacuation by the British. Many of the Zulus perished in the blazing ruins of the roof, their charred and roasted bodies being subsequently discovered. Meanwhile an equally heroic action had been enacted in another part of the hospital by William and Robert Jones. Seven patients were under their care, and these two men defended them to the last, succeeding in saving six of them. The seventh, Sergeant Maxwell, was delirious, and when his brave comrades had dressed him he refused to be moved. After saving the other six, Robert Jones returned to save him by force, but found the Zulus had stabbed him as he lay on the bed. William Allen and Frederick Hitch kept the open space between the hospital window and the inner defence clear, enabling the patients to be brought safely across from the burning building. Under a raking fire they held their post against terrible odds, and both received severe wounds, but persevered in their heroic duty. Later on, when so badly wounded as to be almost incapacitated, they braved the bullets and rain of spears showered all around them, and carried ammunition to their comrades during some hours of the defence. Amid the hail of missiles which beat upon the gallant defenders of the barricades there was one heroic figure moving from point to point, taking no active part in the defence, and with no excitement of battle to sustain him. It was Surgeon-Major James Henry Reynolds, who worked calmly and devotedly, ministering help to those struck down. During those long hours of desperate battle he earned his Cross repeatedly, and when not actually attending to the wounded, busied himself in carrying ammunition to those at the barricade. His example of cool bravery was the admiration of all. Another brave man among many was Corporal Schiess, of the Natal Native Contingent. He noticed that one Zulu in particular was doing great damage from behind an ant hill, crept along the barricade far out, and under fire, and after a short time was able to shoot this Zulu marksman. Before he returned he disposed of two others in a similar way. Three times he leapt on to the top of the wall of sacks, stabbed a Zulu and

The Defence of Rorke's Drift

sprang back, in spite of the fact that he had just come out of hospital when the attack commenced, having been previously severely wounded in the foot.

The garrison had now been forced to retreat behind the inner line of defence into the half of the laager against the opposite mission building, and a breach made in the barricade of this half, to render possible the retreat of the garrison with the sick, had to be desperately defended throughout the remainder of the attack. Night had now fallen. The Zulus upon all sides continued, with unabated fury, their combined attack upon the remaining portion of the laager. The blazing roof of the hospital threw a lurid glare upon the scene, and showers of burning sparks fell in a fierce rain upon the conflict and confusion beneath, while high into the air rose a great volume of smoke, flaming with the reflection of the fire underneath, and shone in the night, visible from far in the surrounding country. It was this glare that attracted the attention of Lord Chelmsford and his force, telling them of the attack upon Rorke's Drift, and filling them with apprehension for the fate of their comrades of the garrison.

To the last this terrible conflict remained a hand-to-hand struggle against odds. The Zulus swarmed into the space between the inner barricade of the hospital, and attempted, by force of numbers, again and again to overwhelm the garrison. But, hard pressed as they were, their daring spirit remained undiminished; after hours of hopeless battle, men were found to follow Hook, in a charge through the mass of their foes, to bring in the water-carts, abandoned in the retreat, the necessity for which was absolute, to mitigate the suffering of the sick and wounded men within the laager. This brave act was successfully accomplished without any loss to this sortie of a forlorn hope.

Until 4 o'clock in the morning the fighting continued. Then, after some desultory firing, the enemy withdrew over the hill. Fearing a fresh attack, the position was strengthened, the weapons of the dead Zulus were collected, and a message was sent to Helpmakaar for reinforcements. About 6 a.m. another large body of Zulus appeared in sight, but shortly afterwards Lord Chelmsford's column was sighted coming towards the Post. The heroic little garrison was relieved. The total number present during the defence was eight officers, ninety-six non-commissioned officers and men, and thirty-five non-commissioned officers and men sick. Their losses were fifteen killed and two died of wounds received. The official number of Zulus killed is given as 350, this being the number found around the defences, but many more were afterwards found some distance from the Post, bringing the number up to 600.

History of the Victoria Cross

JOHN ROUSE MERRIOTT CHARD
(LIEUTENANT, AFTERWARDS COLONEL)
ROYAL ENGINEERS

Photo by HAWKE, *Plymouth.*

This officer was in command of the Rorke's Drift Post on January 22, 1879, when, with about a hundred men, mostly of the 24th Regiment, the position was attacked by 4,000 Zulus. Throughout the entire defence, which lasted from 4 p.m. till daybreak next morning, Colonel Chard directed the operations with the most heroic bravery. The Lieut.-General in command of the troops reported that "had it not been for the fine example and excellent behaviour of these two officers[1] under the most trying circumstances, the Defence of Rorke's Drift Post would not have been conducted with that intelligence and tenacity which so essentially characterized it"; also "that its success must, in a great degree, be attributable to the two young officers who exercised the chief command on the occasion in question."

The Defence of Rorke's Drift will go down to posterity as one of the finest examples of British heroism, and the names of Chard and Bromhead will hold a prominent position in the annals of the British Army. The late Queen Victoria caused their names to be inscribed on the colour pole of the 24th Regiment, together with those of Lieutenants Melvill and Coghill, who fell so heroically on the banks of the Buffalo River on the same day, while endeavouring to save the colours of the regiment from the enemy after the Massacre of Isandlwana.

Colonel Chard, son of Mr. W. W. Chard, of Pathe, Somerset, and Mount Tamar, Devon, was born in 1847. Educated at Plymouth New Grammar School, Cheltenham, and Woolwich, he entered the Royal Engineers in 1868. He was stationed at Bermuda for some time, ultimately going to South Africa on the outbreak of the Zulu War. After the Defence of the Drift, for which, in addition to the Victoria Cross, he was promoted Captain and Brevet-Major, he became ill of fever, and went to Ladysmith to recruit his health, but recovered sufficiently to take part in the battle of Ulundi. Towards the end of 1879 he was ordered home, and on his arrival at Plymouth was met by a tele-

---
[1] Lieutenants Chard and Bromhead.

The Zulu War

gram from the late Queen and received by her at Balmoral. He retired from the service in August, 1897, and died at Hatch Beauchamp Rectory, near Taunton, Somerset, on November 1, 1897.

GONVILLE S. BROMHEAD
(LIEUTENANT, AFTERWARDS MAJOR)

24TH REGIMENT

Photo by ELLIOTT & FRY.

IN the Defence of Rorke's Drift Post, on January 22, 1879, Lieutenant Bromhead was associated with Lieutenant Chard, and the eulogistic remarks made by the Lieut.-General in Command on that officer, were made to apply equally to him. By his splendid example of courageous bearing he inspired his men in the magnificent defence of the barricade, where, with rifle and bayonet, he assisted to repel the terrific and continuous attacks made for hours by the Zulus.

His name, together with those of Chard, Melvill, and Coghill, are inscribed upon the colour pole of the 24th Regiment, and will go down to posterity associated ever with one of the grandest achievements of British arms. In addition to being awarded the Victoria Cross, he was promoted Captain and Brevet-Major.

Was the son of Sir Gonville Bromhead, Bart., and died in Lucknow, India, on February 10, 1891.

JAMES HENRY REYNOLDS
(SURGEON-MAJOR, NOW LIEUT.-COLONEL)

ARMY MEDICAL DEPARTMENT

ON January 22, 1879, during the Defence of Rorke's Drift, Lieut.-Colonel Reynolds behaved with conspicuous bravery, attending to the wounded under a heavy cross-fire from the Zulus on the hills above the Post, and a continual shower of assagais from those attacking the barricades. When not actually engaged in his humane task, he carried ammunition to the men from the magazine.

History of the Victoria Cross

Photo by LAMBERT, WESTON & SON, *Folkestone.*

Son of Mr. L. Reynolds, J.P., of Dalyston House, Granard, Ireland, Colonel Reynolds was born at Kingstown, Dublin, on February 3, 1844. Educated at Castle Knock and Trinity College, Dublin, he entered the Medical Staff Corps as Assistant-Surgeon, March 31, 1868, becoming Surgeon March 1st, 1873; Surgeon-Major (for distinguished field service), January 23, 1879; Lieut.-Colonel, April 1, 1887; and attained substantive step (Brigade-Surgeon Lieut.-Colonel) December 25, 1892, retiring in 1896. Served in the Kaffir War of 1877-8, and in Zulu War; besides Rorke's Drift, was present at the battle of Ulundi. Possesses the South African Medal with three dates—1877-8-9—being equivalent to three clasps, and also the Gold Medal of the British Medical Association for his services at Rorke's Drift. During his second year's service received the approbation of the Commander-in-Chief (Lord Sandhurst), for services rendered during a severe outbreak of cholera in India in the 36th Regiment. Colonel Reynolds is now (although on retired list) in Medical Charge of the Royal Army Clothing Factory, London.

JAMES LANGLEY DALTON

(ACTING ASSISTANT)

COMMISSARIAT AND TRANSPORT DEPARTMENT
(AFTERWARDS COMMISSARIAT STAFF CORPS)

Photo by DEBENHAM, *Southsea.*

THE successful defence of Rorke's Drift on January 22, 1879, was in a great measure due to this officer, who, on hearing the news that the Zulus were marching on the Post, devoted his energies and resource to the construction of the barricades. He was at the corner of the hospital when the first onslaught was made by the dense mass of Zulus, and his unerring aim and cool courage did much to contribute to the repulse of, and heavy loss inflicted on, the enemy at that point. One

The Zulu War

Zulu had sprung on to the barricade, and, having seized the rifle of one of the defenders, was about to assagai him, when Dalton rushed forward and saved the man's life by shooting the Zulu. During the Defence he was very severely wounded, but continued at his post until the Zulus retired. In spite of the invaluable work done by Dalton, the War Office ignored his merits, and it was not until many months after — in November, 1879 — that they were awakened to the fact that his bravery had been overlooked, and he would have been left unrewarded had not the facts been laid before Parliament, and pressure of public opinion been brought to bear in his favour.

Dalton had been a Sergeant-Major in the British Army before the war. He died at Portsmouth in April, 1887.

WILLIAM ALLEN

(CORPORAL, AFTERWARDS SERGEANT-INSTRUCTOR OF MUSKETRY)

24TH REGIMENT

To this man's undaunted bravery at the Defence of Rorke's Drift, January 22, 1879, when, with Frederick Hitch, he held a most dangerous and difficult position, the removal of the wounded and sick patients from the burning hospital across to the Inner Defence was able to be accomplished. Severely wounded, he still held his post, raked by a heavy fire from the Zulus on the adjacent hill. When the wounded had been removed and his post was no longer tenable, he served out ammunition to the holders of the barricade.

Unfortunately this brave man is no longer on the List, having died some few years ago.

FREDERICK HITCH

(PRIVATE)

2ND BATT. 24TH REGIMENT

On January 22, 1879, at the Defence of Rorke's Drift, Hitch was associated

History of the Victoria Cross

Photo by COLLIER, *Birmingham.*

with William Allen (V.C.) in a most courageous defence of a dangerous and important position. By their steady fire the two men held open the communication between the Hospital and the Inner Defence, enabling the wounded to be carried across, when the Zulus had set light to the thatched building. He was very badly hit by a roughly-made Zulu bullet, which inflicted a fearful gash in his shoulder, no less than thirty-six pieces of bone being taken away afterwards from the wound. He was presented with the Cross by Queen Victoria at Netley Hospital on his return in the summer of 1879.

Born at Southgate in Middlesex, November 28, 1856. Previous to the Zulu War, he had served through the Kaffir War of 1877–8, and since leaving the Army has held various positions of responsibility, chief among them that of one of the " Right of the Line " Corps of Commissionaires, stationed at the Imperial Institute, and also at the United Service Institute, Whitehall. Hitch, though his arm has lost a great deal of its former power, may now often be seen in London, driving his smart cab, with which (possessing two horses of his own) he makes a comfortable living.

HENRY HOOK

(PRIVATE)

24TH REGIMENT

Photo by CHAFFIN, *Taunton.*

THE heroic conduct of Private Henry Hook on January 22, 1879, and his superhuman efforts in saving the wounded from the burning hospital will be found fully related in the account of the Defence of Rorke's Drift Post.

He was born at Churcham, Gloucestershire, and served for five years in the Monmouthshire Militia before joining the 24th Regiment. Served through the Kaffir War, 1877–8, and for his bravery at Rorke's Drift was presented with the Victoria Cross by Lord Wolseley on August

The Zulu War

3, 1879. Has served in the Volunteers, and at present is Sergeant in the 1st Volunteer Battalion Royal Fusiliers, and one of the staff at the British Museum.

ROBERT JONES
(PRIVATE)

2ND BATT. 24TH REGIMENT

DECORATED for conspicuous bravery and devotion to the wounded at Rorke's Drift, January 22, 1879. Privates Robert and William Jones, posted in a room of the Hospital facing the hill, kept up a steady fire against enormous odds, and while one worked to cut a hole through the partition into the next room, the other shot Zulu after Zulu through the loopholed walls, using his own and his comrade's rifle alternately when the barrels became too hot to hold owing to the incessant firing. By their united heroic efforts six out of seven patients were saved by being carried through the broken partition. The seventh, Sergeant Maxwell, being delirious, refused to be helped, and on Robert Jones returning to take him by force he found him being stabbed by the Zulus on his bed.

Robert Jones died in London only a few years ago.

WILLIAM JONES
(PRIVATE)

2ND BATT. 24TH REGIMENT

To the heroic efforts of this man and his namesake Robert Jones, six out of seven patients were saved from the burning Hospital at Rorke's Drift on January 22, 1879. The fate of the seventh, together with the courageous defence of both these men, in a room of the building, against tremendous odds, is described in the record of Robert Jones.

History of the Victoria Cross

F. C. SCHIESS
(CORPORAL)
NATAL NATIVE CONTINGENT

THE heroic share of Corporal Schiess in the splendid Defence of Rorke's Drift was only tardily recognized by the authorities, and the same pressure was brought to bear upon them as was necessary in the case of James Dalton (V.C.), before his undoubted merits were rewarded. By birth a Swede, he was one of the wounded in the Hospital when the news was brought that the Zulus were marching on the Drift, and in spite of a severe and painful injury to his foot, he came from his bed and took part in the heroic defence. His conduct at the barricades was brave to a degree. On one occasion he leapt on to the wall of mealie-bags, stabbed a Zulu, and sprang down again, repeating the performance three times in succession.

JOHN WILLIAMS
(PRIVATE)
2ND BATT. 24TH REGIMENT

AT the defence of Rorke's Drift, January 22, 1879, John Williams was posted with two other men in a distant room of the Hospital, and by his heroic bravery and devotion was the means of saving the lives of two patients. When the Zulus had fired the Hospital, he broke a way through the partition and succeeded in getting them through into the next room. His courageous conduct, when afterwards associated with Private Hook (V.C.), is detailed in the chapter on the Defence of Rorke's Drift.

ANTHONY BOOTH
(COLOUR-SERGEANT)
80TH REGIMENT

AFTER the appalling disaster of Isandlwana seven weeks previously, it was inconceivable that any body of our men should have formed a laager

The Zulu War

at any place in Zululand without adequate precaution against surprise. Yet such actually happened on March 11 and 12, 1879, when about twenty wagons, carrying provisions for the garrison at Luneberg, were laagered up on the Intombi River, only a solitary sentry being placed on watch during the night, and in spite of the fact that Umbelini, a notoriously evil-disposed Zulu chief, was close at hand in his kraal. Besides the convoy-guard, there was only a company of the 80th Regiment under Captain David B. Moriarty, as a protection, this officer having taken the handful of men out of Luneberg to meet the wagons a day or so earlier. In the middle of the night the sentry was set upon, but contrived to fire a shot and warn the camp. Four thousand Zulus were, however, upon them, and a general massacre ensued. A few survivors on the opposite bank of the Intombi River opened fire, but 200 of the enemy got across. The lieutenant in command of this small party of survivors rode off to Luneberg for assistance, leaving them without any commanding officer, but Booth rallied his men, ten only in number, and showed so bold a front, that, though the enemy followed for three miles, he was able to bring his little party back to Luneberg and even secure the safety of a few more who escaped from the slaughter on the left bank. His resolute valour was the means of saving the lives of any who eventually reached Luneberg, for had he not acted with such presence of mind and conspicuous courage in the face of terrible odds, not one man would have lived to tell the tale.

HENRY LYSONS

(Lieutenant) 2nd Batt. The Cameronians (Scottish Rifles); Now Lieut.-Colonel, 1st Bedfordshire

On March 28, 1879, Sir Evelyn Wood, V.C., in command of the mounted men, taking part in the assault of the Inhlobane Mountain, noticed that much loss was being caused to our men by some Zulus who had taken up a strong position in some caves, from which they commanded the spot where some of our wounded were lying. He therefore ordered their dislodgment.

History of the Victoria Cross

Photo by HEATH, *Plymouth.*

Some delay taking place in carrying it out, Captain the Honourable Ronald Campbell, Coldstream Guards, with Lieutenant Lysons and Private Edmund Fowler, " advanced in a most courageous manner over a mass of fallen boulders and between rocks which led to a cave in which the enemy lay hidden." There being only room for one man to pass at a time, they had to advance in single file, and the first to reach the cave was Captain Campbell. On seeing him the Zulus fired, shooting him dead, upon which Lysons and Fowler sprang forward, and with great gallantry drove them from their stronghold. Afterwards Lysons remained at the cave's mouth while Captain Campbell's body was carried down the hill.

Lieut.-Colonel Lysons, son of the late Sir Daniel Lysons, of Crimean fame, was born at Morden, Surrey, on July 13, 1858. Educated at Wellington, he joined the 90th Light Infantry in 1878, serving through the Zulu War as A.D.C. to Sir Evelyn Wood, V.C., taking part in the affairs of Zungen Nek, and the Inhlobane Mountain, and the battles of Kambula and Ulundi, being twice mentioned in despatches and obtaining medal and clasp. Served through the Soudan War, 1884-5, obtaining medal, clasp and bronze star with Egyptian Army.

Photo by OLDHAM, *Colchester.*

EDMUND FOWLER

(PRIVATE) 90TH PERTHSHIRE VOLUNTEER LIGHT INFANTRY (THE SCOTTISH RIFLES); NOW SERGEANT THE ROYAL IRISH

THIS gallant soldier was associated with Lieutenant (now Lieut.-Colonel) Lysons, in a most courageous act at the Inhlobane Mountain, Zululand, March 28, 1879. Fuller details are given in the record of that officer.

The Zulu War

REDVERS HENRY BULLER, C.B.

(CAPTAIN AND BREVET-LIEUT.-COLONEL, NOW GENERAL, THE RIGHT HONOURABLE, G.C.B., G.C.M.G., P.C.)

60TH RIFLES

Photo by ELLIOTT & FRY.

THE Zulu War of 1879, though successfully carried out in the end, was responsible for terrible loss of life during the short time occupied in forcing the Zulus to submission. The disaster at Isandlwana was terrible enough, that at Intombi followed soon after, and the affair at the Inhlobane Mountain narrowly escaped equalling the first-named in appalling consequences. Hearing that vast herds of cattle were on the top of the Mountain, a raid upon them was arranged, and, on March 28, 500 mounted men set off to bring them down. The ascent of the side approached was so steep, that it was hardly passable for horses, but they succeeded in gaining the summit, and had commenced to drive the herds together, when Sir Redvers Buller saw, about six miles away, a force of 20,000 Zulus advancing upon him. This impi was known to be "on the way" from Ulundi, but it was never imagined that it could compass the distance in so short a time. There was now nothing for our men but a hasty retreat, and down the precipitous paths they had ascended (the easier road on the other side, which they had intended to use being now blocked by the enemy) men and horses struggled, fell, and crowded together. The advanced Zulus promptly fell upon them, assagaied the horses, and speared every man they could reach, and it was during this terrible time that Captain Buller performed the many heroic acts for which he was deservedly awarded the Cross.

Captain D'Arcy, Lieutenant Everitt, and a trooper of the Frontier Light Horse, were all, one after another, rescued by him from the ferocious Zulus, when their horses had been shot or stabbed to death. Rallying his men, he rode, time after time, at the hordes of the infuriated enemy, and by his personal courage, cool behaviour, and undaunted resolution, held them in check and covered the retreat. Captain Thomasson, in his work on the Zulu Campaign, says that Buller is known to have saved six men that day, but it would be impossible to tell how many more owed their lives to his orders and example. Streatfield, another chronicler of that war, says that Buller was "a splendid worker, and never seemed to tire, however great the amount of hard work, and wherever the stiffest amount of work was, he was sure to be found. In action, if you could ascertain for certain where most bullets were flying, you would be pretty safe in betting that Buller would be in the middle of it."

Born December 7, 1839, Sir Redvers Buller is the son of the late James Wentworth Buller. Educated at Eton, he entered the 60th Rifles in 1858, serving in the China War, 1860; Red River Expedition, 1870; Ashanti War, 1874; Kaffir War, 1878; Zulu War, 1879; Boer War, 1881, acting in the latter as Chief of Staff. Was in Intelligence Department during Egyptian War, 1882, taking part in the battles of Kassassin and Tel-el-Kebir, for which he was mentioned in despatches, received the medal and clasp, 3rd class Osmanieh, Khedive's Star, and was created K.C.M.G. Served in Soudan Expedition, 1884, mentioned twice in despatches, and promoted Major-General. Was Chief of Staff in Soudan (Nile), 1884–5, again mentioned in despatches and created K.C.B. Quartermaster-General, 1887; Under-Secretary for Ireland, 1887; Adjutant-General, 1890–7, and in command at Aldershot, 1898–9. On the outbreak of war in South Africa in 1899, commanded the forces at the commencement of the troubles in that country, and, later on, acted as General Officer commanding in Natal, conducting the operations for the relief of Ladysmith, which, with that dogged and resolute way so characteristic of him, he successfully accomplished.

WILLIAM KNOX LEET

(MAJOR, AFTERWARDS MAJOR-GENERAL, C.B.)

1st Batt. 13th Prince Albert's Somersetshire Light Infantry

On March 28, 1879, the fighting on the Inhlobane Mountain, under Sir Evelyn Wood, was so severe that a retirement was deemed advisable. During the retreat the Zulus continuously harassed our men. The 13th Light Infantry formed part of the small force. Towards evening Lieutenant A. M. Smith, Frontier Light Horse, had his horse shot from under him, and, being closely pursued by the enemy, was on the point of being speared, when Major Leet, galloping to his rescue, took him up behind him, riding with him

The Zulu War

Photo by LAFAYETTE, *Dublin.*

under rifle-fire and a shower of assagais to a place of safety.

During the Indian Mutiny General Leet served with marked distinction, both with his battalion under Lord Mark Kerr, and as a Staff Officer to several columns towards the end of the campaign, being twice mentioned in general orders. Served in South Africa, 1878, against Sekukuni, and also in the Expedition to Mandalay, 1886–7, in both latter campaigns being mentioned in despatches. Was in 1887 created a Companion of the Bath, and died on June 29, 1898, aged 65. (Born November 3, 1833.)

EDWARD STEVENSON BROWNE

(LIEUTENANT, NOW BRIGADIER-GENERAL, C.B.)

1ST BATT. 24TH REGIMENT

DECORATED for his bravery at Inhlobane Mountain, in Zululand, March 29, 1879, when, during the disastrous retreat of our force, he twice rode back towards the pursuing Zulus and assisted an unmounted man to escape.

Brigadier-General Browne entered the Army in 1871, and since 1902, has commanded the 5th Army Corps at York.

Photo by DOWNEY, *London*

LORD WILLIAM LESLIE DE LA POER BERESFORD

(CAPTAIN, AFTERWARDS COLONEL, K.C.I.E.)

9TH (QUEEN'S ROYAL) LANCERS

PREVIOUS to the battle of Ulundi, which broke the Zulu power and brought that sanguinary war to a close, a reconnaissance was made across the White Umvolosi River on July 3, 1879. The cavalry having pushed

History of the Victoria Cross

Photo by MAULL & FOX.

far out towards Ulundi, thousands of Zulus, hidden up to that moment in deep hollows, opened a brisk fire on our men. The " retire " was sounded, and at that instant Sergeant Fitzmaurice, of the 24th, was thrown from his horse, severely injured and partially stunned, and, the Zulus being now only a few yards away, his fate seemed sealed. Lord William Beresford then rode back, cut his way to the man, took him up on his horse and brought him away safely. This task was rendered all the more dangerous and difficult owing to the fact that Fitzmaurice twice nearly pulled him off the saddle, but Sergeant O'Toole rendered valuable assistance by helping to keep the man on the horse, at the same time checking the advance of the nearest Zulus with his carbine. O'Toole was deservedly awarded the Victoria Cross also, thanks to Lord William speaking on his behalf, for when commanded to Windsor to receive the decoration, he told Her late Majesty that he could not in honour receive the recognition of his services unless it were shared in by Sergeant O'Toole, who, he generously affirmed, deserved infinitely greater credit than any which might attach to himself, and the next *Gazette* announced O'Toole's reward.

Colonel Lord William Leslie de la Poer Beresford, third son of the Rev. John de la Poer, fourth Marquess of Waterford, was born on July 20, 1847. Educated at Eton, he entered the 9th Lancers in 1867 as Cornet, obtained his commission as Lieutenant in 1870, and his Captaincy in 1876. Was an A.D.C. to Lord Lytton, Viceroy of India, from the end of 1875 to October, 1881. Served through the Jowaki Expedition, 1877–8, this being his first active service. Besides the Zulu War, he served with the gallant Lancers in the Afghan War, being present at the capture of Ali Musjid, and from 1881 to 1894 was Military Secretary to the successive Viceroys of India, Lords Dufferin and Lansdowne. Became Major in 1884, and served with the Burmese Expedition, being mentioned in despatches and receiving Brevet of Lieut.-Colonel. Became Colonel in January, 1891. Died December 28, 1900.

The Zulu War

EDMUND O'TOOLE
(SERGEANT)
FRONTIER LIGHT HORSE

IN the Zulu War of 1879, a reconnaissance was made, prior to the battle of Ulundi, on July 3, 1879. When ordered to retire, vast hordes of Zulus advancing towards the mounted men, Sergeant Fitzmaurice was injured by his horse falling and rolling on him. Lord William Beresford rode back and took him up in front of him, but the enemy were now only a short distance from them and O'Toole kept them in check, shooting many with his carbine. Fitzmaurice, however, was so stunned by his fall that he could not keep upon the horse, and nearly dismounted Lord William, upon which O'Toole threw away his carbine and together they were able to rescue him. (See also account of Lord William Beresford.)

CECIL D'ARCY
(CAPTAIN)
FRONTIER LIGHT HORSE

ON July 3, 1879, during the reconnaissance before Ulundi by the Mounted Corps, Trooper Raubenheim, of the Frontier Light Horse, fell from the saddle as the rest were retiring. Notwithstanding the proximity of the Zulus, who were rushing towards them, Captain D'Arcy waited until his companion had mounted behind him and then proceeded to ride away, but the horse kicked both men off. Raubenheim was stunned, so D'Arcy tried to lift the man into the saddle again, heroically making several attempts, though the Zulus were getting nearer and nearer; but at last, finding he was powerless to do so, he was obliged to leave him. It was a miraculous escape for Captain D'Arcy as, when he started to save himself, the Zulus had actually closed upon him.

Captain D'Arcy's life was saved by Sir Redvers Buller, V.C., during the Zulu War.

THE BASUTO WAR
and
OPERATIONS AGAINST SEKUKUNI
1879 and 1881

PETER BROWN
(TROOPER)
CAPE MOUNTED RIFLES

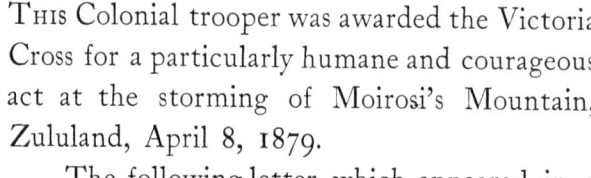

THIS Colonial trooper was awarded the Victoria Cross for a particularly humane and courageous act at the storming of Moirosi's Mountain, Zululand, April 8, 1879.

The following letter, which appeared in a Cape newspaper, gives the details of his heroic act and the subsequent disposal of the Victoria Cross he so well deserved. The second paragraph appeared in the *Cape Argus* of August, 1895, but the first bore no name or date when it came into the author's hands, though probably it issued from the same source—

I

" It may interest you to hear how Peter Brown won his Victoria Cross. Everybody who knows the circumstances under which he got it believes that no man ever deserved the decoration better than he did, if as well. He was a rough, ignorant, but excessively manly and kind-hearted man ; exactly the sort of man so well described by the late Sir Hastings Doyle in his well-known poem, 'The Private of the Buffs.' I am certain that Brown did not know of the existence of such a decoration as the Victoria Cross when he performed the signal act of valour that got it for him, and this, of course, made his conduct all the more admirable. He was one of the advanced party of stormers in the assault made on Moirosi's Mountain stronghold, on the 8th of April, 1879. In rushing up to the assault, several men (officers, non-commissioned officers and privates) fell, killed and wounded. Three wounded men crept to the shelter of a small rock that lay in the middle of a perfectly open space, not twenty yards from the lower tier of *schanzen*. The stormers had passed on to the left of this open space, and were trying to scale defences on the flank of the position, when these three men began to cry piteously for water.

"It appeared to be certain death to go to them, as the open space, where this sheltering stone lay, was completely swept by the fire of all the *schanzen* on that part of the mountain. Their screams, however, became quite heart-rending, and after a minute or two Brown said with an oath, 'I can't stand this any longer; has any one any water?' He was handed a tin canteen half full of water, and he coolly walked across the open space, knelt down beside the rock, and, without making the slightest attempt to shelter himself, began to pour water into the mouth of one of the wounded men; while doing this a bullet broke his arm; he quietly picked up the canteen and went on pouring the water into the man's mouth with his other hand, and almost immediately a second bullet struck him in the leg, and he fell over amongst the men to whose help he had gone.

"It is impossible to imagine an act of more deliberate self-sacrifice, coupled with absolutely dauntless bravery, than that performed by Peter Brown.

"(Signed) J. M. GRANT,
"Lieut.-Colonel Commanding C.M.R."

II

From the *Argus* (Cape), August, 1895—

"At a recent Parade sale, Trooper Brown's Victoria Cross, together with the '77, '78, '79 war medal and clasp, were put up to auction, and knocked down to a bidder at twenty-five shillings. Twenty-five shillings was the exact price of the rarest distinction that can be conferred on a Briton for doing his duty on the field of battle. The purchaser, a captain in the Cape Town Highlanders, who says he would give his own right hand for such a distinction, purposes presenting the Cross and medal to the Commanding Officer of the C.M.R., and in so doing he is taking the only right and proper course. The little story is its own moral, and we leave our readers to follow out the reflections which it may awaken. Of one thing we may be certain—that the dead trooper's Cross and medal will not again come beneath the hammer of the auctioneer. The Commanding Officer of the C.M.R. will see to that."

ROBERT GEORGE SCOTT

(SERGEANT, NOW LIEUT.-COLONEL)

Cape Mounted Rifles

Photo by MIDDLEBROOK, *Kimberley.*

DECORATED for a particularly fine act of courage and devotion on April 8, 1879, during an attack on Moirosi's Mountain. The enemy were concentrating a very severe fire upon our men from behind a line of stone barricades, and it was impossible for the Colonials to reply in any effective manner. Seeing the serious state of affairs, Robert George Scott, then a Sergeant in the Colonial Corps, volunteered to creep up to the enemy's defences and fling time-fuse shells into their midst. He, first, caused all his men to retire under cover, lest any shell should burst prematurely—by which precaution he probably saved many of their lives—and then, under a hail of lead, deliberately advanced under the enemy's defences, and twice attempted to throw the shells over. The second time, owing to some defect in the fuse which he had lighted, the shell burst almost in his hands, blowing the right one to pieces, and severely wounding him in the left leg.

During the Boer War, 1899–1902, he served with the Kimberley Light Horse.

EDMUND BARON HARTLEY

(SURGEON-MAJOR, NOW COLONEL, C.M.G.)

Cape Mounted Rifles

DECORATED for his great bravery in attending the wounded during the unsuccessful attack on Moirosi's Mountain, Basutoland, June 5, 1879. Corporal A. Jones fell, severely wounded, and, in spite of the very heavy fire from the enemy, Surgeon-Major Hartley crossed the open ground and carried the wounded man to shelter. Having done this, he continued ministering

The Basuto War

Photo by WALERY, London.

to the other injured among the storming party, exposing himself freely and fearlessly during his devoted duties.

Colonel Edmund Baron Hartley (C.M.G. 1900) has been Principal Medical Officer, Cape Colonial Forces, since 1878. Son of Dr. Edmund Hartley. Was born on May 6, 1847, at Ivy Bridge, Devon, receiving his medical education at St. George's Hospital, London. M.R.C.S. England; L.R.C.P. Edinburgh. From 1867 to 1869 was a clerk in H.M. Inland Revenue; 1874-7 was District Surgeon in Basutoland, joining, in the latter year, the Colonial Forces, with which he served during the next four years in the Galeka, Gaika, Moirosi, Tembu and Basuto Campaigns. He next saw active service in 1897, in Bechuanaland, where he was wounded; and later, in 1900, in South Africa, against the Boers. For his services he was created C.M.G.

FRANCIS FITZPATRICK

(PRIVATE)

94TH REGIMENT (NOW 2ND BATT. CONNAUGHT RANGERS)

SEKUKUNI'S TOWN was the stronghold of a native chief in South Africa who caused us much trouble to reduce and capture in 1879, long after the Zulu War was ended, and out of which it arose. On November 28, Lieutenant J. C. Dewar, King's Dragoon Guards, fell severely wounded. He was, with the exception of Private Fitzpatrick and Private Flawn (to whom the Victoria Cross was also awarded), practically alone, having under his command only six of the native contingent. These were proceeding to carry him down a steep hill, when suddenly about forty of the enemy, spear in hand, appeared in pursuit, whereupon the wounded officer was dropped and deserted by all but the two Irishmen, one of whom bore him on his back, while the other fired at the oncoming enemy. Alternately, one bearing and the other defending, he was eventually carried off into safety.

THOMAS FLAWN
(PRIVATE)

94TH REGIMENT (NOW 2ND BATT. CONNAUGHT RANGERS)

At the attack on Sekukuni's Town, South Africa, on November 28, 1879, Flawn, with Private Fitzpatrick (V.C.), saved the life of Lieutenant Dewar, King's Dragoon Guards. Further details of this gallant act are given in the record of Private FitzPatrick (V.C.).

JOHN FREDERICK McCREA
(SURGEON)

1ST REGIMENT, CAPE MOUNTED YEOMANRY

On January 14, 1881, during the action against the Basutos at Tweefontein, near Thaba Tsen, Surgeon McCrea behaved with very great bravery and devotion to the wounded. The enemy had charged with the greatest determination, forcing the Burghers to retire with a loss of sixteen killed and twenty-one wounded. Among the latter was a man named Aicramp, who had been shot and lay some considerable distance away, but McCrea went to his assistance under a heavy fire, and, with the help of Captain Buxton, of the Mafeteng Contingent, carried him to the shelter of an ant-heap, and then returned for a stretcher. While again cross-

The Basuto War

ing the open space he was severely wounded in the right breast by a bullet, but still continued in his duties with the Ambulance, and carried many wounded from the field. He paid little attention to his own injury, and was forced to dress it as well as he could later on, as no other medical officer was present. The *Gazette* stated that, had it not been for his exertions, the sufferings of the wounded would have been greatly aggravated and many more lives lost.

He died in Africa in the summer of 1894.

THE NAGA HILLS (INDIA) EXPEDITION
1879—1880

RICHARD KIRBY RIDGEWAY
(CAPTAIN, NOW COLONEL)
BENGAL STAFF CORPS

ON November 22, 1879, during the attack on Konoma, in the Naga Hills Expedition, Captain Ridgeway displayed very great bravery in charging up to a barricade and, under a very severe fire, attempting to tear down the planking surrounding it. During this brave act he was severely wounded in the left shoulder by a rifle bullet.

Colonel Ridgeway, son of R. Ridgeway, Esq., F.R.C.S., was born in Co. Meath, Ireland, on August 18, 1848. Educated privately and at R.M.C., Sandhurst, he joined the 96th Regiment in January, 1868, and the Indian Staff Corps 1872. Passed Staff College 1883. From 1874 to 1880 was Adjutant of the 44th Goorkha Rifles. Served through the Naga Hills Expedition of 1875, and that of 1879; Manipur, 1891; Tirah, 1897.

THE BOER REVOLT

1880—1881

JAMES MURRAY
(LANCE-CORPORAL)
94TH REGIMENT (NOW 2ND BATT. CONNAUGHT RANGERS)

AT Elandsfontein, near Pretoria, January 16, 1881, Murray and his comrade, John Danaher, advanced for 500 yards into the open, under heavy fire, to rescue two men of the 2nd Royal Scots Fusiliers—Byrne and Davis—who had been severely wounded. No sooner had they started forward than Murray's horse was shot under him; still, without hesitation, he proceeded on foot. "We both," writes Murray, "reached them together, and, on stooping to raise Byrne's head, I was shot through the body, the ball entering my right side and passing out near the spine. Seeing how useless it was for Danaher to remain, I ordered him to secure my carbine and escape. Byrne breathed his last, by my side, soon after. Davis and I were taken prisoners, and, together with Byrne's body, carried in a bullock hide to the Boer camp on the mountain top, where we were well treated. They kept us there twenty-six hours. By the courtesy of the Boer commandant, we were then permitted to return to Pretoria, under a flag of truce, bringing with us the body of our poor comrade. Davis died five days afterwards."—Extract from a letter dated Dublin, March 25, 1891.

Photo by Ellis, *Malta.*

JOHN DANAHER

(PRIVATE)

NOURSE'S HORSE (AFTERWARDS 94TH REGIMENT)

THE Victoria Cross was conferred upon this brave soldier for his gallantry at Elandsfontein, near Pretoria, January 16, 1881, when, with Lance-Corporal Murray (V.C.), he advanced under heavy fire to the rescue of two men of the Royal Scots Fusiliers. The details of the act are given in the record of Lance-Corporal Murray.

JAMES OSBORNE

(PRIVATE)

2ND BATT. 58TH (NORTHAMPTONSHIRE) REGIMENT

ON February 22, 1881, during the action at Wesselstroom, Private Osborne rode towards a party of forty-two Boers, and, under a heavy fire, picked up Private Mayes, who was lying wounded, and carried him back to camp.

The Boer Revolt

ALAN RICHARD HILL
(LIEUTENANT, NOW MAJOR ALAN RICHARD HILL-WALKER, RETIRED)
58TH THE RUTLAND (NOW 2ND BATT. NORTHAMPTON) REGIMENT

Photo by DOWNEY, *London.*

ON January 28, 1881, during the action of Laing's Nek, Lieutenant Hill remained behind after the retreat had been ordered, and attempted to carry Lieutenant Baillie, who had been severely wounded. Being unsuccessful in getting the injured officer on to a horse, he was forced to carry him in his arms, and during this humane action Lieutenant Baillie was again hit, and this time mortally wounded. After this, in spite of the heavy fire from the enemy, Lieutenant Hill twice returned on to the open ground, each time rescuing a wounded man.

Major Alan Richard Hill-Walker, V.C., son of the late Captain Hill, Chief Constable North Riding of Yorkshire, was born on July 12, 1859. Educated at Richmond (Yorkshire) and privately. In 1877 joined the North Yorks Rifles, and in 1879 the 58th Regiment, with which gallant Corps he served through the Zulu War of 1879, and the Boer War of 1881, taking part in the Battles of Ingogo, Majuba Hill (where he was severely wounded), and Laing's Nek, mentioned in despatches, and where his V.C. was won as described above. In 1883-5 he served in Natal, Cape Town and South Africa; was Adjutant 3rd and 4th Battalions Northampton Militia, 1887-92; Station Staff Officer at Bangalore during the next three years; officiating A.A.G. in Mandalay, 1897; took part in the Tirah Campaign and the march down the Bara Valley, 1897.

History of the Victoria Cross

JOHN DOOGAN
(PRIVATE)
(LATE) 1ST DRAGOON GUARDS

ON January 28, 1881, at the action of Laing's Nek, Major Brownlow was dismounted during a charge, owing to his horse being shot. Doogan, who was the Major's servant, seeing the precarious position of his master, rode to his assistance, and though himself severely wounded, sprang from his horse to induce him to accept his mount, receiving another wound while engaged in this gallant act.

Photo by ADAMS, Reading.

JOSEPH JOHN FARMER
(CORPORAL)
ARMY HOSPITAL CORPS

ON February 27, 1881, during the battle of Majuba Hill, when our men were driven back, the Boers rushed forward and, disregarding the rules of modern warfare, commenced firing at the wounded whom Farmer was attending. He held up a white handkerchief in order to induce the Boers to stop firing in his direction, but immediately was shot through the hand. Nothing daunted, and determined to do his best for those in his charge, he seized the handkerchief again in his unwounded hand, but instantly a bullet passed through it, rendering him powerless to continue.

Photo by MALTBY, Chelsea.

This brave man, owing to his wounds, has now left the service and follows the occupation of house painter in London. He was born in London on May 5, 1854, and his Cross was presented to him by Queen Victoria at Osborne on August 9, 1881.

THE EGYPTIAN WAR

1882

ISRAEL HARDING

(GUNNER)

H.M.S. "ALEXANDRA," ROYAL NAVY

Photo by SIMONDS, *Portsmouth.*

ON July 11, 1882, the guns of H.M.S. *Alexandra* were pounding the forts of Alexandria, and a 10-inch spherical shell struck the side of the ship, passed through it and lodged on the main deck. Hearing some one shout "There is a live shell just above the hatchway," Harding dashed up the ladder from below, and saw the shell with the fuse burning. Without any hesitation he threw some water over it, then, picking it up, he placed it in a tub standing close by, thereby saving many lives which would undoubtedly have been lost had it been given time to explode. He was at once promoted Chief Gunner.

History of the Victoria Cross

FREDERICK CORBETT

(PRIVATE)

3RD BATT. 60TH KING'S ROYAL RIFLE CORPS

On August 5, 1882, the Mounted Infantry, to which Corbett was attached, made a reconnaissance upon Kafr Dowar. They came under a severe fire from the enemy, and Lieutenant Howard-Vyse was mortally wounded. He fell in the open, in a very exposed position, and, there being no time to move him, Corbett asked for, and was granted, leave to stay at his side and endeavoured to stop the bleeding of his officer's wound. Although a target for the rifles of the enemy, who poured a constant fire upon him, he did not move until the Mounted Infantry retired to where he was kneeling, when he assisted in carrying the officer from the field.

WILLIAM MORDAUNT MARSH EDWARDS

(LIEUTENANT, NOW MAJOR)

74TH REGIMENT (2ND BATT. HIGHLAND LIGHT INFANTRY)

At the battle of Tel-el-Kebir, on September 13, 1882, Lieutenant Edwards displayed great courage in leading a party of his men to the attack on a redoubt. He outdistanced his followers and dashed alone into the Egyptian Battery, killed the officer in charge, and was knocked down by a gunner. Three of his men arriving at that moment saved him from being killed.

Major Edwards, son of H. W. B. Edwards, Hardingham Hall, was educated

Photo by HAWKE, *Plymouth.*

The Egyptian War

at Eton and Trinity College, Cambridge. Gazetted Sub-Lieutenant (unattached) 1876. Joined 74th Highlanders 1877. Served in Straits Settlements and Hong Kong; Egypt, 1882, in which, in addition to the Victoria Cross, he received the medal and clasp and Khedive's Star; India, 1884-9. Five years Adjutant of 3rd Battalion Highland Light Infantry. Retired November, 1896. Appointed H.M. Honourable Corps of Gentlemen at Arms, 1899.

THE SOUDAN WAR
1884
(Red Sea Littoral)

ARTHUR KNYVET WILSON
(CAPTAIN, NOW ADMIRAL, K.C.B., K.C.V.O.)

ROYAL NAVY

Photo by HAWKE, *Plymouth.*

ON February 29, 1884, at the battle of El-Teb, Captain Wilson, on the staff of Rear-Admiral Sir William Hewett (V.C.), attached himself, during the advance, to the right half battery, Naval Brigade, in the place of Lieutenant Royds, R.N., who had been mortally wounded. As our troops closed on the enemy's Krupp battery, the Arabs charged out on to the corner of the square, and the full force was received by the detachment who were dragging the Gardner gun. Captain Wilson dashed out to the front, and attacked several Arabs single-handed. His sword, during the fight, was broken, but he attacked the savages with his fists. By the diversion caused by his gallant action, time was given to some of the York and Lancaster Regiment to come to the support with their bayonets.

Sir Redvers Buller, V.C., in command, stated that but for the courageous action of Captain Wilson some of the detachment must have been speared. Although himself wounded, he continued with the half-battery during the day.

Sir Arthur Wilson, born March 4, 1842, served in the Crimean War; the China War, 1858; the Egyptian Campaign, 1882; and Soudan, 1884.

The Soudan War

Was A.D.C. to the Queen, 1892–5, and a Lord Commissioner of the Admiralty and Comptroller of the Navy, 1897–1901. Since the latter year has been in command of the Channel Squadron.

WILLIAM THOMAS MARSHALL
(QUARTERMASTER-SERGEANT, NOW MAJOR)

19TH HUSSARS

Photo by GILL, Colchester.

DURING the charge of the Cavalry at El-Teb, on February 29, 1884, Lieut.-Colonel Barrow, 19th Hussars, severely wounded and unhorsed, lay on the ground surrounded by the enemy. Quartermaster-Sergeant Marshall, who had stayed behind with him, seized him by the hand, dragged him through the enemy back to the regiment and saved his life.

Born on December 5, 1854, Major Marshall joined the 19th Hussars in 1873. Served through the Egyptian War of 1882, and received his Commission in 1885.

THOMAS EDWARDS
(PRIVATE)

42ND ROYAL HIGHLANDERS (THE BLACK WATCH)

AT the battle of Tamaai on March 13, 1884, Edwards was attached to the Naval Brigade as mule-driver. The enemy directed a particularly fierce attack on the guns, and, at one of them, Edwards was standing with Lieutenant Almack, R.N., when a hand-to-hand fight took place. The Lieutenant was killed, as also was one of the bluejackets, but Edwards bayonetted two Arabs and, though severely wounded by a spear, rejoined the ranks and did excellent service in the defence of the guns.

History of the Victoria Cross

PERCIVAL SCROPE MARLING
(LIEUTENANT) 60TH THE KING'S ROYAL RIFLE CORPS
(NOW LIEUT-COLONEL, C.B., 18TH HUSSARS)

Photo by ELLIS, Baker Street.

On March 13, 1884, at the battle of Tamaai, Private Morley (35th Regiment) was severely wounded. Lieutenant Marling at once rode up, and had the injured man placed on the saddle in front of him, but he immediately fell off. Thereupon Lieutenant Marling dismounted, and, giving up the horse, succeeded in carrying him for eighty yards into safety, the enemy being close upon him and keeping up a sharp fire.

Lieut.-Colonel Marling, son of Sir William Marling, was born in Gloucestershire, March 6, 1861. Educated at Harrow and R.M.C., Sandhurst. Served through the Boer War, 1881; present at Laing's Nek and Ingogo engagements. Through Egyptian Campaign of 1882, present at the battles of Tel-el-Mahuta, Kassassin, and Tel-el-Kebir. In Suakim Campaign, battle of El-Teb, and relief of Tokar, actions of Tamaai, and Tamanib; Khartoum Expedition, 1884; battle of Abu-Klea, El-Gubat, and Metemmeh, and through the many actions fought under Sir H. Stewart. Major, August, 1896. On the outbreak of the Boer War embarked for South Africa, taking part in the operations extending over 1899–1900.

THE NILE EXPEDITION

1884—1885

ALBERT SMITH
(GUNNER)
ROYAL ARTILLERY

ON January 17, 1885, the Soudanese broke our square, and the soldiers were compelled to fall back slightly. By this a gun was left in a comparatively unprotected position, and a native rushed at Lieutenant Guthrie, who was in command of it, and who, at that moment, was superintending its working. Being unarmed, he would certainly have been speared had not Smith warded off the blow with a handspike, which momentary diversion gave the officer time to draw his sword and by a blow bring the Soudanee to the ground. In falling, however, the savage cut at him with a long knife, which Smith again warded off, not, however, in time to prevent the infliction of a severe wound in the officer's thigh. The native was then killed by Smith, but Lieutenant Guthrie died a few days afterwards from his wound.

BURMA

1889

JOHN CRIMMIN

(SURGEON, NOW LIEUT.-COLONEL, C.I.E.)

"Non-combatants" run a good deal more risk in the course of their duties than the world generally is aware of, and it is well when a gallant deed, such as that which earned Surgeon Crimmin the coveted distinction of the Victoria Cross, draws public attention to the dangers that are braved by the nominally non-fighting portion of our forces. Surgeon Crimmin, born on March 19, 1859, is a Dublin man, and a Licentiate of the Royal College of Surgeons, Ireland, and of the King and Queen's College of Physicians, Ireland. He entered the Indian Medical Service in 1882, passing out of Netley fifth on the list. He was senior medical officer to the expeditionary force against the rebellious Karens at the end of 1888, and it was in a skirmish with the rebels on January 1, 1889, that he earned his V.C. "I especially wish to bring Surgeon Crimmin to the notice of the Brigadier-General," wrote the officer commanding the Mounted Infantry, "for the gallant way in which he attended the wounded under a heavy fire. At one time, while attending an injured man, he was surrounded by the enemy, and defended himself and the wounded man, killing some of the Karens." It was recorded also that Surgeon Crimmin was as capable in the hospital as on the battlefield. "His arrangements for the comfort and disposal of the sick and wounded were," says Brigadier-General Collett, "as perfect as the circumstances of the time permitted." Became Surgeon-Major on September 30, 1894, and Lieut.-Colonel in 1902. Was Civil Surgeon at Rutnagherry, and is now Health Officer of the Port of Bombay.

Burma

FERDINAND SIMEON LE QUESNE
(SURGEON-CAPTAIN, NOW MAJOR)
ROYAL ARMY MEDICAL STAFF

Photo by HAWKE, *Plymouth.*

DURING the attack on the village of Tartan, on May 4, 1889, a young officer, William Graham Michel (of the 2nd Norfolk, or 9th Regiment) was mortally wounded. Surgeon-Captain Le Quesne remained for some minutes with him, within five yards of the loopholes of the enemy's stockade, whence proceeded a hail of lead. While dressing the wounds of another officer soon afterwards, Dr. Le Quesne was himself severely wounded.

Born at Jersey, December 25, 1863, Major Le Quesne is the son of the late Lieut.-Colonel G. N. Le Quesne. Served in the Chin Looshai (1890), and Wunthoo (1891) Campaigns; also through the Boer War, 1899–1902. Educated at King's College Hospital, London, of which he is Honorary Fellow.

THE MANIPUR (N.E. INDIA) RISING
1891

CHARLES JAMES WILLIAM GRANT
(LIEUTENANT, NOW MAJOR)
INDIAN (MADRAS) STAFF CORPS, FORMERLY 12TH (THE SUFFOLK) REGIMENT

Photo by STEREOSCOPIC CO., *London.*

THE decoration was gained by Lieutenant Grant in the outbreak which occurred at Manipur, a small native State at the foot of the Eastern Himalayas. While at Tummu, a small military station, news was brought him of the massacre of the residents at the former place on the night of March 24–25, 1891, and of the danger the survivors, if any, were in. Promptly taking with him eighty native soldiers, he marched day and night through Northern Burma, reached Thobal, near Manipur, and from March 31 held it against the whole Manipuri army until relieved on April 9. For this he was awarded the Cross, and promoted Captain and Major on May 26, two months after his gallant exploit.

Major Grant is son of Lieut.-General D. G. S. St. J. Grant, late Madras Staff Corps. Was born at Bourtie, Aberdeenshire, on October 14, 1861; educated privately and at R.M.C., Sandhurst. Joined Suffolk Regiment on May 10, 1882, the Madras Staff Corps two years later—May 10, 1884; and the 2nd Burma Battalion in 1890. In 1891 was A.D.C. to the Commander-

The Manipur (N.E. India) Rising

in-Chief in Madras, Lieut.-General Hon. Sir J. C. Dormer; A.A.G. Madras District, 1897. Served through the Burma Expedition, 1885–87. Promoted Major, May 10, 1900.

In the Manipur Rising, in the fighting subsequent to the occurrence above related, he had his horse shot under him, and was himself severely wounded. All the surviving faithful and heroic men who accompanied him on his march to Thobal were decorated with the Order of Merit.

THE HUNZA NAGAR (N.W. INDIA) EXPEDITION
1891

FENTON JOHN AYLMER
(CAPTAIN, NOW COLONEL)
ROYAL ENGINEERS

Photo by HARRINGTON & NORMAN, *Calcutta.*

ON December 2, 1891, an Expedition sent into the Hunza Nagar country arrived at the Nilt Fort. Our force consisted of about a thousand men, mostly Kashmir Imperial Service Troops, and sixteen British officers. The Fort which had to be attacked, standing at the extremity of a ledge which overhung the Nilt *nullah*, was protected on three sides by a precipice, and the only approach to the gate had been strongly defended by *abattis* of branches. It was impossible to bring the mountain-guns to bear on this part, owing to the impracticability of dragging them up the cliffs which overlooked it, and for a long time a hot rifle-fire was kept up by our men, which was equally severely replied to by the enemy from their loopholed stronghold. At length it was resolved to take the Fort by storm, and, to enable an entry to be made, the great gate had to be blown in. This dangerous duty was entrusted to Captain Aylmer, in command of the Engineers, and he was supported by a hundred Goorkhas, under Lieutenants Boisragon (V.C.) and Badcock. While the Goorkhas hacked at the branches of the *abattis* to make an entrance, the three officers, with a small handful of men,

The Hunza Nagar (N.W. India) Expedition

sprang through the opening and forced the gate of the outer wall. Captain Aylmer then, in a most cool and courageous manner, advanced under heavy fire and placed the charge of gun-cotton against the main gate, lighted the fuse, during which he was shot in the leg, and retired to await the explosion. For some reason the charge failed to ignite, upon which he returned, arranged the charge afresh, and re-lit the fuse. He was again severely injured in the hand by a rock hurled from above by one of the enemy. The explosion, which now took place, sufficed to blow in the gate, and the officers, followed by their men, dashed through and commenced a terrific hand-to-hand combat with the defenders, who, after a most desperate resistance, were driven from the Fort. Captain Aylmer, though again severely wounded, fired nineteen shots with his revolver, killing several of the enemy, and remained fighting, until at last, owing to loss of blood, he had to be carried out of action.

The following is another account of his marvellous pluck, and athletic prowess, given in *The Relief of Chitral* by Captains G. J. and F. E. Younghusband—

"During the construction, a very prompt and plucky act on Major Aylmer's part saved the life of a soldier. About a mile up stream, where the first floating bridge had been constructed, a flying-bridge and rafts were still working backwards and forwards to supply the Guides with their wants on the other bank. One of these rafts, on which were two men of the Devonshire Regiment Maxim Gun Detachment, got accidentally overturned, and the boatmen and oars were washed away. The two soldiers managed to climb on to the raft and were carried down stream at a great pace. General Gatacre, seeing the accident, immediately galloped down to the site of the new bridge to give warning, in the hopes of saving the men. Meanwhile one of them had made an attempt to jump on shore and had been swept away and drowned, and the survivor on the raft came flying down the torrent. With the greatest presence of mind Major Aylmer immediately slipped down a slack wire that was across the river and just managed to grab the soldier as he shot past. The raft was immediately after dashed to pieces on the rocks below. With considerable difficulty they were both hauled on shore and it was then found that the Major was badly bruised and cut by the wire. The Royal Humane Society's medal has been given for many a less distinguished act of bravery, yet I do not think that, in the stir of passing events, it actually occurred to any of the spectators to send the recommendation home."

Fenton John Aylmer, 2nd son of the late Captain F. J. Aylmer, 97th Regiment, was born at Hastings, April 5, 1862. Educated privately. Joined Royal Engineers, 1880. Served in India since 1883; has been A.A.G., and acted as

History of the Victoria Cross

A.Q.M.G. and D.Q.M.G., Army Headquarters. Served in Burma Expedition, 1886-7 (despatches, medal and clasp); Hazara Expedition, 1891 (despatches, clasp); Hunza Expedition, 1891-2 (despatches, clasp, V.C., Brevet-Major); Isazai Expedition, 1892; Chitral Expedition, 1895 (despatches, medal and clasp, Brevet-Lieut.-Colonel). At present A.Q.M.G. Madras Command (Ootacamund).

GUY HUDLESTON BOISRAGON
(LIEUTENANT, NOW MAJOR)
INDIAN STAFF CORPS

Photo by DICKENSON, *New Bond Street.*

On December 2, 1891, at the capture of the Nilt Fort, this officer displayed great bravery in leading the assault, through very severe difficulties, to the inner gate. Finding his force insufficient, he went back under a heavy cross-fire and collected more men with whom he returned to the relief of the first party, now sorely pressed. With the additional help he had obtained, the enemy were driven from the Fort. A more detailed account of the action is given in the record of Captain Aylmer (V.C.).

Major Boisragon, son of Major-General H. F. M. Boisragon, was born at Kohat, Punjab, on November 5, 1864. Educated at Charterhouse and Sandhurst, joined the 10th (Lincolnshire) Regiment in 1885 and the 5th Goorkhas, 1887. Became Captain, 1896; Major, 1903. Served through the Hazara Expeditions of 1888 and 1891, with the two Miranzai Expeditions, 1891; also in that in Waziristan, 1894-5. Took part in the fighting on North-West Frontier, 1897; the operations in the Sarnana and Kurram Valley; Tirah Expedition, 1897-8; and operations against the Khani Khel Chamkhannis.

JOHN MANNERS SMITH
(LIEUTENANT, NOW MAJOR, C.I.E.)
INDIAN (BENGAL) STAFF CORPS, FORMERLY 9TH THE NORFOLK REGIMENT

Decorated for conspicuous bravery at the attack and capture of a strong position occupied by the enemy near Nilt, in the Hunza Nagar country,

The Hunza Nagar (N.W. India) Expedition

Photo by BOURNE & SHEPHERD, *India.*

on December 20, 1891. From their almost inaccessible position, the enemy had barred the advance of our men for seventeen days, but they were eventually dislodged by two parties of fifty Rifles, the first being under the command of Lieutenant John Manners Smith. For nearly four hours he steadily moved his handful of men from point to point on the face of an almost precipitous cliff, whenever he was able to avoid the showers of rocks hurled upon him from the enemy above; and during the entire time he was quite unable to defend himself from any attack the enemy might choose to make. Eventually the summit of the cliff was reached, which was within a few yards of the tribesmen's *sangars*, into which he led his gallant little band and shot the first man with his revolver. The *Gazette* states that it was entirely due to the splendid leading of this officer, together with the coolness and dash he displayed, that a success was obtained.

Born at Lahore, August 30, 1864, son of the late Charles Manners Smith, F.R.C.S., Major Smith was educated at Trinity College, Stratford-on-Avon; King Edward VI School at Norwich, and the R.M.C., Sandhurst. Lieutenant in the Norfolk Regiment, 1883-8, joining the Indian Staff Corps, and serving with the 3rd Sikhs and 5th Goorkha Rifles, 1885-7. On the mission of Sir Mortimer Durand to Sikkim in 1888 and to Cabul in October, 1893, this officer formed one of the staff, being created C.I.E. for his services. He has held political appointments in the East from 1889-98, taking part in the Isazai and Tirah Expeditions.

THE WEST AFRICAN (RIVER GAMBIA) EXPEDITION

1892

WILLIAM JAMES GORDON
(LANCE-CORPORAL)
1ST BATTALION WEST INDIA REGIMENT

Photo by DANIELS, *Tachbrook Street, London.*

ON March 13, 1892, an attack was made on the town of Toniataba, in West Africa. Major G. C. Madden, who commanded the troops, was superintending a party of twelve men who were trying to break down the South Gate of the town with a huge beam which they were using as a battering-ram. The Major's back was, for a moment, turned to the Gate, when, suddenly, several musket-barrels, not more than two or three yards from him, were pushed through two rows of loopholes, which up to that moment had been masked. In an instant Gordon called to his officer to "Look out," and, pushing him aside, flung himself between him and the muskets, which were at that moment fired, the contents of one of them entering Gordon's lung. His quick act of heroic devotion undoubtedly saved the life of Major Madden.

BURMA

1893

OWEN EDWARD PENNEFATHER LLOYD
(SURGEON-MAJOR, NOW LIEUT.-COLONEL)
ARMY MEDICAL STAFF

Photo by KLIER, *Rangoon.*

ON January 6, 1893, a severe attack was made on the Sima Post by Kachins. The commanding officer, Captain Morton, was wounded, upon which Surgeon-Major Lloyd, accompanied by Subadar Matab Singh, ran at once to his assistance and, on reaching him, sent the Subadar back for help, remaining with him, and attending to his injuries. During this time, Lloyd was himself severely wounded; the enemy were within ten or fifteen paces of him, and they killed three men and a bugler. On the help he had sent for arriving, he assisted in carrying him back to the Fort, where, however, in spite of their efforts, in a few minutes he expired. The Subadar and five Sepoys who assisted were all awarded the Order of Merit.

Lieut.-Colonel Lloyd, son of the late Major M. Pennefather Lloyd, late 59th Regiment, was born on January 1, 1854. Educated at Fermoy College, Cork, he is a member of the Royal Irish University. Is L.R.C.S., L.R.C.P., L.M., Edinburgh. On August 4, 1878, joined the R.A.M.C., serving through the Zulu War, and the operations against Sekukuni. Transvaal War, 1881-2, taking part in the siege of Standerton. Was Medical Officer to the Franco-British Boundary Commission to the Mekong River, 1894-5, and since 1898 has been in medical charge of the Burma-China Boundary Commission.

CHITRAL (FORT)

1895

HARRY FREDERICK WHITCHURCH

(SURGEON-CAPTAIN, NOW SURGEON-MAJOR)

INDIAN (BENGAL) MEDICAL SERVICE; 24TH BENGAL NATIVE INFANTRY

Photo by NICHOLLS, *Sandown.*

On March 3, 1895, the garrison of Chitral Fort made a *sortie*. When about one-and-a-half miles from the Fort, Captain Baird was mortally wounded, and Surgeon-Captain Whitchurch went to his assistance. The enemy, in great strength, had now succeeded in forcing their way through the fighting-line. Darkness had set in, and, with only a small handful of Goorkhas and men of the 4th Kashmir Rifles, they were completely isolated from assistance. Placing the wounded officer in a dhoolie, they then attempted to return. The Goorkhas most bravely clung to their load until three of them were killed and a fourth severely wounded, upon which Surgeon Whitchurch took Baird upon his back and continued the journey. Unable to take a direct road, they were obliged to make their way by a circuitous route of three miles, exposed to a raking fire from the enemy who were posted on all the surrounding cliffs and walls, and it was only the darkness that prevented the total annihilation of the devoted little band. Time after time, in order to force a way over some walls held by a more than usually obstinate group of the enemy, Whitchurch had to lay down his burden, and charge with his men, after which he would pick him up and make his way on a little further. Eventually the Fort was

Chitral (Fort)

reached, with but seven men, whose devotion to their wounded officer has seldom been equalled. Just as the doctor reached the Fort, Baird was hit for the third time, the bullet striking him in the face, and, in spite of every care, he died next day. Before his death, however, he was able to tell of the heroic devotion of Surgeon Whitchurch, being anxious it should not go unrecognized.

Captain Younghusband in his story of Chitral says that Mr. Robertson, Political Agent, wrote in his report to Government saying, " It is difficult to write temperately about Whitchurch," and men who have themselves won the Victoria Cross have said that never has it been more gallantly earned than on this occasion.

Dr. Whitchurch, son of Mr. F. Whitchurch, of Sandown, Isle of Wight, was born on September 22, 1866. Educated in England, France and Germany. Entered St. Bartholomew's Hospital, 1883 ; and the Indian Army, 1888, serving in the Looshai Expedition and the relief of Aijal and Changsil, Defence of Malakand ; relief of Chakdara, North-West Frontier of India, 1897-8 ; China, 1901, taking part in relief of Pekin Legations.

THE MATABELE REBELLION

1896

HERBERT STEPHEN HENDERSON
(TROOPER)
BULUWAYO FIELD FORCE

Photo by TURNER, *Buluwayo.*

WHEN the Matabele broke out into rebellion in 1896, Henderson joined the Rhodesia Horse as a scout, and accompanied Captain Macfarlane's party which rode to the rescue of some settlers living in isolated districts. At daybreak, on March 30, the party was suddenly fired upon by Matabele in ambush, and Henderson, with a fellow-trooper named Celliers, forming the advance guard, were cut off from the rest. Celliers was shot through the knee, and his horse, being hit in five places, after going a short distance fell dead. Left alone with Celliers, Henderson dismounted, put him on to his own horse, and, in this manner, travelling by night and hiding by day, walking alongside, supporting his comrade who was enduring untold agonies, they at last reached Buluwayo, absolutely exhausted, thirty-five miles from where he had started on his devoted and heroic task. When one realizes that the enemy was swarming around them, that these men were without food (except a few sour plums) from daylight on the Sunday, when Celliers was shot, until the Wednesday morning; that his friend was in such pain that he implored to be left behind, and that the risk of capture and death by fiendish methods was with them every moment of those long hours, it

The Matabele Rebellion

will not be considered too much to say that his heroic act ranks among the most worthy for which the Victoria Cross has been bestowed. But, unhappily, in spite of the care with which he was guarded and tended by his friends, Celliers died on May 16, 1896, in hospital, having had to undergo amputation of the leg, owing to the length of time which elapsed from the day he was wounded to the date when the operation was performed.

Herbert Stephen Henderson, son of Mr. William Henderson, of Bishop Street Engineering Works, Glasgow, was born at Hillhead, Glasgow, on March 30, 1875. Educated at Kelvinside Academy. Served for some years with Engineers in Glasgow. In 1892 went to the Rand goldfields, being connected with some well-known mines. In 1894 started for Rhodesia and volunteered, on the outbreak of the Rebellion, as a Scout. Was presented with the Victoria Cross by Lord Milner at the opening of the Buluwayo Railway in 1896.

FRANK WILLIAM BAXTER

(TROOPER)

BULUWAYO FIELD FORCE

THE Victoria Cross would have been awarded to Frank William Baxter had he survived. There are few cases on record to equal the heroism, devotion, and nobility of heart displayed by this trooper, who on April 22, 1896, gave up his horse to his wounded friend to save him from falling into the hands of the Matabele, and, remaining on foot himself, was assagaied.

The following account of the occurrence is taken from Mr. F. C. Selous' book, *Sunshine and Storm in Rhodesia*—

"When the Scouts were recalled, and commenced to retire from the Umguza, after having driven a body of natives from its shelter, as I have already related, they were suddenly fired on by a party of Matabele who had taken up a position amongst some bush to the left of their line of retreat. The foremost amongst the Scouts galloped past this ambush, but Captain Grey, with a few of those in the rear, halted and returned the enemy's fire. Trooper Wise was the first man hit, and seems to have received his wound from behind, just as he was mounting his horse, as the bullet struck him high in the back, and, travelling up the shoulder-blade, came out near the collar-bone. At this instant Wise's horse stumbled, and then, recovering itself, broke away from its rider, galloping straight back to town, and leaving the wounded man on the ground. A brave fellow named Baxter at once dismounted and put Wise on his own horse, thus saving the latter's life, but, as it proved, thereby sacrificing his own. Captain Grey and Lieutenant Hook at once went to Baxter's assistance, and they got him along as fast as they could, but the Kaffirs had now closed on them, and were firing out of the bush at very close quarters. Lieutenant Hook was shot from behind, the bullet entering the right buttock and coming out near the groin, but most luckily, though severing the sciatic nerve, just missing both the thigh-bone and the femoral artery. Nearly at the same time, too, a bullet just grazed Captain Grey's forehead, half stunning him for an instant. 'Texas' Long, a well-known member of the Scouts, then went to Baxter's assistance, and was helping him along, when a bullet struck the dismounted man in the side, and he at once let go of Long's stirrup leather and fell to the ground. No further assistance was then possible and poor Baxter was killed by the Kaffirs immediately afterwards. Whilst these brave deeds were being performed, Lieutenant Fred Crewe, with some others of the Scouts, amongst whom I may mention Button and Radermeyer, were keeping the Kaffirs in check and covering the retreat of the wounded men. Just as Lieutenant Hook got near to Crewe, his horse was shot through the fetlock and buttock at the same time, and, rolling over, threw Hook to the ground, causing him at the same time to drop his rifle. Hook got on his legs and was hobbling forward when Crewe said to him, 'Why don't you pick up your rifle?' 'I can't,' was the answer; 'I'm too badly wounded.' 'Are you wounded, old chap,' said Crewe; 'then take my horse, and I'll try and get out of it on foot.' Crewe then assisted Hook to mount his horse, and fought his way back on foot, only escaping with his life by a miracle, keeping several Kaffirs who were very near him, but who had no guns, at bay with his revolver, whilst he retreated backwards. So near were these men to him, that one of them, as he turned, threw a heavy *knob-kerry* at him, which struck him a severe blow in the back. Nothing could have saved him had not the Kaffirs been constantly kept in check by the steady fire of Radermeyer, Button, Jack Stuart, and others of the Scouts, and also by a cross-fire from some of the Colonial Boys, directed by Captain Fynn and Lieutenant Mullins.

"The splendid gallantry and devotion to one another shown by Captain Grey and his officers and men on this day will ever be remembered in Rhodesia as amongst the bravest of the brave deeds performed by the colonists in the suppression of the present Rebellion. Such acts, too, speak for themselves, and bear eloquent, if silent, testimony against the cruel and malicious calumnies on the character of the white settlers in Matabeleland which have so frequently disgraced the pages of a widely-read, if generally despised, weekly journal.

The Matabele Rebellion

"As soon as Grey's Scouts and the Colonial Boys had reached the guns, these latter were limbered up, and the whole patrol retired slowly on Buluwayo, the Matabele making no attempt to follow. Indeed, their loss must have been severe, and had Grey's Scouts and the Colonial Boys only been supported instead of being recalled, the Matabele would never have rallied, but would have been kept on the run and killed in large numbers by the mounted men. At least this is my view, and it has been thoroughly borne out by the experience gained in subsequent fights during this campaign.

"Our loss on this day was, Baxter killed, and Wise and Hook wounded amongst Grey's Scouts, while five or six of the Colonial Boys were wounded, but none dangerously. Wise has long ago recovered from his wound and Lieutenant Hook is in a fair way to do so. I have forgotten to mention that my horse must have been captured by the Matabele as he did not return to Buluwayo and has not since been heard of. The lucky savage into whose hands he fell, became possessed at the same time of a very good saddle and a brand new Government coat."

RANDOLPH COSBY NESBITT

(CAPTAIN)

MASHONALAND MOUNTED POLICE, NOW IN BRITISH SOUTH AFRICA POLICE

Photo by BASSANO, *London.*

DURING the native insurrection in Mashonaland in 1896, many of the homesteads were sacked, and the settlers with their families murdered, before help could be sent to them, living as they did, in many cases, in isolated districts, miles from their nearest neighbours. In June, 1896, Mr. Judson, director of telegraphs at Salisbury, had ridden with a patrol to effect the relief of the miners at the Alice Mine in the Mazoe Valley, but on reaching them found himself powerless to bring them away through the hordes of savages, and was compelled to remain in laager with them. On the 19th Captain Nesbitt, when out with a patrol of thirteen men, came across a runner from Mr. Judson, bearing a note to Judge Vincent to the effect that to relieve them, one hundred men and a

Maxim gun were required. Reading it to his thirteen men, Captain Nesbitt asked them if they would accompany him to endeavour to rescue the beleaguered party, a question answered readily enough, and at once the gallant little band set off. They fought their way through the enemy and eventually reached the laager, and putting the three women who were with the miners into an armoured wagon, commenced the return journey, again fighting heavily. Through the masses of savages who barred their way the little band of brave men steadily penetrated, the enemy often creeping through the long grass and when quite close firing at the wagon. By the bravery of these colonists and the skilful and courageous leading of Captain Nesbitt, at length they were all brought safely into Salisbury with the loss of only three men killed and five wounded, eight horses killed and seven wounded. The action of Captain Nesbitt and his thirteen men stands prominently out among the many brave deeds performed by our colonists during those troublous times.

Born at Queenstown in Cape Colony, on September 20, 1867, Captain Nesbitt is the son of Major C. A. Nesbitt. Educated at St. Paul's School, in London, he joined the Cape Mounted Rifles, August 10, 1885, and served through the Mashona Expedition of 1890, being promoted Lieutenant (Police) in September, 1891. Held the appointment of Chief Constable at Fort Peddie, in the Cape, in March, 1892, till April, 1893. Returned to Mashonaland at the end of that year and became Inspector of the Mounted Police in that region and appointed J.P. in 1895. Served in Gazaland, 1894, on special service. Attained his present rank on June 1, 1895. During the Boer War, 1899–1902, was in command of a squadron of B.S.A.P. under Generals Plumer and Baden-Powell, in the Transvaal.

PUNJAB FRONTIER

1897—1898

EDMOND WILLIAM COSTELLO

(LIEUTENANT, NOW CAPTAIN)

INDIAN STAFF CORPS

Photo by MAYALL, *Piccadilly.*

On the night of July 26, 1897, during the fighting at the Malakand, Lieutenant Costello, with the assistance of two Sepoys, saved the life of a wounded Lance-Havildar, who was lying sixty yards away on the football field. At the time of this gallant act, the field was swarming with the enemy's swordsmen and a heavy rifle-fire directed upon it.

Edmond Costello, son of Surgeon-Colonel Costello, I.M.S., was born on August 7, 1873. Educated at Beaumont and Stonyhurst College, he joined the 14th West Yorkshire in August, 1892, and was attached to the 22nd Punjab Infantry in 1894. During Malakand Campaign was twice wounded.

ROBERT BELLEW ADAMS

(MAJOR AND BREVET-LIEUT.-COLONEL, NOW LIEUT.-COLONEL, C.B.)

INDIAN STAFF CORPS

At Nawa Kili, in Upper Swat, North-West Frontier of India, on August 17, 1897, Lieut.-Colonel Adams and some of the Guides started in pursuit of the tribesmen after the action of Landakai, and it is believed that the horse of Lieutenant R. T. Greaves bolted with his rider. When near-

History of the Victoria Cross

Photo by WALERY, London.

ing the enemy, Greaves was shot through the body and fell to the ground, being quickly surrounded by the tribesmen. Major Adams, Lieutenants McLean and Fincastle, seeing Greaves' predicament, rode to his rescue and succeeded in recovering his body. They drove off the enemy, but Greaves was killed by another shot just as they commenced to carry him away. Major Adams most bravely stood between the enemy and McLean and Fincastle while these two officers were attempting to put their wounded friend on to one of their horses. Lieutenant McLean was mortally wounded while engaged in this humane act.

Robert Bellew Adams was born in 1856, and entered the Army in 1876, becoming Captain, 1887; Major, 1896. Served in the Afghan War, 1879, and Chitral Relief Force, 1895. Is A.D.C. to His Majesty the King. Was presented with the Victoria Cross by the late Queen Victoria at Windsor, on July 9, 1898. At present serving at Mardan in India.

ALEXANDER EDWARD MURRAY, VISCOUNT FINCASTLE

(LIEUTENANT, NOW CAPTAIN)

16TH LANCERS

Photo by DICKENSON, New Bond Street.

ASSOCIATED with Colonel R. B. Adams (V.C.), in the gallant attempt to save the life of Lieutenant Greaves, of the Guides, at Nawa Kili, Upper Swat, India, on August 17, 1897.

Born on April 22, 1871, son of the Earl of Dunmore, Viscount Fincastle joined the 16th Lancers in 1891, becoming Captain, October 17, 1899. Was A.D.C. to the Viceroy of India, 1894. Served in Dongola Expedition, 1896, and Boer War, 1899–1902, commanding Fincastle's Horse during that time.

Punjab Frontier

HECTOR LACHLAN STEWART MacLEAN
(LIEUTENANT)

INDIAN STAFF CORPS

THIS officer, had he survived, would have been awarded the Victoria Cross for his gallant conduct on August 17, 1897, in Upper Swat, India, when, as recorded in the account of Colonel Adams (V.C.), he attempted to save the life of Lieutenant Greaves. Lieutenant MacLean had served in the Hazara Expedition.

Photo by MILNE & SON, *Blairgowrie.*

THOMAS COLCLOUGH WATSON
(LIEUTENANT, NOW CAPTAIN)

ROYAL ENGINEERS

ON September 16, 1897, Lieutenant Watson, while at the attack on the village of Bilot in the Mamund Valley, collected a few men of the Buffs and Bengal Sappers and led them into the burning village, in order to dislodge some of the enemy who were inflicting loss on our troops. With conspicuous courage he made two gallant attempts, but was, on both occasions, repulsed and severely wounded.

Captain Watson, born on April 1, 1867, entered the Army in 1888, and was promoted to his present rank on November 19, 1898.

JAMES MORRIS COLQUHOUN COLVIN
(LIEUTENANT, NOW BREVET-MAJOR)

ROYAL ENGINEERS

ON September 16, 1897, at the village of Bilot, in the Mamund Valley, Indian Frontier, Lieutenant Colvin, after Lieutenant Watson (V.C.) had been incapacitated from his wounds, continued in the attempt to drive out the

Photo by FALL, Baker Street, London.

enemy from the burning village. His conduct was most brave, and his devotion to his men most noticeable, as, during the whole affair, a very heavy fire was kept up against them by the enemy.

Born at Bijnor, India, on August 26, 1870, Major Colvin is the son of Mr. J. C. Colvin, late Bengal Civil Service. Educated at Charterhouse and Royal Military Academy, he joined the Royal Engineers in 1889, becoming Lieutenant in 1892; Captain, April 1, 1900; and Brevet-Major, August, 1902, for his services in South Africa as an officer on special service. Took part in the Chitral Relief Force, 1895; Malakand Field Force, 1897 (mentioned in despatches); Buner Field Force, 1898; and South Africa, 1901–2.

JAMES SMITH

(CORPORAL)

THE BUFFS (EAST KENT REGIMENT)

ON the night of September 16, 1897, Lieutenant Watson (V.C.) called for volunteers to enter the burning village of Bilot (North-West Frontier of India), and drive the enemy out with the bayonet. Corporal Smith followed his officer, and was particularly noticeable for his gallant conduct on that occasion. Later, although wounded, he continued firing coolly and steadily, and assisted in removing the wounded to a place prepared for their reception. The officer afterwards left to obtain assistance for the wounded, leaving Corporal Smith in charge of the men; and during his absence Smith directed the fire of his party, exposing himself freely in order to watch the enemy, who were unable to take the position, which was held most gallantly.

Punjab Frontier

HENRY SINGLETON PENNELL
(LIEUTENANT, NOW CAPTAIN)
SHERWOOD FORESTERS (DERBYSHIRE REGIMENT)

ON October 20, 1897, during the attack on the Dargai Heights, Captain W. E. G. Smith, of the Derbyshire Regiment, was shot, and Lieutenant Pennell, under a terrific hail of bullets, ran to him, and twice attempted, in a most brave manner, to carry him into shelter. It was only when he found that the officer was dead that he desisted from any further attempts.

Son of Mr. Edwin Pennell, of Dawlish, in Devonshire, Captain Pennell was born on June 18, 1874. Educated at Eastbourne College, he joined the Derbyshire Regiment in 1893; promoted to 1st Lieutenant, 1896; Captain, 1900. Served in Tirah Campaign, 1897-8, being mentioned in despatches as well as gaining the Victoria Cross, which was presented to him by Lieut.-Colonel Dowse at Bareilly, North-West India, on September 2, 1898. Took part in the Boer War, 1899-1902, being twice mentioned in despatches. Was severely wounded during the Relief of Ladysmith.

G. FINDLATER
(PIPER)
GORDON HIGHLANDERS

THE historic and superb storming of the Dargai Heights took place on October 20, 1897. Piper Findlater was shot through both feet, but sat up, under a terrific fire, and continued playing the regimental march in order to encourage his comrades in the charge. Decorated at Netley Hospital by Her late Majesty Queen Victoria.

History of the Victoria Cross

Photo by PARISIAN PHOTO CO., *Edinburgh.*

E. LAWSON
(PRIVATE)
GORDON HIGHLANDERS

DECORATED for his conspicuous bravery at the assault of the Dargai Heights on October 20, 1897. Under a terrific fire from the enemy he carried Lieutenant Dingwall, who was severely wounded, from an open spot to a safer position. Afterwards he acted in a similarly brave manner towards Private McMillan, and during his heroic action was wounded in two places.

S. VICKERY
(PRIVATE, NOW CORPORAL)
DORSETSHIRE REGIMENT

DECORATED for his courageous conduct on October 20, 1897, at the storming of the Dargai Heights, when he ran down the slope, under a very severe fire, to the help of a wounded soldier whom he subsequently carried back to shelter. Later on, when with Brigadier-General Kempster's column in the Waran Valley, he became separated from his company and was attacked by three of the enemy, all of whom he killed.

Photo by FREKE, *Cardiff.*

THE KHARTOUM EXPEDITION
(Omdurman)
1898

PAUL ALOYSIUS KENNA
(CAPTAIN, NOW MAJOR)
21ST LANCERS

Photo by ELLIOTT & FRY.

ON September 2, 1898, at the battle of Khartoum, Major Crole Wyndham's horse was killed in the charge of the 21st Lancers, and he was in a most dangerous position, until Captain Kenna rode to him, and, taking him up behind him, rode into safety. When the charge was over, he returned, and assisted Lieutenant De Montmorency (V.C.), in his heroic endeavour to rescue the body of Lieutenant Grenfell.

Major Kenna, born on August 16, 1862, is the son of Mr. James Kenna. Was educated at St. Augustine's College, Stonyhurst, and Sandhurst, passing from the latter into the 2nd West Indian Regiment in 1886. After two years' service in the West Indies and West Africa, joined the 21st Lancers. Served as Assistant Provost-Marshal in South Africa, 1899-1902. Served in Somaliland Campaign, 1904. Received the Royal Humane Society's Medal in 1895 for jumping off Carlisle Bridge into the Liffey to rescue a drowning man.

History of the Victoria Cross

THE HONOURABLE RAYMOND HARVEY LODGE JOSEPH DE MONTMORENCY

(LIEUTENANT, AFTERWARDS CAPTAIN)

21ST LANCERS

Photo by CHARLETON, *Newbridge.*

On September 2, 1898, during the battle of Khartoum, Lieutenant de Montmorency, when the charge of the 21st Lancers had taken place, returned to the help of Lieutenant R. G. Grenfell, who had fallen wounded and was lying surrounded by a number of Dervishes. Finding, on reaching him, that the officer was dead, he endeavoured to put the body on a horse, but the animal broke away, and he would himself have been killed but for the help of Corporal Swarbrick and Captain Kenna (V.C.).

He was son of the late General Viscount Frankfort de Montmorency, and was born on February 5, 1867. Entered the 21st Lancers September, 1887, became Lieutenant 1889, Adjutant 1893, Captain 1899. While serving in the Boer War, 1899–1902, he was killed on February 23, 1900, when in command of the corps of scouts which bore his name.

THOMAS BYRNE

(PRIVATE)

21ST LANCERS

On September 2, 1898, at the battle of Khartoum, during the celebrated charge of the 21st Lancers, Lieutenant the Honourable R. F. Molyneux had been wounded, dismounted and disarmed, and was being attacked by Dervishes. Byrne, though himself severely wounded, went to the officer's rescue, attacked those surrounding him, receiving another severe injury, and by his brave exertions enabled the officer to escape.

Photo by SUMNER, *Oxford.*

The Khartoum Expedition (Omdurman)

NEVILL MASKELYNE SMYTH

(CAPTAIN, NOW MAJOR)

2ND DRAGOON GUARDS

ON September 2, 1898, at the battle of Khartoum, an Arab " ran amok " among the camp followers. Captain Smyth, seeing that some of them must be killed if he were not promptly stopped, rode up, met the Arab's charge and killed him, receiving a spear-wound in the arm. This gallant action saved at least one of the camp followers from death.

Son of the late Sir Warington Smyth, F.R.S., of Marazion, in Cornwall, Major Smyth was born in London on August 14, 1868. Educated privately and at R.M.C., he joined the 2nd Dragoon Guards in 1888 at Sialkot, and served on the Afghan Frontier (Zhob Valley Expedition) in 1890; through the Dongola Expedition, 1896; (battles of Firket, and Hafir; occupation of Dongola); Soudan Campaign, 1897 (bombardment of Metemmeh); battles of Atbara and of Khartoum; Soudan Campaign, 1899 (battle of Gedid); Boer War, 1899–1902, serving in Major Lawley's column. Promoted Captain in December, 1897, Major in October, 1903.

THE KHARTOUM EXPEDITION
(Gedarif-Kassala)
1898

THE HONOURABLE ALEXANDER GORE ARKWRIGHT HORE-RUTHVEN
(CAPTAIN, 3RD BATT. HIGHLAND LIGHT INFANTRY)
LIEUTENANT, 79TH CAMERON HIGHLANDERS

Photo by SHARP, *Hamilton, N.B.*

ON September 22, 1898, at the battle of Gedarif, an Egyptian officer had fallen wounded within fifty yards of the Dervishes, who were advancing, firing and charging. Captain Hore-Ruthven picked him up and carried him towards the 16th Egyptian Battalion, several times laying down his burden to fire at the enemy, in order to keep them in check, and succeeded in getting him into safety.

Born at Windsor, July 6, 1872, Captain the Hon. Hore-Ruthven is the son of the 8th Baron Ruthven. Educated at Eton, he joined the 3rd Batt. H.L.I. in 1891, was attached to the Egyptian Army in the Soudan in 1898, and during the battle of Gedarif and other engagements commanded the camel corps. Was three times mentioned in despatches. Gazetted to 79th Cameron Highlanders in 1899.

CRETE

1898

WILLIAM JOB MAILLARD, M.D.
(SURGEON)
ROYAL NAVY

Photo by WEST, *Southsea.*

ON September 6, 1898, H.M.S. *Hazard* landed some men at Candia during the troubles in that place, whereupon a terrific hail of bullets greeted them, and Arthur Stroud, A.B., fell back into the boat seriously wounded, as the rest sprang ashore. Surgeon Maillard, in spite of the rain of lead directed on him, returned, and endeavoured to carry the man, who was then dying, into shelter, but the boat got adrift, and from so unstable a platform he found it impossible. When he returned to his post, his clothes were riddled with bullets, but he was fortunately unhurt.

William Job Maillard, educated at Kingswood School, Bath; Dunheved College, Launceston; Guy's Hospital, London (M.R.C.S., L.R.C.P.), entered the Navy, August 22, 1889, and for his gallant services was promoted Staff-Surgeon on June 2, 1899. Was presented with the Victoria Cross by the late Queen at Windsor on December 15, 1898.

He retired in 1902, and died at Bournemouth on September 10, 1903, aged 40.

THE BOER WAR

1899-1902

CHARLES FITZCLARENCE
CAPTAIN, ROYAL FUSILIERS
(NOW MAJOR, IRISH GUARDS)

THE Victoria Cross was awarded to this officer for three distinct acts of bravery during the siege of Mafeking. On October 14, 1899, Captain FitzClarence, with his squadron of the Protectorate Regiment, which consisted of only partially-trained men who had not before been under fire, went out to render assistance to an armoured train, sent out from the town. The Boers were numerically far superior, and the position began to look very serious for the squadron, who at one time were completely surrounded. Captain Fitz-Clarence, however, handled his men in so splendid a manner, and inspired them with such confidence by his calm bearing and personal courage, that they succeeded in relieving the armoured train, and inflicted, besides, a severe loss on the enemy, accounting for fifty killed and a great number wounded, the moral effect of which had a most important bearing in later actions with the enemy. Again, on October 27, 1899, he led a night *sortie* and attacked the enemy's trenches. A hand to hand combat ensued with the bayonet, and the enemy were driven out with great loss. He was the first in the trench, and killed four Boers himself with his sword. Major-General R. S. S. Baden-Powell, in command at Mafeking, reported that but for the personal bravery and dash of this officer, the attacks would have been failures, with heavy loss of life and prestige on our part as a result. On December 26, 1899, Captain FitzClarence was conspicuous for his spirit, leading and bravery during the action at Game Tree, near Mafeking, in which engagement he was severely wounded through both legs.

Born on May 8, 1865, Major FitzClarence is the son of Captain the Hon. George FitzClarence, R.N., third son of the first Earl of Munster.

The Boer War

Educated at Eton and Wellington College, he entered the Royal Fusiliers November 10, 1886, serving for some years with the Egyptian Army, but the investment of Mafeking, in which he so greatly distinguished himself, was his first active service. In October, 1900, he was transferred to the Irish Guards, being, in the following month, promoted Major by brevet. Is a Staff College officer, and at present Major of Brigade at Aldershot.

MATTHEW FONTAINE MAURY MEIKLEJOHN
(CAPTAIN)
2ND BATT. GORDON HIGHLANDERS

Photo by FAIRWEATHER, *St. Andrews.*

On October 21, 1899, at the battle of Elandslaagte, almost at the beginning of the Great War (and just before Sir George White, V.C., was forced into Ladysmith to stand a siege of 118 days), the Boer position had been captured, but a heavy cross-fire was poured upon our men from a kopje in advance of us, which was about to be taken by assault. The fire was so terrific that the Highlanders, whose leaders had been shot down, commenced to waver. Captain Meiklejohn, seeing at once the critical position, sprang forward, calling on his men to follow him. Although falling desperately wounded almost at once, his conspicuous bravery and fearless example had the effect of steadying the men, who advanced to the assault and captured the kopje.

Captain Meiklejohn, son of the late J. M. D. Meiklejohn, Professor of Education at St. Andrew's University, was born on November 20, 1870, and entered the Gordon Highlanders (92nd) on June 17, 1891, with which gallant body of men he fought in the Chitral Relief Force, 1895, on the Punjab Frontier, and through the Tirah Expedition, 1897-98, being wounded during the latter campaign. Promoted Captain 1899. For his services in India he wears the (new) Indian Medal and three clasps. The wound he received at Elandslaagte caused him to lose his right arm almost at the shoulder. In 1901 was Garrison-Adjutant at St. Helena, whence he returned to enter the Staff College.

History of the Victoria Cross

WILLIAM ROBERTSON

(SERGEANT-MAJOR, NOW QUARTERMASTER AND HON. LIEUTENANT)

2ND GORDON HIGHLANDERS

Photo by DAVIDSON, *Dumfries.*

At the battle of Elandslaagte, October 21, 1899, during the final and decisive advance on the Boer position, Sergeant-Major Robertson led each successive rush of his battalion, exposing himself fearlessly to the enemy's artillery and rifle-fire in order to encourage the men. When the main position had been captured, he led a small party to seize the Boer camp, which operation was successfully carried out, and though a deadly cross-fire was poured upon him and his men, he continued to hold on to the position, encouraging them until he was dangerously wounded in the body and sustained a compound fracture of the left arm.

William Robertson, son of Mr. John Robertson, of Dumfries, was born at Greyfriars, Dumfriesshire, on February 27, 1865. Enlisted in the 2nd Gordons at Devonport, December 1, 1884, rising to warrant rank in 1895, and Quartermaster 3rd Gordons May 12, 1900.

After some years of service in India, landed in South Africa on October 8, 1899, two days before the Boer Ultimatum to Great Britain, proceeding immediately to Ladysmith, in the defence of which he took part after recovery from his wounds received at Elandslaagte, and for which he possesses a clasp to his medal as well as those for Elandslaagte and Cape Colony.

On Christmas Day, 1900, after his return home, was presented, in recognition of his bravery and distinguished services, with the freedom of his native town, having, four months previously, received the Victoria Cross from the hands of Her late Majesty Queen Victoria, at Windsor Castle.

The Boer War

R. JOHNSTONE
(CAPTAIN)
IMPERIAL LIGHT HORSE

Photo by ELLIOTT & FRY, *London.*

THE act for which this gallant officer was awarded the Victoria Cross is described in the record of Captain Mullins (V.C.). Both officers were serving at the time with the Imperial Light Horse, whose deeds place them second to none of the Irregular Troops raised during the Boer War. They were recruited mostly, if not entirely, of men from the gold mines of the Rand, and were commanded by Colonel Chisholm, and Majors Karri-Davis and Sampson, the two latter well-known in connexion with their part during the Jameson Raid, and their subsequent incarceration in Pretoria Gaol by Krüger.

C. H. MULLINS
(CAPTAIN, NOW MAJOR, C.M.G.)
IMPERIAL LIGHT HORSE

Photo by BASSANO, *London.*

AT the battle of Elandslaagte, October 21, 1899, where the "Charge" of that name was so gallantly carried out, a forward movement was met by a terrific fire at almost point-blank range, and for a moment the advance was in danger of being checked. Captains Mullins and R. Johnstone most bravely rushed forward, rallying the men, the former officer being wounded during this devoted action. By their heroic act, at a most critical moment, the intended flanking movement was unimpeded, allowing this operation, which decided the issue of the battle, to be successfully carried out. Reference to Captain Johnstone is made above.

History of the Victoria Cross

JOHN NORWOOD

(SECOND-LIEUTENANT, NOW LIEUTENANT)

5TH (PRINCESS CHARLOTTE OF WALES') DRAGOON GUARDS

Photo by LAFAYETTE.

ON October 30, 1899, a small patrol under Lieutenant Norwood was sent out from Ladysmith, and, coming under a heavy fire from a large body of the enemy posted on a ridge, were retiring at full speed, when a trooper fell from his saddle, wounded. In spite of the rain of bullets directed at him, Lieutenant Norwood rode back for three hundred yards to the fallen man, dismounted, and carried him on his back until he could place him out of range, when he mounted his horse, which he had, during this gallant act, led with his free hand, and rejoined his troop.

Lieutenant John Norwood, son of J. Norwood, Esq., of Pembury Lodge, near Beckenham, was educated at Abbey School, Rugby, and Oxford, and entered the 5th Dragoon Guards February 8, 1899.

ERNEST BEACHCROFT BECKWITH TOWSE

(CAPTAIN, RETIRED)

1ST GORDON HIGHLANDERS

THE first act of this brave officer for which he was mentioned in connexion with the award of the Victoria Cross, was at Magersfontein, December 11, 1899, when he heroically endeavoured, during the retirement, to carry out of action Colonel Downman, who had been mortally wounded. Being unable, however, to accomplish this, he supported him until Colour-Sergeant Nelson and Lance-Corporal Hodgson came to his assistance. The second act was on April 30, 1900, on Mount Theba, where, with twelve men, he took his stand on a plateau which fully one hundred and fifty of the enemy were endeavouring to reach. Neither side seemed to have noticed the proximity of the other, until about one hundred yards apart. The Boers then dashed forward to within forty yards, calling on Captain Towse and his little party to surrender, to which the Highland officer replied by an order to his men to open fire, charging

The Boer War

Photo by WINTER, *Derby.*

forward at the oncoming enemy, who were driven off, in spite of their very superior strength in numbers. Just at the last, this gallant officer was shot through both eyes, which entirely destroyed his sight.

Captain Towse was born on April 23, 1864, and educated at Wellington College. Entered the Wilts Regiment December 16, 1885, and was posted to the Gordons January 2, 1886, with which splendid corps he served in the Relief of Chitral, 1895, and, two years later, on the Punjab Frontier. Promoted Captain 1896. He received the Victoria Cross from the hands of the late Queen Victoria, by whom, in 1900, he was appointed Sergeant-at-Arms. In 1902 he was re-appointed Sergeant-at-Arms to H.M. the King, and in 1903 became one of the Hon. Corps of Gentlemen-at-Arms.

Photo by ELLIOTT, *Aldershot.*

HENRY EDWARD MANNING DOUGLAS, D.S.O.

(LIEUTENANT, NOW CAPTAIN)

ROYAL ARMY MEDICAL CORPS

AT the battle of Magersfontein, December 11, 1899, when the Highland Brigade was so terribly cut up, Lieutenant Douglas was conspicuous for his devoted attendance to the wounded. Under a pitiless sleet of bullets, he advanced on to the open plain and attended to the wounds of Captain W. E. Gordon, Major Robinson, and many other stricken men. His bravery was not confined only to this occasion, for during the day he behaved as bravely in other actions in which he was engaged.

History of the Victoria Cross

This young Army doctor, son of Mr. George A. Douglas, of Kingston, Jamaica, entered the medical branch of the Service July 28, 1899, and was promoted Captain July 27, 1902. On his return to this country he did duty for some time at St. George's Barracks, London, proceeding in October, 1903, on active service to Africa with General Egerton's command in Somaliland.

JOHN DAVID FRANCIS SHAUL

(CORPORAL, NOW BAND SERGEANT)

HIGHLAND LIGHT INFANTRY

Photo by PLUMMER, *Forest Gate.*

At the battle of Magersfontein, December 11, 1899, when the Highlanders were mown down by the terrific rifle-fire of the Boers, Corporal Shaul's bravery and humane conduct were so conspicuous that, not only was he noticed by his own officer, but even those of other regiments remarked upon it. At one critical time he was specially prominent in encouraging his men to advance across the bullet-swept open ground, setting them a splendid example by his own behaviour. He was in charge of the stretcher-bearers—a very important duty—and was most conspicuous in dressing the wounds of the injured. In one case he went to a wounded man, and, with the utmost coolness and deliberation, sat down by him and attended to him, in spite of the hail of bullets which kept raining around him. He continually went from one man to another, wherever he could mitigate suffering.

Sergeant Shaul is the son of Sergeant John Shaul, 2nd Batt. Royal Scots, who served his country in the Crimea and in China, 1860. He was born at King's Lynn, Norfolk, September 11, 1873, educated at the Duke of York's School, Chelsea, and at the age of fifteen joined the First H.L.I., with which he served in Crete during the fighting in 1898. He fought in South Africa from the commencement to the end of the Boer War, receiving both medals and five clasps. His commanding officers at Magersfontein were Lieutenant-Colonel H. R. Kelham, C.B., and Major T. Richardson, D.S.O., and the Victoria Cross was presented to him by H.R.H. the Duke of York at Pietermaritzburg, August 14, 1901.

The Boer War

WALTER NORRIS CONGREVE
(CAPTAIN, NOW LIEUT.-COLONEL, M.V.O.)
2ND RIFLE BRIGADE

Photo by KNIGHT, *Aldershot.*

ON December 15, 1899, at the battle of Colenso Bridge, during the early part of Buller's advance to the relief of Ladysmith, the guns of the 14th and 66th Batteries R.F.A. had dashed forward, far in advance of their flank supports, and opened fire on the Boer position. Without shelter of any description, and in full view of the enemy strongly entrenched, they became the object of as fearful and pitiless a storm of bullets and shell as any battery has had to face in modern war.

The horses were torn to pieces, the gunners littered the ground around the guns, but, with that dogged and stolid endurance, and that incapability of the British soldier to know when he is beaten, officers and men, with a heroism unsurpassed before or since, worked their guns in a desperate and hopeless endeavour to turn the tide. At last hardly enough remained to serve the guns, and any attempt to bring relief from the donga, five hundred yards to the rear, seemed only to increase the blizzard of shot and shell which swept, without intermission, the space between the donga and the guns. Soon the batteries had *no one* to serve them, and they were deserted, but there were some heroic spirits who echoed Colonel Long's words, uttered as they removed him from the storm-stricken gun by which he had fallen, " Abandon be damned ! we don't abandon guns ! " General Buller, on hearing of the disaster, called for volunteers to attempt to bring them in. His call was readily answered by, among others, Captain Schofield, Captain Congreve, Captain Reed and Lieutenant Roberts, son of the Commander-in-Chief. Captain Schofield got together his team, and was able to bring in one of the only two guns which were saved. Captain Congreve and Lieutenant Roberts started out on their almost hopeless task, getting as far as hooking a second gun to a limber, and, though it was brought back, it cost the life of Lieutenant Roberts, who fell mortally wounded. Captain Congreve, badly wounded, made for the donga, but he saw his brother officer fall, and bravely returned through the hell of fire and brought him into shelter. Captain Reed brought up three teams to see what could be done at this point, and heroically dashed for the guns, but the horses could not be induced to face the storm, and, as men were falling fast at every attempt, no further endeavour was made and the remaining guns had to be abandoned. Corporal Nurse, for his gallant services during the awful ordeal, was, with the four officers, awarded the Victoria Cross. Further details of Captains Schofield and Reed, Lieutenant Roberts and Corporal Nurse are given under their respective headings.

Captain Congreve, son of the late William Congreve, J.P., of Congreve, Staffordshire, was born on November 20, 1862. Educated at Harrow, he entered the Rifle Brigade February 7, 1885, becoming Captain in December, 1893, Major in the regiment and Army Lieut.-Colonel December 21, 1901. Served on the Staff in South Africa as A.M.S. and private secretary to Lord Kitchener, after which, in November, 1902, he became Assistant Military Secretary and A.D.C. to H.R.H. the Duke of Connaught in Ireland, being made a member of the Royal Victorian Order by His Majesty the King when on a visit to that country in 1903.

HAMILTON LYSTER REED

(CAPTAIN)

7TH BATTERY, ROYAL FIELD ARTILLERY

Photo by WERNER, *Dublin.*

THE Victoria Cross was awarded to Captain Reed for his conspicuous bravery during the heroic attempt to save the guns at Colenso, December 15, 1899, and a detailed account of the affair will be found in the record of Captain Congreve (V.C.).

Captain Reed, son of Sir Andrew Reed, K.C.B., C.V.O., late Inspector-General Royal Irish Constabulary, was born on May 23, 1869, and, after graduating at Woolwich, entered the Royal Artillery February 17, 1888, becoming Captain in 1898. During the Boer War was, at first, Adjutant of Brigade Division R.F.A. and later D.A.A.G. on the Staff of the G.O.C. Orange River Colony. Took part in the operations in Natal, including action at Colenso, where he gained the Victoria Cross, the relief of Ladysmith, actions of Spion Kop, Vaalkranz, Tugela Heights, Pieter's Hill, Laing's Nek, Belfast and Lydenburg. Was presented with the Victoria Cross at Ladysmith on March 4, 1900, by Sir Redvers Buller, V.C.

The Boer War

THE HONOURABLE F. H. S. ROBERTS
(LIEUTENANT)
KING'S ROYAL RIFLE CORPS

Photo by STEREOSCOPIC Co., *London.*

SON of Field-Marshal the Earl Roberts, V.C., K.G., Commander-in-Chief. Born at Umballa, India, January 8, 1872, he entered the King's Royal Rifle Corps June 10, 1891, and, during the four following years, was on active service on the North-West Frontier of India—including Chitral, receiving medals and clasps and being mentioned in despatches. His heroic bravery at Colenso, December 15, 1899, for which, had he survived, he would (according to the *Gazette*) have received the Victoria Cross—now possessed by his family—is detailed in the account given under the heading of Captain Congreve (V.C.).

The gun, in the saving of which Lieut. Roberts lost his life, has been presented to his gallant father as a family heirloom by the War Office authorities.

HARRY NORTON SCHOFIELD
(CAPTAIN, NOW MAJOR)
ROYAL FIELD ARTILLERY

Photo by BASSANO, *London.*

THE act for which Captain Schofield was awarded the Victoria Cross is given in greater detail in the record of Captain Congreve, together with whom and Lieutenant Roberts, Corporal Nurse and Captain Reed he made a heroic attempt to save the guns at Colenso, December 15, 1899.

Born on January 29, 1865, Major Schofield entered the Royal Artillery February 15, 1884, becoming Captain February, 1893, and Major February, 1900. He was, in the first instance, gazetted to the Order for Distinguished Service, but,

History of the Victoria Cross

in the *Gazette* of August 30, 1901—nearly two years after his brave conduct at Colenso—the bronze Victoria Cross was substituted for that of the Gold Cross of the D.S.O.

WILLIAM BABTIE, C.M.G.
(MAJOR, NOW LIEUT.-COLONEL)
ROYAL ARMY MEDICAL CORPS

Photo by ELLIOTT & FRY.

ON December 15, 1899, at the battle of Colenso, the wounded of the 14th and 66th Batteries R.F.A. were without medical assistance. They had been carried to a donga in rear of the guns, which, as detailed in the account of Captain Congreve (V.C.), had suffered so fearfully from the enemy's shell and rifle fire. On assistance being sent for, Major Babtie, Staff Officer to P.M.O. Natal Army, rode across the open ground, his pony being hit three times, and attended to the sufferers under fire which was directed on any one exposing himself. This he was obliged to do in passing from one wounded man to another. Later on he went out and assisted Captain Congreve when that officer heroically brought in the late Hon. F. H. S. Roberts (V.C.)

Born on May 7, 1859, Lieutenant-Colonel Babtie is the son of Mr. John Babtie, J.P., of Dunbarton. Educated at Glasgow University (M.B. 1880), he entered the Army Medical Service on July 30, 1881, and was promoted Major from July 30, 1893. Served in Crete, 1897-98, as Senior Medical Officer, and for his services during the International Occupation was created C.M.G. In South Africa he took part in all the actions for the relief of Ladysmith, and subsequent operations in Natal and the Eastern Transvaal (despatches, *London Gazette*). Promoted Lieut.-Colonel November 29, 1900. Queen's medal with five clasps. Has served as Assistant Director-General A.M.S. on the Headquarters Staff of the Army since June 1, 1901. Is a Knight of Grace of the Order of St. John of Jerusalem in England. Ptesented with the Victoria Cross by Earl Roberts at Pretoria in October, 1900.

The Boer War

GEORGE EDWARD NURSE

(CORPORAL, NOW SERGEANT)

66TH BATTERY, ROYAL FIELD ARTILLERY

Photo by KAINES, *Guernsey.*

THE heroic action in which Corporal Nurse gained the Victoria Cross is described in the account given of Captain Congreve, with whom he was associated in attempting the rescue of the guns at Colenso. In addition to the first battle on the Tugela, he has fought almost through the whole four Colonies, from Durban on the east to Mafeking (Relief) on the north-west.

Born at Enniskillen, Ireland, April 14, 1873, son of Charles Nurse, of Cobo Hotel, Guernsey. After undergoing a course of higher class education at the Chamberlain Academy, Guernsey, joined the Royal Artillery, enlisting at St. George's Barracks, London, January 6, 1892; served in Ireland till May, 1897, proceeding to South Africa with his unit, which was commanded on "Black Friday," December 15, 1899, by Major W. Foster, under Colonel Long, with General Hildyard in brigade command. His Cross was presented to him at Ladysmith by General Sir Redvers Buller, V.C., under whose supreme command it was so nobly gained.

GEORGE RAVENHILL

(PRIVATE)

2ND BATT. ROYAL SCOTS FUSILIERS

Photo by COYNE, *Pietermaritzburg.*

ON the disastrous December 15, 1899, at Colenso, when the guns of the 14th and 66th Batteries R.F.A. had to be abandoned, owing to the awful fire concentrated upon them by the Boers, Ravenhill was one of the heroic band of men who made the brave attempt to save them, and one of the few who escaped the hail of lead and lived to tell the tale. He was also with the party who eventually succeeded in saving one.

History of the Victoria Cross

A more detailed account of the affair is given in the record of Captain Congreve.

George (not Charles, as gazetted) Ravenhill is a Warwickshire man, although currently reported as hailing from Ayr, having been born at Birmingham on February 21, 1872, his father being Mr. T. Ravenhill, Warren Road, Washwood.

At Birr, Ireland, in May, 1889, he joined the 1st battalion of his regiment, with which he served afterwards in India for close on six years, and with the sister battalion for two years on the veldt. Possesses the Queen's and the King's medals, with clasps, for relief of Ladysmith, Transvaal and Cape Colony.

At Colenso he gained the Cross under command of Colonel E. E. Carr, C.B., and in General Geoffrey Barton's brigade, the decoration being presented to him by H.R.H. the Duke of York on June 4, 1901, at Pietermaritzburg.

He was once wounded at Colenso, shot through the forearm.

Was also awarded the medal for distinguished conduct, which was, however, cancelled on being gazetted to the Victoria Cross, even though the medal was for a different action—the battle of Fredricksbad.

HORACE ROBERT MARTINEAU
(SERGEANT)
PROTECTORATE REGIMENT

THE gallant defence of Mafeking, during a long and weary siege of seven months, will ever stand out as one of the bright episodes of the Great Boer War. Many a *sortie* was made during the early days of the siege, and many a stubborn fight strained the resources of the hard-pressed little garrison far away on the limitless African veldt.

In the action at Game Tree, on December 26, 1899, the "retire" had been sounded, but Sergeant Martineau remained behind, and took up Corporal Le Camp, whom he saw had been shot, close in front of the Boer trenches. While trying to get him under shelter, half dragging, half carrying him, Martineau received a wound in the side, but, such was his devotion to his fellow-soldier, that he paid no attention to his own condition and suffering, but proceeded to attend to his friend's wounds, after which he helped him, little by little, towards cover, until he himself was again wounded. Thoroughly exhausted by the strain of carrying his friend, the second wound prevented any further action on his part, and he sank down, powerless to proceed further. He was, altogether, wounded three times, once so seriously that it resulted in his left arm having to be amputated.

Horace Robert Martineau, son of Mr. William Martineau, of Hornsey, was born on October 31, 1874, in Bayswater, London. Educated chiefly at University College School, after which he went to South Africa. On the outbreak of the Matabele Rebellion, accompanied Major-General Baden-Powell in his successful campaign to subdue them. In 1889, when the war clouds began to gather and Krüger grew more obstinate, Martineau volunteered into the Protectorate Regiment from Cape Town, his services prior to that time having been with the Cape Police. He has now given up soldiering, and holds a very good position in the African Boating Company, a large and influential concern at Durban.

H. E. RAMSDEN

(TROOPER)

PROTECTORATE REGIMENT

On December 26, 1899, during the heavy fighting at Game Tree, near Mafeking, as described in the account of Sergeant Martineau, after the order to retire had been given, Trooper H. E. Ramsden took up his brother (Trooper A. E. Ramsden), who had been shot through both legs and was lying some ten yards only from the main Boer trench, and carried him for eight hundred yards under a heavy fire, putting him down from time to time to rest, till they met some men who helped to convey him to a place of safety.

This is the second Victoria Cross awarded to a soldier for saving his own brother's life, the first having been awarded to Sir C. J. S. Gough.

History of the Victoria Cross

SIR JOHN PENISTON MILBANKE, BART.
(LIEUTENANT, NOW CAPTAIN)
10TH (THE PRINCE OF WALES' OWN ROYAL) HUSSARS

WHILE on a reconnaissance near Colesberg, on January 5, 1900, a small patrol of the 10th Hussars were retiring, and the horse of one of the men was unable to keep up with the rest. Sir John Milbanke, although severely wounded, rode back to him, took him upon his own horse, and brought him back to the camp. The man he rescued was, at the time, close to a party of Boers who had galloped near, and, dismounted, were firing heavily on any one within range.

Sir John Milbanke, son of Sir Peniston Milbanke, 9th Baronet, was born on October 9, 1872. After serving in the 3rd Royal Sussex Regiment for some years, entered the 10th Hussars, November 23, 1892, rising to Captain, April 17, 1900, while serving on the staff of Sir John French.

ROBERT JAMES THOMAS DIGBY JONES
(LIEUTENANT)
ROYAL ENGINEERS

LIEUTENANT ROBERT JAMES THOMAS DIGBY JONES was killed in action during the great assault on Ladysmith, on January 6, 1900, after successfully defending Waggon Hill West with a few men for twelve hours under desperate conditions, displaying conspicuous bravery and gallant conduct throughout.

Sir George White, in his despatch (*London Gazette*, February 8, 1901), stated he " would have had great pleasure in recommending Lieutenant Digby Jones and Trooper Albrecht for the distinction of the Victoria Cross had they survived."

In the *London Gazette* of August 8, 1902,

The Boer War

it was announced that the King was graciously pleased to direct that the Victoria Cross earned by Lieutenant Digby Jones, Trooper Albrecht, and four others should be sent to their representatives. (See Appendix II.

Lieutenant Digby Jones accompanied the 23rd Field Company R.E. (under the command of Major S. R. Rice, R.E.) to Natal in June, 1899, proceeding straight to Ladysmith, where he was employed in the construction of a Hospital in the camp (afterwards abandoned when the siege commenced) and afterwards on the defences of the town.

He was mentioned in Sir George White's despatch (December 11, 1899) for having successfully destroyed the 4.7 Boer gun on Surprise Hill, during the sortie from Ladysmith on December 10, 1899, under the command of Colonel Metcalfe, with some 500 men of the Rifle Brigade. Newspaper correspondents afterwards mentioned that the first fuse inserted was defective, and that " Lieutenant Digby Jones went back at the risk of death or mutilation and inserted another," which successfully destroyed the gun, which had been causing much annoyance to the garrison.

He was again mentioned in despatches (Sir George White, February 8, 1901) in connexion with the " Assault on Ladysmith, January 6, 1900."

On the evening of the 5th January, Lieutenant Digby Jones had been sent to Waggon Hill West in command of a working-party, consisting of thirty Sappers, some bluejackets, Gordon Highlanders and Imperial Light Horse, to make an emplacement for a 4.7 gun. At about 2.45 a.m. on the 6th, they were surprised by the Boers, and, after ordering the men to stand to arms, Digby Jones, at once, himself extinguished the lanterns which were giving a line for the enemy's fire. There they made a most gallant stand till about 5.30 a.m., when reinforcements arrived.

Later on, when all the officers of the Gordons and Imperial Light Horse had either been killed or wounded, he took command, and, rallying the hard-pressed men again and again, kept the crest of the hill.

Space does not allow of mention of all that is recorded, but a brief summary of an incident mentioned by Major Rice (C.R.E., Ladysmith) may be given.

The sudden appearance of a party of Boers on that part of the hill had caused its worn-out defenders to retire in disorder, when Digby Jones got his first intimation of the presence of the enemy, under De Villiers, on the crest, in the shape of a shot over the parapet at a distance of only a few feet, which killed 2nd Corporal Hunts, R.E. In a moment Digby Jones picked up a rifle, and, dashing round the end of the emplacement, shot De Villiers, Lance-Corporal Hockaday at the same time shooting De Jaegers. Digby Jones was then heard to say, " What's up ? The Infantry have gone." A man replied, " There is an order to retire, sir." Digby Jones said, "I have no order to retire," and at once ordered bayonets to be fixed, and, calling his men to follow him, led them (with 2nd Lieutenant Denniss, R.E.) to the charge, reoccupying the firing line in front of the emplacement.

Later on, while leading his men forward, he was struck in the throat by a bullet and was instantly killed.

A study of the position shows of what vital importance the tenure of Waggon Hill West was to the safety of Ladysmith; so much so that the *South African Review* (February 24, 1900), in a paragraph on Lieutenant Digby Jones, says, "So far as can be humanly judged it was this officer who *saved Ladysmith* and the British arms from the mortification of a defeat and its incalculable consequences." And the *Army and Navy Gazette* (July 5, 1902), from which portions of the preceding account are borrowed, says, "General Ian Hamilton, who had witnessed his intrepid and resourceful conduct through the day, had decided to recommend him for the Victoria Cross, which was fully approved by Sir George White, and, subsequently, brought forward in his despatch." This fine young soldier was only twenty-three years of age.

His brother officer, 2nd Lieutenant G. B. Denniss, hearing Digby Jones was down, went out on the ridge, which was swept by the enemy's fire, to search for him, and was, unfortunately, shot while performing this deed of mercy.

Quoting from a correspondent, the *Army and Navy Gazette* (January 27, 1900), says, "Lieutenant Digby Jones' name will stand out in the history of the siege of Ladysmith as one who set a brilliant example to all about him, and brought no little credit on the corps of Royal Engineers. He did his duty nobly to the end!"

Lieutenant Digby Jones was the second son of Charles Digby Jones, of Chester Street, Edinburgh. He was born September 27, 1876, educated first at Alnmouth, Northumberland, and afterwards at Sedbergh School, Yorkshire (going there in May, 1890, and leaving in December, 1893), where he won the Sedgwick Mathematical prize in 1893, and was in the 1st XV. for football, and the 2nd XI. at cricket.

He passed into Woolwich in 1894, thirty-fourth in order of merit, when bifurcating for Royal Engineers was fifth, and passed out sixth in the Royal Engineer Division, obtaining his commission on August 5, 1896. After completing his course of instruction at the S.M.E., Chatham, he was posted to the 23rd Field Company R.E.

He was a good all-round athlete, being especially prominent in his golf and skating. At the former he won the Boys' Scratch Medal at North Berwick two years in succession, and while at Chatham was secretary of the R.E. Golf Club,

The Boer War

forming one of the team in the annual inter-regimental matches with the Royal Artillery in the years '97, '98, and '99, doing the best round for the Sappers in the latter year. He was also secretary of the R.E. Rugby Football Club while at Chatham, and was one of its foremost players.

He is buried in Ladysmith Cemetery, and a cairn was erected by the 23rd Field Company R.E. on the spot where he fell, as a memorial to him and to those Sappers who fell near him on Waggon Hill. In addition to a brass tablet put up in St. Mary's Cathedral, Edinburgh, by his parents and brothers, his old Scottish schoolfellows erected one in the Parish Church at Alnmouth.

In the *History of the Royal Military Academy* (written by Captain Guggisberg, R.E.) it states:—" In the Spring term, 1901, the octagon of the west library was turned into a kind of Sapper Valhalla. The walls were covered with handsome oak panels, on which were inscribed, in gold letters, the names of dead and gone engineers who had distinguished themselves in the service of their country, ranging from Waldivus, Ingeniator (1086) to a brave young subaltern, Digby Jones, V.C. (Ladysmith, 1900)." There are only 120 names on these panels.

By a strange coincidence his younger brother, Lieutenant Owen G. Digby Jones, was commissioned to the Royal Engineers on the very day his brother was killed (January 6, 1900).

He had many relatives who served in the Army with distinction, amongst whom may be mentioned—

(i.) *His Grand-Uncle*—Major-General John Christie, C.B., A.D.C. to Queen Victoria, who raised the 1st Bengal Cavalry, better known as "Christie's Horse," in 1838, which he commanded to the end of the Afghan War. Seven medals.

(ii.) *His Cousin*—Major-General John Moore Graham, who served through the Indian Mutiny and received through the Secretary of State for India, the "most gracious approbation of Her Majesty" for services performed during that period.

(iii.) *His Cousin*—Lieut.-Colonel Robert Hope Moncreiff Aitken, V.C., who earned the Victoria Cross on six different occasions during the siege of Lucknow, and was ten times mentioned in despatches.

History of the Victoria Cross

JAMES EDWARD IGNATIUS MASTERSON
(LIEUTENANT, NOW CAPTAIN AND BREVET-MAJOR)
1ST BATT. DEVONSHIRE REGIMENT

ON January 6, 1900, after seven weeks of continual bombardment and all the privations of a close siege, the Boers found Sir George White's gallant garrison as stubborn as ever, and, with Buller's battalions steadily, though slowly, creeping to its relief, they began to entertain doubts whether Ladysmith would fall as easily as they had once expected. They therefore determined on a general assault on the town, hoping that disease and starvation had sapped the strength of the defending garrison. Though the British ranks had been sadly thinned since the commencement of the siege, the indomitable pluck of the British had in no way diminished, and, second to none, the Devonshire Regiment acquitted itself on that day, in a manner worthy of its best traditions. At Waggon Hill, three of its companies, one of which was led by Lieutenant Masterson, made a dash for a ridge, strongly held by the enemy, and captured it, but became at once exposed to a terrible fire from the right and left front. The position becoming almost untenable, Lieutenant Masterson undertook to convey a message to the Imperial Light Horse, a hundred yards distant, to direct their attention to the left front, and endeavour to check the enemy's fire from that point. The ground which he had to traverse was absolutely without cover, and swept by a galling fire, and before he had crossed it he was shot in both thighs. With undaunted courage, struggling up, he contrived to crawl along and deliver his message before falling exhausted in the trench held by our men. By his heroic devotion, Masterson was the means of saving many lives.

Major Masterson, born on June 25, 1862, enlisted at an early age in the 87th Royal Irish Fusiliers, with which famous regiment he fought at Tel-el-Kebir, gaining medal with clasp, and Khedive's Star. Commissioned into the Devonshire Regiment in 1891, he served in the operations in Burma (medal and clasp); and in 1897–8 took part in the fighting on the North-West Frontier of India (medal and two clasps). This officer's career is one of the many instances—from Luke O'Connor onwards—in which men, who in their early days

The Boer War

served as private soldiers, have gained the Victoria Cross and eventually risen to high rank.

J. PITTS
(PRIVATE)
1ST BATT. MANCHESTER REGIMENT

THE Victoria Cross was awarded to Private Pitts for his indomitable courage and endurance on January 6, 1900, when, with Private Robert Scott (V.C.), he held a sangar on Caesar's Camp, during the attack on the garrison of Ladysmith. Further details of the affair are given in the record of Robert Scott.

ROBERT SCOTT
(PRIVATE)
1ST BATT. MANCHESTER REGIMENT

Photo by MILES, *Haslingden.*

THE dogged endurance of our soldiers under adverse circumstances has been often remarked upon, and the conduct of Private Scott furnishes an example of it which has seldom, if ever, been excelled. During the great attack on Ladysmith, January 6, 1900, when the fortunes of the hard-pressed and starving garrison so often hung in the balance, Caesar's Camp came in for its share of the work and danger. In one of the sangars Privates Scott and Pitts resolutely maintained their position, and for fifteen hours, without food or water, kept up a hot fire on the Boers, who, having shot all the fourteen men in the sangars on the immediate left, occupied their positions and poured a continuous and heavy fire on these two brave soldiers.

Robert Scott is a "Lancashire lad," having been born at Haslingden on June 4, 1874. On February 2, 1895, he entered the Manchester Regiment, with which he was serving in Natal on the outbreak of hostilities, October, 1899; served throughout the siege of Ladysmith, and during that long time of privation and danger was never once absent from duty. Possesses the Queen's and King's medal with many clasps, including almost the first and the last—Elandslaagte and Belfast.

The officer under whom he served during the great attack on the town was Lieutenant R. Hunt-Grubbe, and the Victoria Cross was pinned on his breast by Lord Kitchener on June 8, 1902, at Pretoria.

History of the Victoria Cross

FRANCIS NEWTON PARSONS
(LIEUTENANT)
44TH (ESSEX) REGIMENT

On March 3, 1900, Lieut.-General Sir Thomas Kelly-Kenny recommended this officer for the Victoria Cross on account of his humane and devoted action during the battle of Paardeberg, February 18, 1900, when he went to the assistance of Private Ferguson, 1st Batt. Essex Regiment, who had been wounded and fallen in an exposed place. After dressing his wounds, he twice, under a terrific fire, went to the river bank to fetch water for him, subsequently carrying him to a place of safety. It is sad to have to relate that this gallant officer was killed at Dreifontein, on March 10, 1900, being again on that occasion noticed for his conspicuous bravery.

Lieutenant Parsons was the son of Dr. C. Parsons, of Dover. He was born on March 23, 1875, entered the 1st Essex Regiment (44th) on February 29, 1896, and attained the rank he held at his death on March 1, 1898. His name is recorded, together with those of seven officers, one warrant officer, and 198 non-commissioned officers and men, on a tablet in the garrison church at Warley Barracks, placed there in memory of those of the Essex Regiment who gave their lives in their country's cause in the Boer War. The tablet was unveiled by Sir Evelyn Wood, V.C., in 1903.

H. ALBRECHT
(TROOPER)
IMPERIAL LIGHT HORSE

On January 6, 1900, at Waggon Hill, during the great assault upon Ladysmith by the Boers, Albrecht behaved with the greatest bravery in leading a party of men who were dashing for the top of the hill to seize the position before the enemy could do so.

Lieutenant Digby-Jones (V.C.), referred to elsewhere, shot the leading Boer, the two next being disposed of by Albrecht, who, during the stubborn fight which took place, unfortunately met his death.

The Boer War

The *Gazette* states that, but for this, the Victoria Cross would have been conferred upon him. Further details of the manner in which he was killed are given in the record of Lieutenant Digby Jones, V.C. (See also Appendix II).

ALFRED ATKINSON
(SERGEANT)
1ST BATT. YORKSHIRE REGIMENT

Photo by PRICE, *Jersey.*

DURING the battle of Paardeberg, on February 18, 1900, Sergeant Atkinson exposed himself to the heavy fire of the enemy to procure and carry water to the wounded. Seven times he repeated this devoted act, and at the last attempt he was shot through the head, dying a few days after.

In a letter from the Adjutant of his battalion he is reported as having been a most exemplary soldier and excellent non-commissioned officer.

Born at Armley, Leeds. He rejoined the Colours from the Reserve at the call of duty in October, 1899, and was entitled to the Queen's medal with clasps for Kimberley (Relief) and Paardeberg, where he fell.

He was the son of Farrier-Major James Atkinson, "H" Battery, 4th Brigade Royal Artillery (who is stated to have been one of the party who captured the original cannon from which the Victoria Cross is now cast), and in accordance with the regulation of August 8, 1902, his Cross is now in the possession of his father.[1]

A. E. CURTIS
(PRIVATE, NOW CORPORAL)
2ND BATT. EAST SURREY REGIMENT

AT Onderbank Spruit, on February 23, 1900, Colonel R. H. W. H. Harris, C.B., was severely wounded, and lay during the whole day in an exposed position, and under a heavy fire from the Boers posted behind a breastwork

---

[1] Appendix II.

History of the Victoria Cross

Photo by COYNE, Pietermaritzburg.

at short range. They fired at any one who gave any sign of life, and Colonel Harris was hit eight or nine times. Curtis made several ineffectual attempts to reach the wounded officer, and at last succeeded in doing so. Notwithstanding the fire directed upon him, Curtis attended to the Colonel's wounds, gave him a drink from his flask and endeavoured to carry him to shelter. Finding he was not equal to the task, he called for help, upon which Private Morton immediately dashed out, and in spite of the Colonel's entreaties to them to leave him and not risk their lives, the two men succeeded in carrying him to cover.

The Victoria Cross was presented to him at Pietermaritzburg on August 14, 1901, by H.R.H. the Duke of York.

EDGAR THOMAS INKSON

(LIEUTENANT, NOW CAPTAIN)

ROYAL ARMY MEDICAL CORPS

Photo by ELLIOTT & FRY, London.

THE Victoria Cross was awarded to this officer for a humane and devoted act at Hart's Hill, Colenso, February 24, 1900. Lieutenant J. G. Devenish (1st Royal Inniskilling Fusiliers), having been severely wounded and unable to move, was lying exposed to a very heavy fire. Lieutenant Inkson, seeing his danger, carried him for 400 yards through the hail of lead poured upon them, and, in spite of the absence of cover for the entire distance, succeeded in conveying him to a place of safety.

Captain Edgar Thomas Inkson, son of Surgeon-Major-General Inkson, R.A., was born at Nyne Tal, India, on April 5, 1872. After passing through University College

The Boer War

Hospital, London, was gazetted Surgeon, July 28, 1899, just ten weeks before the war, and was almost at once sent out to South Africa. He took part in every action for the relief of Ladysmith—from Colenso to the finish, at the end of February, with Fitzroy Hart's, or the Irish Brigade, being twice named in despatches. For his services he has been awarded—in addition to the Victoria Cross—both medals and many clasps. Although daily under fire for weeks together was never once wounded, even though in medical charge with the batteries at Colenso. On return from active service, eighteen months after being gazetted, was presented with the Victoria Cross, at St. James' Palace, by H.M. The King, May 13, 1902.

W. FIRTH

(SERGEANT)

1st Batt. Duke of Wellington's West Riding Regiment

Photo by Elliott, *Aldershot.*

At Plewman's Farm, near Arundel, Cape Colony, February 24, 1900, Sergeant Firth gained the Victoria Cross for two acts of bravery and devotion.

Lance-Corporal Blackman had been wounded and was lying in the open not more than five hundred yards from the enemy, who were keeping up a severe fire on all around. Firth, scorning the bullets aimed at him and his burden, carried the wounded man to cover.

Shortly afterwards, 2nd Lieutenant J. H. B. Wilson fell dangerously wounded, and, in spite of the proximity of the Boers, who had advanced quite close to our firing-line, Firth carried the officer over the crest of the ridge to shelter, receiving a bullet through the eye and nose while engaged in his humane task.

History of the Victoria Cross

Photo by HELSBY, *Beresford Road, N.*

J. J. CLEMENTS
(CORPORAL)
RIMINGTON'S GUIDES

NEAR Strijdenburg, on February 24, 1900, Corporal Clements, by an act of splendid pluck and dash, turned the tables very completely on a party of five Boers. He lay wounded, shot through the lungs, when the Boers came towards him and called on him to surrender. Instead of submitting, he dashed at the party, shot three of them with his revolver, and forced the entire five to surrender to him and two other men of the Guides. The Victoria Cross was presented to him in London on July 1, 1902, at the same time as Lieutenant F. W. Bell (V.C.).

CONWYN MANSEL-JONES
(CAPTAIN)
WEST YORKSHIRE REGIMENT

ON February 27, 1900, at the attack on Terrace Hill, north of the Tugela, Natal, a terrific shell and rifle fire was directed on the companies of the West Yorkshire Regiment, which for the moment checked their advance. Captain Mansel-Jones, by his courageous initiative, gave confidence to his men, and, although he fell severely wounded, the companies took the ridge without any further check. It was "this officer's self-sacrificing devotion to duty at a critical moment" which prevented the whole attack being possibly checked.

The Boer War

Born in 1871, Captain Mansel-Jones entered the Army in 1890, becoming Captain in 1899. Served in the Ashanti Campaign of 1895–6.

H. ENGLEHEART

(SERGEANT)

10TH (THE PRINCE OF WALES' OWN ROYAL) HUSSARS

Photo by SINCLAIR, *Canterbury.*

IN the dawn of March 13, 1900, the party that had successfully destroyed the railway north of Bloemfontein had to charge through a Boer piquet, besides getting over four deep spruits, in order to creep back through the Boer lines. At the last of these Sapper Webb's horse fell, and consequently he was left in a precarious position.

In the face of a deadly shell and rifle fire, notwithstanding the great risk of being cut off and captured, Sergeant Engleheart returned to Sapper Webb's assistance.

Some time was lost getting the man and horse out of the spruit, and the position became momentarily worse owing to the rapid advance of the Boers.

At last, however, he was successful, and, retiring slowly to cover Webb's retreat, he was able to get him safely back to the party. Shortly before this had taken place Sergeant Engleheart had shown great gallantry in dashing into the first spruit, approachable only in single file, which was still held by a party of Boers who were hesitating whether to fire or fly. Had they been given time to rally they would certainly have destroyed our small lot of men, outnumbered as they were by four to one.

H. Engleheart, son of the late Mr. Francis Engleheart, formerly a member of the Stock Exchange, and grandson of N. B. Engleheart, Esq., Blackheath, the last of the Queen's Proctors, was born on November 14, 1864. He was presented with the Victoria Cross by the late Queen Victoria on December 15, 1900, being centre man of the last five of her soldiers on whose breasts the aged Sovereign pinned her Cross.

History of the Victoria Cross

EDMUND JOHN PHIPPS-HORNBY
(MAJOR, NOW LIEUT.-COLONEL)
"Q" BATTERY ROYAL HORSE ARTILLERY

Photo by ELLIOTT & FRY.

On March 31, 1900, a force under General Broadwood was falling back upon Bloemfontein from Thabanchu. It crossed the Modder River and bivouacked at 4.30 a.m. When the Boers attacked at 5.45 a.m., the convoy of about 100 wagons was hurried away towards Bloemfontein along the road which traversed a large open plain about one-and-a-half miles in diameter, across which, at right angles, ran a donga, and through this the wagons began to pass. The guns of "Q" and "U" Batteries followed in line. From the statement of some Boer prisoners, who said that they had been present on the occasion, it would appear that a large party of them had been making their way to Thabanchu and marched across this spruit straight into our camp. They promptly beat a hasty retreat and got into the drift just before daylight, and, as the convoy came up, disarmed the drivers, took them prisoners, and packed each wagon on. Various statements have been made as to what actually happened at this moment. One version is that Major Phipps-Hornby, being told that the enemy were in the drift, promptly galloped his battery away to bring it into action, and that the noise caused thereby told the Boers that they were detected, and they at once opened a terrific fire on all who had not passed the drift. However, it is certain that no sooner had the battery commenced to dash away than the enemy concentrated a furious fire upon the frantic horses and their gallant drivers and gunners. One gun and one wagon, their horses mown down, were left behind. Reaching a spot about 800 yards distant, the remaining guns were unlimbered and came into action, firing steadily. The horses were taken behind some unfinished railway sheds some distance away. So terrible was the fire, that every man round one of the guns was hit, and, at two of them, only one man was left to serve each, and one to bring up ammunition for both. Soon, of all the officers who had come into action, Major Phipps-Hornby was the only one left.

The Boer War

The ground was littered with dead and dying men, the bullets were rattling on the guns like hail, and every time that limbers with ammunition were brought up, the horses were all killed. Word was presently sent to retire and save the guns if possible, and, as the fire was too hot for the horses to face, it was resolved to try to drag them back by hand. Four guns were hauled to shelter in this way, and it was then necessary to bring in the limbers. The work was so terribly hard, and the distance so considerable, that volunteers were called for to take out horses for the purpose. Two limbers were brought in by this means and two more partly by horses and partly by hand. One gun and one limber still remained in the open, and, though four heroic attempts were made, the horses were killed each time, and, finally, they had to be abandoned. The rescued guns had one by one been sent to a place of safety, where the Battery was reformed. Under a deluge of shot and shell, such as perhaps has only been equalled by that faced by the 14th and 66th Batteries at Colenso, the heroism displayed by all ranks was so magnificent that it was impossible to select any individual for special reward, and the Commander-in-Chief decided to act in accordance with Rule 13 of the Victoria Cross Warrant, which resulted in the decoration being awarded to Major Phipps-Hornby, Sergeant Parker, Gunner Lodge and Driver Glasock. That so many guns were saved under such terrible circumstances, and such a frightful fire from the enemy, and that the little force was extricated from the dangerous position in which it was placed, was very greatly due to the heroism and individual example of Major Phipps-Hornby, who was in command, and who most fearlessly exposed himself during the terrible ordeal.

Colonel Phipps-Hornby, son of Admiral of the Fleet Sir Geoffrey Phipps-Hornby, G.C.B., was born December 31, 1857, at Lordington, Sussex. Entered the Royal Artillery in 1877, his first service being in the Bechuanaland Expedition, 1884-5. Became Major, December 11, 1895; Brevet-Lieut.-Colonel—for distinguished service—November 29, 1900; and was, from April 12 following, until attaining the rank of Lieut.-Colonel in the Regiment, A.D.C. to the Commander-in-Chief, Earl Roberts, V.C.

History of the Victoria Cross

Photo by WHITLOCK, *Birmingham.*

C. PARKER

(SERGEANT)

"Q" BATTERY ROYAL HORSE ARTILLERY

THE heroic act in which Sergeant Parker took part will be found described in detail in the record of Major Phipps-Hornby. The bravery exhibited by all concerned in the affair at Korn Spruit on March 31, 1900, was so marked as to render it impossible to single out any individual for special merit. Therefore the Commander-in-Chief decided to treat the case as coming under Rule 13 of the Victoria Cross Warrant, and Sergeant Parker was elected by the non-commissioned officers of the Battery as the representative they considered most worthy of the decoration.

ISAAC LODGE

(GUNNER, NOW BOMBARDIER)

"Q" BATTERY ROYAL HORSE ARTILLERY

THE Victoria Cross was awarded to this gunner for his heroic bravery in saving the guns at Korn Spruit, a description of which is given in the sketch of Major Phipps-Hornby (V.C.).

Isaac Lodge was born at Great Canfield on May 6, 1866, enlisted in the R.G.A. on December 29, 1888, and transferred to the Royal Horse Artillery in February, 1889; posted to "B" Battery, and transferred five years later to the now historic "Q" Battery. During the early days of the war, he saw very active service in Cape Colony, Transvaal, and Orange Free State, including the relief of Kimberley, and the bombardment of the victors of Magersfontein at Paardeberg, for which he was awarded the Queen's medal and four clasps.

Photo by CHARLETON, *Newbridge.*

The Boer War

H. H. GLASOCK
(DRIVER)
"Q" BATTERY ROYAL HORSE ARTILLERY

Photo by CHARLETON, *Newbridge.*

THE episode of saving the guns at Korn Spruit on March 31, 1900, will rank in the annals of the British Army with the heroic act at "Maiwand," in the Afghan War, when James Collis and Patrick Mullane earned their Crosses so worthily. A full description of the Korn Spruit affair and the heroism displayed by Glasock, Parker, Lodge, and Major Phipps-Hornby, will be found in the record of the last named. The conduct of all concerned was so splendid that it was impossible to choose any individual as more worthy of the distinguished decoration than any of the others engaged, therefore the Commander-in-Chief decided to treat the case of the Battery as one of collective gallantry under Rule 13 of the Victoria Cross Warrant, and Driver Glasock was selected by the drivers of the Battery as the man they considered most deserving of the award.

FRANCIS AYLMER MAXWELL, D.S.O.
LIEUTENANT, INDIAN STAFF CORPS,
(ATTACHED TO ROBERTS' LIGHT HORSE)
(NOW BREVET-MAJOR, 18TH BENGAL LANCERS)

THE heroic episode of saving the guns at Korn Spruit, on March 31, 1900, has already been described in the record of Major Phipps-Hornby, but with the names of those mentioned therein the list of heroes on that occasion does not end. Lieutenant Maxwell, though not belonging to the famous "Q" Battery, was present also at the affair, and was specially mentioned by Lord Roberts, for " the greatest gallantry and disregard of danger." On five different occasions he went out to face the blizzard of lead " and assisted in bringing in two guns and three limbers, one of which he, Captain Humphreys, and some gunners, dragged in by hand." And in their company

History of the Victoria Cross

Photo by ELLIOTT & FRY, *London.*

he again went out to endeavour to bring in the last gun, remaining there exposed to shot and shell, till the attempt had to be abandoned. The notification in the *Gazette* recording the act for which Lieutenant Maxwell was awarded the Cross, makes reference to the gallantry displayed by him during the Chitral Campaign, 1895, when he removed the body of Lieut.-Colonel F. D. Battye of the Guides under a very heavy fire from the enemy, " for which, though recommended, he received no reward." This official statement of an act of gallantry in a previous campaign, included in the notification of that for which the Cross is awarded in a later one, has not occurred before in the Victoria Cross records.

Born on September 7, 1871, Lieutenant Maxwell in 1891 became 2nd Lieutenant 2nd Batt. Royal Sussex Regiment (107th), from which, as Lieutenant, he entered the Indian Staff Corps, December, 1903; was promoted, for his distinguished services, Brevet-Major in 1902, and appointed A.D.C. to Lord Kitchener. For services on the Indian Frontier, he was decorated with the D.S.O. and holds the Frontier medal and clasps, to which he has now added both the South African medals with many clasps. Was decorated with the Victoria Cross by H.R.H. the Duke of York, at Pietermaritzburg, August 14, 1901.

Photo by RUSSELL & SONS, *London.*

WILLIAM HENRY SNYDER NICKERSON

(LIEUTENANT, NOW CAPTAIN)

ROYAL ARMY MEDICAL CORPS (ATTACHED TO MOUNTED INFANTRY)

AT Wakkerstroom, on April 20, 1900, as the infantry were advancing to the support of the mounted troops, Captain Nickerson carried out his duties in a conspicuously courageous manner, in one instance especially, remaining by a wounded man after attending to his injuries, in spite of the dreadful rifle-fire, until he was able to remove him to a place of safety.

The Boer War

Captain Nickerson, son of the Rev. D. Nickerson, Chaplain H.M. Forces, was born on March 27, 1875. Educated at Portsmouth Grammar School, he took his degree of M.B. Ch.B. at Owen's College, Manchester, in 1896, and entered the R.A.M.C., July 27, 1898. For his distinguished services was promoted Captain on November 29, 1900.

HARRY CHURCHILL BEET

(CORPORAL, NOW SERGEANT)

1ST BATT. NOTTINGHAM AND DERBYSHIRE REGIMENT (MOUNTED INFANTRY)

Photo by DEALE, *Bloemfontein.*

NEAR Wakkerstroom, on April 22, 1900, No. 2 Mounted Infantry Co. (1st Derbyshire) and two squadrons Imperial Yeomanry were obliged to retire from their position, being under a ridge strongly held by the enemy. An Imperial Yeoman, Corporal Burnett, being shot, was left on the ground, on seeing which Beet went back, dragged him to cover, and attended to his wounds, keeping up whenever able such a hot fire on the enemy that they were prevented from approaching the post till after darkness had set in, when Dr. Wilson, Imperial Yeomanry, took charge of the wounded man. Not only during the retirement, but throughout the whole afternoon, Beet was exposed to a heavy fire.

Son of Mr. J. A. Beet, sculptor, of Brackendale Farm, near Bingham, Notts, where he was born on April 1, 1873. Joined the Sherwood Foresters, February 18, 1892, embarking for India January, 1894, serving throughout the fighting on the Punjab Frontier, 1897–8 (medal and two clasps). During active service in South Africa was once wounded, December 9, 1901; was promoted Sergeant by Lord Kitchener for service in the field, April 4, 1900, gaining his Victoria Cross as above described while under immediate command of Captain P. Leverson-Gower, and Column-Commander Lieut.-Colonel Sitwell, D.S.O. The decoration was presented to him at the capital of Natal, August 14, 1901, by H.R.H. the Duke of York.

History of the Victoria Cross

JOHN FREDERICK MACKAY
(CORPORAL)
GORDON HIGHLANDERS (NOW LIEUTENANT KING'S OWN SCOTTISH BORDERERS)

Photo by LAFAYETTE.

ON May 29, 1900, during the action at Crow's Nest Hill, near Johannesburg, Lieutenant Mackay was conspicuous for his humanity and brave conduct, attending to the wounded, and giving them every help in his power, in spite of being far from any cover, and within a short range of the Boers. He also carried one man from the open ground to shelter, under a very heavy fire.

Lieutenant Mackay, formerly a student at Trinity College, Dublin, entered the Army as a private soldier, enlisting into the 1st Gordons, serving with that distinguished corps against the Chitralese in 1895, and on the Punjab Frontier, 1897–8, including the storming of Dargai, obtaining the special Frontier medal and clasps. His commission in the K.O.S.B. was signed just fourteen months after he won the Victoria Cross (July 27, 1901).

FRANK HOWARD KIRBY
(CORPORAL, NOW SERGEANT-MAJOR)
ROYAL ENGINEERS

ON June 2, 1900, Kirby was one of a party who had been sent out to cut the Delagoa Bay Railway. While retiring, they were hard pressed by a large number of Boers, both mounted and on foot, and several small rearguard actions were fought. During one of these, one of the men had his horse shot under him, and he commenced to try and catch up his troop, running after them on foot, under a full fire of the enemy. Kirby turned and rode back to him, and succeeded in getting him on to his horse, all the time under a heavy fire, at quite close range, after which he rode back with him, over the rising ground, to where the rearguard had taken up a fresh position.

Frank Howard Kirby, born at Thane, Oxfordshire, November 12, 1871, son of Mr. W. H. Kirby of that town, was educated at Alleyn's School, Dulwich, and entered the Royal Engineers at St. George's Barracks, London, on August 8, 1892.

He embarked for South Africa, upon his first active service, on October 29, 1899, gaining, almost at once, the Medal for Distinguished Conduct—blowing up the railway near Bloemfontein, March, 1900. During the campaign he gained, under the immediate command of Colonel A. Hunter-Weston, D.S.O., the King's and Queen's Medal and six clasps. The *Gazette* states that the occasion described above was the third upon which Kirby displayed great gallantry in the face of the enemy. He was frequently named in despatches, was promoted Sergeant-Major in the field by Lord Roberts (July, 1900), being presented with the Victoria Cross by H.R.H. the Duke of Cornwall and York at Cape Town, on August 19, 1901.

CHARLES WARD

(PRIVATE)

2ND BATT. YORKSHIRE LIGHT INFANTRY

Photo by SWITHENBANK, *Chapel Allerton.*

AT Lindley, on June 26, 1900, where so many of our brave men fell, about 500 of the enemy succeeded in getting to close quarters with a picket, which was attacked from three sides. Both the officers were wounded, and every man, with the exception of six, was placed *hors-de-combât*. A reinforcement to save the post was absolutely necessary, but a message to that effect would have to be taken to the signalling station. Ward volunteered to do this, but, as it meant almost certain death to any man attempting it, his gallant offer was at first refused. He, however, insisted on being allowed to go, and, with 150 yards of open ground to cross, swept by the heavy rifle-fire of the Boers, succeeded in reaching the signallers. His message delivered, he resolved to return again, risking his life with the object of encouraging his few remaining comrades to maintain their defence, by assuring them that the much needed help was asked for and would soon be at hand. He contrived to reach the hard-pressed post again, but not before being severely wounded.

Charles Ward, son of Mr. George Ward, was born at Leeds, July 10, 1877, being educated at Primrose Hill School in that city. On April 29, 1897, he enlisted into the 1st Batt. Yorkshire Light Infantry—the old 51st of Peninsula and Waterloo fame—with which, under Colonel G. P. F. Byng, he served for two years, joining the 2nd Battalion at Wynberg, Cape Colony. Owing to his severe wound he has only two clasps to his medal, Cape Colony and Free State. When he gained the Victoria Cross his Company and Commanding Officers were Captain Wittycombe and Lieut.-Colonel Barter, C.B., with Major-General A. H. Paget, C.V.O., as Chief. So highly was Ward's conduct appreciated that the citizens of Leeds, on his discharge from the service, presented him with a testimonial and £600, together with a commemorative medal in gold by Mr. William Owen.

ARTHUR HERBERT LINDSEY RICHARDSON
(SERGEANT)
LORD STRATHCONA'S CORPS

Photo by STUART *Brompton Road.*

On July 5, 1900, at the action of Wolve Spruit, about fifteen miles north of Standerton, a small party of Lord Strathcona's Corps, about thirty-eight in number, came to close quarters with about eighty of the enemy. The Colonials came under a very fierce fire, and, on the order to retire being given, Richardson rode back and took up a man who had been hit in two places, and who was dismounted, his horse having been shot, and carried him out of range of the Boers. A heavy fire was brought to bear on him at the time, the enemy being only 300 yards distant, and the horse he rode was wounded and could only proceed slowly.

The Boer War

WILLIAM EAGLESON GORDON
(CAPTAIN)
GORDON HIGHLANDERS

On July 11, 1900, at Leehoehoek (or Dornboschfontein), a spirited action was fought against the Boers, whose fire at only 850 yards was so terribly severe that the Artillery horses were unable to stand against it. Captain Gordon, however, determined to attempt to drag one of the guns into shelter by hand. To accomplish this, a drag-rope had first to be fastened to it, which task of fearful risk, by reason of the hail of lead raining on any one exposing himself, he elected to carry out himself. Calling for volunteers, and instructing them to dash out on the instant he should sign to them that all was ready, he made for the gun, fastened the rope to it, signalled to his men, who promptly doubled out, and all commenced hauling. Of the gallant band, three men were severely, and Captain Younger mortally, wounded; whereupon, seeing that further attempts would only mean increased casualties, Captain Gordon ordered the remainder under cover of a kopje, saw personally to the wounded, and then himself retired. During the entire affair his conduct is described as having been *most admirable*, the handling of his men as *masterly*, and his devotion, on every occasion under fire, *most remarkable*. (See account of Captain Younger, V.C.)

Captain W. E. Gordon is the son of the late W. E. Gordon, M.D., of Bridge-of-Allan, Stirlingshire, where he was born on May 4, 1866. Educated at Edinburgh University; entered the 1st Gordon Highlanders, then in Ceylon, on June 6, 1888. His first active service was with the Chitral Relief Expedition in 1895, for which he was awarded the (new) Frontier Medal and two clasps (Malakand Pass). Two years later he served through the Tirah Campaign, being present at the storming of the Dargai Heights (clasp to medal). Was Adjutant of his battalion during the Boer War, being dangerously wounded at Magersfontein, December 11, 1899; twice mentioned in despatches; received Queen's and King's medal with seven clasps and the Victoria Cross, which latter decoration was placed on his breast by Lord Kitchener at Pretoria on Peace Thanksgiving Day, June 1902.

DAVID REGINALD YOUNGER
(CAPTAIN)
GORDON HIGHLANDERS

ON July 11, 1900, during the action near Leehoehoek, Captain Younger, finding that the Artillery horses were unable to stand the accurate and terribly severe fire of the enemy, went out with a few men and succeeded in dragging an Artillery wagon into shelter by hand. Later on, he was one of those who, at the call of Captain Gordon (V.C.), volunteered to endeavour to drag in one of the guns by hand, during which attempt he was mortally wounded. (See account of Captain Gordon.)

Born on March 17, 1871, Captain Younger, after serving as an officer of the Duke of Edinburgh's Edinburgh Artillery, commissioned as 2nd Lieutenant into the Gordon Highlanders on December 23, 1893, fighting at Chitral and on the Punjab Frontier, 1895, 1897–8, including the gallant and historic assault and capture of the Dargai Heights, in October, 1897. The medal and three clasps were obtained by him for these trying services, and, but for his sad but heroic death, the Victoria Cross, as stated in the *Gazette*, would have been his to wear. It has now been delivered to his relatives in accordance with the Regulation approved by H.M. The King in 1902.[1]

N. R. HOWSE
(CAPTAIN)
NEW SOUTH WALES MEDICAL STAFF CORPS

ON July 24, 1900, at the action of Vredefort, Captain Howse went forward to a man lying severely wounded, and, taking him up, carried him some consider-

[1] See Appendix II.

The Boer War

able distance to shelter, during which humane act he came under a very severe cross-fire from the Boers. The decoration was presented to Captain Howse by Sir Frederick Darling, Governor of New South Wales, on February 8, 1902, at Sydney.

WILLIAM HOUSE
(PRIVATE)
2ND BATT. ROYAL BERKSHIRE REGIMENT

Photo by DEE, *Reading.*

ON August 2, 1900, it was resolved to make an attack upon the Boer position at Mosilikatse Nek, and, for the purpose of ascertaining a better idea of the enemy's force, a sergeant was sent forward to reconnoitre. Before he could, however, rejoin his comrades, he was seen by the enemy, who, opening fire, wounded him most severely. He lay on the open ground, in full view of the Boer marksmen, who kept up a hail of bullets on and around him. House, though cautioned that almost certain death lay before him, sprang out from the cover, behind which he and the rest of the troops were concealed, and attempted to carry in his wounded comrade. While making this heroic attempt he himself was badly shot, and, though lying fully exposed, in his turn, to the Boer rifle-fire, called to his comrades not to come to his assistance until the advance was made. This act, for which he was awarded the Victoria Cross, was performed under the immediate command of Captain Sir Edward Pasley, Bart., Sir Ian Hamilton being Chief.

William House, son of Mr. Thomas House, of Park Lane, Thatcham, Berkshire, was born at that place on October 7, 1879, enlisted into the Royal Berkshire Regiment on November 3, 1896, and was duly gazetted to the roll of the Victoria Cross on his twenty-third birthday, October 7, 1902. Besides this coveted decoration, he possesses both medals for the South African War and many clasps. Received the Victoria Cross at the hands of H.M. the King on October 24, 1902, in London.

History of the Victoria Cross

T. LAWRENCE
(SERGEANT)

17TH LANCERS

Photo by BEAUFORT, *Birmingham.*

ON August 7, 1900, Sergeant Lawrence was on patrol duty with Private Hayman, when they were attacked by about fourteen of the enemy. Private Hayman's horse was hit, and in falling threw its rider, dislocating his shoulder. Lawrence went at once to his comrade's help, dragged him from under the wounded animal, set him on his own horse, telling him to ride towards the picket. He then took Hayman's carbine, and, with his own as well, kept the enemy at a distance until the wounded man was safely out of range, when he commenced to retire on foot, followed by the Boers for two miles, and keeping them off until he received assistance.

The Victoria Cross, so nobly earned, was presented to Sergeant Lawrence by H.M. the King in London on August 12, 1902.

HARRY HAMPTON
(SERGEANT, NOW SERGEANT-INSTRUCTOR IN MUSKETRY)

1ST BATT. LIVERPOOL REGIMENT

ON August 21, 1900, Sergeant Hampton was in command of a party of mounted infantry at Van Wyk's Vlei, and had been holding an important position for a considerable time against very heavy odds. They were at length compelled to retire, but he saw all his men safely into cover before he would leave, and then, although himself severely wounded in the head, went to the assistance of Lance-Corporal Walsh, who was too badly injured to keep up with the rest, and supported him until the man was killed by another shot, he himself receiving a second wound shortly after.

The Boer War

Photo by BIRTLES, *Warrington*.

Sergeant Hampton, son of Mr. Samuel Hampton, of Crown Terrace, Richmond, Surrey, was born at that place December 14, 1870. Entered the 1st Batt. King's Liverpool Regiment at Aldershot, March 10, 1889, rising to the rank of Corporal in exactly two years. Saw service in the West Indies and Nova Scotia from 1891 to 1897, and in South Africa from the latter year till almost the close of the war. His Commanding Officers on the day he won the Victoria Cross were Brevet-Major C. J. Steavenson and Major (now Colonel Sir) H. K. Stewart, K.C.B., and the decoration was presented to him by H.M. the King at St. James' Palace in December, 1901.

H. J. KNIGHT

(CORPORAL)

1ST BATT. THE KING'S LIVERPOOL REGIMENT; NO. 1 COMPANY 4TH DIVISION MOUNTED INFANTRY

ON August 21, 1900, during operations near Van Wyk's Vlei, Corporal Knight and four men were occupying a position behind some rocks, to cover the rear of a detachment of their company, which, under Captain Ewart, D.S.O., was holding the right of the line. Being attacked on the right by about fifty Boers, Knight's little band of four men were almost surrounded at very close quarters by the enemy. Ordering them to retire one by one to a more sheltered position, he stayed at his post for nearly an hour, covering Captain Ewart's force, during which two of his men were shot. Placing one of them in a secure place he left him there, carrying the other for two miles on his back, the whole time being under a very hot fire from the enemy.

Photo by SOUTHWELL, *Battersea*.

History of the Victoria Cross

WILLIAM HEATON

(PRIVATE, NOW SERGEANT)

1ST BATT. THE KING'S LIVERPOOL REGIMENT

Photo by GARDINER, *Ormskirk.*

AT Geluk, on August 23, 1900, Private Heaton's company, while advancing in front of the general line held by our troops, was surrounded, and, coming under a raking fire, was suffering most severely. The position becoming serious, the Commanding Officer requested Heaton to convey a message back, explaining the precarious situation in which the company stood, and asking for relief. At the greatest possible risk, Heaton successfully accomplished his mission, and there is no doubt that but for his great courage in undertaking so hazardous a duty, his company would have had a very heavy death-roll and been forced to surrender.

GUY G. E. WYLLY

(LIEUTENANT)

TASMANIAN IMPERIAL BUSHMEN

ON September 1, 1900, when a foraging party was near Warm Bad, Lieutenant Wylly was one of the advanced scouts. While passing through a narrow and thickly-wooded defile, they were suddenly fired upon, at a very short range, by the Boers.

Being well hidden by the trees, it was impossible for the enemy to be exactly located, or for our men to fire with any effect; and, being much exposed, six, including Lieutenant Wylly, were hit, out of the little party of eight. Corporal Brown was badly hurt in the leg, and his horse shot, seeing which, though wounded himself, Wylly went to the man's assistance, helped him up on to his own horse, and took shelter behind some boulders, from which he opened a sharp fire on the enemy to cover the retreat of the rest of his party.

Colonel Hickman, D.S.O. (Worcestershire Regiment), reports that Wylly's brave action saved Brown from being killed or taken prisoner, and, in firing to cover the retreat of the rest, at the grave risk of being himself cut off, he was the means of saving others of his party from a similar fate.

The Boer War

Born in 1883, Lieutenant Wylly is the son of Major E. Wylly, late Leinster Regiment and Indian Staff Corps, and grandson of the late Mr. Robert Clerk, of Westholme, Somerset, and Sergeant-at-Arms to the House of Assembly, Hobart, Tasmania. Has been gazetted to the Royal Berkshire Regiment.

J. H. BISDEE
(PRIVATE)
TASMANIAN IMPERIAL BUSHMEN

ON September 1, 1900, Bisdee was one of the advanced scouts near Warm Bad (at the same time as Lieutenant Wylly (V.C.), who so gallantly distinguished himself on that occasion). As related in the account of that officer, the party were passing through a narrow gorge and were suddenly fired at by some Boers in ambush, six of the eight men being wounded, including Wylly and another officer. The horse of the latter was hit, and bolted, upon which Bisdee gave his stirrup-leather to his officer with the object of helping him out of action, but the latter's wounds being too severe to allow of his getting on in this fashion, Bisdee dismounted, placed him on the horse, mounted behind him, and helped him out of range of the Boers, who kept up a hot fire on the two men, both of whom were, during Bisdee's gallant act, in a very exposed place.

Private Bisdee is the son of the late Mr. J. Bisdee, of Hutton, Weston-super-Mare.

E. DURRANT
(PRIVATE)
2ND BATT. RIFLE BRIGADE

WHEN one considers the terrible surroundings of a battle-field, the awful spectacle of dead and dying men, the strain on the nerves, the excitement and noise of firing, it is not strange to hear of any soldier succumbing to the mental strain involved. At Spion Kop, while men were being literally torn to pieces by shell-fire, it has been placed on record that some of our men were seen wandering about calmly as if among the peaceful fields of England, and it is not difficult to realize that men, in the midst of such awful carnage, became battle-dazed and temporarily deranged. Such a case occurred at Bergendal, on August 27, 1900, when a soldier, Acting-Corporal Wellar, having been wounded, became dazed, and getting up from the firing-line, commenced to run towards the enemy. Private Durrant, seeing the man's condition, started after him, caught and, pulled him down, endeavouring to quieten him, but, finding this too severe a task to accomplish alone, he carried the man for two hundred yards under a tremendous fire, and placed him in a safe position, afterwards returning to his place in the fighting-line.

EDWARD DOUGLAS BROWN
(MAJOR)
(NOW LIEUT.-COLONEL EDWARD DOUGLAS BROWN-SYNGE-HUTCHINSON)
14TH HUSSARS

Photo by KNIGHT, *Aldershot.*

ON October 13, 1900, at Geluk, where Private Heaton gained the Victoria Cross so gallantly in the previous August, the enemy got within 400 yards of our men, opening a heavy fire on them. Sergeant Hersey's horse had been shot, leaving him in imminent danger of sharing the same fate, which he would almost certainly have done but for Major Brown, who, waiting till the last squadron had retired, rode back, and, assisting him to mount behind, brought him safely out of range of the Boers. Shortly afterwards this brave officer also saved the life of Lieutenant J. G. Browne, by holding his horse when it had become almost unmanageable owing to the heavy fire concentrated on it and its rider, and, but for Major Brown's assistance, it could not have been mounted. Subsequently, Lance-Corporal Trumpeter Leigh owed his life to the conspicuous daring of this officer, who carried him out of action, thus making the third he had saved that day.

Major (now Colonel) Brown, son of the late Major David Philip Brown, 7th Hussars, was born on March 6, 1861. Was educated at Edinburgh

The Boer War

Academy, Windermere College, United Service College, and Westward Ho! He received his first commission as Lieutenant in the 18th Hussars, November, 1883, in which he became Captain in less than five years—August 8, 1888—and in his present regiment March, 1889. From January 1, 1890, to December 31, 1894, was Commandant of the Aldershot School of Instruction for Yeomanry, attaining the rank of Major and Brevet-Lieut.-Colonel on January 28, 1899. Mentioned three times in despatches during the Boer War, and has seven clasps to his medal for South Africa.

ALEXIS C. DOXAT

(LIEUTENANT)

3RD BATT. IMPERIAL YEOMANRY

Photo by LAFAYETTE.

On October 20, 1900, near Zeerust, when with a party reconnoitring a position held by about one hundred Boers on the ridge of some kopjes, Lieutenant Doxat's men came under a very severe fire at about three hundred yards range. They then retired, but one of them, having lost his horse, was in a most precarious position, the Boers keeping up a hot fire on him. Lieutenant Doxat promptly galloped back to him, took him on his own horse and rode with him out of range.

Mr. Alexis Doxat, son of Mr. Edmund Doxat, of Wood Green Park, Hertfordshire, was born at Surbiton, Surrey, on April 9, 1867. Educated at Norwich Grammar School and Philberd's, Maidenhead. Was a Captain in the Dalston Militia under Colonel Somerset, C.B., and Lieut.-Colonel Bowles, M.P., passing successfully the Auxiliary School of Instruction and the Hythe Musketry School. On the outbreak of the Boer War, Lieutenant Doxat left the Stock Exchange, of which he was a member, and proceeded to South Africa with Lord Scarborough's detachment. Took part in Lord Methuen's advance from Boshof in May, 1900, and in September joined General Douglas' column as personal A.D.C., acting chiefly as reconnaissance officer. The Victoria Cross was presented to him at Marlborough House on December 17, 1901, by H.M. the King.

History of the Victoria Cross

HAMPDEN ZANE CHURCHILL COCKBURN
(LIEUTENANT, NOW MAJOR)
ROYAL CANADIAN DRAGOONS

Photo by LYONDE, *Toronto.*

On November 7, 1900, at Komati River, the guns were in great danger of being captured by the Boers, but Lieutenant Cockburn behaved with conspicuous coolness and bravery, and, with only a few men, held off the enemy long enough to enable the guns to be got successfully away to safety, not, however, without severe loss among his gallant followers, all of whom were killed, wounded, or taken prisoners, he himself being wounded.

Major Cockburn is the son of Mr. George Ralph Richardson Cockburn, now a Director of the Ontario Bank in Toronto, and for many years M.P. for that city, as well as Principal of Upper Canada College. Born on November 19, 1867, he was educated at Upper Canada College (Toronto), and Rugby School, England. On November 20, 1891, entered Governor-General's Body Guard as 2nd Lieutenant, and early in 1900 volunteered for service in South Africa, where, in addition to the Victoria Cross, he gained the Queen's Medal with clasps for Cape Colony, Diamond Hill, Johannesburg, and Orange Free State, in all of which actions, and during the entire service (when the regiment marched 1,700 miles and took part in forty-five engagements), he commanded a troop. The officers under whose command the Victoria Cross was gained by him were Colonel Lessard, in command of unit, and Major-General Smith-Dorrien, G.O.C., and it was presented to him by H.R.H. the Duke of Cornwall and York at Toronto on October 11, 1901, as was also, on the same occasion, a sword of honour voted to him by the council of that city. Major Cockburn possesses also the Royal Canadian Humane Society's medal for having, at great personal risk, saved the lives from drowning of two brothers, Robert and James Harris, in Lake Rosseau, on September 20, 1897.

The Boer War

RICHARD ERNEST WILLIAM TURNER, D.S.O.
(LIEUTENANT, NOW LIEUT.-COLONEL, QUEEN'S OWN CANADIAN HUSSARS)
ROYAL CANADIAN DRAGOONS

Photo by MONTMINY & Co., *Quebec.*

AT Komati River, November 7, 1900, when the Canadians did such splendid work—as, indeed, they did throughout the whole of their South African service—Lieutenant Turner's conduct was particularly noticeable, especially when the Boers made a most determined attack upon the guns, very nearly succeeding in capturing them. Although he had been twice wounded earlier in the day, Lieutenant Turner dismounted, deployed his men at close quarters, repelled and finally repulsed the Boers, and it was to the courageous initiative and splendid handling of the gallant men by himself and Lieutenant Cockburn (V.C.), and the brave conduct of Sergeant Holland (V.C.) (to whom reference is made elsewhere), that the saving of the guns was chiefly due.

Son of Richard Turner, Esq., of Quebec, where he was born on July 25. 1871, Colonel Turner entered the Queen's Own Canadian Hussars on April 22, 1892. The senior officers under whom the Cross was gained were Major-General Smith-Dorrien and Colonel Lissard, C.B. Possesses the Coronation Medal in addition to that for South Africa (Queen's) with six clasps. The Cross was presented to him by H.R.H. the Prince of Wales at Quebec during His Royal Highness's visit to the Dominion in 1902. Three times "named" in despatches, and severely wounded.

History of the Victoria Cross

E. HOLLAND
(Sergeant)
Royal Canadian Dragoons

Photo by Pittaway, Ottawa.

On November 7, 1900, during the operations at Komati River, Sergeant Holland was associated with Lieutenants Cockburn and Turner in the splendid work done by those officers and their men on that day. When the Boers attacked, and nearly captured, the two 12-pounder guns, it was greatly owing to the fine work done by Holland with a Colt-gun that the enemy were kept in check; and later, finding them so close upon him that there was no chance of his escaping with the gun and carriage, owing to his horse being too exhausted, with the utmost coolness and self-possession, he lifted the gun off the carriage, mounted the horse, and rode away with it under his arm.

CHARLES THOMAS KENNEDY
(Private)
1st Batt. Highland Light Infantry

Photo by Dunbar, Edinburgh.

On November 22, 1900, during the engagement at Dewetsdorp, one of Kennedy's comrades was so severely shot that, without the best medical assistance, it was certain he must bleed to death. Notwithstanding that from Gibraltar Hill, where he was posted, the distance to the hospital was nearly a mile, the entire ground being swept by the Boer rifle-fire, Kennedy carried him all this way on his back and succeeded in placing him in safety, where requisite attention was promptly obtained.

Next day, an urgent and important message was required to be conveyed to the officer commanding, but, to reach him, an open space would have had to be crossed, swept by rifle-fire and almost certain death to any one attempting it. Kennedy volunteered the well-nigh impossible task, and, though he heroically started on his mission, he was unsuccessful, being shot through the body and severely wounded before he had covered twenty yards. Under the skilful treatment he received at the hands of Dr. Possnet, and the careful nursing of Sister Dempster, he recovered to wear the Victoria Cross he so well earned.

Charles Kennedy, son of Mr. C. Kennedy, of Foss, Perthshire, was born at Edinburgh, January 6, 1876. Joined the 1st Battalion Highland Light Infantry on September 17, 1891, and proceeded to India in February, 1894. With the 2nd Battalion he fought on the Punjab Frontier, 1897-8, obtaining medal with clasp. In the South African War he was mentioned in Lord Roberts' despatches, and took part in six battles and several minor actions, from Modder River to Dewetsdorp, where he won his Victoria Cross, which was presented to him on December 16, 1901, at St. James' Palace by H.M. the King.

DONALD FARMER

(SERGEANT)

1ST BATT. THE QUEEN'S OWN CAMERON HIGHLANDERS

Photo by Coyne, Pietermaritzburg

When, on December 13, 1900, General Clements' camp at Nooitgedacht was attacked by a large force of Boers, Lieutenant Sandilands, of the Camerons, took fifteen men and went to the assistance of a picket which was hard pressed, having lost in killed or wounded the greater number of its men. The enemy, posted behind trees, opened fire on the little party at about twenty yards range, killing two men and wounding five, including Lieutenant Sandilands. Farmer at once went to the officer's assistance, and, under a very heavy fire, carried him to shelter, after which he returned to the fighting-line, being, with the rest of his party, after a desperate resistance, taken prisoner.

The Victoria Cross awarded him for this humane act was presented to him by H.R.H. the Duke of York at Pietermaritzburg, August 14, 1901.

History of the Victoria Cross

J. BARRY

(PRIVATE)

1ST BATT. ROYAL IRISH REGIMENT

Photo by NIELSEN, *Kilkenny.*

ON January 7, 1901, during the attack on Monument Hill, Private Barry was near the Maxim gun when his party was surrounded and threatened by the Boers. To save it from falling into the enemy's hands and being used against our own men, he heroically smashed the breach of it, rendering it quite useless, and, while engaged in this devoted action, was killed. The Victoria Cross, as stated in the *Gazette*, would have been awarded to him had he survived, but it was handed to his relatives by the authorities in accordance with the new regulation framed by the Secretary of State for War in 1902.[1]

W. J. HARDHAM

(FARRIER-MAJOR, NOW LIEUTENANT)

4TH NEW ZEALAND CONTINGENT

THE case of this non-commissioned officer is typical of the devotion shown by Englishmen to one another in times of peril, and is one of many instances that occurred during the Boer War. On January 28, 1901, Hardham was in command of a section which became engaged with one of the roving bands of the enemy who kept up for so many months a kind of "guerilla" warfare, and gave us so much trouble to stamp out. Our men were forced to retire, and, just before the movement commenced, Trooper McCrae was wounded, and his horse killed. Seeing the man's plight, Hardham rode to him under a

Photo by HELSBY, *Beresford Road, Canonbury.*

[1] Appendix II.

The Boer War

most galling fire, dismounted, and, helping him on to his own horse, ran by his comrade's side until he had seen him out of danger. Received the Victoria Cross at the hands of H.M. the King, on July 1, 1902, in London.

WILLIAM BERNARD TRAYNOR
(SERGEANT)
2ND BATT. WEST YORKSHIRE REGIMENT

Photo by DUNCAN, *Hull.*

ON the night of February 6, 1901, Bothwell Camp was attacked by a large force of Boers. Under a very heavy fire, Traynor dashed out of his trench and went to the help of a man who had been shot, but, on the way to reach him, was severely wounded and prevented from carrying his comrade to a place of safety. Finding himself powerless to attempt alone what he had intended, he called for assistance, whereupon Corporal Lintott ran to him and together they contrived to carry the injured man to cover. Notwithstanding his serious wound, Traynor remained in command of his section, cheering his men and encouraging all by his devoted example, until, finally, the attack failed and the enemy drew off.

Traynor, though born in Hull, December 31, 1870, is of Irish extraction, being son of Mr. Francis Traynor, of Monaghan. When in his eighteenth year, November 14, 1888, he enlisted into the West York Regiment, serving for some years in India, and from 1899 to 1901 in South Africa, receiving the Queen's medal and clasps for the Relief of Ladysmith, Tugela Heights, Spion Kop, Laing's Nek, Transvaal and Orange Colony.

His Company and Commanding Officers when he gained the Cross were Lieutenant G. L. Crossman, D.S.O., and Lieut.-Colonel W. Fry, C.B., and the well-earned decoration was presented to him by Colonel Edward Stevenson Browne—himself a Victoria Cross winner in the Zulu War of 1879—on July 2, 1902, at York.

Owing to the seriousness of his wound Traynor was invalided in 1902, and now holds a post at Dover Castle.

Corporal Lintott, who so nobly answered his comrade's call for assistance, was awarded the medal for Distinguished Conduct, and promoted Sergeant by Lord Kitchener.

History of the Victoria Cross

FREDERIC BROOKS DUGDALE

(LIEUTENANT)

5TH (ROYAL IRISH) LANCERS

ON March 3, 1901, when in command of an outpost near Derby, Lieutenant Dugdale received orders to retire his men. His party came under a very heavy fire from the Boers at a range of about 250 yards, and three men and a horse were wounded. Riding up to one of the injured men, Lieutenant Dugdale dismounted and put him on to his own horse, ran and caught a riderless horse near by, mounted it, and rode to another helpless man, took this one up behind him and rode with both men out of action.

Lieutenant Dugdale was the son of Colonel J. Dugdale, of Sezincot, Gloucestershire, and was born at Burnley on October 21, 1877. Educated at Marlborough and Christ Church, Oxford, he entered the Army in October, 1899, as 2nd Lieutenant in the 5th Lancers, and at once left England to join his regiment, which, on his arrival in South Africa, was taking part in the defence of Ladysmith. He was employed with the relieving force under Sir Redvers Buller, and was promoted Lieutenant in May, 1900. Served under Sir John French in Cape Colony. Received the King's and Queen's medal, and clasps for Tugela Heights, Orange Free State, Relief of Ladysmith, Laing's Nek, and Belfast. The Cross was presented to this young and promising officer by H.M. the King on October 24 1902, but, on the 13th of the following month, he was killed in the hunting-field while riding with the North Cotswold Hounds.

The Boer War

F. W. BELL
(LIEUTENANT)
WEST AUSTRALIAN MOUNTED INFANTRY

Photo by HELSBY, *Beresford Road, N.*

LIKE our other colonies, Australia sent her contingents of gallant sons to answer the call of the mother-country in time of need, a silent and grim reminder to those who talk of England's isolation. Among the Australian contingent was Lieutenant Bell, and at Brakpan, on May 16, 1901, he was with his company holding the right flank during a sharp encounter with our mobile enemy. When obliged to retire, Bell saw a trooper, dismounted and in imminent danger, owing to the heavy fire poured on all within range. Turning back, he took the man up on his horse, but the double weight was more than the poor jaded animal could bear, and, before it had carried them many yards, it fell, and thus left both men in jeopardy. Without a thought for his own safety, Bell ordered the trooper to escape as best he could, he meanwhile, keeping up a sharp fire on the enemy, held them in check and covered the man's retreat. The Victoria Cross was presented to him in London on July 1, 1902, by H.R.H. the Prince of Wales.

GUSTAVUS HAMILTON BLENKINSOPP COULSON, D.S.O.
(LIEUTENANT AND ADJUTANT)
KING'S OWN SCOTTISH BORDERERS (7TH MOUNTED INFANTRY)

ON May 18, 1901, while engaged with his corps in fighting a rear-guard action, Lieutenant Coulson, who had rallied his men and saved a Maxim gun from falling into the enemy's hands, saw that the horse of Corporal Cranmer had been shot, leaving his rider powerless to keep up with the rest of his troop, and in imminent danger of being killed by the Boers, who were rapidly approaching. Despite the heavy fire brought to bear upon him, this young

History of the Victoria Cross

Photo by LAFAYETTE.

officer rode to his corporal, took him upon his own horse and rode back towards his men. Hardly had they succeeded in getting any distance before the horse was shot, and, falling, threw both men to the ground, whereupon Lieutenant Coulson ordered Cranmer to mount and ride for safety, adding that he would look after himself and do the best he could. Cranmer succeeded in mounting the horse, which had not been so severely wounded as at first appeared, and reached the column in safety. Lieutenant Coulson's position, however, was momentarily becoming more serious; seeing which, Corporal E. Shaw, of the Lincolns (7th Mounted Infantry), rode back to him and took him upon his horse, being himself almost at once shot through the body, Lieutenant Coulson also being badly hit at the same time. Their wounds caused both men to fall from the horse, that of Lieutenant and Adjutant Coulson proving fatal. Though this gallant young soldier never lived to wear the Victoria Cross he had so nobly won, the decoration was handed to his relatives after his death.[1]

Lieutenant Coulson was the only son of H. J. W. Coulson, of Newbrough Hall, Northumberland, and great-grandson of Colonel Blenkinsopp Coulson, of Blenkinsopp Castle, Northumberland—one of a family of distinguished soldiers. He was born at Wimbledon, Surrey, on April 1, 1879, educated at Winchester, and joined the 4th Batt. (Princess of Wales') Yorkshire Regiment, but left it when twenty years of age to enter the Scottish Borderers (July, 1899). In the following January he proceeded on active service to South Africa, gaining the medal and five clasps and the D.S.O. On many occasions (the *Gazette* states) he behaved with great coolness and gallantry under fire, being mentioned in despatches by both Lords Roberts and Kitchener. The act for which the Victoria Cross was awarded him was performed under the immediate command of Major F. C. Lloyd (of the Lincolns) and Colonel T. D. Pilcher, C. B., A.D.C. (now 2nd Bedfordshire).

[1] See Appendix II.

The Boer War

JAMES ROGERS
(SERGEANT)
SOUTH AFRICAN CONSTABULARY

ON June 15, 1901, Colonel Sitwell's column was operating near Thaba 'Nchu, and, during a skirmish, about sixty Boers suddenly attacked a small party of our rear-guard, consisting of Lieutenant F. Dickinson and seven of the South African Constabulary, among the latter being Sergeant Rogers. The officer's horse was shot, causing him to follow his men on foot, but Rogers, seeing this, returned to him, pulled him up on to his horse, and rode with him for over half a mile till cover was reached, firing continuously at the enemy. He then returned to within 400 yards of the enemy, and brought away, one after the other, two of his comrades whose horses were shot; and, not content with saving these three lives, occupied himself with riding after two horses which had broken away riderless, brought them back, and helped two more of his comrades to mount them, thus being the means of saving five men by his own individual exertions. The fire of the enemy was very hot during all this time, and the Boers were so close that many called on him to surrender, to which he paid no heed but continued firing whenever possible.

Photo by KELSBY, *Beresford Rd., Canonbury.*

W. J. ENGLISH
(LIEUTENANT)
2ND SCOTTISH HORSE

THIS young officer belonged to one of the corps raised during the Boer War—a corps, as its name implies, of men from that part of Great Britain celebrated for their hardiness and fighting powers. This grand body of men has, however, been disbanded since peace was restored in South Africa, but its achievements will not be easily forgotten. At Vlakfontein the Boers made a most determined attack upon our position, the extreme right of which was held by Lieutenant English and five men. Though of his small party two were killed and two wounded, the position was most gallantly held " owing to this officer's personal pluck." As time

History of the Victoria Cross

went on, ammunition ran short, and he went for a fresh supply to the next party, having to cross over fifteen yards of open ground, within thirty yards of the enemy, under a very heavy fire.

Received the Victoria Cross at the hands of H.M. the King on July 1, 1902, in London.

H. G. CRANDON
(PRIVATE)

18TH (PRINCESS OF WALES') HUSSARS

Photo by CHAPMAN, *Swansea.*

AT Springbok Laagte, on July 4, 1901, Privates Crandon and Berry were scouting, when suddenly a party of the enemy opened fire upon them from a range of only 100 yards. Berry was shot in the right hand and left shoulder, his horse at the same time falling. Crandon rode to his friend, gave him his own horse, and for more than 1,000 yards ran by his side till he had succeeded in getting him to safety, all the time under a heavy fire from the enemy.

ALEXANDER YOUNG
(SERGEANT-MAJOR)

CAPE POLICE

THE action of Ruiter's Kraal was fought on August 13, 1901, and several surrounding kopjes were held by small parties of Boers. Sergeant-Major Young and a small handful of men rushed one of these kopjes, which was held by Commandant Erasmus and about twenty Boers. On Young's party gaining the top, the enemy were seen galloping away to join their friends on another hill, and to prevent their doing so, Young dashed in pursuit, followed by his little band, whom he outstripped, coming up with the enemy fully fifty yards in advance of any of his men. He

Photo by SIMMONS, *Galway.*

The Boer War

dashed among the Boers, shot one of them, and captured their Commandant, being fired at by the latter three times before he was able to take him prisoner.

LLEWELLYN ALBERIC EMILIUS PRICE-DAVIES, D.S.O.
(LIEUTENANT, NOW CAPTAIN)
KING'S ROYAL RIFLE CORPS

AT Blood River Poort, on September 17, 1901, the Boers had overwhelmed the right of the British column, and some 400 of them galloped round the flank and rear of the guns, charged the drivers (who were trying to get the guns away), calling upon them to surrender. Lieutenant Price-Davies, hearing the order given to open fire upon the Boers, at once drew his revolver and dashed in among them, firing in a most gallant and desperate manner to save the guns. He was immediately shot and knocked off his horse, but happily was not mortally wounded, although he had ridden without hesitation to what seemed almost certain death.

Lieutenant Price-Davies, son of Lewis Richard Price-Davies, of Marrington Hall, Cherbury, Salop, was born on June 30, 1878; educated at Marlborough, and entered the Royal Rifles, February 23, 1898. Served in South Africa, as Adjutant to Smyth's Mounted Infantry, 1899–1902, receiving both medals, mention in despatches and four clasps. For his distinguished service in the earlier phase of the war, during which he was three times wounded, he was created a member of the D.S.O. Lord Kitchener presented him with the Victoria Cross at Pretoria, on June 8, 1902.

F. G. BRADLEY
(DRIVER)
69TH BATTERY ROYAL FIELD ARTILLERY

THE operations during the latter part of the Boer War were extended even into Zululand (where so many Crosses were won in 1879), and a sharp action was fought at Itala, on September 26, 1901. Ammunition was running short among those posted at the top of a steep hill, and, to get the necessary supply to them involving great risk of life, Major Chapman called for volunteers for the work. Driver Lancashire and Gunner Bull instantly answered to the call and started across the open space of about one hundred and fifty yards, swept by a pitiless fire. Half-way across, Lancashire was shot, and fell, whereupon Bradley and Gunner Rabb rushed out from their cover, and carried him under shelter.

Bradley then started in his turn and endeavoured to carry up the ammunition, succeeding with the help of Gunner Boddy in accomplishing the task.

Lancashire, Bull, Rabb and Boddy, for their brave services were awarded the medal for Distinguished Conduct in the Field.

W. BEES
(PRIVATE)
1st BATT. DERBYSHIRE REGIMENT

Photo by FROST, *Loughborough.*

BEES was attached to one of the Maxim guns which suffered severely during the action at Moedwil, on September 30, 1901. Of the nine men serving the gun, six were hit and lay badly wounded. Unable to bear their cries for water any longer, Bees determined to try to procure some from a spruit about five hundred yards away in front of the gun, and held by the Boers. Under a raking fire he doggedly went forward and succeeded in filling a camp kettle, having during this devoted mission to pass—in going and returning—within one hundred yards of some Boers posted behind rocks, and, though the vessel he carried was hit by several bullets, he contrived to reach his comrades and give them the relief they so sorely needed.

The Boer War

LESLIE CECIL MAYGAR
(LIEUTENANT)
5TH VICTORIAN MOUNTED RIFLES

AT the action of Geelhoutboom, November 23, 1901, one of our detached posts was in danger of being outflanked, upon which Lieutenant Maygar rode forward with orders to its officer to retire. While this was being done, when about two hundred yards from the enemy, one of the men had his horse shot, on seeing which Lieutenant Maygar lifted him up on to his own horse. The animal, however, bolted and got into swampy ground, and they were obliged to dismount. Seeing that it was unable to bear the weight of both, Lieutenant Maygar put the trooper on the horse, ordered him to ride for cover, and, under a heavy fire, made his way to shelter on foot.

Lieutenant Leslie Cecil Maygar, son of Mr. Edwin Willis Maygar, formerly of Bristol, was born on May 26, 1871, at "The Dean" Station, Victoria, New South Wales. Educated privately. Entered the Victorian Mounted Rifles, March 1, 1891, and served in South Africa from February 1, 1901, to July 31, 1902, gaining, besides the Victoria Cross, the King's, and the South African medal with clasps for Transvaal, Orange River Colony and Cape Colony, Served under Major Daly, O.C., 5th V.M.R., and Colonel Pulteney. The Cross was presented to him at Pretoria on June 8, 1902, by Lord Kitchener.

History of the Victoria Cross

THOMAS JOSEPH CREAN

(SURGEON-CAPTAIN)

1ST IMPERIAL LIGHT HORSE

On December 18, 1901, during the action with De Wet at Tygerskloof, Surgeon Crean displayed the greatest devotion to the wounded, when only 150 yards distant from the Boers. In spite of the heavy fire concentrated on his position, he ministered to the sufferers in the fighting line, although badly wounded himself, and only gave up when hit for the second time, receiving a severe wound from which, though considered mortal at the time, he fortunately recovered.

Surgeon-Captain Crean, son of Thomas Crean, Esq., Barrister-at-Law, of North Brook Road, Dublin, was born on April 19, 1873. Educated at the Royal College of Surgeons in Dublin, he joined the Imperial Light Horse as a trooper on the outbreak of hostilities. Was commissioned in March, 1900, and appointed Captain in 1900. Gave up squadron command in June, 1901, and became Surgeon-Captain. Gazetted Captain R.A.M.C. on September 3, 1902. Took part in the battle of Elandslaagte, where he was wounded. Served through the siege of Ladysmith, taking part in all engagements during its defence. Later, was employed during operations in the Transvaal and Orange River Colony, and in the relief of Mafeking. Possesses Queen's and King's medals with five clasps, and a testimonial of the Royal Humane Society. The Victoria Cross was presented to him by H.M. the King at St. James' Palace on March 13, 1902.

He also possesses the Arnott medal.

The Boer War

ALFRED ERNEST IND

(SHOEING SMITH)

Royal Horse Artillery, X.I. Section Pompoms

Photo by Lamb, *Tetbury.*

On December 20, 1901, a sharp action was fought in the Orange River Colony, at a place called Tafelkop. So fierce and accurate was the fire of the enemy, that the whole of those serving the Pompom had, with the exception of Ind, been shot down. Disregarding his comrades' fate, Ind stuck to his post, firing into the advancing Boers until the last possible moment. So heroic was his behaviour on this occasion, that Captain Jeffcoat, mortally wounded as he was, signified his wish that Ind's conduct be brought to the notice of his superior officer, and, eventually, to the authorities, for not only had he, on this special occasion, behaved with conspicuous bravery, but on every one in which he had been engaged since his section had been in action.

Alfred Ernest Ind is the son of Mr. George Ind, of Tetbury, Gloucestershire, where he was born on September 16, 1872. Entered the Royal Horse Artillery on February 19, 1901, being promoted Corporal subsequent to the action above described. For his services during the war has been awarded the Queen's and King's medal with clasps to each, and is now a member of that celebrated battery known as the "Chestnut Troop." He was once wounded, and four times mentioned in despatches, including that in which he was named for the Victoria Cross, which was pinned to his breast at Buckingham Palace, November 26, 1902, by H.M. the King.

History of the Victoria Cross

A. MARTIN-LEAKE
(SURGEON-CAPTAIN)
SOUTH AFRICAN CONSTABULARY

Photo by DOWNER, *Watford.*

AT the action of Vlakfontein, February 8, 1902, this medical officer behaved with very great bravery, and devotion to the wounded, on many occasions. He went forward—into the fighting line—to the assistance of one of them, attending to him under a very heavy fire from about forty Boers, at a range of only 100 yards. Having done all he could for this man, he turned to an officer who had been severely wounded, and, in devoting his attention to him, was shot three times, and only ceased when, through sheer exhaustion, he was compelled to do so. Of the eight men at this point, every one was wounded, and when offered water to relieve his own sufferings, the doctor refused it until satisfied that all the others had been first served.

ASHANTEE

1900

JOHN MACKENZIE
(SERGEANT, 2ND BATT. 78TH HIGHLANDERS;
EMPLOYED WITH THE WEST AFRICAN FRONTIER FORCE)
NOW CAPTAIN, ROYAL SCOTS (OR LOTHIAN) REGIMENT

ON June 6, 1900, at Dompoassi, in Ashantee, Sergeant Mackenzie displayed great courage under a severe fire. He worked two Maxim guns with exemplary coolness and steadiness, and received a severe wound while so doing, but afterwards volunteered to clear the stockades, putting himself at the head of the men, and, by a splendid charge, driving the enemy headlong into the bush.

Captain Mackenzie, at the age of eighteen (in August, 1887), enlisted into the Seaforth Highlanders, the depôt of which he joined at Fort George, Inverness, and was on December 8 posted to the 1st Battalion (72nd), then stationed at Edinburgh Castle. In May, 1891, he obtained his first stripe, which, on becoming a 78th man, in India, early in 1892, he relinquished, and remained for close upon a year a " full private." Became Corporal in May, 1897, in which year (November) he was posted to the Lagos Regiment, on the West Coast of Africa, being promoted Sergeant in his own regiment in March, 1899. As a lance-corporal, took part in the relief of Chitral, with the 78th, in the spring of 1895 (first medal and clasp).

During his service in West Africa he has taken part in three distinct campaigns, being on each occasion named in despatches, and (1897) awarded the medal for Distinguished Conduct in the Field. Was badly wounded at the relief of Kumasi, the campaign in which he pre-eminently distinguished himself. On November 29, 1900, was commissioned as 2nd Lieutenant into the Black Watch, in which he became Lieutenant in October, 1903, and was on January 22, 1904, promoted Captain into the 1st Royal Scots, or Lothian Regiment, thus rising from the rank of Sergeant (on the Supernumerary list too) to that of Company Commander in little more than three years.

CHARLES JOHN MELLISS
(CAPTAIN)
INDIAN STAFF CORPS

Photo by ELLIOTT & FRY, *London.*

WHEN employed with the West African Frontier Force, Captain Melliss behaved with great gallantry at Obassa, on September 30, 1900. Seeing that the enemy were in great numbers, and about to offer a stubborn resistance, he collected as many men as he could find at the moment, and led them through the bush in a charge against the natives, at a point where he saw they were most strongly united. His courageous conduct, and that of his men, drove the enemy off for a moment, but a hand-to-hand fight soon took place. He ran his sword through a native who had fired at him, being shot himself in the foot, which paralysed the limb, but his wild rush had had the desired effect, and the enemy broke into a panic and fled, pursued by the Sikhs, who slew a great number. On three previous occasions Major Melliss was noticed for his courageous conduct.

Son of Lieut.-General G. J. Melliss, I.S.C., Major Melliss was born in 1862. Entered the Army in 1882 (East York's Regiment), and became Captain, 1893. Served in East Africa, 1896, and against the Mazrui rebels; also on the North-west frontier of India, 1897–8, and the operations in the Kurram Valley, 1897. Tirah Campaign, 1897–8, being present at the storming of

Ashantee

Dargai. Took part in the actions in the Bara Valley and in the relief of Kumassi, 1900, obtaining his Brevet of Lieut.-Colonel, and being twice mentioned in despatches. In Sir John Willcock's despatch of December 25, 1900, the following reference to him is made—

" Although this officer (Captain Melliss) has been awarded the Victoria Cross for valour, his work throughout the campaign has been so valuable and conspicuous, that I sincerely trust he will be noted for higher promotion, on attaining the rank of Major, which he is now near. He has eighteen years service, but is held back by the rules for promotion in the Indian Staff Corps."

CHINA

1900

LEWIS STRATFORD TOLLEMACHE HALLIDAY
(CAPTAIN, NOW BREVET-MAJOR)
ROYAL MARINE LIGHT INFANTRY

Photo by MAULL & FOX, *London.*

IN June, 1900, in spite of the great war taking place in South Africa, the attention of this country was anxiously directed to another quarter of the world, where it was feared a terrible tragedy had been, or was, taking place. The Chinese had broken out into rebellion against the Europeans in their country, and the Legations in Pekin were hemmed in by Boxers, who directed a heavy fire against the insufficiently protected buildings. On the 24th an attack was made on the west wall of the British Legation, and the Boxers set light to the stable quarters and occupied some buildings adjoining. After this had with great difficulty been put out, those in the Legation came under a severe fire from the enemy at very close quarters, and it was resolved to force them to evacuate the cover they had secured. Captain Halliday, after a hole had been made through the wall of the Legation, led twenty marines in a gallant dash at the enemy, and a hand-to-hand fight quickly ensued, in which he was shot through the left shoulder from a Boxer only a few feet from him, receiving a most dangerous wound, the bone of his shoulder being smashed, and part of the lung torn away. Despite the serious-

China

ness and pain of his wound, Captain Halliday killed three of his foes, and then, finding he was unable to proceed further, ordered his men to go on without him, and refused any assistance in getting to the hospital, lest by allowing any one to help him, he might lessen the force necessary to drive out the Boxers.

Major Lewis S. T. Halliday, son of Lieut.-Colonel Stratford Charles Halliday, R.A., was born at Medstead, Hants, on May 14, 1870. Educated at Elizabeth College, Guernsey, he entered the Royal Marine Light Infantry on September 1, 1889, becoming Captain on January 31, 1898, and Major by Brevet for distinguished field service, September 12, 1900.

On May 29, 1900, he landed at Taku from H.M.S. *Orlando*, in command of fifty men R.M.L.I., and proceeded to Pekin as Legation Guard, in the defence of which he won his Victoria Cross in the way described. He obtained also the China medal with clasp, inscribed, " Defence of Legation," and he now commands the unit of his corps on board the *Empress of India*.

BASIL JOHN DOUGLAS GUY
(MIDSHIPMAN, NOW LIEUTENANT)

H.M.S. " BARFLEUR," ROYAL NAVY

Photo by RUSSELL, *Southsea.*

On July 13, 1900, during the attack on Tientsin City in China, the Naval Brigade came under a very heavy cross-fire, several men being hit. One of them, Able Seaman J. McCarthy, falling when about fifty yards from cover, Mr. Guy went to his assistance, and, seeing him desperately wounded, tried to carry him into shelter, but was not strong enough to do so. He, nevertheless, stayed by him, binding up his wound, and, as by this time the rest of his party had reached cover, the entire fire of the enemy from the city wall was concentrated on them both. So terrific was the hail of lead that the ground around them was literally ploughed up. Mr. Guy then ran to cover to obtain assistance, and, the bearers coming up, he dashed out with them and assisted in putting McCarthy on to a stretcher and carrying him in. The seaman was however, unfortunately, again shot, and died just as he reached cover.

Born on May 9, 1882, Mr. Guy is the son of the Rev. Douglas Sherwood

History of the Victoria Cross

Guy, Vicar of Sedbergh. Entered the *Britannia* on January 15, 1897, passing out to the *Barfleur* in 1898, and has served since then entirely in the East. On July 15, 1903, was promoted Lieutenant for his services, and received the Victoria Cross from the hands of H.M. the King on March 8, 1902, at Keyham Barracks. This is the first Cross gained in the Navy since His Majesty's Accession, and the forty-first awarded to members of the senior service since the institution of the decoration.

SOMALILAND

1902—1903

ALEXANDER STANHOPE COBBE, D.S.O.
(CAPTAIN, LOCAL LIEUT.-COLONEL)

INDIAN ARMY

Photo by ELLIOTT & FRY.

At the action of Erego, in Somaliland, on October 6, 1902, some of the companies had retired, and Captain Cobbe was left by himself in front of the line with a Maxim gun, which he brought in quite alone and worked in a most gallant manner at a most critical period of the fight. He also, when an orderly had fallen wounded, went out and brought him in, although he was exposed to a very heavy fire both from the enemy, only about twenty yards from him, and from his own men who had retired about the same distance in the rear.

Born on June 5, 1870, Captain Cobbe is the son of the late Lieut.-General Sir A. H. Cobbe. Educated at Wellington, he entered the South Wales Borderers (24th Regiment) as 2nd Lieutenant in 1889, obtained his Lieutenancy in 1892, transferring to the Indian Staff Corps in the same year, and was gazetted Captain from September 21, 1900. Served in the Chitral Relief Force, 1895, being mentioned in despatches; the South Angoniland Expedition, 1898;

History of the Victoria Cross

and the Expedition against Kwamba, 1899, being again mentioned. During his service in Ashantee in 1900 was severely wounded, and received the D.S.O. The Victoria Cross was presented to him by General Manning on February 22, 1903, at Obbia.

JOHN EDMOND GOUGH
(CAPTAIN AND BREVET-MAJOR, NOW BREVET-LIEUT.-COLONEL)
RIFLE BRIGADE

Photo by SYMONDS, *Portsmouth.*

IN the account of the act on April 22, 1903, for which Captain Rolland was awarded the Victoria Cross, mention is made of Captain Gough, but it was not until some time afterwards that the great bravery displayed by this officer was brought to the notice of the authorities, who promptly awarded him the decoration he so thoroughly deserved. Captain Gough was at the time in command of the column, and although he reported the heroic conduct of Captains Rolland and Walker, no knowledge of his own bravery on the same occasion was brought to light until eye-witnesses of his action reported it to headquarters.

Lieut.-Colonel Gough, born on October 25, 1871, is the son of General Sir Charles John Stanley Gough, V.C., who gained his Victoria Cross in the Indian Mutiny, 1857-8, by several acts of conspicuous daring. He is also nephew of General Sir Hugh Henry Gough, V.C., who gained the Victoria Cross for bravery at Alum Bagh in 1857, and Lucknow, 1858, and thus establishes a record, for no other family has ever yet possessed three members of the decoration. He was appointed 2nd Lieutenant in the Rifle Brigade on March 12, 1892; became 1st Lieutenant, December 6, 1893; Captain, December 5, 1898; Brevet-Major (for distinguished service in South Africa—Boer War), November 29, 1900; and in addition to being awarded the Victoria Cross was promoted Brevet-Lieut.-Colonel to date April 22, 1903. His other war services include the expeditions against Chikusi and Chilwa in British Central Africa, the Nile Expedition of 1898, and South Africa, 1899-1902 (Lombards Kop, Ladysmith, Laing's Nek, Belfast and

Somaliland

Lydenburg). He received the Victoria Cross at the hands of H.M. the King on February 29, 1904, at St. James' Palace.

The late Mr. W. T. Maud, artist correspondent of the *Graphic*, during the fight at Daratoleh sent home the following account of the incident, and it will be seen, in the last two paragraphs, how Major Gough, while bringing forward the bravery of his fellow-officers, kept back any reference to his own gallant conduct—

" Owing to shortness of ammunition, and the large number of our wounded, Major Gough now decided to retire to Danop. After four hours' fighting, the enemy's fire was slackening, but it had not been silenced. Accordingly a final charge was made from the front and left faces, led by Captains Walker and Townshend.

" At 2.30 the retreat commenced in square formation, the dead and wounded being tied on camels. The enemy immediately pressed upon the rear-guard, which, owing to the thick bush, got considerably in rear of the main column. Captain Bruce, R.A., staff officer to Major Gough, who was with the rear-guard, was wounded at twenty yards' distance, falling on the path, unable to move. With him were Captains Walker and Rolland, of the Intelligence Department, two Yaos, one Sikh, and one man of the Somali Camel Corps. Meantime the column, unaware of what had happened, was getting further away. Captain Rolland ran back 500 yards, and returned with a Bikanir camel for Bruce, while Captain Walker and the men remained with Bruce, keeping off the enemy. This they successfully accomplished, but not before Bruce was hit again and the Sikh wounded. But for this gallant conduct, Bruce would have fallen into the enemy's hands."

In a subsequent message, despatched from Bohotle on April 28, when his despatches were no longer subject to Major Gough's censorship, Mr. Maud wrote as follows—

" My despatch from Danop, dated April 23, describing the action of Daratoleh, was censored by Major Gough, who passed everything written therein except mention of himself in connexion with the rescue of Captain Bruce.

" As a matter of fact, Gough personally directed the rear-guard action, and joined Captain Walker, two Yaos, one Sikh, and one man of the Somali Camel Corps in keeping back the enemy with rifle-fire until Rolland returned with the camel. Gough then helped to place Bruce upon it. Poor Bruce was unconscious and mortally wounded, and died soon afterwards."

History of the Victoria Cross

CLEMENT LESLIE SMITH
(LIEUTENANT)

46TH REGIMENT; 2ND BATT. DUKE OF CORNWALL'S LIGHT INFANTRY

Photo by KIRK, *Cowes.*

On January 10, 1904, during the Somaliland Campaign, the enemy made a sudden and desperate onslaught upon the 5th Somali Mounted Infantry at Jidballi. Under cover of the surrounding bushes, which were close to our force, and supported by rifle-fire, many succeeded in getting right in amongst our men. In the hand-to-hand fighting which ensued Rahamat Ali, a Hospital-Assistant, was severely wounded. Lieutenant Smith, serving with the Somali Mounted Infantry, and Lieutenant J. R. Welland, M.D., of the Royal Army Medical Corps, endeavoured to save the life of the wounded man, and made heroic attempts to place him upon a horse and get him away from the enemy. Hemmed in now on all sides, they were unable to do so, and the unfortunate man was killed. The *Gazette* states that "Lieutenant Smith then did all that any man could do to bring out Doctor Welland, helping him to mount a horse, and, when that was shot, a mule. This also was hit and Doctor Welland was speared by the enemy. Lieutenant Smith stood by Doctor Welland to the end, and, when that officer was killed, was within a few paces of him, endeavouring to keep off the enemy with his revolver. At that time the *dervishes* appeared to be all round him, and it was marvellous that he escaped with his life."

Clement Leslie Smith, born on January 17, 1878, is the son of Canon Clement Smith, M.V.O., M.A., Rector of Whippingham and Chaplain-in-Ordinary to H.M. the King. Became 2nd Lieutenant in the 5th Vol. Batt. Hampshire Regiment, October 21, 1896, and on May 5, 1900, was commissioned into the 2nd Batt. Duke of Cornwall's Light Infantry. Early in 1901 was selected for special service in South Africa and employed as Railway Staff officer, receiving the Queen's medal and three clasps. In May, 1903, was selected for special service in Somaliland.

WILLIAM GEORGE WALKER

(CAPTAIN)

INDIAN ARMY

(SERVING WITH THE BIKANIR CAMEL CORPS)

ASSOCIATED with Captain Rolland (V.C.) in an act of conspicuous devotion and courage in saving the body of Captain Bruce during the fight at Daratoleh in the Somaliland Campaign, on April 22, 1903. Fuller details are given in the account of Captain Rolland and Major J. E. Gough (V.C.).

Captain Walker, son of the late Deputy-Surgeon W. Walker, M.D., LL.D., of the Indian Medical Service, was born in 1863, educated at Haileybury, and entered the Army in 1885, becoming Captain, 1896. He served through the Miranzai (1891) and Waziristan (1894) Expeditions.

GEORGE MURRAY ROLLAND

(CAPTAIN)

INDIAN ARMY

(INTELLIGENCE OFFICER SERVING WITH THE BERBERA-BOHOTLE FLYING COLUMN)

ON April 22, 1903, in Somaliland, during the return of Major Gough's column to Danop, the rear-guard was left far behind the rest of the column, and Captain Bruce was mortally wounded. They were almost surrounded by the enemy who were swarming in the bush, very thick at this part, and while a heavy fire was kept up against them Captains Rolland and Walker (V.C.), with two men of the King's African Rifles, one Sikh and one Somali of the Camel Corps, stood by the wounded officer to save him from falling into the enemy's hands.

Captain Rolland afterwards ran back 500 yards to the column, now fast disappearing in the distance, unaware of what was taking place, and returned with assistance to carry away Captain Bruce, and, by his and his fellow-soldiers' great courage and devotion, the body of that officer was saved from mutilation by the savages. Captain Rolland's account of the incident, published in one of the newspapers of August 10, 1903, is set out here in full.

Captain George Murray Rolland, son of the late Major Patrick Murray Rolland, R.A., was educated at Harrow and Sandhurst, afterwards joining the

History of the Victoria Cross

Bedfordshire Regiment. In 1889 he joined the 1st Bombay Infantry, becoming Captain in November 1900.

From the "Daily Graphic" of August 10, 1903.

"The following interesting extracts from a letter written by Captain George Murray Rolland, 1st Bombay Grenadiers, Intelligence Officer, serving with the Berbera-Bohotle Flying Column, on whom the Victoria Cross has just been conferred for conspicuous gallantry at the battle of Daratoleh, have been sent to us for publication—

"'It was a grand fight, and for four hours our little band of 200 stood shoulder to shoulder in a tiny little square, barely thirty yards on each side, with a hail of bullets falling all round us. Our ammunition was running short, so at 2.30 a.m. (the action began at 10.30 a.m.) Major Gough decided to retire. A horde of savages followed us for three more hours, coming within fifteen to thirty yards of us. It was a tight corner. Major Gough is a splendid soldier, so cool and calm; he is a grand fellow. Poor Captain Bruce and I were on the rear-guard together—both Harrow boys. The bush was so dense we could scarcely see a yard in it. We were left behind with four men; so Bruce called out, "Rolland, come along with those men," and we retired slowly, firing as we went. A savage crept up close to the path along which we were marching; owing to the dense grass and bush we did not notice it. Poor Captain Bruce suddenly threw up his arms and fell on his face, shot through the body. The bullet entered his right side and passed out by the left. I saw the savage moving off; my carbine was on him in a second, and he rolled over. I can't tell whether he was actually the man who shot Captain Bruce, but I saw no other, so think it must have been him. I ran to Captain Bruce and raised him up, turning him on to his back. He was bleeding terribly, and I saw at a glance it was a mortal wound. I dragged him a little out of the path, which was much exposed to the enemy's fire, and undid his collar, taking off his bandolier, revolver and belt, while the four brave men covered me with their fire and kept the enemy in check, who were yelling with delight as they saw one white man dying and another close to him, and they kept calling out to each other (I was told afterwards by the Somali who fought by me that they were saying that they had got us all, and to come on and spear us). Captain Bruce was a very heavy man, of nearly 14 stone, and I am only 9¼ stone, so I could not lift him. None of the men could stop firing to help me, or the enemy would have been on us, so I shouted to the disappearing column, "Halt in front!" It was then out of sight, slowly retiring along the winding path, and

Somaliland

we were practically cut off. It was a moment of great despair, as I thought my shout had not been heard.

"'The enemy were now pressing us very hard, so I had to stop attending to poor Captain Bruce, and emptied the magazine of my carbine at them. Then I fired off my revolver and emptied that too. Suddenly Captain Bruce stood up, and I rushed to hold him up. He walked two steps forward, and fell on his face again. I tried to break his fall, and he brought me down too—he was too heavy for me. I again turned him on to his back. He opened his eyes and spoke to me (his last words), "They have done for me this time, old man!" From now to his death he was practically unconscious. To my infinite relief I then saw Captain Walker trekking towards me. He and I tried to carry Captain Bruce, but it was no use, so then I left them and ran back 400 yards or more to where the rear-guard was, to fetch help. It was a terribly long run, and I thought I must get hit every moment, as the bullets fell splashing round me. I seized a Bikanir camel, and was running back with it, when Major Gough came up and asked what was the matter. I told him, and he rushed back to Captain Bruce. I followed slower, as the led camel refused to step out, and I could not induce mine to hurry up—in fact he was frightened, and did not like to leave his friends.

"'I reached the little group, and made the camel sit down, and we lifted up Captain Bruce, Major Gough at his head, and Captain Walker and I at his feet. While doing so three bullets struck the ground between us. One went through poor Captain Bruce's leg, but he was too far gone to feel it. Then the Sikh, who had done his duty nobly, had his arm smashed by a fourth bullet. We had to throw Captain Bruce on to the camel anyhow, and as we did so the poor fellow died. The two Yaos (Africans), the Somali, and the Sikh made up the four who helped us, and they did their work well. It was a wonder to me that out of our little group only the Sikh was wounded. I thought all the time that not one of us would escape, and that we should have all fallen. However, we saved Captain Bruce's body, and we could only regret that we could not save his life; but I knew when he fell that he had received his death-wound, and that all we could save from falling into the enemy's hands would be his body, and I thank God we were able to do that, for he would have been mutilated had those savages got hold of him. He was a dear chap, a great friend of mine, and an old Harrow chum. R.I.P.

"'Well, we were not left alone till 5.30 p.m., and then the enemy drew off. It was the hardest day of my life. I fired and fired in that fight, till my rifle was boiling hot; even the woodwork felt on fire. Up to 3 a.m. a few biscuits and cocoa, then a twenty-five mile ride, a seven hours' fight, and

History of the Victoria Cross

twenty-five miles back to camp, i.e. fifty miles that day; twenty-five hours without food of any kind, between the 3 a.m. biscuits and cocoa on the 22nd to the 4 a.m. dinner on the 23rd. Oh, the thirst of that day! I had two water-bottles on my camel, and drained them both. Hunger I did not feel. That march home was a terrible one! The smell of the dead bodies and the blood on our empty stomachs made us feel so sick, and as I rode up and down from the front to the rear of the column and back I passed the bodies of Captains Bruce and Godfrey tied on to camels, and swaying about helplessly. Oh, it was a heart-rending sight to me to see all that remained of two strong, healthy men, who only that morning were so full of life and spirits! We reached Danop again at 2 a.m., and when I got off my camel I reeled from tiredness, which up to then I had not felt. However, I was given brandy and water, and then I had to go off and arrange for our dead to be laid out and placed under a guard for that night, to prevent hyenas attacking them. The wounded had to be looked to and made comfortable. Next morning at 8 a.m. we buried Captains Bruce and Godfrey side by side, just as they were, in their khaki uniforms. Major Gough read the service, and we all stood round. It was a most impressive funeral; a soldier's always is, but this one was unusually so. Not one of us could have spoken after it was over without breaking down, and we all walked away from the grave with silent, bowed heads. Half an hour later we were all ourselves again, for there is not time in a soldier's life for grief. We were one and all busy with our respective work. I had only one suit of khaki with me, so, as it was covered with blood, I had to go and have it washed and dried, and went about practically naked while it took place.'"

NIGERIA

1903

WALLACE DUFFIELD WRIGHT
(LIEUTENANT, NOW CAPTAIN)
THE QUEEN'S (ROYAL WEST SURREY) REGIMENT; (NORTHERN NIGERIA REGIMENT)

Photo by LAFAYETTE.

ON February 26, 1903, during the Kano-Sokoto Expedition in West Africa, Lieutenant Wright, with only one officer and forty men, made a most gallant stand for two hours against the repeated charges of 1,000 of the enemy's cavalry and 2,000 infantry, inflicting such losses upon them that they were forced to retire, upon which his little party pursued them until they broke into full retreat. The *Gazette* states that the success of this affair was greatly due to Lieutenant Wright's personal example and skilful leadership.

Captain Wright, son of Mr. J. S. Wright, was born at Gibraltar on September 20, 1875, entering the 2nd Queen's Regiment on December 9, 1896, becoming Captain in 1903. With less than a year's service took part in the Malakand and Tirah Campaigns, in which he was severely wounded, and in Northern Nigeria, 1901–3, being again wounded. For these services he has been awarded the Indian medal (1895) with clasps for Punjab Frontier and Tirah, and the African "General Service" medal with two clasps. The officers under whose command he gained the Victoria Cross were Colonel Morland, C.B., D.S.O., and Brigadier-General Kemball, C.B., D.S.O., and the decoration was presented to him by H.M. the King at Buckingham Palace on November 5, 1903.

Appendix I

THE VICTORIA CROSS WARRANTS

I

War Department,
February 5, 1856.

The Queen has been pleased, by an instrument under her Royal Sign Manual, of which the following is a copy, to institute and create a new Naval and Military Decoration, to be styled and designated " The Victoria Cross," and to make the rules and regulations therein set forth under which the said Decoration shall be conferred.

Victoria, by the grace of God of the United Kingdom of Great Britain and Ireland, Queen, Defender of the Faith, etc., to all to whom these presents shall come, Greeting.

Whereas We, taking into Our Royal Consideration that there exists no means of adequately rewarding the individual gallant services either of officers of the lower grades in Our Naval and Military Service, or of warrant and petty officers, seamen, and marines, in Our Navy, and non-commissioned officers and soldiers in Our Army; and whereas the third class of Our Most Honourable Order of the Bath is limited, except in very rare cases, to the higher ranks of both Services, and the granting of Medals, both in Our Navy and Army, is only awarded for long service or meritorious conduct, rather than for bravery in action or distinction before an enemy, such cases alone excepted where a general medal is granted for a particular action or campaign, or a clasp added to the medal for some special engagement, in both of which cases all share equally in the boon, and those who by their valour have particularly signalised themselves, remain undistinguished from their comrades; now, for the purpose of attaining an end so desirable as that of rewarding individual instances of merit and valour, We have instituted and created, and by these presents, for Us, Our Heirs and Successors, institute and create a new Naval and Military Decoration, which We are desirous should be highly prized and eagerly sought after by the officers and men of Our Naval and Military Services, and are graciously pleased to make, ordain, and establish the following rules and ordinances for the government of the same, which shall from henceforth be inviolably observed and kept:—

Firstly.—It is ordained, that the distinction shall be styled and designated " The Victoria Cross," and shall consist of a Maltese cross of Bronze, with Our Royal Crest in the centre, and underneath which an escroll bearing the inscription " For Valour."

Secondly.—It is ordained, that the Cross shall be suspended from the left breast, by a blue riband for the Navy and by a red riband for the Army.

Thirdly.—It is ordained, that the names of those upon whom We may be pleased to confer the Decoration shall be published in the *London Gazette*, and a registry thereof kept in the Office of Our Secretary of State for War.

Fourthly.—It is ordained, that any one who, after having received the Cross, shall

Appendix I

again perform an act of bravery, which, if he had not received such Cross, would have entitled him to it, such further act shall be recorded by a Bar attached to the riband by which the Cross is suspended, and for every additional act of bravery an additional Bar may be added.

FIFTHLY.—It is ordained, that the Cross shall only be awarded to those officers or men who have served Us in the presence of the enemy, and shall have then performed some signal act of valour, or devotion to their country.

SIXTHLY.—It is ordained, with a view to place all persons on a perfectly equal footing in relation to eligibility for the Decoration, that neither rank, nor long service, nor wounds, nor any other circumstance or condition whatsoever, save the merit of conspicuous bravery shall be held to establish a sufficient claim to the honour.

SEVENTHLY.—It is ordained, that the Decoration may be conferred on the spot where the act to be rewarded by the grant of such Decoration has been performed, under the following circumstances :—I. When the Fleet or Army, in which such act has been performed, is under the eye and command of an Admiral or General Officer commanding the Forces. II. Where the Naval or Military force is under the eye and command of an Admiral or Commodore commanding a squadron or detached naval force, or of a General commanding a corps, or division, or brigade on a distinct and detached service, when such Admiral, Commodore, or General Officer shall have the power of conferring the Decoration on the spot, subject to confirmation by Us.

EIGHTHLY.—It is ordained, where such act shall not have been performed in sight of a Commanding Officer as aforesaid, then the claimant for the honour shall prove the act to the satisfaction of the Captain or Officer commanding his ship, or to the Officer commanding the regiment to which the claimant belongs, and such Captain, or such Commanding Officer shall report the same through the usual channel to the Admiral or Commodore commanding the force employed in the service, or to the Officer commanding the forces in the field, who shall call for such description and attestation of the act as he may think requisite, and on approval shall recommend the grant of the Decoration.

NINTHLY.—It is ordained that every person selected for the Cross, under Rule Seven, shall be publicly decorated before the naval or military force or body to which he belongs, and with which the act of bravery for which he is to be rewarded shall have been performed, and his name shall be recorded in a General Order, together with the cause of his especial distinction.

TENTHLY.—It is ordained that every person selected under Rule Eight shall receive his Decoration as soon as possible, and his name shall likewise appear in a General Order as above required, such General Order to be issued by the naval or military Commander of the Forces employed on the service.

ELEVENTHLY.—It is ordained that the General Orders above referred to shall from time to time be transmitted to Our Secretary of State for War, to be laid before Us, and shall be by him registered.

TWELFTHLY.—It is ordained that as cases may arise not falling within the rules above specified, or in which a claim, though well founded, may not have been established on the spot, We will, on the joint submission of Our Secretary of State for War and of our Commander-in-Chief of Our Army, or on that of Our Lord High Admiral or Lords Commissioners of the Admiralty in the case of the Navy, confer the Decoration, but never without conclusive proof of the performance of the act of bravery for which the claim is made.

Appendix I

THIRTEENTHLY.—It is ordained that, in the event of a gallant and daring act having been performed by a squadron, ship's company, a detached body of seamen or marines, not under fifty in number, or by a brigade, regiment, troop, or company, in which the Admiral, General, or other Officer commanding such forces, may deem that all are equally brave and distinguished, and that no special selection can be made by them: then in such case, the Admiral, General, or other Officer commanding, may direct, that for any such body of seamen or marines, or for every troop or company of soldiers, one Officer shall be selected by the Officers engaged for the Decoration; and in like manner one Petty Officer or Non-Commissioned Officer shall be selected by the Petty Officers and Non-Commissioned Officers engaged; and two Seamen or Private Soldiers or Marines shall be selected by the Seamen, or private soldiers, or marines, engaged, respectively, for the Decoration; and the names of those selected shall be transmitted by the Senior Officer in command of the naval force, brigade, regiment, troop, or company, to the Admiral or General Officer commanding, who shall in due manner confer the Decoration as if the acts were done under his own eye.

FOURTEENTHLY.—It is ordained that every Warrant Officer, Petty Officer, Seaman or Marine, or Non-commissioned Officer, or Soldier who shall have received the Cross, shall, from the date of the act by which the Decoration has been gained, be entitled to a Special Pension of Ten Pounds a year, and each additional Bar conferred under Rule Four on such Warrant or Petty Officers, or Non-commissioned Officers or Men, shall carry with it an Additional Pension of Five Pounds per annum.

[In reply to a question asked in the House of Commons on June 13, 1898, Mr. Brodrick, Under Secretary of State for War, stated:—" In reference to soldiers earning the Victoria Cross, who, from old age or infirmity not due to their own fault, may be in poor circumstances and unable to earn a living, it has been decided that at the Secretary of State's discretion the sum of £50 a year may be granted by way of pension in lieu of the £10 which has accompanied the Victoria Cross since its institution."]

FIFTEENTHLY.—In order to make such additional provision as shall effectually preserve pure this most honourable distinction, it is ordained, that if any person on whom such distinction shall be conferred be convicted of treason, cowardice, felony, or of any infamous crime, or if he be accused of any such offence and doth not after a reasonable time surrender himself to be tried for the same, his name shall forthwith be erased from the registry of individuals upon whom the said Decoration shall have been conferred by an especial Warrant under Our Royal Sign Manual, and the pension conferred under Rule Fourteen shall cease and determine from the date of such Warrant. It is hereby further declared that We, Our Heirs and Successors, shall be the sole judges of the circumstances demanding such expulsion; moreover, We shall at all times have power to restore such persons as may at any time have been expelled, both to the enjoyment of the Decoration and Pension.

Given at our Court at Buckingham Palace, this Twenty-ninth day of January, in the nineteenth year of Our reign, and in the year of Our Lord one thousand eight hundred and fifty-six.

By Her Majesty's command,
(*Signed*) PANMURE.

TO OUR PRINCIPAL SECRETARY OF STATE FOR WAR.

Appendix I

II

London Gazette,
August 10, 1858.

By a Warrant under Her Royal Sign Manual August 10, 1858, Her Majesty was pleased to direct that the Victoria Cross should be conferred subject to the rules and ordinances already made on Officers and Men of Her Majesty's Naval and Military Services who may perform acts of conspicuous courage and bravery under circumstances of extreme danger, such as the occurrence of a fire on board ship, or of the foundering of a vessel at sea, or under any other circumstances in which through the courage and devotion displayed life or public property might be saved.

III

From the *London Gazette* of July 8, 1859.

War Office,
July 6, 1859.

The Queen having been graciously pleased by a Warrant under Her Royal Sign Manual bearing date December 13, 1858, to declare that Non-Military Persons who, as Volunteers, have borne arms against the mutineers, both at Lucknow and elsewhere, during the late operations in India, shall be considered as eligible to receive the decoration of the Victoria Cross, subject to the rules and ordinances already made and ordained for the Government thereof, provided that it be established in any case that the person was serving under the orders of a General or other Officer in command of Troops in the Field when he performed the Act of Bravery for which it is proposed to confer the decoration; Her Majesty has accordingly been pleased to signify Her intention to confer this high distinction on the undermentioned gentlemen, etc., etc.

(Then follow the names of Kavanagh and Mangles, with the act for which they were decorated.)

IV

The Royal Warrant.

January 1, 1867.

The Queen has been pleased by an instrument under Her Royal Sign Manual of which the following is a copy to direct that the decoration of the Victoria Cross may be conferred on persons serving in the local forces of the Colony of New Zealand or who may hereafter be employed in the local forces raised or which may be raised in the Colonies and their Dependencies generally. Victoria, by the Grace of God, of the United Kingdom of Great Britain and Ireland, Queen, Defender of the Faith: To all to whom these presents shall come, Greeting. Whereas, by a warrant under Her Royal Sign Manual, countersigned by one of our principal Secretaries of State, and bearing date at our Court at Buckingham Palace, the 29th day of January, 1856, in the nineteenth year of our reign, We did constitute and create a new naval and military decoration, to be styled and designated the Victoria Cross, which decoration We expressed Our desire should be highly prized and eagerly sought after by the officers and men of Our naval and military services, and did also make, ordain and establish the rules and ordinances therein set forth for the Govern-

Appendix I

ment of the same, to be thenceforth inviolably observed and kept. And whereas, during the progress of the operations which We have undertaken against the Insurgent native tribes in Our Colony of New Zealand, it has happened that persons serving in the Local Forces of our said Colony have performed deeds of gallantry, in consideration of which they are not, according to the strict provisions of our said recited warrant, eligible for this high distinction. Now know ye, that We, of Our especial grace, certain knowledge, and mere motion, have thought fit hereby to signify Our Royal Will and Pleasure, that the said decoration may be conferred on such persons aforesaid, who may be qualified to receive the same in accordance with the rules and ordinances made, ordained, and established, by Us for the Government thereof, by our said recited warrant, and We do by these presents for Us Our Heirs and Successors, ordain and appoint that it shall be competent for such persons aforesaid to obtain the said decoration, in the manner set forth in the rules and ordinances referred to, or in accordance with such further rules and ordinances as may hereafter be made and promulgated by Us, Our Heirs and Successors, for the government of the said decoration, provided that it be established in any case that the person was serving with Our Troops, under the orders of a general or other officer, under circumstances which would entitle an officer, or soldier of our Army to be recommended for the said decoration, in accordance with the rules and ordinances prescribed in our said recited warrant, and provided also that such person shall be recommended for it by such General or other Officer. And We do further, for Us, our Heirs and Successors, ordain and appoint that the said decoration may also be conferred, in accordance with the rules and ordinances prescribed in our said recited warrant, and subject to the provisoes aforesaid, on such persons as may be qualified to receive the same in accordance with the said rules and ordinances who may hereafter be employed in the Local Forces raised, or which may be raised, in Our Colonies and their dependencies, and who may be called upon to serve in co-operation with Our Troops, in military operations which it may be necessary to undertake for the suppression of rebellion against Our authority, or for repelling invasion by a foreign enemy.

Given at Our Court at Osborne House, at Isle of Wight, this first day of January, one thousand eight hundred and sixty-seven in the thirtieth year of Our reign.

By Her Majesty's Command,

(*Signed*) J. PEEL.

V

Royal Warrant.

Qualification required for the decoration of the Victoria Cross.

(This Warrant applies also to the Auxiliary and Reserve forces.)

Victoria R.

Whereas doubts have arisen as to the qualification required for the decoration of the Victoria Cross, and whereas the description of such qualification in our Warrant of 29th day of January, 1856, is not uniform, Our Will and Pleasure is that the qualification shall be " conspicuous bravery or devotion to the country in the presence of the enemy," and that Our Royal Warrant of the 29th day of January, 1856, shall be read and interpreted accordingly.

It is Our further Will and Pleasure that officers and men of Our Auxiliary and

Appendix I

Reserve Forces (Naval and Military) shall be eligible for the decoration of the Victoria Cross under the conditions of the said Warrant, as amended by this, Our Warrant.

Given at Our Court at Osborne, this 23rd day of April, 1881, in the 44th year of Our reign.

By Her Majesty's Command,
HUGH C. E. CHILDERS.

VI

WAR OFFICE,
August 24, 1881.

THE Queen having been graciously pleased by warrant under Her Royal Sign Manual bearing date August 6, 1881, to direct that the decoration of the Victoria Cross shall be conferred on members of the Indian Ecclesiastical Establishments who may be qualified to receive the same in accordance with the rules, etc., provided that it be established in any case that the person was serving under the orders of a General or other Officer in command of Troops in the Field when he performed the act of bravery for which it is proposed to confer the decoration. [Here follows the announcement of the award to the Rev. J. W. Adams.]

APPENDIX II

The following announcement appeared in the *London Gazette* of August 8, 1902 :—

"The King has been graciously pleased to approve of the Decoration of the Victoria Cross being delivered to the *representatives* of the undermentioned officers, non-commissioned officers and men who fell during the recent operations in South Africa, in the performance of acts of valour, which would, in the opinion of the Commander-in-Chief of the Forces in the Field, have entitled them to be recommended for that distinction had they survived :—

"D. R. YOUNGER, Captain, Gordon Highlanders.

"R. J. T. DIGBY JONES, Lieutenant, Royal Engineers.

"H. ALBRECHT, Trooper 459, Imperial Light Horse.

"G. H. B. COULSON, Lieutenant and Adjutant, King's Own Scottish Borderers, 7th Mounted Infantry.

"A. ATKINSON, Sergeant 3264, Yorkshire Regiment.

"J. BARRY, Private 3733, 1st Batt. Royal Irish Regiment."

APPENDIX III

N.W.P. AND OUDH PROVINCIAL MUSEUM

EXTRACT from the Proceedings of Meeting 2 of 1896–7, held on March 24, 1897.

3. *Department of Indian History since 1500 A.D. Portrait of the late Thomas Henry Kavanagh and his Victoria Cross.*

Mr. Constable, advancing towards a small table, draped with a "Union Jack" flag, placed in front of Thorwaldsen's bust of His Majesty King Ghazi-ud-din Haidar, stated that he now had the great honour of announcing to the meeting a very important accession to the Museum collections illustrating the History of India since 1500 A.D., in the shape of an original water-colour painting of the late Thomas Henry Kavanagh, V.C., in the disguise he wore when he left the Residency to guide Sir Colin Campbell's relieving army into Lucknow, together with the Victoria Cross he had won by that deed of heroism, an exploit which was admirably described in the printed account of it pasted on to the back of the portrait as follows:—

THOMAS HENRY KAVANAGH, V.C.

The Residency of Lucknow was besieged from June 30, 1857, by mutineers and rebels in the proportion of thirty to one of the defenders.

Generals Outram and Havelock, with over 2,000 troops, fought their way through the city on September 26 to rescue the garrison and return to Cawnpore.

But they, too, were surrounded and obliged to defend themselves in places adjoining the Residency Entrenchment, and on reduced rations both forces subsisted on the provisions of the original garrison as the Generals brought none.

The situation was very critical by November, and, to be successful, the relief, said to be coming from Cawnpore, must be sure and quick. Provisions and ammunition existed only for a few days more.

Thinking over the situation, Mr. Kavanagh decided that the early success of the relieving force of 4,000 men would be secured if the Commander-in-Chief had a guide conversant with the city and environs, with the positions occupied by the enemy, and with their character, in whom he could repose confidence. He therefore volunteered on November 8 to leave the defences to

Appendix III

convey information to Sir Colin Campbell, and help him as his guide. Sir James Outram at first considered the enterprise impossible, but Mr. Kavanagh's confidence assured him, and he saw the importance of giving such assistance to the Commander-in-Chief.

Mr. Kavanagh is an Irishman from Westmeath; he is tall, his complexion is fair, his eyes are blue, and his hair brown, and he wore a short beard, and was then thirty-six years old. His face, hands, and throat and hair were blackened with a cork dipped in oil and burnt at a candle, and he wore the dress of a Mohammedan irregular soldier, a *nondescript*. The dress in the photograph[1] is the one he wore.

He left the Residency after dark on November 9; walked near fifteen miles through houses and fields; was twice stopped by mutineers, and satisfied their curiosity without exciting suspicion; and by sunrise he delivered to Sir Colin Campbell a note from Sir James Outram, telling him the object of Mr. Kavanagh's escape, and to have confidence in him. Misr. Kanouji Lal, a Brahman, accompanied Mr. Kavanagh, who attributes much of his success to the courage and intelligence of this devoted servant of Government.

By midday on November 10, a message was sent to Sir James Outram from the Alambagh (a fortified garden near two miles outside the city) by a *Semaphore* on the roof of the garden house, informing him of the safe arrival of Mr. Kavanagh; and his wife was then, for the first time, told of his escape.

On the afternoon of November 17, Mr. Kavanagh ran alone in advance of the relieving force to the nearest post of the Residency, and led over Sir James Outram, through the fire of the enemy, to Sir Colin Campbell, when the two Generals met for the first time in their lives, and in the din of war; and the besieged were saved.

Sir Colin Campbell acknowledged Mr. Kavanagh's services thus:—"This escape, at a time when the entrenchment was closely invested by a large army, and communication, even through natives, was almost impossible, is, in Sir Colin Campbell's opinion, one of the most daring feats ever attempted; and the result was most beneficial, for in the immediate subsequent advance on Lucknow of a force under the Commander-in-Chief's directions, the thorough acquaintance with the localities possessed by Mr. Kavanagh, and his knowledge of the approaches to the British position were of the greatest use; and His Excellency desires to record his obligations to this gentleman, who accompanied him throughout the operations, and was ever present to afford valuable information."

These relics, which it was no exaggeration to term the most precious which the Museum would ever possess, were presented to it by Hope Kavanagh, Esq., District Superintendent of Police, Allahabad, in response to a suggestion made to him on the 1st inst. by Mr. Constable, who had felt that relics such as these could have but one fitting resting-place—Lucknow—where they would be regarded, he was sure, by Briton and loyal Indian alike, as National property, and an incentive to duty in all spheres of life.

The verso of the bar of the Cross was inscribed—

"THOS. H. KAVANAGH, Esq.,
　　Asst. Commr. in Oude."

and in the centre of the verso of the Cross itself—

"8 Novr.
1857."

[1] *Sic*, because the above printed description was used by the late Mr. Kavanagh to paste on to the back of photographs, cabinet size, of the water-colour portrait by Lawless that he was wont to give to his

Appendix III

the day of the month being, it may be, a clerical or engraver's error; as it was on the night of the 9*th* of November, 1857, that Kavanagh left the Residency, accompanied by Misr. Kanouji Lal, the Brahman. Although it was on the 8*th* that he *volunteered*, it was a fact worth noting here that it was on the 9*th* of November, 1882, that Kavanagh died, aged sixty-two, while resting, when *en route* for India, at Gibraltar, in the house of his friend, the late Lord Napier of Magdala, then the Governor and Commander-in-Chief of that garrison. (Mr. Kavanagh died on the 11th, not the 9th.—P.A.W.)

The portrait, a full-length miniature on a cabinet sized card, which was always considered an admirable likeness of the 1857 Kavanagh as he appeared in his disguise, was the work of Matthew James Lawless, a well-known subject painter, who from 1858 to 1863 was a constant exhibitor at the Royal Academy. He also made many designs for wood engravings, and died in London in the autumn of 1864, aged twenty-eight years.

It was painted in London in 1860, when Kavanagh received the Cross from the hands of Our Gracious Queen and Empress, and is happily in excellent preservation. At the foot are these words, " Lawless to his friend Lucknow Kavanagh." On the right (the spectator's), the painter's monogram surmounting the date of painting, 1860.

A friend of the late Mr. Kavanagh had joined with Mr. Constable in providing a suitable case for the portrait and Cross, and Mr. Constable now begged leave to propose that these relics be deposited in the large room of the King's Library, the one used for this meeting, there to be kept for ever, the case being fixed to a small marble slab to be built into the north wall of the room, at a place now indicated to the meeting, which would all be done at the expense of those who would provide the case.

Mr. Constable then presented to the Museum for formal record all the correspondence he had had with Mr. Hope Kavanagh, who, in the course of it, had informed him that the tulwar, pistol, and shield his father bore on that memorable night, together with the other articles of his disguise, had been presented to the Dublin Museum some years ago. It thus happened that the country of Kavanagh's birth, and the Indian city where he spent much of his working life, and where his supreme deed of heroism was wrought, divide the honour of possessing relics, the right of which may, it is hoped, serve to keep alive for ever the memory of one of Ireland's bravest sons; of one of India's loyal Brahmans.

Resolved:—That the cordial thanks of the Museum Committee be conveyed to Mr. Hope Kavanagh for his presentation of these very important historical records of his late father's career.

Also, that Mr. Constable be thanked for his action in the matter.

Further resolved that these relics be placed in the position proposed by Mr. Constable, and agreed to by the Meeting.

True Extract.

A. FUHRER, Ph.D.,
Curator and Secretary,
Provl. Mus. Committee, Lucknow.

friends. A copy, with an ink line through "photograph," and the word *picture* in ink below, is pasted on to the back of the original water-colour portrait.

Lucknow,
March 15, 1897.

A. C.

Appendix III

No. 60 of 1897.

From THE CURATOR AND SECRETARY,
PROVINCIAL MUSEUM COMMITTEE,
LUCKNOW,

To HOPE KAVANAGH, Esq.,
DISTRICT SUPERINTENDENT OF POLICE,
ALLAHABAD.

Dated LUCKNOW, *March* 24, 1897.

SIR,—

I am directed by the Committee of Management to convey to you their cordial thanks for the presentation of the very important relics and records of your late father's career. I have the honour to forward for your information an extract from the Proceedings of Meeting No. 2, held on March 24, 1897.

I have the honour to be, Sir,
Your most obedient Servant,
A. FUHRER, Ph.D.,
Curator and Secretary,
Provl. Museum Committee, Lucknow.

APPENDIX IV

Official Report of Lieutenant John R. M. Chard, the officer in command during the Defence of Rorke's Drift, Zulu War, 1879.

Rorke's Drift,
January 25, 1879.

Sir,—

I have the honour to report that on the 22nd inst. I was left in command at Rorke's Drift by Major Spalding, who went to Helpmakaar to hurry in the Company 24th Regiment, ordered to protect the ponts.

About 3.15 p.m. on that day I was at the ponts when two men came riding from Zululand at a gallop and shouted to be taken across the river.

I was informed by one of them, Lieutenant Adendorff, of Lonsdale's Regiment (who remained to assist in the defence), of the disaster at Isandlwana Camp, and that the Zulus were advancing on Rorke's Drift. The other, a Carabineer, rode off to take the news to Helpmakaar.

Almost immediately I received a message from Lieutenant Bromhead, commanding the Company 24th Regiment at the Camp near the Commissariat Stores, asking me to come up at once.

I gave the order to inspan, strike tents, put all stores, etc. into the wagon, and at once rode up to the Commissariat Store, and found that a note had been received from the 3rd Column to state that the enemy were advancing in force against our post, which we were to strengthen and hold at all costs.

Lieutenant Bromhead was most actively engaged in loop-holing and barricading the store building and hospital, and connecting the defence of the two buildings by walls of mealie bags and two wagons that were on the ground. I held a hurried consultation with him and with Mr. Dalton of the Commissariat (who was actively superintending the work of defence, and whom I cannot sufficiently thank for his most valuable services), entirely approving of the arrangements made. I went round the position, and then went down to the ponts and brought up the guard of 1 sergeant and 6 men, wagon, etc. I desire here to mention the offer of the punt-man Daniels and Sergeant Milne, 3rd Buffs, to move the punts in the middle of the stream and defend them from their decks with a few men.

We arrived at the post about 3.30 p.m. Shortly after, an officer of Durnford's Horse arrived and asked for orders. I requested him to send a detachment to observe the drifts and punts and throw out outposts in the direction of the enemy, and check his advance as much as possible, falling back upon the post when forced to retire and assist in its defence.

I requested Lieutenant Bromhead to post his men, and having seen him and every man at his post, the work once more went out.

Appendix IV

About 4.20 p.m. the sound of firing was heard behind the hill to our south. The officer of Durnford's returned reporting the enemy close upon us, and that his men would not obey his orders, but were going off to Helpmakaar, and I saw them, apparently about 100 in number, going off in that direction.

About the same time Captain Stephenson's detachment of Natal Native Contingent left us, as did that officer himself.

I saw that our line of defence was too extended for the small number of men now left us, and at once commenced a retrenchment of biscuit boxes. We had not completed a wall two boxes high when, about 4.30 p.m., 500 or 600 of the enemy came in sight round the hill to our south, and advanced at a run against the south wall. They were met by a well-sustained fire, but, notwithstanding their heavy loss, continued the advance to within fifty yards of the wall, when they were met with such a heavy fire from the wall and cross fire from the store that they were checked, but taking advantage of the cover afforded by the cookhouse, ovens, etc., kept up a heavy fire. The greatest number, however, without stopping, moved to the left around the hospital and made a rush at our NW. wall of mealie bags, but after a short but desperate struggle were driven back with heavy loss into the bush around the work. The main body of the enemy were close behind, and had lined the ledge of rock and caves, overlooking us about 400 yards to our south, from where they kept up a constant fire, and advancing more to their left than the first attack, occupied the garden, hollow road, and bush in great force.

Taking advantage of the bush, which we had not time to cut down, the enemy were able to advance under cover close to our wall, and in this part soon held one side of the wall while we held the other. A series of desperate assaults were made, extending from the hospital along the wall as far as the bush reached; but each was most splendidly met and repulsed by our men with the bayonet, CORPORAL SCHIESS, N.N.C., greatly distinguishing himself by his conspicuous gallantry.

The fire from the rocks behind us, though badly directed, took us completely in reverse, and was so heavy that we suffered very severely, and about 6 p.m. were forced to retire behind the retrenchment of biscuit boxes.

All this time the enemy had been attempting to force the hospital, and shortly after set fire to its roof. The garrison of the hospital defended it room by room, bringing out all the sick who could be moved before they retired, Privates WILLIAMS, HOOK, R. JONES, and W. JONES, 24th Regiment, being the last men to leave holding the doorway with the bayonet, their own ammunition being expended. From the want of interior communication and the burning of the house, it was impossible to save all. With most heartfelt sorrow I regret we could not save these poor fellows from their terrible fate.

Seeing the hospital burning and the desperate attempts of the enemy to fire the roof of the stores, we converted two mealie-bag heaps into a sort of redoubt, which gave a second line of fire all round, ASSISTANT COMMISSARY DUNNE working hard at this, though much exposed, and rendering valuable assistance. As darkness came on we were completely surrounded, and after several attempts had been gallantly repulsed, were eventually forced to retire to the middle, and then the inner wall of the kraal on our East. The position we then had we retained throughout. A desultory fire was kept up all night, and several assaults were attempted and repulsed; the vigour of the attack continuing until after

Appendix IV

midnight, and men, firing with the greatest coolness, did not waste a single shot; the light afforded by the burning hospital being of great help to us.

About 4 a.m., 23rd inst., the firing ceased, and at daybreak the enemy were out of sight over the hill to the south-west.

We patrolled the grounds, collecting the dead Zulus, and strengthened the arms of our defences as much as possible.

We were removing the thatch from the roof of the stores when, about 7 a.m., a large body of the enemy appeared on the hills to the south-west. I sent a friendly Kaffir, who had come in shortly before, with a note to the officer commanding at Helpmakaar, asking for help.

About 8 a.m. the third column appeared in sight, the enemy, who had been gradually advancing, falling back as they approached.

I consider the enemy who attacked us to have numbered about three thousand.

We killed about three hundred and fifty.

Of the steadiness and gallant behaviour of the whole garrison I cannot speak too highly. I wish especially to bring to your notice the conduct of—

LIEUTENANT BROMHEAD, 2nd Batt. 24th Regiment, and the splendid behaviour of his Company B, 2nd Batt. 24th Regiment.

SURGEON REYNOLDS, A.M.D., in his constant attention to the wounded under fire where they fell.

ACTING COMMISSARIAT OFFICER DALTON, to whose energy much of our defences were due, and who was severely wounded while gallantly assisting in the defence.

ASSISTANT COMMISSARY DUNNE.

ACTING STOREKEEPER BYRNE (killed.)

COLOUR-SERGEANT BOURNE, 2nd Batt. 24th Regiment.

SERGEANT WILLIAMS, ,, ,, ,, ,, (wounded dangerously).

SERGEANT WINDRIDGE, 2nd Batt. 24th Regiment.

CORPORAL SCHIESS, 2nd Batt. 3rd Natal Native Contingent (wounded).

1395 PRIVATE WILLIAMS, 2nd Batt. 24th Regiment.

593 PRIVATE JONES, ,, ,, ,, ,,

PRIVATE McMAHON, Army Hospital Corps.

716 PRIVATE R. JONES, 2nd Batt. 24th Regiment.

,, H. HOOK.

,, ROY, 1st Batt. 24th Regiment.

Total present at Rorke's Drift January 22, 1879: 8 Officers, 96 Non-Com. Officers and Men; 35 Non-Com. Officers and Men sick; total, 139.

The following is a list of the killed:—

SERGEANT MAXFIELD, 2nd Batt. 24th Regiment.

PRIVATE SCANLAN.

,, HAYDEN.

,, ADAMS.

,, COLE.

,, FAGAN.

,, CHICK.

Appendix IV

1398 Private Williams, 2nd Batt. 24th Regiment.
,, Nicholls, 1st ,, ,, ,,
,, Horrigan, ,, ,, ,, ,,
,, Jenkins, ,, ,, ,, ,,
Mr. Byrne, Commissariat Department.
Trooper Hunter, Natal Mounted Police.
,, Anderson, Natal Native Contingent.
One Private (native), ,, ,, ,,
Total, 15.

Twelve wounded, of whom two have since died, viz. :—
Sergeant Williams, 2nd Batt, 24th Regiment.
Private Beckett, 1st ,, ,, ,,
Making a total killed of 17.

I have, etc.,
(*Signed*) JOHN R. M. CHARD,
Lieut. R.E.

To Colonel Glyn, C.B.,
Commanding 3rd Column.

APPENDIX V

From the diary of LIEUT.-COLONEL J. H. Reynolds, V.C., report sent to C.O. on the defence of Rorke's Drift.

(Kindly placed at the Author's disposal.)

On January 22 (1879) at about 12.30 p.m., we were surprised at Rorke's Drift by hearing big guns in our neighbourhood, and almost immediately I commenced climbing up the big hill of Oscarberg, in company with the Missionary Witt and Mr. Smith (afterwards), Army Chaplain. We expected to get a view of what was happening, but on looking across the Buffalo river from the top we discovered that Isandlwana Mountain (five miles away) shut from our view the scene of action. Three more reports of big guns were distinctly audible after we completed the ascent, there being, I should say, a quarter of an hour interval between. At 1.30 a large body of natives marched over the slope of Isandlwana in our direction, their purpose being evidently to examine ruined kraals and ravines for hiding fugitives. These men we took for our own Native Contingent. Soon afterwards appeared three[1] horsemen on the Natal side of the river galloping in the direction of our post, and feeling they might possibly be messengers for additional medical aid, I hurried down to the hospital and (arrived) there as they rode up. They looked frightfully scared, and I was startled to find one of them riding Surgeon-Major Shepard's pony. Their report was the camp at Isandlwana had been taken by the enemy and all our men massacred, that no power could stand against the enormous numbers of the Zulus, and there was nothing left for every one but to fly for our lives. I could get no account of Dr. Shepard[2] except that his pony had been found loose, but ready saddled. My first move was to consult with Lieutenant Bromhead and Acting-Commissary Dalton, Lieutenant Chard not having as yet joined us from the Pontoon. We quickly decided that, with barricades well placed around our position, a stand could best be made where we were. Just at this period Mr. Dalton's[3] energies were invaluable. Without the smallest delay, which would have been so fatal for us, he called upon the men (all eager for doing) to carry the mealie sacks here and there for defences, and it was charming to find in a short time how comparatively protected we had made ourselves. Lieutenant Chard, commanding, was present at the commencement of this work, and directed principally the lines of defence. He approved also of the hospital being taken in, and between the convalescent patients (eight or ten) orderlies, and myself, we loopholed the building and made a continuation of the Commissariat defences round the hospital. It occupied, however, a wretched position, having a garden and shrubbery close by, which afterwards proved so favourable to the enemy.

---

[1] The official report says "two."—P. A. W.
[2] Was killed at Isandlwana while attending to a wounded man.—P. A. W.
[3] Assistant-Commissary James Langley Dalton, V.C.—P. A. W.

Appendix V

Comparing our prospect with that of the Isandlwana affair, we felt that the mealie barriers might afford us a moderately fair chance. The patients, I must mention, were retained in the hospital, although situated at our weak end, as every part of the Commissariat House was already crowded with stores. But we did not consider either building would be taken unless with the fall of the whole place.

When our plans of temporary defence were nearly completed, I was relieved by seeing Mr. Witt and Mr. Smith safely inside. They had, just then, returned from the hill, where they remained up to a late moment, continuing to believe that the natives I before alluded to were our own men.

Mr. Witt was at this moment making preparations to ride away. Mr. Smith said he should have to remain, as his Kaffir groom had bolted and taken with him the horse.

About 3.30 the enemy made their appearance in a large crowd on the hospital side of our post, coming on in skirmishing order at a slow slinging run. We opened fire on them from the hospital at 600 yards, and although the bullets ploughed through their midst and knocked over many, there was no check or alteration made in their approach. They seemed quite regardless of the danger, and, what struck me as most strange, they had no war-cry, nor did they at this time fire a single shot in return. As they got nearer they became more scattered, but the large bulk rushed for the hospital and the garden in front. My attention being altogether directed for a while to these points, I cannot state with authority whether the Zulus, whom I, shortly afterwards, saw in a large number in the opposite, or north, side of our fort, got there by extending this body, or if they came independently from the opposite direction, thereby carrying out their reputed mode of attack in a bull's-horn fashion. However it was, we found ourselves quickly surrounded by the enemy, with their strong force holding the garden. From all sides, especially the garden and shrubbery, they poured on us a continuous fire, until at last they forced themselves in the latter place so daringly, that numbers of them climbed over the mealie sacks in front of the hospital, and drove the defenders back behind a retrenchment of biscuit boxes, hastily formed, with much forethought and judgment, by Lieutenant Chard. I discovered afterwards that this officer, when planning our defences, reckoned on the assistance of the Basutos, who deserted at the last moment. It followed from this, that our men, at first, had to be distributed over so large an area in proportion to our number, as dangerously to weaken any one point, and render it unequal to repel a determined rush. But for this retrenchment our position could not have held out five minutes longer. A heavy fire from behind it was resumed with renewed confidence, and with little confusion or delay, thus checking the natives from getting in amongst us, and, at the same time, permitting a semi-flank fire, from another part of the fort, to play on the enemy, as they now and then made forward dashes. At this time, too, the loopholes in the hospital were made great use of, so that the combined fire had the desired effect of keeping the Zulus at bay. It was, however, only temporary. After a short respite, they came on again with redoubled vigour. Some of them gained the hospital verandah, and there got hand-to-hand with our men defending the doors. Once again the enemy were completely driven back to find shelter in the garden, but others soon pressed forward in their stead, and, having occupied the verandah in larger numbers than before, pushed their way right into the hospital. Confusion on our side naturally followed, and every one escaped as best he could into the contracted laager. It was quite impossible to save the patients unable to

Appendix V

move, as the only easy exit from hospital was in front. Private Hunter, Natal Mounted Police, was killed in the attempt. During this partial success of the enemy, very heavy firing was being made on our fort from all sides, and it was in this period we sustained our principal loss in killed and wounded. The engagement continued till about 7 p.m., and then, when we were beginning to consider our situation somewhat desperate, the fire from our opponents appreciably slackened, giving us some time for reflection.

Lieutenant Chard here again shone in resource. Anticipating the probability of the Zulus making one more united dash for the fort, and possibly an entrance, he converted an immense stack of mealies standing in the middle of our enclosure, and originally cone-fashioned, into a comparatively safe place for a last retreat. I would explain that the top of the cone was removed, and a number of sacks taken out from the heart of what remained, forming a sheltered space sufficient to accommodate about forty men, and in a position for making good shooting. Mr. Dunne, Commissariat Officer, assisted in the construction. Just as it was completed, smoke from the hospital appeared and shortly burst into flames. The light from it, however, proved advantageous to us (as it showed us the position of the enemy), a matter which the Zulus must have recognized themselves, as no further attack was made from that quarter. During the whole night following, desultory (firing) went on, but nothing of a continued or determined effort was again attempted by the enemy. About 6 a.m. we found, after careful reconnoitring, that all the Zulus, with exception of a couple of stragglers, had left our immediate vicinity, and soon afterwards a large body of men were seen at a distance in Zululand marching towards us. For a long time, and even after we distinguished red coats through field-glasses, we believed them to be the enemy, some of them, perhaps, dressed in kits of those men who fell at Isandlwana. Indeed, we could not think otherwise, as the Basuto officer who escaped with his men from Isandlwana and joined us the night before reported that the General's party had been broken up into small lots, each trying to escape into the colony. Not until the mounted Infantry in advance crossed the drift about a quarter of a mile off were we convinced of our relief. Then we gave them three cheers, and really felt that it was all right for us. I do not think it possible that men could have behaved better than did the 2/24 and A.H. Corps, who were particularly forward, as well as odds and ends of other regiments who happened to be at Rorke's Drift on that night.

APPENDIX VI

Report of COLONEL GLYN, C.B,. commanding No. 3 Column, to Lord Chelmsford, commanding the Forces in South Africa, showing how the Queen's Colour of the 1st Batt. 24th Foot, which had been lost on January 22, has since been recovered, and giving an account of the gallant behaviour of Lieutenant and Adjutant Melvill and Lieutenant Coghill of that Regiment until they met their deaths in the endeavour to save this Colour from falling into the enemy's hands.

RORKE'S DRIFT, BUFFALO RIVER,
February 21, 1879.

SIR,—

I have the honour to report that on January 22 last, when the camp at Isandlwana was attacked by the enemy, the Queen's Colour of the 1st Batt. 24th Regiment was in the camp, the head-quarters and five companies of the regiment being there also.

From all the information I have been since able to obtain, it would appear that when the enemy had got into the camp, and when there was no longer any hope left of saving it, the Adjutant of the 1st Batt., Lieutenant Melvill, departed from the camp on horseback, carrying the Colour with him in hope of being able to save it.

The only road to Rorke's Drift being already in possession of the enemy, Lieutenant Melvill and the few others who still remained alive struck across country for the Buffalo river, which it was necessary to cross to reach a point of safety. In taking this line, the only one possible, ground had to be gone over which, from its ruggedness and precipitous nature, would under ordinary circumstances, it is reported, be deemed almost utterly impossible for mounted men.

During a distance of about six miles Lieutenant Melvill and his companions were closely pursued, or, more properly speaking, accompanied by a large number of the enemy, who, from their well-known agility in getting over rough ground, were able to keep up with our people though the latter were mounted, so that the enemy kept up a constant fire on them, and sometimes even got close enough to assegai the men and horses.

Lieutenant Melvill reached the bank of the Buffalo and at once plunged in, horse and all; but being encumbered with the Colour, which is an awkward thing to carry even on foot, and the river being full and running rapidly, he appears to have got separated from his horse when he was about half-way across.

He still, however, held on resolutely to the Colour, and was being carried down stream when he was washed against a large rock in the middle of the river.

Lieutenant Higginson, of the Natal Native Contingent, who had also lost his horse

Appendix VI

in the river, was clinging to this rock, and Lieutenant Melvill called to him to lay hold of the Colour. This Lieutenant Higginson did, but the current was so strong that both officers, with the Colour, were again washed away into still water.

In the meantime Lieutenant Coghill, 1st Batt. 24th Regiment, my orderly officer, who had been left in camp that morning when the main body of the Force moved out, on account of a severe injury to his knee, which rendered him unable to move without assistance, had also succeeded in gaining the river bank, in company with Lieutenant Melvill. He too had plunged at once into the river, and his horse had carried him safely across, but on looking round for Lieutenant Melvill and seeing him struggling to save the Colour in the river, he at once turned his horse and rode back into the stream again to Lieutenant Melvill's assistance.

It would appear that now the enemy had assembled in considerable force along their own bank, and had opened a heavy fire on our people, directing it more especially on Lieutenant Melvill, who wore a red patrol jacket. So that when Lieutenant Coghill got into the river again, his horse was almost immediately killed by a bullet. Lieutenant Coghill was thus cast loose in the stream also, and, notwithstanding the exertions of both these gallant officers, the Colour was carried off from them, and they themselves gained the bank in a state of extreme exhaustion.

It would appear that they now attempted to move up the hill from the river bank towards Helpmakaar, but must have been too much exhausted to go on, as they were seen to sit down to rest again. This, I sorely regret to say, was the last time these two most gallant officers were seen alive.

It was not for some days after the 22nd that I could gather any information as to the probable fate of these officers. But immediately I discovered in what direction those who had escaped from Isandlwana had crossed the Buffalo I sent, under Major Black, 2nd Batt. 24th Regiment, a mounted party, who volunteered for this service, to search for any trace that might be found of them.

This search was successful, and both bodies were found where they were last seen as above indicated.

Several dead bodies of the enemy were found about them, so that they must have sold their lives dearly at the last.

As it was considered that the dead weight of the Colour would cause it to sink in the river, it was hoped that a diligent search in the locality where the bodies of these officers were found might lead to its discovery. So Major Black again proceeded on the 4th inst. to prosecute this search.

His energetic efforts were, I am glad to say, crowned with success, and the Colour, with the ornaments, case, etc., belonging to it were found, though in different places in the river bed.

I cannot conclude this report without drawing the attention of His Excellency the Lieut.-General Commanding, in the most impressive manner which words can command, to the noble and heroic conduct of Lieutenant and Adjutant Melvill, who did not hesitate to encumber himself with the Colour of the Regiment in his resolve to save it, at a time when the camp was in the hands of the enemy and its gallant defenders killed to the last man in its defence, and when there appeared but little prospect that any exertions that Lieutenant Melvill could make would enable him to save even his own life. Also, later on, to the noble

Appendix VI

perseverance with which, when struggling between life and death in the river, his chief thoughts to the last were bent on the saving of the Colour.

Similarly, I would draw His Excellency's attention to the equally noble and gallant conduct of Lieutenant Coghill, who did not hesitate for an instant to return, unsolicited, and ride again into the river, under a heavy fire of the enemy, to the assistance of his friend, though at the time he was wholly incapacitated from walking, and but too well aware that any accident that might separate him from his horse must be fatal to him.

In conclusion I would add that both these officers gave up their lives in the truly noble task of endeavouring to save from the enemy's hands the Queen's Colour of their Regiment, and, greatly though their sad end is to be deplored, their deaths could not have been more noble or more full of honour.

I have, etc.,
(*Signed*) R. T. GLYN,
Colonel Commanding 3rd Column.

HORSE GUARDS,
WAR OFFICE,
April 21, 1879.

From SIR M. A. DILLON, Major-General, Military Secretary.
To SIR JOHN JOSCELYN COGHILL, Bart.

SIR,—

I am directed by the Field Marshal Commanding-in-Chief to inform you that His Royal Highness perused with melancholy interest the report forwarded to him by Lord Chelmsford from Colonel Glyn, showing how the Queen's Colour of the 1st Battalion 24th Foot would have fallen into the hand of the enemy on January 22 but for the gallant behaviour of your son Lieutenant Coghill, and Adjutant Melvill of that Regiment.

His Royal Highness, in communicating this Dispatch to you, desires me to assure you of his sincere sympathy with you in the loss of your son, whose gallant death in the successful effort to save the Colour of his Regiment has gained him the admiration of the Army.

It is gratifying to His Royal Highness to inform you that if your son had survived it was Her Majesty's intention to confer upon him the Victoria Cross, and a notification to that effect will be made in the *London Gazette*.

I have the honour, etc., etc.,
(*Signed*) M. A. DILLON,
M.-Genl.

Copy of GENERAL PONSONBY's letter to SIR HASTINGS DOYLE.

MY DEAR DOYLE,—

The Queen commands me to send you the enclosed extract of a letter from the Empress Eugénie, which Her Majesty thinks the relations of Lieutenant Coghill may like to read (p. 402).

To-day the Colours of the 1st Batt. 24th were brought here for the Queen's inspection, when she placed on the Queen's colour a wreath in remembrance of the gallant conduct of the two officers who saved their Colours, but lost their lives in doing so.

Yours very truly,
HENRY PONSONBY.

Appendix VI

Extract of a letter from the Empress Eugénie to The Queen, dated Maritzburg, June 20, 1880.

"Nous avons plaçe les couronnes dont nous étions chargées sur la tombe des Lieuts. Coghill et Melvill.

"Si, comme je le crois, les morts voyent ce qu'on fait pour eux, ils seront heureux de ne pas être oubliés par leur souveraine, eux qui ont donné leur vie pour sauver son drapeau.

Le site est magnifique et très sauvage, quelques mètres de plus, ils auraient sans doute été sauvés—c'est encore la perte de leurs chevaux qui causa leur mort.

EUGÉNIE.

We have placed the wreaths, with which we were entrusted, upon the grave of Lieutenants Coghill and Melvill.

If, as I believe, the dead see what one does for them, they will be happy in the thought that they have not been forgotten by their Sovereign, they who have given their lives to save Her Colour.

The spot is grand and very wild; a few yards further and they would, no doubt, have been saved—it was the loss of their horses which brought about their death.

Appendix VII

Active service of John Paton, V.C., while serving in the Campaigns of Turkey, the Crimea, and India, from February, 1854, till July, 1856; and from June, 1857, till March, 1860, viz. :—

Battle of Alma.
Battle of Balaclava.
Siege of Sebastopol, from October 17, 1854, till September 9, 1855.
Taking Bonnee Bridge.
Attack on Allumbagh.
Storming Jellallabad Fort.
Storming Martinière, November 14, 1857
Storming Secundrebagh Fort.
Storming Shah Nujjiff Fort.
Storming Mess-house Fort.
Storming Mossebagh Fort.
Relief of Lucknow.
Relief of Cawnpore.
Siege of Cawnpore.
Battle of Cawnpore.
Battle of Seriagat.
Battle of Kalinady Bridge.
Storming of Futtegurh.
Siege of Lucknow.
Storming Martinière, March 17, 1858.
Storming Begum Palace.
Capture of Lucknow.
Attack on Roda Mowh.
Battle of Alligunge.
Battle of Barriely.
Battle of Pusgoine.
Battle of Tillah.
Storming Mithowlie Fort.
Battle of Bishwa.
Capture of Barriely.
Storming Dalkushaguh.

Prior to the Crimean War, the 42nd, 79th, and 93rd Highlanders were formed into the Highland Brigade. They landed in the Crimea on Septemper 8, 1854, and on the 18th, marched for the Alma, fighting the battle of that name on the 20th. Marched to Balaklava on the 22nd, being left there in charge of the Harbour, shipping and stores. The rest of the troops marched to attack Sebastopol. On the 25th Paton's Brigade fought at Balaklava and stood in the historic "*thin red line*" to face the whole of the Russian Cavalry. On September 7, 1855, marched to the front to take part in the storming of Sebastopol. Returned home at the beginning of 1856. Early in 1857 were ordered to proceed to China, but, on reaching the Cape, found orders awaiting them to proceed as quickly as possible to India, where the Mutiny had broken out. Arrived at Calcutta at the end of October, and at once marched on Lucknow, reaching there on November 15, and on the same day took part in some hard fighting with the enemy's outposts. Next day the Secundra Bagh was stormed, 2,000 Sepoys being killed. The Shah Nujjiff was then attacked, during which Paton performed the courageous and valuable action for which he was awarded the Victoria Cross.

THE VICTORIA CROSS

BY BRANCHES OF THE SERVICE

THE ROYAL (AND LATE INDIAN) NAVY

Lucas, C. D.	Bomarsund, Baltic	1854
Bythesea, J. Johnstone, W.	Wardo Island, Baltic	1854
Peel, W.	Sebastopol, Inkerman, Redan	1854–5
Hewett, W. N. W.	Sebastopol and Inkerman	1854
Daniel, E. St. J.	Inkerman and Redan	1854–5
Gorman, J. Reeves, T. Scholefield, M.	Inkerman	1854
Sullivan, J.	Sebastopol	1855
Buckley, C. W.	Genitchi and Taganrog	1855
Burgoyne, H. T. Robarts, J.	Genitchi	1855
Cooper, H.	Taganrog	1855
Curtis, H. Raby, H. J. Taylor, J.	Sebastopol	1855
Trewavas, J.	Genitchi	1855
Ingoueville, G.	Viborg, Baltic	1855
Sheppard, J.	Sebastopol (harbour)	1855
Kellaway, J.	Marioupol	1855
Day, G. F.	Genitchi (twice)	1855
Commerell, J. E. Rickard, W.	Spit of Arabat	1855
Salmon, N. Harrison, J. Young, T. J. Hall, W.	Lucknow (No. 2)	1857
Mayo, A.	Dacca (Bengal)	1857
Robinson, E.	Lucknow (No. 3)	1858
Chicken, G. B.	Suhijnee (Bengal)	1858
Odgers, W.	New Zealand (Taranaki)	1860

The Victoria Cross by Branches of the Service

Hinckley, G.	China (Fung Wha)	1862
Mitchell, S.	New Zealand (Tauranga)	1864
Seeley, W.	⎫	
Boyes, D. G.	⎬ Japan (Simono Seki)	1864
Pride, T.	⎭	
Harding, I.	Egypt (Alexandria)	1882
Wilson, A. K.	Soudan (El-Teb)	1884
Maillard, W. J.	Crete (Candia Harbour)	1898
Guy, B. J. D.	China (Tientsin)	1900

The Royal Marine Artillery.

Wilkinson, T.	Sebastopol	1855
Dowell, G. D.	Viborg (Baltic)	1855

The Royal Marine Light Infantry.

Prettyjohn, J.	Inkerman	1854
Halliday, L. S. T.	China (Pekin)	1900

CAVALRY.

1st The King's Dragoon Guards.

Doogan, J.	Laing's Nek (Natal)	1881

2nd Dragoon Guards, Queen's Bays.

Blair, R.	Boolundshuhur	1857
Anderson, G.	⎫ Sundella	1858
Monaghan, T.	⎭	
Smyth, N. M.	Omdurman	1898

5th Princess Charlotte of Wales' Dragoon Guards.

Norwood, J.	Ladysmith	1899

2nd Dragoons—Royal Scots Greys.

Grieve, J.	⎫ Balaklava	1854
Ramage, H.	⎭	

The Victoria Cross by Branches of the Service

4TH QUEEN'S OWN HUSSARS.

Parkes, S. . . . . . . Balaklava 1854

5TH ROYAL IRISH LANCERS.

Dugdale, F. B. . . . Derby, South Africa 1901

6TH INNISKILLING DRAGOONS.

Mouat, J. . . . . . Balaklava 1854

7TH QUEEN'S OWN HUSSARS.

Banks, W. G. H. . . . Lucknow (No. 3) 1858
Fraser, C. C. . . . . The Raptee River (Nepal) 1858

8TH KING'S ROYAL IRISH HUSSARS.

Champion, J. . . . . Beejapore and Gwalior 1858
Heneage, C. W. . . .
Pearson, Jno. . . . .
Hollis, G. . . . . . } Gwalior 1858
Ward, J. . . . . . .

9TH QUEEN'S ROYAL LANCERS.

Jones, A. S. . . . . Delhi (Budlekeserai) 1857
Hartigan, H. . . . . Budlekeserai and Agra 1857
Hancock, T. . . . . Delhi 1857
Purcell, J. . . . . . Delhi 1857
Donohoe, P. . . . .
Kells, R. . . . . . } Boolundshuhur 1857
Roberts, J. R. . . . .
Freeman, J. . . . . Agra 1857
Spence, D. . . . . . Shumsabad 1858
Goat, W. . . . . .
Rushe, D. . . . . . } Lucknow (No. 3) 1858
Newell, R. . . . . .
Beresford, W. L. De La P. Ulundi (near), Zululand 1879

The Victoria Cross by Branches of the Service

10TH PRINCE OF WALES'S OWN ROYAL HUSSARS.

Milbanke, J. P.	Colesberg (South Africa)	1900
Engleheart, H.	Bloemfontein (South Africa)	1900

11TH PRINCE ALBERTS' OWN HUSSARS.

Dunn, A. R.	Balaklava	1854

13TH HUSSARS.

Malone, J.	Balaklava	1854

14TH KING'S HUSSARS.

Leith, J.	Betwah, India	1858
Brown, E. D. (now Brown-Synge-Hutchinson)	Geluk, South Africa	1900

16TH QUEEN'S LANCERS.

Fincastle, A. E.	Landakai (Punjaub Frontier)	1897

17TH DUKE OF CAMBRIDGE'S OWN LANCERS.

Berryman, J.		
Farrell, J.	Balaklava	1854
Wooden, C.		
Wood, H. E.	Sindwaho and Sindhora, India	1858–9
Lawrence, T.	Essenbosch (South Africa)	1900

18TH THE PRINCESS OF WALES'S HUSSARS.

Crandon, H. G.	Springboklaagte	1901

19TH ALEXANDRA PRINCESS OF WALES'S OWN HUSSARS.

Marshall, W. T.	El-Teb (Eastern Soudan)	1884

The Victoria Cross by Branches of the Service

21st The Empress of India's Lancers.

Kenna, P. A.		
Montmorency, R.H.L.J. de	Omdurman (Khartoum)	1898
Byrne, T.		

The Royal (and Late Indian) Artillery.

Dickson, C.	Sebastopol	1854
Henry, A.	Inkerman	1854
Miller, F.		
Dixon, M. C.	Sebastopol	1855
Symons, G.		
Arthur, T.	Sebastopol and Redan	1855
Cambridge, D.	The Redan (Sebastopol)	1855
Davis, G.		
Teesdale, C. C.	Kars (Armenia)	1855
Buckley, J.	Delhi (blowing up the Magazine)	1857
Connolly, (I) W.	Jhelum, India	1857
Hills-[Johnes] (I) J.		
Tombs, (I) H.	Delhi, India	1857
Renny, (I) G. H.		
Maude, F. C.	Lucknow (No. 1), India	1857
Olpherts, (I) W.	Lucknow (No. 1)	1857
Thomas, (I) J.	Lucknow (Defence)	1857
Diamond, (I) B.	Boolundshuhur	1857
Fitzgerald, (I) R.		
Miller, (I) J.	Futtehpore	1857
Harrington, (I) H. E.		
Jennings, (I) E.		
Laughnan, (I) T.	Lucknow, Second Relief ("No. 2")	1857
McInnes, (I) H.		
Park, (I) J.		
Roberts, (I) F. S.	Khodagunge	1858
Keatinge (I) R. H.	Chandairee	1858
Brennan, J.	Jhansi	1858
Temple, W.	Rangiriri, New Zealand	1863
Pickard, A. F.		
Manley, W. G. N.	Tauranga, New Zealand	1864
Mullane, P.	Maiwand, Afghanistan	1880
Collis, J.		
Smith, A.	Abu-Klea, Bayuda Desert, Soudan	1885
Reed, H. L.		
Schofield, H. N.	Colenso Bridge, Natal	1899
Nurse, G. E.		

The Victoria Cross by Branches of the Service

Phipps-Hornby, E. J.
Parker, C.
Lodge, I.
Glasock, H. H.
} Korn Spruit, South Africa 1900

Bradley, F. G. . . . . Itala, Zululand (Boer War) 1901
Ind, A. E. . . . . Tafelkop, South Africa 1901

The Royal (and Late Indian) Engineers.

Lennox, W. O. . . . Sebastopol 1854
Lendrim, W. J. . . . Sebastopol (three times) 1855
Macdonald, H. . . . Sebastopol 1855
Elphinstone, H. C. . . Sebastopol 1855
Graham, G. . . . . Sebastopol and Redan 1855
Leitch, P. . . . . . Sebastopol (Redan) 1855
Perie, J. . . . . . Sebastopol (Redan) 1855
Ross, J. . . . . . Sebastopol (twice) and Redan . . . 1855
Home, (I) D. C.
Salkeld, (I) P.
Smith, (I) J.
} Kashmir Gate, Delhi 1857
Thackeray, (I) E. T. . . Delhi 1857
Prendergast, (I) H. N. D. . Mundisore, Rathgur and Betwa (India) 1857
Innes, (I) J. J. McL. . . Sultanpore (India) 1858
Sleavon, M. . . . . Jhansi (India) 1858
Goodfellow, (I) C. A. . . Beyt Fort (India) 1859
Dundas, (I) J.
Trevor, (I) W. S.
} Dewan Giri (Bhootan) 1865
Bell, M. S. . . . . Ordahsu (Ashantee) 1874
Chard, J. R. M. . . . Rorke's Drift (Zululand) 1879
Hart, R. C. . . . . Dakkah (Afghanistan) 1879
Leach, E. P. . . . . Maidanah (Afghanistan) 1879
Aylmer, F. J. . . . . Fort Nilt (Hunza Nagar) 1891
Watson, T. C.
Colvin, J. M. C.
} Bilot (Punjaub Frontier) 1897
Jones, R. J. T. Digby . . Ladysmith (Natal) 1900
Kirby, F. . . . . . Delagoa Bay Railway (Transvaal) . . 1900

The Military Train.

Morley, S.
Murphy, M.
} Azimghur (India) 1858

The Victoria Cross by Branches of the Service

THE FOOT GUARDS.

Grenadier.

Percy, H. H. M	⎫	
Russell, C.	⎬ Inkerman	1854
Palmer, A.	⎭	
Ablett, A.	Sebastopol	1855

Coldstream.

Goodlake, G. L.	Sebastopol ("Great Sortie")	1854
Stanlack, W.	Sebastopol (no date)	1854
Strong, G.	Sebastopol (no date)	1855

Scots (*Fusilier*).

Lindsay, [Loyd]—(Lord Wantage), R. J.	⎫ Inkerman also.	
Knox, J. S.	⎬ Alma (together)	
McKechnie, J.	⎥ Knox Redan also, when in Rifle Brigade, 1855	1854
Reynolds, W.	⎭	
Craig, J.	Sebastopol	1855

INFANTRY.

2nd Batt. 1st The Royals (Royal Scots).

Prosser, J.	Sebastopol (twice)	1855

2nd Batt. 2nd Queen's (The Royal West Surrey).

Wright, W. D.	Northern Nigeria	1903

3rd The Buffs (East Kent).

Maude, F. F.	⎫ Sebastopol (Redan)	1855
Connors, J.	⎭	
Smith, Js.	Bilot, Punjaub Frontier	1897

4th The King's Own (Royal Lancaster).

Grady, T.	Sebastopol (twice)	1854

The Victoria Cross by Branches of the Service

5TH THE NORTHUMBERLAND FUSILIERS.

Grant, R.	Alumbagh, Lucknow (No. 1)	1857
McManus, P.	Lucknow (No. 1)	1857
McHale, P.	Lucknow, etc., twice (No. 1)	1857

7TH THE ROYAL FUSILIERS (CITY OF LONDON REGIMENT).

Norman, W.	Sebastopol	1854
Jones, H. M.	Sebastopol ("repeatedly")	1855
Hughes, M.	Sebastopol (twice)	1855
Hope, W.	Sebastopol (Redan)	1855
Hale, T. E.	Sebastopol (often same day)	1855
Ashford, J.	Kandahar	1880
Fitz-Clarence, C.	Mafeking (three times)	1899

8TH THE KING'S (LIVERPOOL REGIMENT).

Hampton, H.	Van Wyk's Vlei, South Africa	1900
Knight, A. J.		
Heaton, W.	Geluk, South Africa	1900

10TH THE (NORTH) LINCOLNSHIRE REGIMENT.

Kirk, J.	Benares, India	1857
Havelock, H. M.	Cawnpore and Lucknow (No. 1)	1857
Dempsey, D.	Relief of Arrah, Lucknow, etc.	1857–8

11TH THE (NORTH) DEVONSHIRE REGIMENT.

Masterson, J. E. I.	Ladysmith (Defence)	1900

13TH PRINCE ALBERT'S SOMERSETSHIRE L.I.

Napier, W.	Azimghur, India	1858
Carlin, P.		
Leet, W. K.	Inhlobana, Zululand	1879

14TH THE PRINCE OF WALES' OWN WEST YORKS REGIMENT.

Mansel-Jones, C.	Terrace Hill (Ladysmith)	1900
Traynor, W. B.	Lake Crissy, South Africa	1901

The Victoria Cross by Branches of the Service

17TH THE LEICESTERSHIRE REGIMENT.

Smith, P.	Sebastopol ("repeatedly")	1855

18TH THE ROYAL IRISH REGIMENT.

Esmonde, T.	Sebastopol (twice)	1855
Shaw, H.	Nukumaru	1865
Barry, J.	Belfast, South Africa	1901

19TH ALEXANDRA PRINCESS OF WALES' OWN YORKSHIRE REGIMENT.

Evans, S.	Sebastopol	1855
Lyons, J.		
Atkinson, A.	Paardeburg, South Africa	1900

21ST THE ROYAL SCOTS FUSILIERS.

Ravenhill, G.	Colenso Bridge, Natal	1899

23RD THE ROYAL WELSH FUSILIERS.

O'Connor, L.	Alma and the Redan	1854-5
Bell, E. W. D.	Alma	1854
Sylvester, W. H.	Sebastopol	1855
Shields, R.		
Hackett, T. B.	Secundra Bagh, Lucknow (No. 2)	1857
Monger, G.		

24TH THE 2ND WARWICK (SOUTH WALES BORDERERS).

Douglas, C. M.		
Bell, D.		
Cooper, J.	Little Andaman Island (Bay of Bengal)	1867
Griffiths, W.		
Murphy, T.		
Gifford, E. F.	Bequah (and whole campaign), Ashantee	1874
Melvill, T.	Isandlwana, Zululand	1879
Coghill, N. J. A.	Buffalo River, Zululand	1879

The Victoria Cross by Branches of the Service

Bromhead, G.
Williams, J.
Hook, H.
Jones, W. } Defence of Rorke's Drift, Zululand 1879
Jones, R.
Allen, W.
Hitch, F.

Brown, E. S. . . . . Inhlobana Mountain (Zulu) 1879

25TH THE KING'S OWN SCOTTISH BORDERERS.

Coulson, G. H. B. . . . Lambrecht Fontein, South Africa 1901

30TH THE CAMBRIDGESHIRE REGIMENT (EAST LANCASHIRE).

Walker, M. . . . . Inkerman and Sebastopol 1854–5

32ND THE CORNWALL (DUKE OF CORNWALL'S) L.I.

Oxenham, W.
Lawrence, S. H. } Lucknow (Defence) 1857
Dowling, W.
Brown, H. G.

33RD THE DUKE OF WELLINGTON'S (WEST RIDING OF YORK) REGIMENT.

Magner, M. } Magdala, Abyssinia 1868
Bergin, J.

Firth, W. . . . . . Arundel, South Africa 1900

34TH THE CUMBERLAND (1ST BORDER) REGIMENT.

Coffey, W. } Sebastopol 1855
Sims, J. J.

Richardson, G. . . . Kewanie, India 1859

39TH THE DORSETSHIRE REGIMENT.

Vickery, S. . . . . Dargai, etc., Punjab Frontier 1897

40TH THE 2ND SOMERSETSHIRE—P.W. VOL. (1ST SOUTH LANCASHIRE).

Lucas, J. . . . . . Huirangi, New Zealand 1861

The Victoria Cross by Branches of the Service

41st The Welsh Regiment.

Rowlands, H.	} Inkerman	1854
Madden, A.		

42nd The Royal Highlanders—Black Watch.

Farquharson, F. E. H.	Lucknow (No. 3)	1858
Simpson, J.		
Davis, J.	Ruhya, India	1858
Spence, E.		
Thompson, A.		
Gardner, W.	Bareilly, India	1858
Cook, W.	Mylah Ghaut, India	1859
Millar, D.		
McGaw, S.	Amoaful, Ashantee	1874
Edwards, T.	Tamai, Soudan	1884

43rd The Monmouthshire (1st Oxford) L.I.

Addison, H.	Kurrerah, India	1859
Smith, F. A.	Tauranga, New Zealand	1864

44th The East Essex (1st Essex) Regiment.

McWheeney, W.	Sebastopol (three times)	1854-5
Rogers, R. M.	Taku Forts, China	1860
McDougall, J.		
Parsons, F. N.	Paardeberg, etc., South Africa	1900

45th The Nottinghamshire (1st Notts and Derbys) Regiment—The Sherwood Foresters.

Beet, H. C.	Wakkerstroom, South Africa	1900
Bees, W.	Moedvil, South Africa	1901

46th The Cornwall (Duke of Cornwall's) L.I.

Smith, C. L.	Jidballi, Somaliland	1904

47th The Lancashire (1st Loyal North Lancs.) Regiment.

McDermond, J.	Inkerman	1854

49th The Hertfordshire P. C. Wales' (1st Royal Berks) Regiment.

Conolly, J. A.	Sebastopol ("Great Sortie")	1854
Owens, J.	Sebastopol ("Great Sortie," etc.)	1854
Walters, G.	Inkerman	1854

52nd The Oxfordshire (2nd Batt.) L.I.

Hawthorne, R.	Delhi, Kashmir Gate	1857
Smith, H.	Delhi	1857

The Victoria Cross by Branches of the Service

53RD THE SHROPSHIRE (1ST BATT. SHROPSHIRE L.I.) REGIMENT.

Dynon, D.	Chota Behar, India	1857
Ffrench, A. K.		
Irwin, C.		
Kenny, J.	} Lucknow (No. 2)	1857
Pye, C.		

55TH THE WESTMORELAND (2ND BORDER) REGIMENT.

Beach, T.	Inkerman	1854
Elton, F. C.	Sebastopol (several times)	1855

57TH THE (WEST) MIDDLESEX REGIMENT.

Gardiner, G.	Sebastopol (twice)	1855
McCorrie, C.	Sebastopol	1855
Down, J. T.	} Pontoko, New Zealand	1863
Stagpoole, D.		

58TH THE RUTLANDSHIRE (2ND NORTHAMPTONSHIRE) REGIMENT.

Hill-[Walker], A. R.	Laing's Nek, Natal	1881
Osborne, J.	Wesselstroom, Transvaal	1881

59TH THE 2ND NOTTS (2ND EAST LANCASHIRE) REGIMENT.

Sartorius, E. H.	Tazi, Afghanistan	1879

60TH THE KING'S ROYAL RIFLE CORPS (FOUR BATTALIONS).

Heathcote, A. S.	Delhi (" whole siege," etc.)	1857
Turner, S.	Delhi	1857
Garvin, S.	} Delhi (" whole siege," etc.)	1857
Thompson, J.		
Sutton, W.	Delhi (twice)	1857
Divane, J.	Delhi	1857
Waller, G.	Delhi (Cabul Gate, etc.)	1857
Bambrick, V.	Bareilly	1858
Buller, R. H.	Inhlobana Mountain, Zulu (three times)	1879
Corbett, F.	Kafr Dowr, Egypt	1882
Marling, P. S.	Tamai, Soudan	1884
Roberts, F. H. S.	Colenso Bridge, South Africa	1899
Price-Davies, L. A. E.	Blood River Poort, South Africa	1901

The Victoria Cross by Branches of the Service

61st The (South) Gloucestershire (2nd Batt.) Regiment.

Reade, H. T.	Delhi (twice)	1857

63rd The West Suffolk (1st Manchester) Regiment.

Scott, R. Pitts, J.	} Ladysmith, Natal	1900

64th The (2nd) Staffordshire (Prince of Wales' North Staffs) Regiment.

Flinn, T.	Cawnpore, India	1857

65th The 2nd Yorks North Riding (1st York and Lancaster) Regiment.

Mackenna, E. Ryan, Jno.	} Cameron Town, New Zealand	1863

66th The Berkshire (2nd Royal Berks) Regiment.

House, W.	Mosilikatse Nek, South Africa	1900

67th The (South) Hampshire Regiment.

Lenon, E. H. Burslem, N. Lane, T. Chaplin, J. W.	} Taku Forts, China	1860

68th The Durham L.I.

Byrne, Jno.	Inkerman	1854
Hamilton, T. de C.	Sebastopol	1855
Murray, Jno.	Tauranga, New Zealand	1864

70th The Surrey (East Surrey) Regiment.

Curtis, A. E.	Onderbrook Spruit (Colenso), South Africa	1900

71st The Highland L.I.

Rodgers, G.	Morar, Gwalior	1858
Shaul, J. F. D.	Magersfontein, South Africa	1899
Kennedy, C.	Dewetsdorp, South Africa	1900

The Victoria Cross by Branches of the Service

71ST–74TH H.L.I. 3RD BATT. ROYAL LANARK MILITIA.

Hore-Ruthven, A. G. A.	Gedarif (Nile Expedition)	1898

72ND THE DUKE OF ALBANY'S OWN (SEAFORTH) HIGHLANDERS.

Cameron, A. S.	Kotah, India	1858
Sellar, G.	Kabul	1879

74TH HIGHLANDERS (2ND H.L.I.).

Edwards, W. M. M.	Tel-El-Kebir, Egypt	1882

75TH THE STIRLINGSHIRE (1ST GORDON HIGHLANDERS) REGIMENT.

Coghlan, C.	Delhi (twice)	1857
Wadeson, R.	Delhi (twice in one day)	1857
Green, P.	Delhi	1857
Findlater, G.	Dargai, Punjab Frontier (India)	1897
Lawson, E.	Dargai, Punjab Frontier (India)	1897
Towse, E. B. B.	Magersfontein and Mount Thaba, South Africa	1899–1900
Mackay, F. J.	Johannesburg, South Africa	1900
Gordon, W. E.	Krugersdorp, South Africa	1900
Younger, R. D.	Krugersdorp, South Africa	1900

77TH THE (EAST) MIDDLESEX REGIMENT.

Park, Jno.	Alma, Inkerman, Sebastopol	1854–5
Wright, A.	Sebastopol and "the whole Crimean War"	1854–5

78TH HIGHLANDERS ROSS-SHIRE BUFFS (2ND SEAFORTH HIGHLANDERS).

Bogle, A. C.	Oonao, India	1857
Crowe, J. P. H.	Busherat-Gunge, India	1857
Macpherson, H. T.	Lucknow (No. 1)	1857
Jee, J.	Lucknow (No. 1)	1857
McMaster, V. M.	Lucknow (No. 1)	1857
Ward, H.	Lucknow (No. 1)	1857
McPherson, S.	Lucknow (No. 1)	1857
Hollowell, J.	Lucknow (No. 1)	1857
Mackenzie, J.	Dompoassi, Ashantee	1900

79TH THE QUEEN'S OWN CAMERON HIGHLANDERS.

Farmer, D.	Nooitgedacht South Africa	1900

The Victoria Cross by Branches of the Service

80th The Staffordshire Volunteers (2nd South Staffs) Regiment.

Wassall, S.	Buffalo River, Zululand	1879
Booth, A.	Intombi River, Zululand	1879

84th The York and Lancaster Regiment.

Boulger, A.	Lucknow and First Relief of, whole time	1857
Mylott, P.	Lucknow—First Relief of; "in every action"	1857
Lambert, G.	Oonao, Bithoor, Lucknow (No. 1)	1857
Holmes, J.	Lucknow (No. 1)	1857
Anson, A. H. A.	Boolundshuhur and Lucknow (No. 2)	1857
Sinnott, J.	Lucknow (2nd Defence)	1857

86th The Royal County Down (2nd Royal Irish Rifles).

Cochrane, H. S.	Jhansi, India	1858
Jerome, H. E.	Jhansi, Chandairee, and "on the Jumna"	1858
Byrne, Js.	} Jhansi, India	1858
Pearson, J. S.		

88th The Connaught Rangers.

Moore, H. G.	Komgha (Gaikaland), South Africa	1877

90th The Perthshire Volunteers L.I. (2nd Scottish Rifles).

Alexander, J.	Sebastopol (twice)	1855
Moynihan, A.	Sebastopol (in the Redan)	1855
Rennie, W.	"Advance on" and Lucknow (No. 1)	1857
Home, A. D.	} Lucknow (No. 1)	1857
Bradshaw, W.		
Guise, J. C.	} Lucknow (No. 2)	1857
Hill, S.		
Graham, P.	Lucknow (No. 2)	1857
Lysons, H.	} Inhlobana Mountains (Zulu)	1879
Fowler, E.		

92nd The Gordon Highlanders.

White, G. S.	Charasiah and Kandahar	1879-80
Dick-Cunyngham, W. H.	Kabul	1879
Meiklejohn, M. F. M.	} Elandslaagte, Natal	1899
Robertson, W.		

The Victoria Cross by Branches of the Service

93RD THE SUTHERLAND HIGHLANDERS (2ND ARGYLL AND SUTHERLAND) THE PRINCESS LOUISE'S.

Stewart, W. G. D.	} Lucknow (No. 2)	1857
Munro, J.		
Paton, J.		
Dunley, J.		
Grant, P.		
Mackay, D.		
McBean, W.	Lucknow (No. 3)	1858

94TH REGIMENT (NOW 2ND CONNAUGHT RANGERS).

Fitzpatrick, F.	} Sekukuni's Town, South Africa	1879
Flawn, T.		
Murray, Js.	Elandsfontein, Transvaal	1881

95TH THE DERBYSHIRE (2ND NOTTS AND DERBY) REGIMENT.

McQuirt, B.	Rowa, India	1858
Pennell, H. S.	Dargai, Punjab Frontier	1897

97TH THE EARL OF ULSTER'S (2ND ROYAL WEST KENT) REGIMENT.

Coleman, J.	Sebastopol	1855
Lumley, C. H.	Sebastopol (the Redan)	1855

THE 1ST BENGAL EUROPEAN FUSILIERS (1ST ROYAL MUNSTER—101ST).

McGuire, J.	} Delhi	1857
Ryan, M.		
Brown, F. D. M.	Narrioul, India	1857
Butler, T. A.	Lucknow (No. 3)	1858

THE 2ND BENGAL EUROPEAN FUSILIERS—2ND ROYAL MUNSTER (104TH).

Cadell, T.	Delhi (Flagstaff Picket)	1857

THE 1ST BENGAL FUSILIERS.

McGovern, J.	Delhi (several occasions)	1857

THE 4TH (IN 1863 LATE) BENGAL EUROPEAN REGIMENT.

Fosbery, G. V.	"Crag Picquet," Umbeyla, India	1863

The Victoria Cross by Branches of the Service

THE 1ST MADRAS FUSILIERS 1ST ROYAL DUBLIN (102ND).

Mahoney, P.	Mungulwar, India (First Relief of Lucknow)	1857
Ryan, J.	} Lucknow (No. 1)	1857
Duffy, T.		
Smith, J.	Lucknow (No. 2)	1857

105TH THE MADRAS L.I. (2ND KING'S YORKSHIRE L.I.).

Ward, C.	Lindley, South Africa	1900

107TH BENGAL INFANTRY (2ND THE ROYAL SUSSEX).

McNeill, J. C.	Ohanpu, New Zealand	1864

109TH BOMBAY INFANTRY (2ND PRINCE OF WALES' LEINSTER REGIMENT, ROYAL CANADIANS).

Whirlpool, F.	Jhansi *and* Lohari, India	1858

THE PRINCE CONSORT'S OWN RIFLE BRIGADE (FOUR BATTALIONS).

Clifford, H. H.	Inkerman	1854
Wheatley, F.	} Sebastopol	1854
Bourchier, C. T.		
Cuninghame, W. J. M.		
Humpston, R.	} Sebastopol	1855
Bradshaw, J.		
McGregor, R.		
Wilmot, H.	} Lucknow (No. 3)	1858
Nash, W.		
Hawkes, D.		
Shaw, S.	Nawabgunge	1858
O'Hea, T.	Danville Railway Station, Canada	1866
Congreve, W. N.	Colenso Bridge, Natal	1899
Durrant, E.	Bergendal, South Africa	1900
Gough, J. E.	Daratholeh, Somaliland	1903

4TH WEST INDIA REGIMENT.

Hodge, S.	Jubabecolong, West Africa	1866

1ST BATT. WEST INDIA REGIMENT.

Gordon, W. J.	Toniataba, West Africa	1892

The Victoria Cross by Branches of the Service

The Commissariat Corps.

Dalton, J. L.	Rorke's Drift, Zululand	1879

The Royal Army Medical Corps (Old and New).*

Reynolds, J. H.	Rorke's Drift, Zululand	1879
Farmer, J. J.	Majuba Hill (Boer, 1881), Natal	1881
Le Quesne, F. S.	Tartun, Burmah	1889
Lloyd, O. E. P.	Sima (outpost), Burmah	1893
Douglas, H. E. M.	Magersfontein, South Africa	1899
Babtie, W.	Colenso Bridge, Natal	1899
Inkson, E. T.	Harts Hill, Colenso (Natal)	1900
Nickerson, W. H. S.	Wakkerstroom, South Africa	1900

The Imperial Yeomanry—3rd Batt.

Doxat, A. C.	Zeerust, South Africa	1900

The Scottish Horse (The Marquis of Tullibardine's Corps).

English, W. J.	Vlakfontein, South Africa	1901

THE INDIAN ARMY—(OLD).

Exclusive of Artillery, Engineers, European Infantry, and Staff Corps.

The 1st Bengal European Light Cavalry.

Gough, H. H.	Lucknow (No. 2 and other occasions)	1857-8

The 5th Bengal European Cavalry.

Gough, C. J. S.	Khurkowdah, Shumsabad and Meangunge, India	1857-8

The 6th Bengal Cavalry.

Sartorius, R. W.	Abogoo, Ashantee	1874

The 1st Punjab Cavalry.

Watson, J.	Lucknow (No. 2)	1857

The 2nd Punjab Cavalry.

Probyn, D. McN.	Agra (and many " gallant deeds ")	1857

The 2nd Bengal Native Infantry.

Travers, J.	Indore, India	1857

* 28 Medical Officers and men (2) altogether. Those not mentioned here are given with their respective regiments.

The Victoria Cross by Branches of the Service

The 4th Bengal Native Infantry.
Aikman, F. R. . . . . Lucknow—near (No. 3) 1858

The 11th (formerly 70th) Bengal Native Infantry.
Phillipps, E. A. L. . . . Delhi ("whole siege," etc.) 1857
Daunt, J. C. C. . . . Chota Behar, etc., India 1857

The 13th Bengal Native Infantry (formerly).
Cubitt, W. G. . . . . Chinhut, Lucknow 1857
Aitken, R. H. M. . . . Lucknow (Defence of) 1857

The 26th Bengal Native Infantry (formerly).
Jarrett, H. C. T. . . . Baroun, India 1858

The 37th Bengal Native Infantry (formerly).
Rosamund, M. . . . Benares, India 1857

The 46th Bengal Native Infantry (formerly).
Brown, S. J. . . . . Seerporah, India 1858

The 56th Bengal Native Infantry (formerly).
Cafe, W. M. . . . . Ruhya, India 1858

The 60th Bengal Native Infantry (formerly).
Shebbeare, R. H. . . Delhi 1857

The 66th (now 1st Ghoorka) Bengal Native Infantry.
Tytler, J. A. . . . . Choorpoorah, India 1858

The 72nd Bengal Native Infantry (formerly).
Lyster, H. H. . . . Calpee, India 1858

The 4th Punjab Infantry.
Pitcher, H. W. . . . "Crag Picquet," Umbeyla, India 1863

The Loodiana Regiment (N.I.)
Gill, P. . . . . . . Benares, India 1857

The Bengal Army (Unposted to a Corps).
Roddy, P. . . . . Kuthirga (and "several occasions"), India . . . 1858

The Victoria Cross by Branches of the Service

THE BENGAL VETERAN ESTABLISHMENT.

Forrest, G.	Delhi (blowing up the Magazine)	1857
Raynor, W.	Delhi (blowing up the Magazine)	1857

BENGAL POLICE BATTALION.

Baker, C. G.	Suhijnee, India	1858

THE BENGAL MEDICAL SERVICE.

Whitchurch, H. F.	Chitral (India)—battle near Fort	1895

THE 19TH MADRAS NATIVE INFANTRY.

Clogstoun, H. M.	Chichumbah, India	1859

THE 2ND BOMBAY LIGHT CAVALRY.

Blair, J.	Neemuch and Jeerum, India	1857

THE 3RD BOMBAY LIGHT CAVALRY.

Moore, A. T.	Koosh-ab, Persia	1857
Malcolmson, J. G.		

THE 20TH BOMBAY NATIVE INFANTRY.

Wood, J. A.	Bushire, Persia	1856

THE 24TH BOMBAY NATIVE INFANTRY.

Kerr, W. A.	Kolapore, India	1857

THE 25TH BOMBAY L.I. (NATIVE INFANTRY.)

Waller, W. F. F.	Gwalior	1858

THE BOMBAY MEDICAL SERVICE.

Crimmin, J.	Lwekaw, Burmah	1889

THE INDIAN MEDICAL ESTABLISHMENT.

Fitzgibbon, A. F.	Taku Forts, China	1860

CHAPLAINS—INDIA (BENGAL).

Adams, J. W.	Kabul	1879

INDIAN (BENGAL) CIVIL SERVICE.

McDonell, W. F.	Relief of Arrah, India.	1857
Mangles, R. L.		
Kavanagh, T. H.	Lucknow, Defence and No. 2	1857

The Victoria Cross by Branches of the Service

THE INDIAN STAFF CORPS (NOW "INDIAN ARMY").

Bengal.

Macintyre, D.	late 6th N.I.	Looshai, India	1872
Channer, G. N.	late 95th Foot	Perak Expedition	1875
Scott, A.	late N.I.	Quetta, Baluchistan	1877
Cook, J.	late N.I.	Peiwar Kotal, Afghan	1878
Hamilton, W. R. P.	late 70th Foot	Futtehabad, Afghan	1879
Ridgeway, R. K.	late 96th Foot	Naga Hills, India	1879
Hammond, A. G.	late N.I.	} Kabul	1879
Vousden, W. J.	late 35th Foot		
Boisragon, G. H.	late 10th Foot	} Hunza Nagar (India)	1891
Smith, J. M.	late 9th Foot		
Costello, E. W.	late 14th Foot	} Punjab Frontier (India)	1897
Adams, R. B.	late 12th Foot		
MacLean, H. L. S.	late 5th Foot		
Maxwell, F. A.	late 107th Foot	Korn Spruit, South Africa	1900
Melliss, C. J.	late 15th Foot	Obassa, Ashantee	1900
Cobbe, A. S.	late 24th Foot	Erego, Somaliland	1902
Walker, W. G.	late 1-12th Foot	} Darathole, Somaliland	1903
Rolland, G. M.	late 2-16th Foot		

Madras.

Grant, C. J. W.	late 12th Foot	Thobal, Manipur	1891

Bombay.

Creagh, O'M.	late 95th Foot	Kam Dakka, Afghan	1879
Chase, W. St. L.	late 15th Foot	Kandahar, Afghan	1880

COLONIAL CORPS—1864 TO 1902.

THE AUCKLAND MILITIA—NEW ZEALAND.

Heaphy, C.	Mangapiko, New Zealand	1864

THE NATAL NATIVE CONTINGENT.

Schiess, F. C.	Rorke's Drift, Zululand	1879

THE CAPE MOUNTED RIFLES.

Scott, R. G.	} Moirosi's Mountain, Basuto	1879
Brown, P.		
Hartley, E. B.		

The Victoria Cross by Branches of the Service

THE FRONTIER LIGHT HORSE (NATAL).

D'Arcy, C.
O'Toole, E.   } Ulundi (near), Zululand 1879

THE 1ST CAPE MOUNTED YEOMANRY.

McCrea, J. F. . . . Tweefontein, Basuto 1881

NOURSE'S HORSE (TRANSVAAL).

Danaher, J. . . . . Elandsfontein, Transvaal 1881

THE BULUWAYO FIELD FORCE.

Henderson, H. S.
Baxter, F. W.   } Bulawayo (near), Matabele 1896

THE MASHONALAND MOUNTED POLICE.

Nesbitt, R. C. . . . Salisbury (near), Matabele 1896

THE IMPERIAL LIGHT HORSE (NATAL).

Mullins, C. H.
Johnstone, R.   } Elandslaagte, Natal 1899
Albrecht, H. . . . . Ladysmith, Natal 1900
Crean, T. J. . . . . Tygerskloof, South Africa 1901

THE PROTECTORATE REGIMENT (NORTH-WEST CAPE COLONY).

Martineau, H. R.
Ramsden, H. E.   } Mafeking, South Africa 1899

RIMINGTON'S GUIDES.

Clements, J. J. . . . Strijdenberg, South Africa 1900

LORD STRATHCONA'S CORPS.

Richardson, A. H. L. . . Standerton, South Africa 1900

THE NEW SOUTH WALES MEDICAL STAFF.

Howse, N. R. . . . Vredefort, South Africa 1900

THE TASMANIAN IMPERIAL BUSHMEN.

Wylly, G. G. E.
Bisdee, J. H.   } Warmbad, South Africa 1900

The Victoria Cross by Branches of the Service

The Royal Canadian Dragoons.

Cockburn, H. Z. C. ⎫
Turner, R. E. W. ⎬ Koomati River, South Africa 1900
Holland, E. ⎭

The 4th New Zealand Contingent.

Hardham, W. J. . . . . Naauwpoort, South Africa 1901

The West Australian Mounted Infantry.

Bell, F. W. . . . . . Brakpan, South Africa 1901

The South African Constabulary.

Rogers, Js. . . . . . Thaba N'Chu, South Africa 1901
Martin-Leake, A. . . . Vlakfontein, South Africa 1902

The Cape Police.

Young, A. . . . . . Ruiter's Kraal, South Africa 1901

The 5th Victoria Mounted Rifles.

Maygar, L. C. . . . . Geelhoutboom, South Africa 1901

Index

The numbers, col. 1, denote the order in which the decoration has been gained : thus Alfred Ablett was, in chronological order, the ninety-fifth winner of the V.C. In events such as Alma, Balaklava, Inkerman, both Reliefs of Lucknow, and some few others, the prefixed number is, in some instances, given by seniority (as Lord Wantage first at Alma), in others in alphabetical order. An asterisk (*) prefixed to name indicates that the man is no longer living. The figures affixed to "Lucknow" refer respectively to First and Second Relief, 25 September and 24 November, 1857, and to siege and capture, March 9 to 19, 1858. The "territorial" designation of each regiment will be found in the list of crosses won "*by regiments*," pp. 403–25.

Order in which each cross has been gained.	Name.	Regiment, Corps, etc.	Campaign, etc., and *place*.	Announced in the London Gazette of	Page.
95	*Ablett, A.	Grenadier Guards	Crimea—*Sebastopol*	Feb. 24, 1857	51
351	*Adams, J. W.	Bengal Ecclesiastical Establishment	Afghan—*Kabul*	Aug. 26, 1881	226–227, 386
417	Adams, R. B.	Queen's Own Corps of Guides (ex 12th Foot)	Punjab Frontier—*Landakai*	Nov. 9, 1897	293–294, 295
291	*Addison, H.	43rd Regiment	Indian Mutiny—*Kurrereah*	Sep. 2, 1859	182
240	*Aikman, F. R.	4th Bengal N.I.	Indian Mutiny—*Lucknow* (No. 3)	Sep. 3, 1858	154
132	*Aitken, R. H. M.	13th Bengal N.I.	Indian Mutiny—*Lucknow* (Defence)	Apl. 17, 1863	72–75, 321
453	*Albrecht, H.	Imperial Light Horse (Natal)	Boer—*Ladysmith*	Aug. 8, 1902	318, 324–325, 387
75	*Alexander, J.	90th Regiment	Crimea—*Redan*, etc.	Feb. 24, 1857	40
367	*Allen, W.	24th Regiment	Zulu—*Rorke's Drift*	May 2, 1879	237–243, 247, 248, 392–398
286	*Anderson, C.	2nd Dragoon Guards	Indian Mutiny—*Sundeela* (Oudh)	Nov. 11, 1862	179
189	*Anson, A. H. A.	84th Regiment	Indian Mutiny—*Bolandshuhur* and *Lucknow* (No. 2)	Dec. 24, 1858	120
70	*Arthur, T.	The Royal Artillery	Crimea—*Sebastopol* and *Redan*	Feb. 24, 1857	38
359	Ashford, T.	7th Regiment	Afghan—*Kandahar*	Oct. 7, 1881	232
458	*Atkinson, A.	19th Regiment	Boer—*Paardeberg*	Aug. 8, 1902	325, 387
407	Aylmer, F. J.	Royal Engineers	Hunza-Nagar—*Nilt*	July 12, 1892	280–282, 282
446	Babtie, W.	Royal Army Medical Corps	Boer—*Colenso Bridge*	Apl. 20, 1900	314
284	*Baker, C. G.	Bengal Police	Indian Mutiny—*Suhijnee*	Feb. 25, 1862	178
272	*Bambrick, V.	60th Regiment	Indian Mutiny—*Bareilly*	Dec. 24, 1858	171
250	*Bankes, W. G. H.	7th Hussars	Indian Mutiny—*Lucknow* (No. 3)	Dec. 24, 1858	161
498	*Barry, J.	18th Regiment	Boer—*Monument Hill, Belfast*	Aug. 8, 1902	352, 387

Index

Order in which each cross has been gained.	Name.	Regiment, Corps, etc.	Campaign, etc., and *place*.	Announced in the London Gazette of	Page.
414	*Baxter, F. W.	Bulawayo Field Force	Matabeleland—*Bulawayo* (near)	May 7, 1897	289–291
29	*Beach, T.	55th Regiment	Crimea—*Inkerman*	Feb. 24, 1857	18
510	Bees, W.	45th Regiment	Boer—*Moedvil*	Dec. 17, 1901	360
471	Beet, H. C.	45th Regiment	Boer—*Wakkerstroom*	Feb. 12, 1901	335
330	Bell, D	24th Regiment	(Bay of Bengal)—*Little Andaman Island*	Dec. 17, 1867	208, 209
9	*Bell, E. W. D.	23rd Regiment	Crimea—*Alma*	Feb. 24, 1857	7
502	Bell, F. W.	West Australian Mounted Infantry	Boer—*Brakpan*	Oct. 4, 1901	328
340	Bell, M. S.	Royal Engineers	Ashantee—*Ordahsu*	Nov. 20, 1874	214–215
380	*Beresford, W. L. de la P.	9th Lancers	Zulu—*Ulundi* (near)	Sep. 9, 1879	255–256, 257
335	*Bergin, J.	33rd Regiment	Abyssinia—*Magdala*	July 28, 1868	210
18	*Berryman, J.	17th Lancers	Crimea—*Balaklava*, etc.	Feb. 24, 1857	12, 13
488	Bisdee, J. H.	Tasmanian Imperial Bushmen	Boer—*Warmbad*	Nov. 13, 1900	345
150	Blair, J.	2nd Bombay Light Cavalry	Indian Mutiny—*Neemuch*, etc.	Feb. 25, 1862	98
190	*Blair, R.	2nd Dragoon Guards	Indian Mutiny—*Boolandshuhur*	June 18, 1858	120–121
146	*Bogle, A. C.	78th Regiment	Indian Mutiny—*Oonao*	Sep. 2, 1859	87
408	Boisragon, G. H.	Bengal Staff Corps (ex Lincoln Regiment)	Hunza-Nagar (India)—*Nilt*	July 12, 1892	280, 282
374	*Booth, A.	80th Regiment	Zulu—*Intombi River*	Feb. 24, 1880	250–251
141	*Boulger, A.	84th Regiment	Indian Mutiny—*Lucknow* (No. 1)	June 18, 1858	84
48	*Bourchier, C. T.	Rifle Brigade	Crimea—*Sebastopol* (Rifle Pits)	Feb. 24, 1857	27
323	*Boyes, D. G.	Royal Navy—H.M.S. *Euryalus*	Japan—*Simono Seki*	Apl. 21, 1865	200, 201
509	Bradley, F. G.	Royal Artillery	Boer—*Itala* (Zululand)	Dec. 27, 1901	359–360
60	*Bradshaw, J.	Rifle Brigade	Crimea—*Sebastopol*	Feb. 24, 1857	33, 34
180	*Bradshaw, W.	90th Regiment	Indian Mutiny—*Lucknow* (No. 1)	June 18, 1858	116
258	*Brennan, J.	Royal Artillery	Indian Mutiny—*Jhansi*	Nov. 11, 1859	165
364	*Bromhead, G.	24th Regiment	Zulu—*Rorke's Drift*	May 2, 1879	237–243, 244, 245, 392–398
211	*Brown, F. D. M.	1st Bengal Fusiliers (101st)	Indian Mutiny—*Narnoul*	Feb. 17, 1860	138
491	Brown, E. D.	14th Hussars	Boer—*Geluk*	Jan. 15, 1901	346–347
383	*Brown, P.	Cape Mounted Rifles	Basutoland—*Moirosi's Mountain*	Apl. 13, 1880	258–260
491	Brown-Synge-Hutchinson; see Edward Douglas Brown				346 to 347
379	Browne, E. S.	24th Regiment	Zulu—*Inhlobana Mountain*	June 17, 1879	255
153	Browne, H. G.	32nd Regiment	Indian Mutiny—*Lucknow* (Defence)	June 24, 1862	100
282	*Browne, S. J.	46th Bengal N.I.	Indian Mutiny—*Seerporah*	Mar. 1, 1861	175–176
64	*Buckley, C. W.	Royal Navy—H.M.S. *Miranda*	Crimea—*Genitchi* and *Taganrog* (Azof)	Feb. 24, 1857	35, 36, 37
115	*Buckley, J.	Bengal Ordnance (classed as R.A.)	Indian Mutiny—*Delhi* (*Magazine*)	June 18, 1858	64–66

Index

Order in which each cross has been gained.	Name.	Regiment, Corps, etc.	Campaign, etc., and *place*	Announced in the London Gazette of	Page.
377	Buller, R. H.	60th Regiment	Zulu—*Inhlobana Mountain*	June 17, 1879	224, 253–254, 257, 311, 312, 315
65	*Burgoyne, H. T.	Royal Navy—H.M.S. *Swallow*	Crimea—*Genitchi* (Azof)	Feb. 24, 1857	35, 36, 37, 57
301	*Burslem, N.	67th Regiment	China—*Taku Forts*	Aug. 13, 1861	195, 196
242	*Butler, T. A.	1st Bengal European Fusiliers (101st)	Indian Mutiny—*Lucknow* (No. 3)	May, 6, 1859	155–156
259	*Byrne, James	86th Regiment	Indian Mutiny—*Jhansi*	Nov. 11, 1859	164, 165
30	*Byrne, John	68th Regiment	Crimea—*Inkerman*	Feb. 24, 1857	19
429	Byrne, T.	21st Lancers	Khartum—*Omdurman*	Nov. 15, 1898	300
2	Bythesea, J.	Royal Navy—H.M.S. *Arrogant*	Crimea—(*Baltic*) *Wardo Island*	Feb. 24, 1857	2, 3
124	Cadell, T.	2nd Bengal European Fusiliers (104th)	Indian Mutiny—*Delhi*	Apl. 29, 1862	69
264	Cafe, W. M.	56th Bengal N.I.	Indian Mutiny—*Ruhya*	Feb. 17, 1860	167, 169
98	*Cambridge, D.	Royal Artillery	Crimea—*Sebastopol* (The Redan)	June 23, 1857	52
253	Cameron, A. S.	72nd Regiment	Indian Mutiny—*Kotah*	Nov. 11, 1859	162
263	*Carlin, P.	13th Regiment	Indian Mutiny—*Azimghur*	Oct. 26, 1858	101 167,
276	Champion, J.	8th Hussars	Indian Mutiny—*Gwalior* and *Beejapore*	Jan. 20, 1860	172
341	Channer, G. N.	Bengal Staff Corps (ex 95th Regiment)	Perak—Straits of Malacca (not localised)	Apl. 14, 1876	216
303	Chaplin, J. W.	67th Regiment	China—*Taku Forts*	Aug. 13, 1861	196, 197
363	*Chard, J. R. M.	Royal Engineers	Zulu—*Rorke's Drift*	May 2, 1879	237–243, 244, 245, 392–398
358	Chase, W. St. L.	Bombay Staff Corps (ex 15th Foot)	Afghan—*Kandahar*	Oct. 7, 1881	231–232
285	*Chicken, G. B.	Royal (late Indian) Navy	Indian Mutiny—*Suhijnee*	Apl. 27, 1860	178
462	Clements, J. J.	Rimington's Guides	Boer—*Strijdenberg*	June 4, 1901	328
31	*Clifford, H. H.	Rifle Brigade	Crimea—*Inkerman*	Feb. 24, 1857	19
294	*Clogstoun	19th Madras N.I.	Indian Mutiny—*Chickumbah*	Oct. 21, 1859	183
515	Cobbe, A. S.	Indian Army (ex 24th Regiment)	Somaliland—*Erego*	Jan. 20, 1903	371–372
493	Cockburn, H. Z. C.	Royal Canadian Dragoons	Boer—*Koomati River*	Apl. 23, 1901	348, 349, 350
254	*Cochrane, H. S.	86th Regiment	Indian Mutiny—*Jhansi*	Dec. 24, 1858	163
55	*Coffey, W.	34th Regiment	Crimea—*Sebastopol*	Feb. 24, 1857	31
361	*Coghill, N. J. A.	24th Regiment	Zulu—*Buffalo River*	May 2, 1879	233–235, 236, 399–402
121	Coghlan, C.	75th Regiment	Indian Mutiny—*Budle-ke-serai* (Delhi)	Nov. 11, 1862	67
94	*Coleman, J.	97th Regiment	Crimea—*Sebastopol*	Feb. 24, 1857	51
357	Collis, J.	Royal Horse Artillery	Afghan—*Maiwand* and *Kandahar*	May 17, 1881	231
421	Colvin, J. M. C.	Royal Engineers	Punjab Frontier—*Bilot*	May 20, 1898	295–6

Index

Order in which each cross has been gained.	Name.	Regiment, Corps, etc.	Campaign, etc., and *place*.	Announced in the London Gazette of	Page.
110	*Commerell, J. E.	Royal Navy—H.M.S. *Weser*	Crimea—*Arabat* (Isthmus of—Azof)	Feb. 24, 1857	59–60
442	Congreve, W. N.	Rifle Brigade	Boer—*Colenso Bridge*	Feb. 2, 1900	311–316
135	*Connolly, W.	Bengal Horse Artillery	Indian Mutiny—*Jhelum*	Sep. 3, 1858	76–77
99	*Connors, J.	3rd Regiment	Crimea—*Sebastopol* (The Redan)	Feb. 24, 1857	53
25	*Conolly, J. A.	49th Regiment	Crimea—*Sebastopol* (" The Great Sortie ")	May 5, 1857	16
344	*Cook, J.	Bengal Staff Corps (5th Ghoorkas)	Afghan—*Peiwar Kotal*	Mar. 18, 1879	219–220
292	*Cook, W.	42nd Regiment	Indian Mutiny—*Maylah Ghaut*	June 21, 1859	167, 182, 183
67	*Cooper, H.	Royal Navy—H.M.S. *Miranda*	Crimea—*Taganrog* (Azof)	Feb. 24, 1857	36, 37
331	*Cooper, J.	24th Regiment	(Bay of Bengal) *Little Andaman Islands*	Dec. 17, 1867	208, 209
397	*Corbett, F.	60th Regiment	Egypt—*Kafr dowr* (Alexandria)	Feb. 16, 1883	270
416	Costello, E. W.	Bengal Staff Corps (ex 14th Foot)	Punjab Frontier—*Malakand*	Nov. 9, 1897	292
503	*Coulson, G. H. B.	25th Regiment	Boer—*Lambrecht Fontein*	Aug. 8, 1902	355–356, 387
96	*Craig, J.	Scots Fusilier Guards	Crimea—*Sebastopol*	Nov. 20, 1857	51
506	Crandon, H. G.	18th Hussars	Boer—*Springbok Laagte*	Oct. 18, 1901	358
348	Creagh, O'M.	Bengal Staff Corps (ex 95th Foot)	Afghan—*Kam Dakka*	Nov. 18, 1879	223
512	Crean, T. J.	Imperial Light Horse	Boer—*Tyger's Kloof*	Feb. 11, 1902	362
404	Crimmin, J.	Bombay Medical Service	Burmah—*Lwekaw*	Sep. 17, 1889	276
151	*Crowe, J. P. H.	78th Regiment	Indian Mutiny—*Busherutgunge*	Jan. 15, 1858	99
130	*Cubitt, W. G.	13th Bengal N.I.	Indian Mutiny—*Chinhut* (*Lucknow*)	June 21, 1859	71
49	*Cuninghame, W. J. M.	Rifle Brigade	Crimea—*Sebastopol* (Rifle Pits)	Feb. 24, 1857	28
76	*Curtis, H.	Royal Navy—Naval Brigade	Crimea—*Sebastopol*	Feb. 24, 1857	41, 45, 46
459	Curtis, A. E.	70th Regiment	Boer—*Onderbrookspruit*	Jan. 15, 1901	325–326
366	*Dalton, J. L.	Commissariat Department	Zulu—*Rorke's Drift*	Nov. 18, 1879	237–243, 246–247, 250, 392–398
391	Danaher, J.	Nourse's Horse (S. African)	South Africa (Boer 1881) *Elandsfontein*	Mar. 14, 1882	265, 266
32	*Daniel, E. St. J.	Royal Navy	Crimea—*Inkerman* and *Redan*	Feb. 24, 1857	19
382	*D'Arcy, C.	Frontier Light Horse	Zulu—*Ulundi* (near)	Oct. 10, 1879	253
196	*Daunt, J. C. C.	70th Bengal N.I.	Indian Mutiny—*Chota Behar*, etc.	Feb. 25, 1862	122–123
100	*Davis, Gronow	Royal Artillery	Crimea—*Sebastopol* (the Redan)	June 23, 1857	53
265	*Davis, J.	42nd Regiment	Indian Mutiny—*Ruhya*	May 27, 1859	168
108	*Day, G. F.	Royal Navy	Crimea—*Arabat,*— Isthmus of (Azof)	Feb. 24, 1857	57–58

Index

Order in which each cross has been gained.	Name.	Regiment, Corps, etc.	Campaign, etc., and *place*.	Announced in the London Gazette of	Page.
147	*Dempsey, D.	10th Regiment	Indian Mutiny—*Arrah, Lucknow*, etc.	Feb. 17, 1860	87
191	*Diamond, B.	Bengal Horse Artillery	Indian Mutiny—*Bolandshuhur*	Apl. 27, 1858	121
352	*Dick-Cunyngham W. H.	92nd Highlanders	Afghan—*Kabul* (Sherpur)	Oct. 18, 1881	227–228
11	Dickson, C.	Royal Artillery	Crimea—*Sebastopol* (1st bombardment)	June 23, 1857	8
154	*Divane, J.	60th Regiment	Indian Mutiny—*Delhi*	Jan. 20, 1860	101
58	Dixon, M. C.	Royal Artillery	Crimea—*Sebastopol*	Feb. 24, 1857	32
192	*Donohoe, P.	9th Lancers	Indian Mutiny—*Bolundshuhur*	Dec. 24, 1858	121
394	Doogan, J.	1st Dragoon Guards	South Africa (Boer 1881) *Laing's Nek—Natal*	Mar. 14, 1882	268
329	Douglas, C. M.	24th Regiment	(Bay of Bengal) *Little Andaman Island*	Dec. 17, 1867	207–208, 209
440	Douglas, H. E. M.	Royal Army Medical Corps	Boer—*Magersfontein*	Mar. 29, 1901	309–310
89	Dowell, G. D.	Royal Marine Artillery—H.M.S. *Ruby*	Crimea—*Viborg* (Baltic)	Feb. 24, 1857	48
134	*Dowling, W.	32nd Regiment	Indian Mutiny—*Lucknow* (Defence)	Nov. 22, 1859	76
309	*Down, J. T.	57th Regiment	New Zealand—*Pontoko*	Sep. 23, 1864	187
492	Doxat, A. C.	Imperial Yeomanry	Boer—*Zerust*	Jan. 15, 1901	347
181	*Duffy, T.	1st Madras Fusiliers (102nd)	Indian Mutiny—*Lucknow* (No. 1)	June 18, 1858	117
501	*Dugdale, F B.	5th Lancers	Boer—*Derby*	Sep. 17, 1901	354
326	*Dundas, J.	Royal (late Bengal) Engineers	Bhootan—*Dewangiri*	Dec. 31, 1867	104, 202–203, 203–204
212	*Dunley, J.	93rd Regiment	Indian Mutiny—*Lucknow* (No. 2)	Dec. 24, 1858	138
19	*Dunn, A. R.	11th Hussars	Crimea—*Balaklava*	Feb. 24, 1857	12
489	Durrant, E.	The Rifle Brigade	Boer—*Bergendal*	Oct. 18, 1901	345–346
197	*Dynon, D.	53rd Regiment	Indian Mutiny—*Chota Behar*	Feb. 25, 1862	122, 123
401	Edwards, T.	42nd Regiment	Soudan (Eastern)—*Tamai*	May 21, 1884	273
398	Edwards, W. M. M.	74th Regiment	Egypt—*Tel-el-Kebir*	Feb. 13, 1883	270–271
77	*Elphinstone, H. C.	Royal Engineers	Crimea—*Sebastopol*	June 4, 1858	41
93	*Elton, F. C.	55th Regiment	Crimea—*Sebastopol*	Feb. 24, 1857	50
464	Engleheart, H.	10th Hussars	Boer—*Bloemfontein*	Oct. 5, 1900	329
505	English, W. J.	2nd Scottish Horse (Tullibardine's)	Boer—*Vlakfontein*	Oct. 4, 1901	357–358
78	*Esmonde, T.	18th Regiment	Crimea—*Sebastopol*	Sep. 25, 1857	42
57	*Evans, S.	19th Regiment	Crimea—*Sebastopol*	June 23, 1857	31
497	Farmer, D.	79th Regiment	Boer—*Nooitgadacht*	Apl. 12, 1901	351
385	Farmer, J. J.	Army Hospital Corps (old title)	South Africa (Boer 1881) *Majuba—Natal*	May 17, 1881	268
243	*Farquaharson, F. E. H.	42nd Regiment	Indian Mutiny—*Lucknow* (No. 3)	June 21, 1859	157
20	*Farrell, J.	17th Lancers	Crimea—*Balaklava*	Nov. 20, 1857	13
213	*Ffrench, A K.	53rd Regiment	Indian Mutiny—*Lucknow* (No. 2)	Dec. 24, 1858	138, 139

Index

Order in which each cross has been gained.	Name.	Regiment, Corps, etc.	Campaign, etc., and *place*.	Announced in the London Gazette of	Page.
418	Fincastle, A. E. Visct.	16th Lancers	Punjab Frontier—*Landakai*	Nov. 9, 1897	294
423	Findlater, G.	75th Regiment	Punjab Frontier—*Dargai*	May 20, 1898	297
461	Firth, W.	33rd Regiment	Boer—*Arundel*	June 11, 1901	327
433	Fitz Clarence, C.	7th Regiment	Boer—*Mafeking*	July 6, 1900	304–305
193	*Fitzgerald, R.	Bengal Horse Artillery	Indian Mutiny—*Bolundshuhur*	Apl. 27, 1858	121
304	*Fitzgibbon, A. F.	Indian Medical Establishment	China—*Taku Forts*	Aug. 13, 1861	197
386	Fitzpatrick, F.	94th Regiment	Basutoland—*Sekukuni's Town*	Feb. 24, 1880	261–262
387	Flawn, T.	94th Regiment	Basutoland—*Sekukuni's Town*	Feb. 24, 1880	261–262
234	*Flinn, T.	64th Regiment	Indian Mutiny—*Cawnpore*	Apl. 12, 1859	149
116	*Forrest, G.	Bengal Veteran Establishment	Indian Mutiny—*Delhi Magazine*	June 18, 1858	64–66
320	Fosbery, G. V.	4th Bengal European Regiment	Umbeyla (India)—" *Crag Picquet* "	July 7, 1865	198–199
376	Fowler, E.	90th Regiment	Zulu—*Inhlobana Mountains*	Apl. 7, 1882	252
290	*Fraser, C. C.	7th Hussars	Indian Mutiny—*Raptee River*	Nov. 9, 1860	181–182
201	*Freeman, J.	9th Lancers	Indian Mutiny—*Agra*	Dec. 24, 1858	127
53	*Gardiner, G.	57th Regiment	Crimea—*Sebastopol*	June 4, 1858	30
271	*Gardner, W.	42nd Regiment	Indian Mutiny—*Bareilly*	Aug. 24, 1858	170
128	*Garvin, S.	60th Regiment	Indian Mutiny—*Delhi*	Jan. 20, 1860	71
337	Gifford, E. F. Lord	24th Regiment	Ashantee—*Whole Campaign* and *Becquah*	Mar. 31, 1874	212–213
118	*Gill, P.	Loodiana (India) Regiment	Indian Mutiny—*Benares*	Aug. 24, 1858	66, 67
468	Glasock, H. H.	Royal Horse Artillery	Boer—*Korn Spruit*	June 26, 1900	330–333
241	*Goat, W.	9th Lancers	Indian Mutiny—*Lucknow* (No. 3)	Dec. 24, 1858	155
296	Goodfellow, C. A.	Royal (Bombay) Engineers	Indian Mutiny—*Fort Beyet*	Apl. 17, 1863	184
24	*Goodlake, G. L.	Coldstream Guards	Crimea—*Sebastopol* (twice)	Feb. 24, 1857	14–16, 18
478	Gordon, W. E.	75th Regiment	Boer—*Krugersdorp*	Sep. 28, 1900	339–340
410	Gordon, W. J.	West India Regiment	West Africa—*Toniataba*	Dec. 9, 1892	141, 206, 284
33	*Gorman, J.	Royal Navy	Crimea—*Inkerman*	Feb. 24, 1857	20, 24, 25
152	Gough, C. J. S.	5th Bengal European Cavalry	Indian Mutiny—*Khurkowdah* and thrice later	Oct. 21, 1859	99–100, 135, 317, 372
204	Gough, H. H.	1st Bengal European Light Cavalry	Indian Mutiny—*Lucknow* (twice—'57 and '58)	Dec. 24, 1858	99, 134–135, 372
517	Gough, J. E.	The Rifle Brigade	Somaliland—*Daratoleh*	Jan. 15, 1904	100–135, 372–373, 375–378
13	*Grady, T.	4th Regiment	Crimea—*Sebastopol*	June 23, 1857	9
79	*Graham, G.	Royal Engineers	Crimea—*Sebastopol* (Redan)	Feb. 24, 1857	42

Index

Order in which each cross has been gained.	Name.	Regiment, Corps, etc.	Campaign, etc., and *place*.	Announced in the London Gazette of	Page.
228	*Graham, P.	90th Regiment	Indian Mutiny—*Lucknow* (No. 2)	Dec. 24, 1858	144
406	Grant, C. J. W.	Indian (Madras) Staff Corps (ex 12th Foot)	Manipur (India)—*Thobal*	May 26, 1891	278-297
214	*Grant, P.	93rd Regiment	Indian Mutiny—*Lucknow* (No. 2)	Dec. 24, 1858	139
173	*Grant, R.	5th Regiment	Indian Mutiny—*Alumbagh, Lucknow* (No. 1)	June 19, 1860	111
155	*Green, P.	75th Regiment	Indian Mutiny—*Delhi*	Oct. 26, 1858	101-102, 167
15	*Grieve, J.	2nd Dragoons	Crimea—*Balaklava*	Feb. 24, 1857	10
332	*Griffiths, W.	24th Regiment	(Bay of Bengal)—*Little Andaman Island*	Dec. 17, 1867	208, 209, 236
215	*Guise, J. C.	90th Regiment	Indian Mutiny—*Lucknow* (No. 2)	Dec. 24, 1858	139
480	Guy, B. J. D.	Royal Navy—H.M.S. *Barfleur*	China (1900)—*Tientsin*	Jan. 1, 1901	369-379
230	*Hackett, T. B.	23rd Regiment	Indian Mutiny—*Lucknow* (No. 2)	Apl. 12, 1859	145, 146
101	Hale, T. E.	7th Regiment	Crimea—*Sebastopol*	May 5, 1857	54
219	Hall, W.	Royal Navy—H.M.S. *Shannon's* Brigade	Indian Mutiny—*Lucknow* (No. 2)	Feb. 1, 1859	141, 206
475	Halliday, L. S. T.	Royal Marine L.I.	China (1900)—*Pekin* (The Legation)	Jan. 1, 1901	368-369
63	Hamilton, T. de C.	68th Regiment	Crimea—*Sebastopol*	Feb. 24, 1857	35
347	*Hamilton, W.R.P.	Bengal Staff Corps, "The Guides" (ex 70th Regiment)	Afghan—*Futtehabad*	Oct. 7, 1879	222
354	Hammond, A. G.	Bengal Staff Corps "The Guides"	Afghan—*Kabul*	Oct. 18, 1881	228-229
484	Hampton, H.	8th Regiment	Boer—*Van Wyk's Vlei*	Oct. 18, 1901	342-343
125	*Hancock, T.	9th Lancers	Indian Mutiny—*Delhi*	Jan. 15, 1858	70
499	Hardham, W. J.	4th New Zealand Contingent	Boer—*Naauwpoort*	Oct. 4, 1901	352-53
396	Harding, I.	Royal Navy—H.M.S. *Alexandra*	Egypt—*Alexandria*	Sep. 15, 1882	269
206	*Harrington, H. E.	Bengal Artillery	Indian Mutiny—*Lucknow* (No. 2)	Dec. 24, 1858	136, 137
217	*Harrison, J.	Royal Navy	Indian Mutiny—*Lucknow* (No. 2)	Dec. 24, 1858	140
345	Hart, R. C.	Royal Engineers	Afghan—*Dakkah*	June 10, 1879	220-221
123	*Hartigan, H.	9th Lancers	Indian Mutiny—*Delhi* and *Agra*	June 19, 1860	68-69
385	Hartley, E. B.	Cape Mounted Rifles	Basutoland—*Morosi's Mountain*	Oct. 7, 1881	260-261
143	*Havelock [Allan] H. M.	10th Regiment	Indian Mutiny—*Cawnpore* and *Lucknow* (No. 1)	Jan. 15, 1858	85, 116
246	*Hawkes, D.	The Rifle Brigade	Indian Mutiny—*Lucknow* (No 3)	Dec. 24, 1858	159
160	*Hawthorne, R.	52nd Regiment	Indian Mutiny—*Delhi* (Cashmere Gate)	Apl. 27, 1858	103-106
313	*Heaphy, C.	Auckland Militia, New Zealand	Maori—*Mangapiko River*	Feb. 8, 1867	189

Index

Order in which each cross has been gained.	Name.	Regiment, Corps, etc.	Campaign, etc., and *place*.	Announced in the London Gazette of	Page.
161	Heathcote, A. S.	60th Regiment	Indian Mutiny—*Delhi* ("whole siege")	Jan. 20, 1860	106
486	Heaton, W.	8th Regiment	Boer—*Geluk*	Jan. 18, 1901	344
413	Henderson, H. S.	Bulawayo Field Force	Matabeleland—"*Campbell's Store*"	May 7, 1897	288–289
277	*Heneage, C. W.	8th Hussars	Indian Mutiny—*Gwalior*	Jan. 28, 1859	173, 174
34	*Henry, A.	Royal Artillery	Crimea—*Inkerman*	Feb. 24, 1857	20–21
26	*Hewett, W. N. W.	Royal Navy—H.M.S. *Beagle*	Crimea—"*The Great Sortie*" and *Inkerman*	Feb. 24, 1857	17, 47
393	Hill-Walker, A. R.	58th Regiment	South Africa (Boer 1881) *Laing's Nek*—Natal	Mar. 14, 1882	267
220	*Hill, S.	90th Regiment	Indian Mutiny—*Lucknow* (No. 2)	Dec. 24, 1858	141, 142
138	Hills-Johnes, J.	Bengal Horse Artillery	Indian Mutiny—*Delhi*	Apl. 27, 1858	78–80
306	Hinckley, G.	Royal Navy—H.M.S. *Sphinx*	China (Taepings, 1862)—*Fung Wha*	Feb. 6, 1683	197
368	Hitch, F.	24th Regiment	Zulu—*Rorke's Drift*	May 2, 1879	237–243, 247, 247–248, 392–398
328	*Hodge, S.	4th Batt. West India Regiment	West Africa—*Jubabecolong*	Jan. 4, 1867	141, 206
495	Holland, E.	Royal Canadian Dragoons	Boer—*Koomati River*	Apl. 23, 1901	349, 350
279	*Hollis, G.	8th Hussars	Indian Mutiny—*Gwalior*	Jan. 28, 1859	174
182	*Hollowell, J.	78th Regiment	Indian Mutiny—*Lucknow* (No. 1)	June 18, 1858	117, 118
175	*Holmes, J.	84th Regiment	Indian Mutiny—*Lucknow* (No. 1)	June 18, 1858	112
183	Home, A. D.	90th Regiment	Indian Mutiny—*Lucknow* (No. 1)	June 18, 1858	116, 117–18, 119
157	*Home, D. C.	Bengal Engineers	Indian Mutiny—*Delhi*—Kashmere Gate	June 18, 1858	103–106
369	Hook, H.	24th Regiment	Zulu—*Rorke's Drift*	May 2, 1879	237–243, 248–249, 392–398
80	Hope, W.	7th Regiment	Crimea—*Sebastopol*	May 5, 1857	43, 54
432	Hore-Ruthven, A. G. A.	1st Royal Lanark Militia —H.L.I., 3rd Batt.	Nile (1898)—*Gedarif* (Kasalla)	Feb. 28, 1899	302
482	House, W.	66th Regiment	Boer—*Mosilikatse Nek*	Oct. 7, 1902	341
481	Howse, N. R.	New South Wales Medical Staff	Boer—*Vredefort*	June 4, 1901	340–341
69	*Hughes, M.	7th Regiment	Crimea—*Sebastopol*	Feb. 24, 1857	38
61	*Humpston, R.	The Rifle Brigade	Crimea—*Sebastopol*	Feb. 24, 1857	33, 34
513	Ind, A. E.	The Royal Artillery	Boer—*Tafelkop*	Aug. 15, 1902	363
90	*Ingoueville, G.	Royal Navy—H.M.S. *Arrogant*	Crimea—*Viborg* (Baltic)	Feb. 24, 1857	49
460	Inkson, E. T.	Royal Army Medical Corps	Boer—*Hart's Hill*, *Colenso*	Jan. 15, 1901	326–327
239	Innes J. J. McL.	Royal (Bengal) Engineers	Indian Mutiny—*Sultanpore*	Dec. 24, 1858	153–154
221	*Irwin, C.	53rd Regiment	Indian Mutiny—*Lucknow* (No. 2)	Dec. 24, 1858	142
288	*Jarrett, H. C. T.	26th Bengal N.I.	Indian Mutiny—*Baroun*	June 21, 1859	181

Index

Order in which each cross has been gained.	Name.	Regiment, Corps, etc.	Campaign, etc., and *place*.	Announced in the London Gazette of	Page.
176	*Jee, J.	78th Regiment	Indian Mutiny—*Lucknow* (No. 1)	Nov. 9, 1860	113
207	*Jennings, E.	Bengal Artillery	Indian Mutiny—*Lucknow* (No. 2)	Dec. 24, 1858	137
257	*Jerome, H. E.	86th Regiment	Indian Mutiny—*Jhansi*, etc.	Nov. 11, 1859	164, 165
437	Johnstone, R.	1st Imperial Light Horse (Natal)	Boer—*Elandslaagte*	Feb. 12, 1901	307
3	*Johnstone, W.	Royal Navy—H.M.S. *Arrogant*	Crimea—*Wardo Island* (Baltic)	Feb. 24, 1857	2, 3
122	Jones, A. S.	9th Lancers	Indian Mutiny—*Delhi*	June 18, 1858	68
71	Jones, H. M.	7th Regiment	Crimea—*Sebastopol*	Sep. 25, 1857	39, 54
370	*Jones, R.	24th Regiment	Zulu—*Rorke's Drift*	May 2, 1879	237–243, 249, 392–398
452	*Jones, R. J. T. Digby	Royal Engineers	Boer—*Ladysmith*	Aug. 8, 1902	73, 318–321, 324, 325, 387
371	Jones, W.	24th Regiment	Zulu—*Rorke's Drift*	May 2, 1879	237–243, 249, 392–398
203	*Kavanagh, T. H.	Bengal Civil Service	Indian Mutiny—*Lucknow* (No. 2)	July 8, 1859	128–134, 384, 388–391
249	*Keatinge, R. H.	Bombay Artillery	Indian Mutiny—*Chandairee*	Feb. 25, 1862	160–161
107	*Kellaway, J.	Royal Navy—H.M.S. *Wrangler*	Crimea—*Marioupol* (Azof)	Feb. 24, 1857	57
194	Kells, R.	9th Lancers	Indian Mutiny—*Boolundshuhur*	Dec. 24, 1858	122
427	Kenna, P. A.	21st Lancers	Khartum—*Omdurman*	Nov. 15, 1898	299, 300
496	Kennedy, C.	71st Regiment	Boer—*Dewetsdorp*	Oct. 18, 1901	350–351
222	*Kenny, J.	53rd Regiment	Indian Mutiny—*Lucknow* (No. 2)	Dec. 24, 1858	142
140	Kerr, W. A.	24th Bombay N.I.	Indian Mutiny—*Kolapore* (Bo.)	Apr. 27, 1858	83
473	Kirby, F.	Royal Engineers	Boer—"*Delagoa Bay Railway*"	Oct. 5, 1900	336–337
119	*Kirk, J.	10th Regiment	Indian Mutiny—*Benares*	Jan. 20, 1860	66, 67
485	Knight, H. J.	8th Regiment	Boer—*Van Wyk's Vlei*	Jan. 4, 1901	343
5	*Knox, J. S.	Scots Guards	Crimea—*Alma* and the *Redan*	Feb. 24, 1857	5
145	*Lambert, G.	84th Regiment	Indian Mutiny—*Oonao, Bithoor* and *Lucknow* (No. 1)	June 18, 1858	86
302	*Lane, T.	67th Regiment	China—*Taku Forts*	Aug. 13, 1861	195, 196
208	*Laughnan, T.	Bengal Artillery	Indian Mutiny—*Lucknow* (No. 2)	Dec. 24, 1858	137
136	*Lawrence, S. H.	32nd Regiment	Indian Mutiny—*Lucknow* (Defence)	Nov. 22, 1859	77
483	Lawrence, T.	17th Lancers	Boer—*Essenbosch*	Jan. 15, 1901	342
425	Lawson, E.	75th Regiment	Punjab Frontier—*Dargai*	May 20, 1898	298
346	Leach, E. P.	Royal Engineers	Afghan—*Maidanah*	Dec. 9, 1879	221–222
378	*Leet, W. K.	13th Regiment	Zulu—*Inhlobana Mountains*	June 17, 1879	254–255
81	*Leitch, P.	Royal Engineers	Crimea—*Sebastopol* (Redan)	June 4, 1858	44

Index

Order in which each cross has been gained.	Name.	Regiment, Corps, etc.	Campaign, etc., and *place*.	Announced in the London Gazette of	Page
255	*Leith, J.	14th Hussars	Indian Mutiny—*Betwah*	Dec. 24, 1858	163
52	*Lendrim, W. J.	Royal Engineers	Crimea—*Sebastopol* (three times)	Feb. 24, 1857	29
50	*Lennox, W. O.	Royal Engineers	Crimea—*Sebastopol*	Feb. 24, 1857	28
300	*Lenon, E. H.	67th Regiment	China—*Taku Forts*	Aug. 13, 1861	194, 195
405	Le Quesne, F. S.	Army Medical Staff	Burmah—*Tartun*	Oct. 29, 1889	277
4	*Lindsay [Loyd], R. J., Lord Wantage	Scots Fusilier Guards	Crimea—*Alma* and *Inkerman*	Feb. 24, 1857	4, 5
411	Lloyd, O. E. P.	Army Medical Staff	Burmah—*Sima*	Jan. 2, 1894	285
467	Lodge, I.	Royal Horse Artillery	Boer—*Korn Spruit*	June 26, 1900	330–333
ONE	Lucas, C. D.	Royal Navy—H.M.S. *Hecla*	Crimea—*Bomarsund* (Baltic)	Feb. 24, 1857	1, 36
305	*Lucas, J.	40th Regiment	New Zealand—*Huirangi*	July 19, 1861	185–186
102	*Lumley, C. H.	97th Regiment	Crimea—*Sebastopol* (The Redan)	Feb. 24, 1857	54
72	*Lyons, J.	19th Regiment	Crimea—*Sebastopol*	Feb. 24, 1857	39
375	Lysons, H.	90th Regiment	Zulu—*Inhlobana Mountains*	Apl. 7, 1882	251–252
273	Lyster, H. H.	72nd Bengal N.I.	Indian Mutiny—*Calpee*	Oct. 21, 1859	171
244	*McBean, W.	93rd Regiment	Indian Mutiny—*Lucknow* (No. 3)	Dec. 24, 1858	157–158
87	*McCorrie, C.	57th Regiment	Crimea—*Sebastopol*	Feb. 24, 1857	47
388	*McCrea, J. F.	Cape Mounted Yeomanry	Basutoland—*Tweefontein*	June 28, 1881	262–263
35	*McDermond, J.	47th Regiment	Crimea—*Inkerman*	Feb. 24, 1857	21, 24
59	*Macdonald, H.	Royal Engineers	Crimea—*Sebastopol*	June 4, 1858	33
148	*McDonell, W. F.	Bengal Civil Service	Indian Mutiny—*Arrah*	Feb. 17, 1860	87, 88–95, 96 footnote
299	*McDougall, J.	44th Regiment	China—*Taku Forts*	Aug. 13, 1861	194, 195
339	*McGaw, S.	42nd Regiment	Ashantee—*Amoaful*	Mar. 31, 1874	214
129	*McGovern, J.	1st Bengal Fusiliers (101st)	Indian Mutiny—*Delhi*	June 21, 1859	71
62	*McGregor, R.	The Rifle Brigade	Crimea—*Sebastopol*	Feb. 24, 1857	34
162	*McGuire, J.	1st Bengal European Fusiliers (101st)	Indian Mutiny—*Delhi*	Dec. 24, 1858	107
198	*McHale, P.	5th Regiment	Indian Mutiny—*Lucknow* (No. 1) twice	June 19, 1860	123–126
209	*McInnes, H.	Bengal Artillery	Indian Mutiny—*Lucknow* (No. 2)	Dec. 24, 1858	137
336	*Macintyre, D.	Bengal Staff Corps (2nd Ghurkas)	Looshai (India)—*Lalgnoora*	Sep. 27, 1872	211
472	Mackay, J. F.	75th Regiment	Boer—*Johannesburg*	Aug. 10, 1900	336
223	*Mackay, D.	93rd Regiment	Indian Mutiny—*Lucknow* (No. 2)	Dec. 24, 1858	142
6	*Mackechnie, J.	Scots Guards	Crimea—*Alma*	Feb. 24, 1857	5
307	Mackenna, E.	65th Regiment	New Zealand—*Cameron Town*	Jan. 19, 1864	186
474	Mackenzie, J.	78th Regiment	Ashantee (1900)—*Dompoassi*	Jan. 15, 1901	365–366
419	*MacLean, H. L. S.	Indian Staff Corps Guides (ex 5th Regiment)	Punjab Frontier—*Landakai*	Nov. 9, 1897	294, 295
184	*McManus, P.	5th Regiment	Indian Mutiny—*Lucknow* (No. 1)	June 18, 1858	117, 118, 119

Index

Order in which each cross has been gained.	Name	Regiment, Corps, etc.	Campaign, etc., and *place*.	Announced in the London Gazette of	Page.
177	*McMaster, V. M.	78th Regiment	Indian Mutiny—*Lucknow* (No. 1)	June 18, 1858	114
314	*McNeill, J. C.	107th Bengal Infantry	New Zealand—*Ohaupu*	Aug. 16, 1864	189–190
185	*Macpherson, H. T.	78th Regiment	Indian Mutiny—*Lucknow* (No.1)	June 18, 1858	114
178	*McPherson, S.	78th Regiment	Indian Mutiny—*Lucknow* (No. 1)	Apr. 12, 1859	119
236	*McQuirt, B.	95th Regiment	Indian Mutiny—*Rowa*	Nov. 11, 1859	152
14	*McWheeney, W.	44th Regiment	Crimea—*The entire campaign*	Feb. 24, 1857	10
36	*Madden, A.	41st Regiment	Crimea—*Inkerman*	Feb. 24, 1857	21
334	*Magner, M.	33rd Regiment	Abyssinia—*Magdala*	July 28, 1868	210
171	*Mahoney, P.	1st Madras Fusiliers (102nd)	Indian Mutiny—*Mungalwar*	June 18, 1858	110
431	*Maillard, W. J.	Royal Navy—H.M.S. *Hazard*	(Crete) *Candia*	Dec. 2, 1898	303
114	*Malcolmson, J. G.	3rd Bombay Light Cavalry	Persia—*Koosh-ab*	Aug. 3, 1860	62–63
21	*Malone, J.	13th Hussars	Crimea—*Balaklava*, etc.	Sep. 25, 1857	13
149	Mangles, R. L.	Bengal Civil Service	Indian Mutiny—*Arrah* (Relief of)	July 8, 1859	87, 88, 92, 96–97, 384
315	*Manley, W.G. N	Royal Artillery	New Zealand—*Tauranga*	Sep. 23, 1864	190–191
463	Mansel-Jones C.	14th Regiment	Boer—*Terrace Hill, Colenso*	July 20, 1900	328–329
402	Marling, P. S.	60th Regiment	Soudan (Eastern)—*Tamai*	May 21, 1884	274
400	Marshall, W. T.	19th Hussars	Soudan (Eastern)—*El-Teb*	May 21, 1884	273
449	Martineau, H. R.	The Protectorate Regiment (Cape Colony)	South Africa (Boer)—*Mafeking*	July 6, 1900	316–317
514	Martin-Leake, A.	South African Constabulary	Boer—*Vlakfontein*	May 13, 1902	364
454	Masterson, J. E. I.	11th Regiment	Boer—*Ladysmith*	June 4, 1901	322–323
174	*Maude, F. C.	Royal Artillery	Indian Mutiny—*Lucknow* (No. 1)	June 18, 1858	112, 136
103	*Maude, F. F.	3rd Regiment	Crimea—*Sebastopol* (the Redan)	Feb. 24, 1857	55
469	Maxwell, F. A.	Indian Staff Corps (ex 107th Foot)	Boer—*Korn Spruit*	Mar. 8, 1901	333–334
511	Maygar, L. C.	5th Victoria Mounted Rifles	Boer—*Geelhoutboom*	Feb. 11, 1902	361
233	Mayo, A.	Royal (Indian) Navy	Indian Mutiny—*Dacca*	Feb. 25, 1862	147–148
434	Meiklejohn, M. F. M.	92nd Regiment	Boer—*Elandslaagte*	July 20, 1900	305
490	Mellis, C. J.	Indian Staff Corps (ex 2nd 15th Foot)	Ashantee (1900)—*Obassa*	Jan. 15, 1901	366–367
360	*Melvill, T.	24th Regiment	Zulu—*Buffalo River*	May 2, 1879	233–235, 236, 399–402
451	Milbanke, J. P.	10th Hussars	Boer—*Colesberg*	July 6, 1900	318
293	*Millar, D.	42nd Regiment	Indian Mutiny—*Maylah Ghaut*	June 21, 1859	182, 183

Index

Order in which each cross has been gained.	Name.	Regiment, Corps, etc.	Campaign, etc., and *place*.	Announced in the London Gazette of	Page.
37	*Miller, F.	Royal Artillery	Crimea—*Inkerman*	May 6, 1859	22
202	*Miller, J.	Bengal Ordnance	Indian Mutiny—*Futtehpore*	Feb. 25, 1862	128
316	*Mitchell, S.	Royal Navy—H.M.S. *Harrier*	New Zealand—*Tauranga*	July 26, 1864	190, 191
287	*Monaghan, T.	2nd Dragoon Guards	Indian Mutiny—*Sundeela*	Nov. 11, 1862	179
231	*Monger, G.	23rd Regiment	Indian Mutiny—*Lucknow* (No. 2)	Apl. 12, 1859	145, 146
428	*Montmorency, R H. L. J. de	21st Lancers	Khartum—*Omdurman*	Nov. 15, 1898	299, 300
113	Moore, A. T.	3rd Bombay Light Cavalry	Persia—*Koosh-ab*	Aug. 3, 1860	61-62
343	*Moore, H. G.	88th Regiment	Kaffir—South Africa *Komgha*	June 27, 1879	218
269	*Morley, S	Military Train	Indian Mutiny—*Azimghur*	Aug. 7, 1860	169-170
17	*Mouat, J.	6th Dragoons	Crimea—*Balaklava*	June 4, 1858	11
104	*Moynihan, A.	90th Regiment	Crimea—*Sebastopol* (the Redan)	Feb. 24, 1857	55
356	Mullane, P.	Royal Horse Artillery	Afghan—*Maiwand*	May 17, 1881	230
436	Mullins, C. H.	1st Imperial Light Horse (Natal)	Boer—*Elandslaagte*	Feb. 12, 1901	307
224	*Munro, J.	93rd Regiment	Indian Mutiny—*Lucknow* (No. 2)	Nov. 9, 1860	143
270	*Murphy, M.	Military Train	Indian Mutiny—*Azimghur*	May 27, 1859	170
333	Murphy, T.	24th Regiment	(Bay of Bengal) *Little Andaman Island*	Dec. 17, 1867	208, 209
390	Murray, J.	94th Regiment	South Africa (Boer 1881) *Elandsfontein*	Mar. 14, 1882	265, 266
318	Murray, J.	68th Regiment	New Zealand—*Tauranga*	Nov. 4, 1864	192
142	*Mylott, P.	84th Regiment	Indian Mutiny—July 12 to Sep. 25, 1857, *Lucknow* (No. 1)	Dec. 24, 1858	84
262	Napier, W.	13th Regiment	Indian Mutiny—*Azimghur*	Dec. 24, 1858	166
247	*Nash, W.	The Rifle Brigade	Indian Mutiny—*Lucknow* (No. 3)	Dec. 24, 1858	159
415	Nesbitt, R. C.	Mashonaland Mounted Police	Matabeleland—*Salisbury* (near)	May 7, 1897	291-292
251	*Newell, R.	9th Lancers	Indian Mutiny—*Lucknow* (No. 3)	Dec. 24, 1858	161
470	Nickerson, W. H. S.	Royal Army Medical Corps	Boer—*Wakkerstroom*	Feb. 12, 1901	334-335
51	*Norman, W.	7th Regiment	Crimea—*Sebastopol*	Feb. 24, 1857	25, 29
438	Norwood, J.	5th Dragoon Guards	Boer—*Ladysmith*	July 20, 1900	308
447	Nurse, G. E.	Royal Artillery	Boer—*Colenso Bridge*	Feb. 2, 1900	311-316
8	O'Connor, L.	23rd Regiment	Crimea—*Alma* and the *Redan*	Feb. 24, 1857	6, 322
297	*Odgers, W.	Royal Navy—H.M.S. *Niger*	New Zealand—*Taranaki*	Aug. 3, 1860	185
327	*O'Hea, T.	The Rifle Brigade	(Canada) *Danville Railway Station*	Jan. 1, 1867	205

Index

Order in which each cross has been gained.	Name.	Regiment, Corps, etc.	Campaign, etc., and *place*.	Announced in the London Gazette of	Page.
186	*Olpherts, W.	Bengal Artillery	Indian Mutiny—*Lucknow* (No. 1)	June 18, 1858	115
392	Osborne, J.	58th Regiment	South Africa (Boer 1881)—*Wesselstroom*	Mar. 14, 1882	266
381	*O'Toole, E.	The Frontier Light Horse (Natal)	Zulu—*Ulundi* (near)	Oct. 10, 1879	256, 257
27	*Owens, J.	49th Regiment	Crimea—*Sebastopol* (twice)	Feb. 24, 1857	18
131	*Oxenham, W.	32nd Regiment	Indian Mutiny—*Lucknow* (Defence)	Nov. 22, 1859	72
38	*Palmer, A.	Grenadier Guards	Crimea—*Inkerman*	Feb. 24, 1857	22, 25
10	*Park, J.	77th Regiment	Crimea—*Alma, Inkerman* and *Sebastopol*	Feb. 24, 1857	7
210	*Park, J.	Bengal Artillery	Indian Mutiny—*Lucknow* (No. 2)	Dec. 24, 1858	137, 138
466	Parker, C.	Royal Horse Artillery	Boer—*Korn Spruit*	June 26, 1900	330–333
22	*Parkes, S.	4th Hussars	Crimea—*Balaklava*	Feb. 24, 1857	13
457	*Parsons, F. N.	44th Regiment	Boer—*Paardeberg*, etc.	Nov. 20, 1900	324
225	Paton, J.	93rd Regiment	Indian Mutiny—*Lucknow* (No. 2)	Dec. 24, 1858	143
261	*Pearson, Jas.	86th Regiment	Indian Mutiny—*Jhansi* and *Calpee*	May 1, 1860	166
278	*Pearson, Jno.	8th Hussars	Indian Mutiny—*Gwalior*	Jan. 28, 1859	174
12	*Peel, W.	Royal Navy	Crimea—*Inkerman* and *Sebastopol* (twice)	Feb. 24, 1857	8, 9, 19, 20, 140, 141, 181, 206
424	Pennell, H. S.	95th Regiment	Punjab Frontier—*Dargai*	May 20, 1898	297
39	*Percy, Hon. H. H. M.	Grenadier Guards	Crimea—*Inkerman*	May 5, 1857	23
82	*Perie, J.	Royal Engineers	Crimea—*Sebastopol* (Redan)	Feb. 24, 1857	44
163	*Phillips, E. A. L.	70th (now 11th) Bengal N.I.	Indian Mutiny—*Delhi* (Whole siege, etc.)	Oct. 21, 1859	107
465	Phipps-Hornby, E. J.	Royal Horse Artillery	Boer—*Korn Spruit*	June 26, 1900	330–333
312	*Pickard, A. F.	Royal Artillery	New Zealand—*Rangiriri*	Sep. 23, 1864	188–189
321	*Pitcher, H. W.	4th Punjab Infantry	Umbeyla (India)—"The *Crag Picquet*"	July 19, 1864	199
455	Pitts, J.	63rd Regiment	Boer—*Ladysmith*	July 26, 1901	323
232	Prendergast, H. N. D.	Royal (Madras) Engineers	Indian Mutiny—*Mundisore*, etc., etc.	Oct. 21, 1859	146, 147
40	*Prettyjohn, J.	Royal Marine L.I.	Crimea—*Inkerman*	Feb. 24, 1857	23
508	Price-Davies, L. A. E.	60th Regiment	Boer—*Blood River Poort*	Nov. 29, 1901	359
324	*Pride, T.	Royal Navy—H.M.S. *Euryalus*	Japan—*Simono Seki*	Apl. 21, 1865	200, 201
200	Probyn, D. M.	2nd Punjab Cavalry	Indian Mutiny—*Agra*, etc., etc.	June 18, 1858	126–127
74	*Prosser, J.	1st Regiment	Crimea—*Sebastopol* (twice)	Feb. 24, 1857	40

Index

Order in which each cross has been gained.	Name.	Regiment, Corps, etc	Campaign, etc., and *place*.	Announced in the London Gazette of	Page.
126	*Purcell., J.	9th Lancers	Indian Mutiny—*Delhi*	Jan. 15, 1858	70
229	*Pye, C	53rd Regiment	Indian Mutiny—*Lucknow* (No. 2)	Dec. 24, 1858	145
83	Raby, H. J.	Royal Navy	Crimea—*Sebastopol*	Feb. 24, 1857	41, 45, 46
16	*Ramage, H.	2nd Dragoons	Crimea—*Balaklava*	June 4, 1858	11
450	Ramsden, H E.	The Protectorate Regiment (Cape Colony)	Boer—*Mafeking*	July 6, 1900	317
448	Ravenhill, G.	21st Regiment	Boer—*Colenso Bridge*	June 4, 1901	315–316
117	*Raynor, W.	Bengal Veteran Establishment	Indian Mutiny—*Delhi Magazine*	June 18, 1858	64–66
164	*Reade, H. T.	61st Regiment	Indian Mutiny—*Delhi*	Feb. 5, 1861	108
443	Reed, H. L.	Royal Artillery	Boer—*Colenso Bridge*	Feb. 2, 1900	311–316
41	*Reeves, T.	Royal Navy	Crimea—*Inkerman*	Feb. 24, 1857	20, 24, 25
172	*Rennie, W.	90th Regiment	Indian Mutiny—*Lucknow* twice (No. 1)	Dec. 24, 1858	111
169	*Renny, G. A.	Bengal Horse Artillery	Indian Mutiny—*Delhi*	Apl. 12, 1859	109
365	Reynolds, J. H.	Army Medical Department	Zulu—*Rorke's Drift*	June 17, 1879	237–243, 245–246, 392–398
7	*Reynolds, W.	Scots Guards	Crimea—*Alma*	Feb. 24, 1857	6
477	Richardson, A. H. L.	Lord Strathcona's Corps (Canadian)	Boer—*Standerton*	Sep. 14, 1900	338
295	Richardson, G.	34th Regiment	Indian Mutiny—*Kewanie*	Nov. 11, 1859	184
111	Rickard, W.	Royal Navy—H.M.S. *Weser*	Crimea—*Isthmus of Arabat* (Azof)	Feb. 24, 1857	59, 60
389	Ridgeway, R. K.	Bengal Staff Corps (ex 2nd and 96th Foot)	Naga Hills (India)—*Konoma*	May 11, 1880	264
66	*Robarts, Jno.	Royal Navy—H.M.S. *Miranda*	Crimea—*Genitchi* (Azof)	Feb. 24, 1857	35, 36, 37
444	*Roberts, Hon. F. H. S.	60th Regiment	Boer—*Colenso Bridge*	Feb. 2, 1900	151, 311–316
235	Roberts, F. S. (*Earl*)	Bengal Artillery	Indian Mutiny—*Khodagunge*	Dec. 24, 1858	81, 149–152, 156, 176, 220, 226, 313, 331
195	*Roberts, J. R.	9th Lancers	Indian Mutiny—*Boolundshuhur*	Dec. 24, 1858	122
435	Robertson, W.	92nd Regiment	Boer—*Elandslaagte*	July 20, 1900	306
248	*Robinson, E.	Royal Navy	Indian Mutiny—*Lucknow* (No. 3)	Dec. 24, 1858	160
283	*Roddy, P.	Bengal Army (unattached)	Indian Mutiny—*Kuthirga*	Apl. 12, 1859	177
275	*Rodgers, G.	71st Regiment	Indian Mutiny—*Morar*	Nov. 11, 1859	172
504	Rogers, J.	South African Constabulary	Boer—*Thaba N'Chu*	Apl. 18, 1902	357
298	*Rogers, R. M.	44th Regiment	China—*Taku Forts*	Aug. 13, 1861	139, 194, 195
519	Rolland, G. M.	Indian Army (ex 2nd 16th Foot)	Somaliland—*Daratoleh*	Aug. 7, 1903	372–373, 375–378
220	*Rosamond, M.	37th Bengal N.I.	Indian Mutiny—*Benares*	Aug. 24, 1858	66, 67
92	*Ross, J.	Royal Engineers	Crimea—*Sebastopol* (twice) and *Redan*	Feb. 24, 1857	50

Index

Order in which each cross has been gained.	Name.	Regiment, Corps, etc.	Campaign, etc., and *place*.	Announced in the London Gazette of	Page.
42	Rowlands, H.	41st Regiment	Crimea—*Inkerman*	Feb. 24, 1857	21, 24
252	*Rushe, D.	9th Lancers	Indian Mutiny—*Lucknow* (No. 3)	Dec. 24, 1858	162
43	*Russell, C.	Grenadier Guards	Crimea—*Inkerman*	Feb. 24, 1857	22, 25
	Ruthven—see Hore-Ruthven.				
187	*Ryan, Jno.	1st Madras Fusiliers (102nd)	Indian Mutiny—*Lucknow* (No. 1)	June 18, 1858	117, 118, 119
308	*Ryan, Jno.	65th Regiment	New Zealand—*Cameron Town*	Jan. 19, 1864	186
165	*Ryan, M.	1st Bengal European Fusiliers (101st)	Indian Mutiny—*Delhi*	Dec. 24, 1858	107
158	*Salkeld, P.	Bengal Engineers	Indian Mutiny—*Delhi, Kashmir Gate*	June 18, 1858	103–106
216	Salmon, N.	Royal Navy	Indian Mutiny—*Lucknow* (No. 2)	Dec. 24, 1858	140
350	Sartorius, E. H.	59th Regiment	Afghan—*Shah-jui-Tazi*	May 17, 1881	225
338	Sartorius, R. W.	6th Bengal Cavalry	Ashantee—*Abugoo*, etc.	Oct. 27, 1874	213, 225
372	*Schiess, F. C.	Natal Native Contingent	Zulu—*Rorke's Drift*.	Dec. 2, 1879	237–243, 250, 392–398
445	Schofield, H. N.	Royal Artillery	Boer—*Colenso Bridge*	Aug. 30, 1901	311–316
44	*Scholefield, M.	Royal Navy	Crimea—*Inkerman*	Feb. 24, 1857	20, 25
342	*Scott, A.	Bengal Staff Corps	(Beloochistan)—*Quetta*	Jan. 18, 1878	217
456	Scott, R.	63rd Regiment	Boer—*Ladysmith*	July 26, 1901	323
384	Scott, R. G.	The Cape Mounted Rifles	Basutoland—*Morosi's Mountain*	Oct. 1, 1880	260
322	Seeley, W.	Royal Navy—H.M.S. *Euryalus*	Japan—*Simono Seki*	Apl. 21, 1865	200
353	*Sellar, G.	72nd Regiment	Afghan—*Asami Heights—Kabul*	Oct. 18, 1881	228
441	Shaul, J. D. F.	71st Regiment	Boer—*Magersfontein*	Sep. 28, 1900	310
319	Shaw, H.	18th Regiment	New Zealand—*Nukumaru*	Nov. 28, 1865	192–193
274	*Shaw, S.	60th Regiment	Indian Mutiny—*Nawabgunge*	Oct. 26, 1858	171–172
166	*Shebbeare, R. H.	60th Bengal N.I.	Indian Mutiny—*Delhi*	Oct. 21, 1859	108
91	*Sheppard, J.	Royal Navy—H.M.S. *St. Jean d'Acre*	Crimea—*Sebastopol* (harbour)	Feb. 24, 1857	49
105	*Shields, R.	23rd Regiment	Crimea—*Sebastopol* (Redan)	Feb. 24, 1857	56
266	*Simpson, J.	42nd Regiment	Indian Mutiny—*Ruhya*	May 27, 1859	168
84	*Sims, J. J.	34th Regiment	Crimea—*Sebastopol*	Feb. 24, 1857	46
199	*Sinnott, J.	84th Regiment	Indian Mutiny—*Lucknow* (2nd Defence)	Dec. 24, 1858	126
260	*Sleavon, M.	Royal Engineers	Indian Mutiny—*Jhansi*	Nov. 11, 1859	166
403	Smith, A.	Royal Artillery	Nile Expedition (1884) *Abu-Klea*	May 12, 1885	275
520	Smith, C. L.	46th Regiment	Somaliland—*Jidballi*	June 7, 1904	374–375
317	*Smith, F. A.	43rd Regiment	New Zealand—*Tauranga*	Nov. 4, 1864	191
167	*Smith, H.	52nd Regiment	Indian Mutiny—*Delhi*	Apl. 27, 1858	109
422	Smith, Js.	3rd Regiment	Punjab Frontier—*Bilot*	Apl. 21, 1899	296
159	*Smith, Jno.	Bengal Engineers	Indian Mutiny—*Delhi—Kashmir Gate*	Apl. 27, 1858	103–106
226	*Smith, J.	1st Madras Fusiliers (102nd)	Indian Mutiny—*Lucknow* (No. 2)	Dec. 24, 1858	144

Index

Order in which each cross has been gained.	Name	Regiment, Corps, etc.	Campaign, etc., and *place*.	Announced in the London Gazette of	Page.
409	Smith, J. M.	Bengal Staff Corps (ex 2nd Batt. 9th Foot)	Hunza Nagar—*Nilt*	July 12, 1892	282–283
85	Smith, P.	17th Regiment	Crimea—*Sebastopol*	Feb. 24, 1857	46
430	Smyth, N. M.	2nd Dragoon Guards	Khartum—*Omdurman*	Nov. 15, 1898	301
237	*Spence, D.	9th Lancers	Indian Mutiny—*Shumshabad*	Dec. 24, 1858	152
267	*Spence, E.	42nd Regiment	Indian Mutiny—*Ruhya*	May 27, 1859	167, 169
310	Stagpoole, D.	57th Regiment	New Zealand—*Pontoko*	Sep. 23, 1864	187
28	Stanlack, W.	Coldstream Guards	Crimea—*Sebastopol* (Special duty)	Feb. 24, 1857	18
227	*Stewart, W. G. D.	93rd Regiment	Indian Mutiny—*Lucknow* (No. 2)	Dec. 24, 1858	144
97	*Strong, G.	Coldstream Guards	Crimean—*Sebastopol*	Feb. 24, 1857	52
56	*Sullivan, J.	Royal Navy	Crimea—*Sebastopol*	Feb. 24, 1857	31
156	*Sutton, W.	60th Regiment	Indian Mutiny—*Delhi* (twice)	Jan. 20, 1860	102
106	Sylvester, H. T.	23rd Regiment	Crimea—*Sebastopol* (the Redan)	Nov. 20, 1857	56
68	*Symons, G.	Royal Artillery	Crimea—*Sebastopol*	Nov. 20, 1857	37
86	*Taylor, J.	Royal Navy	Crimea—*Sebastopol*	Feb. 24, 1857	41, 45, 46
109	*Teesdale C. C.	Royal Artillery	Crimea—*Kars* (Armenia)	Sep. 25, 1857	58–59
311	Temple, W.	Royal Artillery	New Zealand—*Rangiriri*	Sep. 23, 1864	188, 189
170	Thackeray, E. T.	Bengal Engineers	Indian Mutiny—*Delhi*	Apl. 29, 1862	110
188	*Thomas, J	Bengal Artillery	Indian Mutiny—*Lucknow* (2nd Defence)	Dec. 24, 1858	119
268	*Thompson, A.	42nd Regiment	Indian Mutiny—*Ruhya*	May 27, 1859	167, 169
139	*Thompson, Js.	60th Regiment	Indian Mutiny—*Delhi*	Jan. 20, 1860	83
137	*Tombs, H.	Bengal Artillery	Indian Mutiny—*Delhi*	Apl. 27, 1858	78, 79, 79–82, 203
439	Towse, E. B. B.	75th Regiment	Boer—*Magersfontein* and *Mount Thaba*	July 6, 1900	308–309
133	*Travers, J.	2nd Bengal N.I.	Indian Mutiny—*Indore*	Mar. 1, 1861	76
500	Traynor, W. B.	14th Regiment	Boer—*Bothwell* (Lake Crissey)	Sep. 17, 1901	353
325	Trevor, W. S.	Royal (late Bengal) Engineers	Bhootan—*Dewan Giri*	Dec. 31, 1867	202, 203–204
88	Trewavas, J.	Royal Navy—H.M.S. *Beagle*	Crimea—*Ginitchi* (Azof)	Feb. 24, 1857	47
494	Turner, R. E. W.	Royal Canadian Dragoons	Boer—*Koomati River*	Apl. 23, 1901	349, 350
127	*Turner, S.	60th Regiment	Indian Mutiny—*Delhi*	Jan. 20, 1860	70
238	*Tytler, J. A.	66th Bengal N.I. (Ghoorkas)	Indian Mutiny—*Choorpoorah*	Aug. 24, 1858	153
426	Vickery, S.	39th Regiment	Punjab Frontier—*Dargai*, etc.	May 20, 1898	298
355	*Vousden, W. J.	Bengal Staff Corps (ex 35th Foot)	Afghan—*Kabul*	Oct. 18, 1881	229–230
144	*Wadeson, R.	75th Regiment	Indian Mutiny—*Delhi*	Dec. 24, 1858	86
45	*Walker, M.	30th Regiment	Crimea—*Inkerman* and *Sebastopol* (twice)	June 4, 1858	25–26
518	Walker, W. G.	Indian Army (ex 1st Batt. 12th Foot)	Somaliland—*Daratoleh*	Aug. 7, 1903	372–373, 375–378
	*Walker-Heneage,—see Heneage				

Index

Order in which each cross has been gained.	Name.	Regiment, Corps, etc.	Campaign, etc., and *place*.	Announced in the London Gazette of	Page.
168	*Waller, G.	60th Regiment	Indian Mutiny—*Delhi* (twice)	Jan. 20, 1860	109
281	*Waller, W. F. F.	25th Bombay N.I.	Indian Mutiny—*Gwalior*	Feb. 25, 1862	175
46	*Walters, G.	49th Regiment	Crimea—*Inkerman*	Feb. 24, 1857	27
	Wantage, *Lord*—see Lindsay				
476	Ward, C.	105th Regiment	Boer—*Lindley*	Sep. 28, 1900	337–338
179	*Ward, H.	78th Regiment	Indian Mutiny—*Lucknow* (No. 1)	June 18, 1858	116
280	*Ward, J.	8th Hussars	Indian Mutiny—*Gwalior*	Jan. 28, 1859	174
362	Wassall, S.	80th Regiment	Zulu—*Buffalo River* (in the)	June 17, 1879	236
205	Watson, J.	1st Punjab Cavalry	Indian Mutiny—*Lucknow*, No. 2 near the "Martinière"	June 18, 1858	135, 136
420	Watson, T. C.	Royal Engineers	Punjab Frontier—*Bilot*	May 20, 1898	295–296
47	*Wheatley, F.	The Rifle Brigade	Crimea—*Sebastopol*	Feb. 24, 1857	27
256	*Whirlpool, F.	3rd Bombay European Regiment (109th)	Indian Mutiny—*Jhansi* and *Lohari*	Oct. 21, 1859	164
412	Whitchurch, H. F.	Indian (Bengal) Medical Service	Chitral (*Attack on Fort* 3.3.1895)	July 16, 1895	286–287
349	White, G. S.	92nd Regiment	Afghanistan—*Charasiah*, '79, *Kandahar* '80	June 3, 1881	223–224, 318, 319, 322
73	*Wilkinson, T.	Royal Marine Artillery	Crimea—*Sebastopol*	Feb. 24, 1857	40
373	Williams, J.	24th Regiment	Zulu—*Rorke's Drift*	May 2, 1879	237–243, 392–398
245	*Wilmot, H.	The Rifle Brigade	Indian Mutiny—*Lucknow* (No. 3)	Dec. 24, 1858	158–159, 159
399	Wilson, A. K.	Royal Navy—H.M.S. *Hecla*	Soudan (Eastern)—*El-Teb*	May 21, 1884	272–273
289	Wood, H. E.	17th Lancers	Indian Mutiny—*Sindwaho* and *Sindhora*	Sep. 4, 1860	180–181, 324
112	*Wood, J. A.	20th Bombay N.I.	Persia—*Bushire*	Aug. 3, 1860	61
23	*Wooden, C.	17th Lancers	Crimea—*Balaklava*	Oct. 26, 1858	14
54	*Wright, A.	77th Regiment	Crimea—*The whole Campaign*	Feb. 24, 1857	30
516	Wright, W. D.	2nd Regiment	Northern Nigeria (not localised)	Sep. 11, 1903	379
487	Wylly, G. G. E.	Tasmanian Imperial Bushmen	Boer—*Warmbad*	Nov. 23, 1900	344–345
507	Young, A.	Cape Police	Boer—*Ruiter's Kraal*	Nov. 8, 1901	358–359
218	*Young, T. J.	Royal Navy—H.M.S. *Shannon*	Indian Mutiny—*Lucknow* (No. 2)	Feb. 1, 1859	141
479	*Younger, D. R.	75th Regiment	Boer—*Krugersdorp*	Aug. 8, 1902	339–340, 387

www.ingramcontent.com/pod-product-compliance
Ingram Content Group UK Ltd.
Pitfield, Milton Keynes, MK11 3LW, UK
UKHW050416240426
12048UKWH00021B/1542